Situated Design Methods

Situated Design Methods

edited by Jesper Simonsen, Connie Svabo, Sara Malou Strandvad, Kristine Samson, Morten Hertzum, and Ole Erik Hansen

The MIT Press
Cambridge, Massachusetts
London, England

This book was set in Stone Sans and Stone Serif by Toppan Best-set Premedia Limited, Hong Kong.

Library of Congress Cataloging-in-Publication Data

Situated design methods / edited by Jesper Simonsen, Connie Svabo, Sara Malou Strandvad, Kristine Samson, Morten Hertzum, and Ole Erik Hansen.
    pages   cm.—(Design thinking, design theory)
Includes bibliographical references and index.
ISBN 978-0-262-02763-2 (hardcover : alk. paper), 978-0-262-54472-6 (pb)
1. Industrial design. I. Simonsen, Jesper, editor of compilation.
TS171.S54   2014
745.2—dc23
2013050860

Contents

Series Foreword

As professions go, design is relatively young. The practice of design predates professions. In fact, the practice of design—making things to serve a useful goal, making tools—predates the human race. Making tools is one of the attributes that made us human in the first place.

Design, in the most generic sense of the word, began over 2.5 million years ago when *Homo habilis* manufactured the first tools. Human beings were designing well before we began to walk upright. Four hundred thousand years ago, we began to manufacture spears. By forty thousand years ago, we had moved up to specialized tools.

Urban design and architecture came along ten thousand years ago in Mesopotamia. Interior architecture and furniture design probably emerged with them. It was another five thousand years before graphic design and typography got their start in Sumeria with the development of cuneiform. After that, things picked up speed.

All goods and services are designed. The urge to design—to consider a situation, imagine a better situation, and act to create that improved situation—goes back to our prehuman ancestors. Making tools helped us to become what we are—design helped to make us human.

Today, the word "design" means many things. The common factor linking them is service, and designers are engaged in a service profession in which the results of their work meet human needs.

Design is first of all a process. The word "design" entered the English language in the 1500s as a verb, with the first written citation of the verb dated to the year 1548. *Merriam-Webster's Collegiate Dictionary* defines the verb "design" as "to conceive and plan out in the mind; to have as a specific purpose; to devise for a specific function or end." Related to these is the act of drawing, with an emphasis on the nature of the drawing as a plan or map, as well as "to draw plans for; to create, fashion, execute or construct according to plan."

Half a century later, the word began to be used as a noun, with the first cited use of the noun "design" occurring in 1588. *Merriam-Webster's* defines the noun as "a particular purpose held in view by an individual or group; deliberate, purposive planning; a mental project or scheme in which means to an end are laid down." Here, too, purpose and planning toward desired outcomes are central. Among these are "a preliminary sketch or outline showing the main features of something to be executed; an underlying scheme that governs functioning, developing or unfolding; a plan or protocol for carrying out or accomplishing something; the arrangement of elements or details in a product or work of art." Today, we design large, complex process, systems, and services, and we design organizations and structures to produce them. Design has changed considerably since our remote ancestors made the first stone tools.

At a highly abstract level, Herbert Simon's definition covers nearly all imaginable instances of design. To design, Simon writes, is to "[devise] courses of action aimed at changing existing situations into preferred ones" (Simon, *The Sciences of the Artificial*, 2nd ed., MIT Press, 1982, 129). Design, properly defined, is the entire process across the full range of domains required for any given outcome.

But the design process is always more than a general, abstract way of working. Design takes concrete form in the work of the service professions that meet human needs, a broad range of making and planning disciplines. These include industrial design, graphic design, textile design, furniture design, information design, process design, product design, interaction design, transportation design, educational design, systems design, urban design, design leadership, and design management, as well as architecture, engineering, information technology, and computer science.

These fields focus on different subjects and objects. They have distinct traditions, methods, and vocabularies, used and put into practice by distinct and often dissimilar professional groups. Although the traditions dividing these groups are distinct, common boundaries sometimes form a border. Where this happens, they serve as meeting points where common concerns build bridges. Today, ten challenges uniting the design professions form such a set of common concerns.

Three performance challenges, four substantive challenges, and three contextual challenges bind the design disciplines and professions together as a common field. The performance challenges arise because all design professions:

1. act on the physical world;
2. address human needs; and
3. generate the built environment.

In the past, these common attributes were not sufficient to transcend the boundaries of tradition. Today, objective changes in the larger world give rise to four substantive challenges that are driving convergence in design practice and research. These substantive challenges are:

1. increasingly ambiguous boundaries between artifacts, structure, and process;
2. increasingly large-scale social, economic, and industrial frames;

3. an increasingly complex environment of needs, requirements, and constraints; and
4. information content that often exceeds the value of physical substance.

These challenges require new frameworks of theory and research to address contemporary problem areas while solving specific cases and problems. In professional design practice, we often find that solving design problems requires interdisciplinary teams with a transdisciplinary focus. Fifty years ago, a sole practitioner and an assistant or two might have solved most design problems; today, we need groups of people with skills across several disciplines, and the additional skills that enable professionals to work with, listen to, and learn from each other as they solve problems.

Three contextual challenges define the nature of many design problems today. While many design problems function at a simpler level, these issues affect many of the major design problems that challenge us, and these challenges also affect simple design problems linked to complex social, mechanical, or technical systems. These issues are:

1. a complex environment in which many projects or products cross the boundaries of several organizations, stakeholder, producer, and user groups;
2. projects or products that must meet the expectations of many organizations, stakeholders, producers, and users; and
3. demands at every level of production, distribution, reception, and control.

These ten challenges require a qualitatively different approach to professional design practice than was the case in earlier times. Past environments were simpler. They made simpler demands. Individual experience and personal development were sufficient for depth and substance in professional practice. While experience and development are still necessary, they are no longer sufficient. Most of today's design challenges require analytic and synthetic planning skills that cannot be developed through practice alone.

Professional design practice today involves advanced knowledge. This knowledge is not solely a higher level of professional practice. It is also a qualitatively different form of professional practice that emerges in response to the demands of the information society and the knowledge economy to which it gives rise.

In a recent essay ("Why Design Education Must Change," *Core77*, November 26, 2010), Donald Norman challenges the premises and practices of the design profession. In the past, designers operated on the belief that talent and a willingness to jump into problems with both feet gives them an edge in solving problems. Norman writes:

In the early days of industrial design, the work was primarily focused upon physical products. Today, however, designers work on organizational structure and social problems, on interaction, service, and experience design. Many problems involve complex social and political issues. As a result, designers have become applied behavioral scientists, but they are woefully undereducated for the task. Designers often fail to understand the complexity of the issues and the depth of knowledge already known. They claim that fresh eyes can produce novel solutions, but then they wonder why these solutions are seldom implemented, or if implemented, why they fail. Fresh eyes can indeed produce insightful results, but the eyes must also be educated and knowledgeable. Designers often lack the requisite understanding. Design schools do not train students about these complex issues, about the interlocking complexities of human and social behavior, about the behavioral sciences, technology, and business. There is little or no training in science, the scientific method, and experimental design.

This is not industrial design in the sense of designing products, but industry-related design, design as thought and action for solving problems and imagining new futures. This new MIT Press series of books emphasizes strategic design to create value through innovative products and services, and it emphasizes design as service through rigorous creativity, critical inquiry, and an ethics of respectful design. This rests on a sense of understanding, empathy, and appreciation for people, for nature, and for the world we shape through design. Our goal as editors is to develop a series of vital conversations that help designers and researchers to serve business, industry, and the public sector for positive social and economic outcomes.

We will present books that bring a new sense of inquiry to the design, helping to shape a more reflective and stable design discipline able to support a stronger profession grounded in empirical research, generative concepts, and the solid theory that gives rise to what W. Edwards Deming described as profound knowledge (Deming, *The New Economics for Industry, Government, Education*, MIT, Center for Advanced Engineering Study, 1993). For Deming, a physicist, engineer, and designer, profound knowledge comprised systems thinking and the understanding of processes embedded in systems; an understanding of variation and the tools we need to understand variation; a theory of knowledge; and a foundation in human psychology. This is the beginning of "deep design"—the union of deep practice with robust intellectual inquiry.

A series on design thinking and theory faces the same challenges that we face as a profession. On one level, design is a general human process that we use to understand and to shape our world. Nevertheless, we cannot address this process or the world in its general, abstract form. Rather, we meet the challenges of design in specific challenges, addressing problems or ideas in a situated context. The challenges we face as designers today are as diverse as the problems clients bring us. We are involved in design for economic anchors, economic continuity, and economic growth. We design for urban needs and rural needs, for social development and creative communities. We are involved with environmental sustainability and economic policy, agriculture competitive crafts for export, competitive products and brands for micro-enterprises, developing new products for bottom-of-pyramid markets and redeveloping old products for mature or wealthy markets. Within the framework of design, we are also challenged to design for extreme situations, for biotech, nanotech, and new materials, and design for social business, as well as conceptual challenges for worlds that do not yet exist, such as the world beyond the Kurzweil singularity—and for new visions of the world that does exist.

The Design Thinking, Design Theory series from the MIT Press will explore these issues and more—meeting them, examining them, and helping designers to address them.

Join us in this journey.

Ken Friedman   Erik Stolterman
Editors, Design Thinking, Design Theory Series

Preface

Design is situated—and thus entails a demand for situated design methods. This book emphasizes the broad scope of situated design by presenting eighteen different situated design methods. We include examples from highly diverse areas such as service and experience, culture, communication, information technology, urban design, environmental studies, and technology studies. The chapters in various ways highlight the situatedness of design and unfold methods to facilitate and conduct situated design processes. The book employs interdisciplinary vocabularies comprising the technical, human, and social sciences, thereby providing a rich and multifaceted understanding of the different ways in which design is much more and much else than the work of traditional craftsmanship-based designers.

In 2010 we published the book *Design Research: Synergies from Interdisciplinary Perspectives* (Simonsen et al. 2010). Our overall intention in that book was to understand the design process better. This we achieved by clarifying features and approaches common to a variety of research disciplines that address design and by undertaking an in-depth exploration of the social processes involved in doing design, as well as analyses of the contexts for the use of design. Thus we focused on the nonroutine and creative aspects of producing, facilitating, encouraging, advancing, and causing a change process that transforms one situation into another, and furthermore acknowledged that results may emerge that were not foreseen as intended outcomes.

In the present book, we continue our interdisciplinary endeavor by exploring design methods. Design methods are important resources for designers, and reflective analyses of the use of design methods are important to understanding the situated manner in which they facilitate design processes. The process of making the book has been highly participatory, with the authors meeting in person and discussing the book at five seminars from 2011 to 2013. At these seminars, we developed and refined the structure, content, and common thread of the book and presented and reviewed draft chapters.

All the chapters are coauthored by scholars from Roskilde University who are engaged in design in their teaching, research, or work as designers. Roskilde University is known as a pioneering university dedicated to interdisciplinary programs based on

problem-based project work (Olesen and Jensen 1999; Mallow 2001; Olsen and Pedersen 2005; Nielsen and Danielsen 2012; Andreasen and Nielsen 2013; Andersen and
Heilesen 2014). Founded in 1972, the university has established a tradition of practice-
oriented research and of study programs based on interdisciplinary analyses of societal
problems. This tradition has recently been manifested in a main subject area of design,
humanities, and technology along with the design-oriented strategic research initiative Designing Human Technologies (RU 2013).

We have been extremely pleased by the constructive comments from MIT Press.
We want to thank the reviewers for their work and have done our utmost to live up
to their high expectations. We hope that you will read the book with the same enthusiasm as we have experienced in writing it.

Jesper Simonsen
Connie Svabo
Sara Malou Strandvad
Kristine Samson
Morten Hertzum
Ole Erik Hansen

References

Andersen, Anders S., and Simon B. Heilesen, eds. 2014. *Problem Based Studies and Project Work.*
New York: Springer.

Andreasen, Lars B., and Jørgen L. Nielsen. 2013. Dimensions of problem based learning: Dialogue
and online collaboration in projects. *Journal of Problem Based Learning in Higher Education* 1 (1):
210–229.

Mallow, Jeffry V. 2001. Student group project work: A pioneering experiment in interactive
engagement. *Journal of Science Education and Technology* 10 (2): 105–113.

Nielsen, Jørgen L., and Oluf Danielsen. 2012. Problem-oriented project studies: The role of the
teacher as supervisor for the study group in its learning processes. In *Exploring the Theory, Pedagogy, and Practice of Networked Learning*, ed. Lone Dirckinck-Holmfeld, Vivien Hodgson, and David
McConnell, 257–272. New York: Springer.

Olesen, Henning S., and Jens H. Jensen, eds. 1999. *Project Studies: A Late Modern University Reform?*
Frederiksberg: Roskilde University Press.

Olsen, Poul B., and Kaare Pedersen. 2005. *Problem-Oriented Project Work: A Workbook.* Frederiksberg: Roskilde University Press.

RU. 2013. *Roskilde University Strategic Research Initiative in Designing Human Technologies.* http://
www.ruc.dk/en/dht.

Simonsen, Jesper, Jørgen O. Bærenholdt, Monika Büscher, and John D. Scheuer, eds. 2010. *Design
Research: Synergies from Interdisciplinary Perspectives.* London: Routledge.

1   Situated Methods in Design

Jesper Simonsen, Connie Svabo, Sara Malou Strandvad, Kristine Samson, Morten Hertzum, and Ole Erik Hansen

1   Introduction

Life in contemporary society is saturated by design. We live in designed environments, we are surrounded by design objects, and in many situations our attention, capacity, and movement are affected by design. Today design penetrates areas far beyond the traditional craftsmanship-based design professions. It takes place in domains as different as health, culture, education, business, transportation, and planning and involves "shaping and changing society" through processes that are at the same time "intentional, situated and emerging" (Simonsen et al. 2010, 203). In addition, design is spreading to universities, which engage in design research and initiate new design-oriented study programs worldwide.

The act of designing involves many participants. As such a participatory endeavor, design can be defined as "a process of investigating, understanding, reflecting upon, establishing, developing, and supporting mutual learning between multiple participants" (Simonsen and Robertson 2012, 2). In this book, we employ the notion of situated design because design processes take place in particular situations and are carried out from embedded positions (Haraway 1988; Suchman 1987, 2007). To say that design is situated is to highlight the interactions and interdependencies between designers, designs, design methods, and the use situation with its actors, activities, structures, particulars, and broader context. Situated design acknowledges the tinkering and negotiation involved in designing things—tangible as well as intangible—and making them happen as intended. Phrased in a slightly different manner, a situated design deals with all the "thinging" that goes into the making of things. Bjögvinsson, Ehn, and Hillgren (2012, 102) emphasize that "things" being designed are not merely objects: "A fundamental challenge for designers and the design community is to move from designing 'things' (objects) to designing Things (socio-material assemblies)."

Design methods are often described as though they are universal and can be applied in the same way across contexts. In this book, we take the reverse point of view and present eighteen situated design methods, all of which acknowledge the situated nature of design. With the expansive development of the design field, design methods have also become multiple and diverse; various domains (re)produce their own ways of designing and ways of approaching design through domain-specific design methods. We acknowledge design methods as a spreading and heterogeneous phenomenon and take an interdisciplinary point of departure by recognizing design as a creative act that combines and merges multiple disciplines. The designed environment may be understood as a field of ongoing engagements and entanglements, in which design processes comprise series of negotiations and rearrangements that introduce new designs and change established designs by combining them in new ways (Highmore 2008, 3). This presents a central challenge for design methods to be able to conceptualize and orchestrate the experience of combinations of designs. It stresses the relational and process-oriented aspects of design and design work and highlights the idea that users of various sorts play central and ongoing roles in the enactment of designs. The user roles include adoption, use, participation, appropriation, tailoring, maintenance, work-arounds, appreciation, and so forth.

In a design-saturated society, design also becomes the subject of university-based research and leads to new educational programs. European design and architecture schools rooted in practice and craftsmanship are increasingly implementing academic criteria in their programs. This reconfiguration of design education revolves around an integration of a traditional academic analysis of a human or societal issue and a creative design solution to this issue. Whereas the traditional academic analysis can draw on established academic conventions (regarding research methods, philosophy of science, and theoretical approach), the design solution is not as easy to account for: How did you come up with your ideas for the design? How did the techniques employed support you in working with these ideas? Why did you choose a specific design over other options? How can you justify the design academically? In short: What is the relation between the analysis of the situation and the resulting design solution? Questions such as these are difficult to answer, and they call for methodological considerations. With this book, we offer a selection of resources for such considerations.

The design methods presented here emerge from a constructive and creative academic community where it is the specific empirical setting that defines the focus of research and the relation between the disciplines. Our book has grown out of an academic tradition focused on the theoretical and methodological aspects of the relation between scientific analysis and design processes. This academic tradition includes collaboration between researchers from different fields and external partners based on an explicit ambition of rethinking the relation between traditional academic curricula, research, and education. Related design study programs include problem orientation, interdisciplinarity, and project work, where the participants' definitions of the problems decide the types of disciplines relevant to the analysis (Andersen and Heilesen

2014). Growing out of this tradition, the chapters in this book take interdisciplinary points of departure in presenting methods and exemplary cases from a variety of design areas, analyzed with vocabularies from a variety of academic disciplines.

This way of studying design is in line with the concept of mode 2 knowledge developed by Gibbons et al. (1994) to define practice-oriented scientific knowledge. It stresses that analysis and design should be carried out in continuous dialogue with the field and in collaboration with participants. This twists the notion that the validity of knowledge is determined solely in the scientific community: for knowledge and design produced in its context of application, the practical applicability is an important criterion for assessing the success and robustness of scientific insight. Thus the scientific quality of analyses and designs is assessed through the involvement of stakeholders and based on contextual criteria.

Another important aspect is the relationship between this kind of design studies and the scientific disciplines. The dialogue between the researchers and the field establishes what scientific knowledge has to be developed and applied. This can lead to multidisciplinary research strategies combining different disciplines, to research strategies that are interdisciplinary in the sense that the development of new scientific knowledge is based on elements from various disciplines, or to an integrated form of interdisciplinarity—also known as transdisciplinarity (Gibbons and Nowotny 2001)—where the engagement with the design field establishes a new kind of scientific knowledge in which no fixed boundaries separate the disciplines.

This book is intended as basic reading for interdisciplinary design programs at undergraduate and graduate university levels. Each chapter presents a situated design method. The methods are the result of experienced design researchers' synthesis of extensive empirical experience and aim to make students and interested practitioners reflect on how to conduct design projects and, especially, how to apply methods in these projects. Learning to master situated design processes requires that descriptions of theoretical, methodological, and empirical knowledge are combined with accounts of actual experiences. Therefore each chapter includes a case, which supports reflection on how to adapt and use the method. To help the reader orient and navigate through the book, the chapters open with a short summary of four questions: *What* kind of method is presented? *Why* is the method relevant and important? *Where* can you use the method? *How* does the method address situatedness?

In the remainder of this chapter, we elaborate on the interconnected themes represented in the title of the book: situated, design, methods. First, we discuss situatedness by outlining four ways of addressing this concept: situated knowledges, situated action, situated learning, and situating contexts. Second, we unfold the notion of design thematically by distinguishing between aspects related to design projects as a whole, collaborative processes, aesthetic experiences, and sustainability. Third, we introduce the eighteen methods and present a navigation table listing central characteristics of each method. An appendix at the end of the book provides questions for each chapter to inspire discussion and reflection.

2 Situated

In this book we emphasize that design methods are situated. There is no one, agreed-on authoritative definition of situatedness. Rather, different researchers have defined and used the concept in related but different ways, as situated knowledges, situated practice, situated learning, and situating contexts.

Donna Haraway (1988) introduced the notion of *situated knowledges*, arguing that knowledge is situated and partial. Knowledge production takes place under specific historical, political, and situational circumstances. These permanent partialities must be taken into account in understanding and relating to knowledge claims. To empha-size this point, Haraway talks about knowledge in the plural, as situated knowledges.

The concept of situated knowledges is an argument against universal knowledge claims, which Haraway sees as irresponsible in the sense that the knowledge producers erase the association between themselves and their claims. By disclaiming the active participation of the knower in constructing her or his representations, knowledge claims appear objective. In Haraway's words, universal knowledge claims are "ways of being nowhere while claiming to see comprehensively" (1988, 584). Importantly, Haraway is similarly critical of relativistic knowledge claims, which evade responsibil-ity by presenting themselves as equally attentive to all possible positions. The associa-tion between the knowers and their claims is again disclaimed, but in contrast to universalism, relativism is "a way of being nowhere while claiming to be everywhere equally" (584). The fundamental similarity of universal and relativistic knowledge claims is that they let knowers escape responsibility for the representations they construct.

As an alternative, Haraway proposes to hold on to the particular, partial, and embedded and thereby to ground knowledge by accounting for how it is locally and historically contingent. In this way, knowledge becomes situated, and knowledge claims become "views from somewhere" (590). If we locate knowledge somewhere in particular, then it is no longer independent of other knowledge claims but involved in a continuous process of joining partial views and living within limits and contra-dictions. This process involves searching for connections and negotiating compro-mises, and it is thereby about the creation and re-creation of knowledges in communities, rather than about isolated individuals' knowledge creation.

Haraway's argument for situated knowledges and against the possibility of universal knowledge has also been developed in relation to design (e.g., Björgvinsson, Ehn, and Hillgren 2012; Büscher et al. 2001; Suchman 2002). For example, Lucy Suchman (2002) suggests considering design as located within networks and practices.

Suchman (1987, 2007) challenges the traditional view on the relationship between plans and action by proposing that plans are merely resources for *situated action*. This means that plans are seen no longer as set procedures simply to be acted out but as guidelines that can be altered in accordance with the situation at hand. The far-reaching implication of this proposal is that the focus shifts from devising plans to acting in concrete situations, the details of which defy any detailed specification in plans. To illustrate the two opposing views on the relationship between plans and action, Suchman (1987, vii; 2007, 24) quotes Gladwin's description of the contrasting ways in which ancient European and Trukese sailors navigated. The European navigator started by devising a plan that prescribed a sequence of actions to follow. If unanticipated conditions occurred, replanning took place, and the new plan was followed. The Trukese navigator, in contrast, started with an objective that remained fixed but merely specified a desired end result. As the voyage proceeded, the Trukese navigator continually adjusted his or her actions in response to the unfolding situation so as to achieve the objective.

Suchman maintains that plans are important resources for action, but the role of plans is fundamentally different from rule following because plans, when viewed as resources, do not in any strong sense determine the course of action. In this way, action is situated in that it is shaped moment by moment in response to local contingencies. Suchman elaborates the relationship between plans and action by an example of planning how to proceed with a canoe trip through a series of rapids. When meeting a challenging series of strong rapids, you might take a break to look at the path ahead and plan your descent. However detailed you make the plan, your actual behavior, once you enter the strong current, will depend on the situation at hand: "The purpose of the plan in this case is not to get your canoe through the rapids, but rather to orient you in such a way that you can obtain the best possible position from which to use those embodied skills on which, in the final analysis, your success depends" (Suchman 1987, 52).

The consequences of Suchman's position with regard to design methods are that methods must be approached as potential resources for the designer to orient by within the local context of the design project. A design method should be seen as a general representation of experiences derived from situated action in past design processes. When used in new design projects, the guidelines provided as part of these methods "must be carefully selected, adapted and appropriated to the specific project and situation at hand" (Bratteteig et al. 2012, 118).

Jean Lave and Etienne Wenger (1991) have coined the term *situated learning*, by which they locate learning in the increased access of learners to participating roles in skilled performances. In this way, they question the idea that effective learning can occur in contexts (such as most schools) separated from the social practice in which learners are trained to perform. Instead Lave and Wenger argue that learning is situated in the sense that it takes place through legitimate peripheral participation in a community of practice.

Legitimate peripheral participation is akin to apprenticeship. It is an integral element of a community of practice, and the learner participates by performing part of the real-world activities performed by the community of practice. The learner's role is legitimate in a double sense. First, the learner is acknowledged as contributing real work that is integral to the practice. Second, the contribution is legitimately peripheral, meaning that the tasks performed by the learner are, initially, simple and intended as much to be vehicles for learning to appreciate the more complex elements of the work. For example, apprentice tailors begin by learning the finishing stages of tailoring, such as ironing finished garments. Ironing is a simple, valuable element of real tailoring but at the same time tacitly makes the apprentice aware of details in the preceding stages of cutting and sewing.

The learning that takes place through legitimate peripheral participation is not confined to the specific tasks performed by the learner. The learner also observes the skilled participants as they perform their tasks, and listens in on their discussions. Witnessing skilled participants as they perform and discuss their work is fundamental to the gradual transition from peripheral to full participation because acquiring a skill involves more than any set of explicit instructions can convey. In addition, it is through the skilled participants' performances and discussions that the standards of full participation are produced.

Rather than assuming a role as teachers, skilled participants in a community of practice are most importantly "embodied exemplars of what apprentices were becoming" (Lave 1996, 153). In other words, the practice with all its constituent tasks and meanings is, normally, performed rather than explicitly explained. Lave (1996) asserts that all knowledge is embedded in context, and, by implication, there is nothing but situated learning. This assertion widens the scope of legitimate peripheral participation from a conceptualization of apprenticeships to a general model of how learning occurs.

Finally, what we call *situating contexts* emphasizes that any design process is embedded in a social context, and the context and the designer's interpretation of it are crucial to the output and outcome of the design process. The relation between actors and contextual structures, including societal institutions, is a debated issue in the social sciences, ontologically as well as epistemologically (e.g., Giddens 1984). Views range from, on the one extreme, an understanding of human action as totally determined by social structures to, on the other extreme, an understanding of society as the result of social interaction. In between, ontological realists argue that the structures are interdependent with the actors' interpretation (Danermark et al. 1997), while ontological constructivists argue that structures consist of collective interpretations (Burr 1995).

In line with Haraway's (1988) understanding of embeddedness, situating contexts entail a focus on how designers interpret and construct the context for the design process to make designs that fit into or stretch the context. Designers are seen as competent actors who operate within the constraints of existing structures. Their practices both influence and are influenced by rules, discourses, and artifacts (Meadowcroft 2007; Shove and Walker 2007). This understanding of how design is situated calls for several types of methods. Interdisciplinary methods are needed to investigate the different ways of understanding the relation between agency and structure, including how design methods must be contextualized depending on the specific situation. Methods to meta-design the context are, in some cases, important to contribute to a process of designing the context and establishing a design space with specific institutions and organizational possibilities to facilitate the design process. Also, methods for reflecting on how to transfer design methods from one context to another are necessary to spread successful ways of working and appreciate the difficulties of doing so.

Situated knowledges, situated action, situated learning, and situating contexts are four interrelated ways of thinking about situatedness. They provide reference points for the treatment of situated design methods in the individual chapters of this book.

A situated design method, following Haraway, implies that design is always carried out with partiality and from a specific, embedded position. Design can only be carried out as "politics and epistemologies of location, positioning, and situating" (Haraway 1988, 589). For instance, partiality, rather than universality or relativity, would be the condition that allows users to be heard and understood in making knowledge claims, as is the case in chapter 8, where experience designs for museums and amusement parks are qualified by stakeholders and users in collaborative workshops. Partiality may also be exercised in the way designers engage with physical surroundings in an ongoing design event. For example, chapter 13 stresses how designers of alternate reality games are continuously receptive to the player's engagement and the properties of the city.

A situated design method in line with Suchman suggests that methods, like plans, are resources for situated action. It follows from viewing design processes as situated action that methods should be seen as ways of supporting design processes, not as recipes for conducting them. While design methods may inspire good questions, they should not be expected to provide authoritative answers. The method in chapter 4 provides four types of resources for situated action: design concepts, design principles, a suggested organization of design projects into four overall phases, and a set of techniques and tools for specific activities.

A situated design method following Lave and Wenger stresses that design processes are embedded in communities of practice. The shared understanding of what should be learned to become skilled is produced through the ongoing practice of the community; it does not exist independently of the community as a curriculum that can be learned before entering the community of practice. By engaging with the community of practice, design projects can be organized as situated learning. In chapter 10, school pupils are involved in a collaborative process of urban design and construction with adult community activists. This process results in the pupils learning, in situ, about how to change their neighborhood. In addition, the adults learn how children and youths can contribute to local development.

A situated design method emphasizing situating contexts deals with the complex relation between the context and the design situation. Such methods involve different actors and stakeholders, as well as societal structures given by institutions, regulation, market mechanisms, and so forth. The challenge is to interpret, work within, and simultaneously reconstruct the context to arrive at a situated design that fits as well as stretches the context. Chapter 17 describes how a designer of an electric car sharing system has to engage in policy processes to establish a taxing system and a parking fee system that makes the design feasible.

Situated design can be conceptualized in multiple ways to address different design agendas, thereby pointing toward diverse design methods. To acquire competence and confidence in conducting situated design, students must undertake design projects that address real-world design problems, preferably in collaboration with, or supervised by, skilled and experienced design researchers. This book provides a portfolio of resources and real-world examples. We present a range of design methods from a community of design researchers with extensive knowledge of cases about information technology, service and experience, communication, culture, health, work life, regional planning and development, urban design, sustainable environmental studies, and more.

3 Design

The book is organized into four parts that target methods for different aspects of design:

• Part I, "Methods for Projects," provides project-level methods for defining the scope of a design project and organizing the activities in a design project. These methods address the project as a whole (chaps. 2–5).
• Part II, "Methods for Collaborative Processes," provides methods for organizing individual design activities as part of design projects. These process-level methods include various techniques, representations, and visualizations (chaps. 6–10).
• Part III, "Methods for Aesthetic Experiences," provides methods targeted at creating experiences rather than supporting goal-directed behavior or the production of tangible products. The design of aesthetic experiences is a fast-growing area involving audiences and participants in the process (chaps. 11–15).

• Part IV, "Methods for Sustainability," presents methods for sustainable production, technological development, and consumption. These macro-level methods target the relations between designs and their societal context (chaps. 16–19).

Part I concerns the design project as a whole. That is, the chapters present methods for defining the scope of a project, organizing the activities in a project, and deriving insights from a project. Methods for projects are needed because it is difficult to organize and conduct projects successfully. This is true for projects run by design practitioners, as evidenced by the large numbers of troubled or even failed projects, as well as for projects run by design students, who conduct projects as a way of learning by doing. While there are numerous reasons for design projects to become troubled and possibly fail, many projects are troubled for similar reasons. It appears that these troubles partly recur because learning across projects is limited, thereby resulting in repetition of similar mistakes rather than in process improvements informed by the lessons learned in past projects (Hertzum 2008). Project methods are a means of targeting recurring reasons for troubled and failed projects. The chapters in this section help designers successfully manage aspects of a project that are related to its situatedness. While it is easy to denounce universalism, the rationale for the described methods is to avoid not just universalism but also relativism and instead provide methods for what could, paraphrasing Haraway (1988), be described as design from somewhere.

The methods in Part I may support and guide action, but they do not in any strong sense determine the course of action. Action is instead contingent on the particulars of a project, and therefore the process of bridging the gap between method and project is one of fitting the method to the particulars of the design situation. To be situated in this way, the method must provide for learning about the particulars of the design situation, as well as for adapting the principles and processes of the method to the situation.

Part II presents methods for organizing specific design activities using various techniques, tools, and visualizations. The goal is to assist the reader in planning, conducting, managing, and evaluating collaborative design processes and to encourage design students and practitioners to do this reflectively, analytically, and experimentally and to use imagination and playfulness.

Collaborative processes include engaging people across disciplines, ages, and contexts. This is achieved by methods that use tools such as online heart rate diagrams to support a constructive atmosphere, affinity diagrams and diagnostic maps to support collective interpretation of qualitative data, tangible design games to imagine user scenarios, and urban architectural design to engage youths in community development. The activities shaped by the methods form a common ground where participants ideally meet on equal terms, with all their differences, and are offered ways to express their opinions and analyze, discuss, model, and reflect on design issues. Visualization plays an important role in materially mediating the collaborative processes, and some chapters explore "difference" as a shaping force in creative design. The focus on the situated, creative, and emergent character of design also fosters consideration of culture and ethics in several chapters.

Part III exemplifies methods with the purpose of inspiring the creation of future aesthetic experiences. Experiences are singular events, and their design must thus have a unique or even surprising character to address audiences in appealing ways. The design object, and even a work of art, is considered in an expanded field where users, audiences, and the social lifeworld engage in the design. The expanded field broadens the perspective and includes more people in the process in addition to conventional actors such as the urban designer, sound designer, game designer, filmmaker, and choreographer.

The chapters in Part III illustrate that the design of aesthetic experiences takes place in messy and situated contexts. Whereas aesthetic design has formerly been associated with the artistic genius alone, here we broaden the perspective. Recent aesthetic theories that emphasize the role of the spectators and their participation (Rancière 2009; Bishop 2012) focus on the sharing of the experience (Pine and Gilmore 1999) and the designer's and artist's engagement with the site, the social and everyday situations (Kwon 1997). Following these perspectives, Part III proposes to see aesthetic design processes as messy and assembled situations that draw things, sites, and people together in unique and singular constellations.

Because aesthetic experience designs often require the presence and participation of an audience, spectator, or player, the potential of a design is actualized in the meeting with the audience. One may even argue that aesthetic experiences can only be partly designed, as their reception depends on the audience and participants and their capacity to engage and interact with the design. Thus the designed experiences do not in any strong sense determine the audience's interpretation. Rather, one could argue that aesthetic experience design opens up the design for interpretation and engagement from audiences and participants broadly conceived.

Part IV considers methods for the design of sustainable products, production, technological systems, consumption, and social development. The chapters have a normative and change-oriented perspective. This implies a focus on designing change agents that intervene in processes of transition, transformation, technological development, consumption, and sociotechnical practices. In addition to addressing the analytic and intervening methods at designers' disposal, the methods here also address how designers can define their roles in such processes.

Design methods for sustainability are needed because our present industrial systems have severe negative effects on the environment. In recent years there has been a focus on global warming owing to the use of fossil fuels, but in general, many important sociotechnical systems (such as energy production, transportation, building, agriculture, and manufacture) use limited resources extensively and give rise to environmental problems as well as social conflicts. Vehicles with more energy-efficient internal combustion engines based on fossil fuels are an example of a new technology that has reduced the use of limited resources per driven kilometer. The overall use of fossil fuels for transportation has, however, increased because of general economic development. The chapters in Part IV argue that the design space for the development of new products and processes has been conceived too narrowly because it has been situated in sociotechnical settings that are not sustainable.

The examined designs are situated in complex social settings. The chapters analyze how design methods are developed to change industrial systems and organizations, and how designers need to understand the cultural, systemic, and organizational context of the change process. Collectively, these chapters emphasize the necessity of understanding the social and technological context for the design processes.

4 Methods

Each chapter in the book presents a situated design method and illustrates it with an empirical case. In the remainder of this chapter, we briefly introduce the eighteen methods. Tables 1.1 to 1.4 provide an overview of the methods to help the reader navigate through the book. The tables, one for each of the book's four parts, outline the methods by indicating their main approach to *situatedness*, the *design* domain and application area addressed in each chapter, and the focus and label of the *method* described.

Part I, on methods for projects, starts with chapter 2, in which Hertzum presents a method for supporting students in thinking about the focus of design projects and devising a project design. A project design is an agreement among the project participants about the focus and structure of their project. Project designs are devised by articulating the project aim and starting to break it down into component activities. The method consists of four questions. Each question targets a different element of the design process and points toward one of four frequent but flawed project designs. Thus the question that a student feels most strongly about points toward a likely project design and also toward the main risk the student must consider in formulating a project.

In chapter 3, Nielsen and Andreasen discuss how students can plan and continually redesign their project work and how researchers and students together can design study processes that stimulate students' engagement, reflection, and creative thinking. The problem- and project-based approach is a way of meeting the challenges faced by the educational system in the transition from an industrial to a knowledge-based society. Problem-based projects are open-ended and directed at handling unknown and dynamic situations. This is relevant for study programs where students are involved in self-directed study practices, and where there is a need for collaboration, flexibility, and implementation of technologies.

In chapter 4, Bødker, Kensing, and Simonsen describe the participatory design method MUST, aimed at early information technology design. The authors present their experiences situating the MUST method to domains and technologies outside its original application area. The method has been used for more than a decade in many university courses and in a large number of private and public companies. Today the method faces challenges such as giving users a say in design when users may be employees as well as consumers, citizens, NGOs, social networks, and so forth. Another challenge is that new technologies imply that design increasingly takes place as part of, or even after, implementation.

In chapter 5, Pries-Heje, Venable, and Baskerville propose and evaluate a soft systems approach to design: the Soft Design Science Methodology (SDSM). SDSM consists of seven activities starting with the specific problem and ending with a constructed, but also generalized, design solution. The methodology is evaluated by applying it retrospectively to a case about improving organizational implementation.

Part II, on methods for collaborative processes, begins with Simonsen and Friberg, who, in chapter 6, present two workshop techniques that support collective analysis of qualitative data. One technique, affinity diagramming, identifies core problems that need to be addressed in the design process. The other technique, diagnostic mapping, describes the problems and how to cope with them. Collective analyses offer all participants a voice, visualize their contributions, combine different actors' perspectives, and anchor the resulting interpretation. The techniques are explained through a case where they were used to analyze how a new electronic medical record introduced life-threatening situations for patients.

Collaborative design processes are influenced by the emotions experienced by the participants. In chapter 7, Christrup presents the Wheel of Rituals, which can be used to create specific states of consciousness in a group of designers. These states can be viewed as a spiral movement into the unknown and are connected to embodied emotions and feelings such as happiness, anger, fear, interest, and anxiety. The rituals can promote states that foster creative progress. The Wheel of Rituals uses light, music, measurement of heart rhythms, and balloons. It is described through a project where students design a performance event with user involvement.

In chapter 8, Gudiksen and Svabo present a method for use in service and experience design. Imagining customer journeys in facilitated workshops is a good way of understanding experiences as they emerge through a series of interactions with various objects, social situations, and physical environments. The method is illustrated by two specific participatory-design journey tools: Journey Touch Points and Pinball Customer Flow. Each tool is applied in collaborative design activities related to museum visits, pop-up marketing, amusement parks, and a food festival.

In chapter 9, Frølunde explores how methods and materials can support visually oriented collaborative and creative learning processes in education. The focus is on facilitating (guiding, teaching) with visual methods to support designerly learning processes. Two cases demonstrate photo elicitation using photo cards, and modeling with LEGO Serious Play sets. Using pragmatic and dialogic learning theories, the author describes a reflexive facilitation practice based on four aspects: situatedness, differences, challenges, and reflexivity. The aim of the chapter is to encourage the reader, whether student or professional, to facilitate with visual methods in a critical, reflective, and experimental way.

In chapter 10, Frandsen and Petersen present Urban Co-creation, a participatory design method for use in urban pedagogy. The method consists of a set of guidelines, tools, and techniques through which school pupils can develop an urban design in a collaborative process with inhabitants and organizations in their neighborhood. The use of the method is exemplified in a case study where youths from a disadvantaged neighborhood in the suburbs of Copenhagen designed and co-constructed colorful and imaginative dustbins to handle problems with local littering. The youths learned about the urban environment by trying to change it, and their neighboring community learned how children and youths can contribute to local problem solving and development.

Part III, on methods for aesthetic experiences, begins with chapter 11, in which Samson outlines a method for assembling urban spaces based on aesthetic materialism. In recent culture-led practices of urban design, designers seek to create urban spaces by following a situated, collective, and aesthetic approach that aims to align with users and existing material and aesthetic resources in the urban environment. Aesthetic judgment is not reduced to the skill of an artistic mastermind alone but rather understood as a dispersed, participatory, and assembled process that emerges from the urban environment.

In chapter 12, Groth presents a method for the early stages of producing portable audio designs like, for example, audio walks and audio guides. She focuses especially on the relationship to specific sites, and how an awareness of the relationship between the site and the audio production can be part of the design process. Such awareness requires paying attention to the specific genre, grasping the complex relationship between the actual and the virtual, and becoming acquainted with the soundscape of the specific site by approaching it both intuitively and systematically. The result is an audio production that narrates the actual through the virtual but also blurs the distinction.

In chapter 13, Kristiansen looks at alternate reality games (ARGs), which are urban games that pretend to be conspiracy theories that really are happening in the players' lives. The games are experienced through events, challenges, and collaborative puzzle solving and may evolve through the engagement of the players. The new design method, Aulaia, addresses the design of ARGs by including directions for generating ideas, exploring sites, writing the narrative, designing the player experience, creating the game challenges, and running and monitoring the game. Urban games are examples of highly situated games, as they depend on contextualized play. Likewise, the design method benefits from both in situ design and situated action.

In chapter 14, Andreasen, Juul, and Rosendahl focus on software-engineering principles. They look at interactive installations that provide embodied, tangible, and immersive experiences. Such installations may deliver light, image, sound, and movement through actuators and may provide interaction through gestures, voice, and sensor signals. The installations are typically driven by specialized software that differs significantly from conventional business software and includes hardware components developed specifically for the installation. With inspiration from conventional software development, interaction design, and creative programming, this chapter considers the development of interactive installations for immersive experiences and their specific design challenges.

In chapter 15, Strandvad presents a pragmatist method for situated experience design. The method derives from empirical studies of film production and performance design and can be seen as a descriptive analysis turned prescriptive. The method consists of three questions to consider when designing an experience: Which techniques are employed as devices? That is, how does conventional wisdom in the field work as a tool to construct the design? Which actors become mediators in the design process? That is, how do various kinds of actors, for example, investors and technical equipment, influence the design process? What program of action does the design outline? That is, what is the intended use that the design aims to realize, and which options for use does the design give? By raising these questions, the method means to assist design processes in action.

Part IV, on methods for sustainability, starts with chapter 16, in which Christensen and Jørgensen examine vehicle design and how vehicle design is constrained by its industrial context. In the auto industry, the development costs of a new product, whether a conventional or electric vehicle, are extremely high. The industry's response is a hybrid design approach, a compromise combining phased and iterative design. On the one hand, finalizing design before production avoids the costs of altering the extremely expensive facilities for mass production of cars. On the other hand, iterative techniques applied in the design phase may provide input about user preferences and inconsistencies in the design.

Hansen and Søndergård continue this endeavor in chapter 17 with a case of emergent design of an urban mobility system based on an electric car sharing system. The authors outline a conceptual and analytic framework for a reflexive design practice for sustainability, including a perspective of structural changes and design as meta-design. They address designing for sustainability as interventions in sociotechnical systems and social practices of users and communities, and they call for reflexive design practices challenging dominant regimes and shaping alternative design spaces. Designers must obtain an ability to contribute to sustainable transition processes, and the chapter addresses design processes aimed at such sustainable transitions enacted in complex social settings with different actors and agendas.

In chapter 18, Christensen, Kjær, and Lybæk discuss design methods that can assist companies and decision makers in reducing or preventing the environmental impacts of products, services, and manufacturing processes. The authors review the most commonly used design methods and approaches in the field, including methods addressing environmental management, life cycle thinking, eco-design, and industrial symbiosis design. The chapter elaborates on how more or less standardized methods are situated when being used by industries in their local context of technology, economy, and situated knowledge.

Finally, the book ends with chapter 19, in which Neisig reflects on how to transfer design methods in a situated way to new organizations, new social environments, or completely different cultural settings. Knowledge about the contextual dependence of design methods and how to cope with this situatedness is important to designers so as to avoid "blindness" when design methods are transferred from one domain to another. Designing for a sustainable transition is necessary to avoid unexpected difficulties. The chapter provides ten recommendations on how to transfer design methods in a situated manner.

Table 1.1

Part I, "Methods for Projects"

Chapter	Situated	Design	Method
Hertzum (chap. 2)	Situated knowledges and action	Design education Problem formulation for student design projects	Maintaining a focus on the entire design project to learn from iterations among its constituent elements *The four-question method for project designs*
Nielsen and Andreasen (chap. 3)	Situated learning and action	Problem- and project-organized studies Project work at a postgraduate master program	Basing design projects on problems to bolster situated learning Recommendations about how to learn from projects *The problem-based approach*
Bødker, Kensing, and Simonsen (chap. 4)	Situated action	Participatory design Health care and energy renovation	Achieving a coherent and anchored vision through genuine user participation and firsthand experience with users' practices *The MUST method for early information technology design*
Pries-Heje, Venable, and Baskerville (chap. 5)	Situated learning and action	Design science research Information technology development in a bank	Merging practical design with design science research to produce more relevant and rigorous designs *The soft design science method*

Table 1.2

Part II, "Methods for Collaborative Processes"

Chapter	Situated	Design	Method
Simonsen and Friberg (chap. 6)	Situated action	Identify, understand, and act on complex design problems Electronic medical records creating life-threatening situations	Using workshop techniques to collectively analyze and interpret qualitative data *Affinity diagramming* and *diagnostic mapping*
Christrup (chap. 7)	Situated action	Situations where a group is working under pressure and stress Idea generation in Performance Design student project	Explicating and reflecting on emotional state to enable creative progress *Wheel of Rituals in design*
Gudiksen and Svabo (chap. 8)	Situated knowledges	Service and experience design Customer journeys in museum and amusement park	Understanding experiences as journeys to grasp their temporality and interactions *Journey touch points and pinball customer flow*
Frølunde (chap. 9)	Situated knowledges and action	Design-oriented education Photo cards and LEGO Serious Play	Using visual materials to support collaborative learning processes in designerly education *The PASIR method*
Frandsen and Petersen (chap. 10)	Situated learning	Participatory urban design Kids design new garbage bins for their local neighborhood	Participating in real-world design activities to educate and empower urban citizens *The Urban Co-Creation method*

Table 1.3
Part III, "Methods for Aesthetic Experiences"

Chapter	Situated	Design	Method
Samson (chap. 11)	Situated knowledges	Spatial design, urban spaces The High Line in Chelsea, the LAK festival, and a DIY initiative in São Paulo	Designing with and for the user to create aesthetic urban experiences *Assembling urban spaces method*
Groth (chap. 12)	Situated knowledges	Portable audio design The audio walk "My Vesterbro" and the audio guide "Do You Remember"	Supporting reflection in audio design to work with the tensions between the real and virtual and between past, present, and future *Design method for audio walks and audio guides*
Kristiansen (chap. 13)	Situated action	Design of urban games Alternate reality games	Arranging game challenges to create collective problem solving, suspense, and progression *The Aulaia method*
Andreasen, Juul, and Rosendahl (chap. 14)	Situated action	Interaction design Interactive installations for, e.g., a bumper car competition	Using software engineering and creative programming to create immersive experiences *Timeboxing model for interactive installations*
Strandvad (chap. 15)	Situated action	Experience design Case studies from film production and performance design	Attending to devices, mediators, and actions to fit creative design processes into universal design methods *The pragmatist method for experience design*

Table 1.4

Part IV, "Methods for Sustainability"

Chapter	Situated	Design	Method
Christensen and Jørgensen (chap. 16)	Situating contexts	Contemporary automobile industry Design and development of new electric car	Combining elements of phased and iterative design to reduce the costs of developing new products *The hybrid design approach*
Hansen and Søndergård (chap. 17)	Situating contexts	Sociotechnical design of infrastructures for transportation Early design stages of the Danish electric vehicle system Cleardrive	Reconfiguring mobility systems and practices to obtain sustainable transition processes *Framework for designing for sustainability*
Christensen, Kjær, and Lybæk (chap. 18)	Situating contexts	Design of industrial systems International standards for resource-efficient industrial systems	Incorporating sustainability in industrial processes to reduce their environmental impacts *Design methods to prevent and reduce environmental problems*
Neisig (chap. 19)	Situating contexts	The transfer of design methods to new social, cultural, and organizational contexts The jam session, living labs, and Cradle2Cradle	Embracing the situatedness of design methods to avoid blindnesses when methods are transferred across contexts *Recommendations on how to transfer design methods*

References

Andersen, Anders S., and Simon B. Heilesen, eds. 2014. *Problem-Based Studies and Project Work*. New York: Springer.

Bishop, Claire. 2012. *Artificial Hells: Participatory Art and the Politics of Spectatorship*. London: Verso.

Bjögvinsson, Erling, Pelle Ehn, and Per-Anders Hillgren. 2012. Design things and design thinking: Contemporary participatory design challenges. *Design Issues* 28 (3): 101–116.

Bratteteig, Tone, Keld Bødker, Yvonne Dittrich, Preben Holst Mogensen, and Jesper Simonsen. 2012. Methods: Organizing principles and general guidelines for participatory design projects. In *Routledge International Handbook of Participatory Design*, ed. J. Simonsen and T. Robertson, 117–144. London: Routledge.

Burr, Vivien. 1995. *An Introduction to Social Constructionism*. London: Routledge.

Büscher, Monika, Satinder Gill, Preben Mogensen, and Dan Shapiro. 2001. Landscapes of practice: Bricolage as a method for situated design. *Computer Supported Cooperative Work* 10 (1): 1–28.

Danermark, Berth, Mats Ekström, Liselotte Jakobsen, and Jan C. Karlsson. 1997. *Explaining Society: An Introduction to Critical Realism in the Social Sciences*. London: Routledge.

Gibbons, Michael, Camille Limoges, Helga Nowotny, Simon Schwartzman, Peter Scott, and Martin Trow. 1994. *The New Production of Knowledge: The Dynamics of Science and Research in Contemporary Societies*. London: Sage.

Gibbons, Michael, and Helga Nowotny. 2001. The potential of transdisciplinarity. In *Transdisciplinarity: Joint Problem Solving among Science, Technology, and Society; An Effective Way for Managing Complexity*, ed. Julie Thompson Klein, Rudolf Häberli, Roland W. Scholz, Walter Grossenbacher-Mansuy, Alain Bill, and Myrtha Welti, 67–80. New York: Birkhäuser, Springer Group.

Giddens, Anthony. 1984. *The Constitution of Society*. Cambridge: Polity Press.

Haraway, Donna. 1988. Situated knowledges: The science question in feminism and the privilege of partial perspective. *Feminist Studies* 14 (3): 575–599.

Hertzum, Morten. 2008. On the process of software design: Sources of complexity and reasons for muddling through. In *Proceedings of the IFIP EIS 2007 Conference on Engineering Interactive Systems*, ed. J. Gulliksen, M. B. Harning, P. Palanque, G. C. van der Veer, and J. Wesson, 483–500. Berlin: Springer.

Highmore, Ben, ed. 2008. *The Design Culture Reader*. London: Routledge.

Kwon, Miwon. 1997. One place after another: Notes on site specificity. *October* 80: 85–110.

Lave, Jean. 1996. Teaching, as learning, in practice. *Mind, Culture, and Activity* 3 (3): 149–164.

Lave, Jean, and Etienne Wenger. 1991. *Situated Learning: Legitimate Peripheral Participation*. Cambridge: Cambridge University Press.

Meadowcroft, James. 2007. Who is in charge here? Governance for sustainable development in a complex world. *Journal of Environmental Policy and Planning* 9 (3): 299–314.

Pine, Joseph B., and James H. Gilmore. 1999. *The Experience Economy*. Boston: Harvard Business School Press.

Rancière, Jacques. 2009. *The Emancipated Spectator*. London: Verso.

Shove, Elizabeth, and Gordon P. Walker. 2007. CAUTION! Transitions ahead: Politics, practice, and sustainable transition management. *Environment and Planning A* 39 (4): 763–770.

Simonsen, Jesper, Jørgen O. Bærenholdt, Monika Büscher, and John D. Scheuer, eds. 2010. *Design Research: Synergies from Interdisciplinary Perspectives*. London: Routledge.

Simonsen, Jesper, and Toni Robertson, eds. 2012. *Routledge International Handbook of Participatory Design*. London: Routledge.

Suchman, Lucy A. 1987. *Plans and Situated Action: The Problem of Human-Machine Interaction*. Cambridge: Cambridge University Press.

Suchman, Lucy A. 2002. Practice-based design of information systems: Notes from the hyperdeveloped world. *Information Society* 18 (2): 139–144.

Suchman, Lucy A. 2007. *Human-Machine Reconfigurations: Plans and Situated Action*. 2nd ed. Cambridge: Cambridge University Press.

I Methods for Projects

2 Project Designs for Student Design Projects

Morten Hertzum

What. This chapter presents a method for supporting students in thinking about the focus of design projects and in devising a project design. A project design is an agreement among the project participants about the focus and structure of their project. Project designs are devised by articulating the project aim and starting to break it down into component activities.

Why. We contend that four frequently used project designs are flawed in the sense that their strength in one area important to design comes at the cost of severe weaknesses in other, equally important, areas. While there are several practical reasons for this state of affairs, student designers should know the flaws inherent in different project designs. In this chapter, we intend (a) to increase the awareness among students and supervisors of the complex considerations involved in the design of projects and (b) to stimulate more reflective discussions of the pros and cons of different project designs by dismantling unrealistic expectations of devising a flawless project design.

Where. This chapter is specifically about project designs for student design projects. The specific focus on student design projects means that the principal rationale for the projects is learning about design. However, student projects rely on learning by doing and thereby blend learning and doing.

How. The method consists of four questions. Each question targets a different element of the design process and points toward one of the four frequent but flawed project designs. Thus the question that a student feels most strongly about points toward a likely project design and also toward the main risk the student must consider in formulating a project.

1   Introduction

A project design sets the focus and structure of a project by articulating the project aim and starting to break it down into component activities. In this chapter, we are specifically concerned with project designs for student design projects. A design project can be broadly defined as a project that aims at "changing existing situations into preferred ones" (Simon 1996, 111), typically by exploiting the possibilities afforded by technology. Our specific focus on student design projects means that the principal rationale for the projects is learning about design, which is sometimes contrasted with doing design. It is, however, a premise for this chapter that the most effective way of learning is by doing. This premise makes design projects central to learning about design. Indeed, half of any study program at our university consists of projects in which the students identify a problem and research it. A core aspect of these projects is that the students themselves form their project groups and identify the focus of their projects. In the design-related study programs, it is therefore imperative that the project designs devised by the students, with support from their project supervisor, capture the essence of design. Otherwise the students will not get exemplary design experiences.

This chapter presents four student project designs that are derived from a simplified model of design projects. Collectively these four project designs capture a large part of the student design projects at our university and, presumably, at many other universities. We contend that all four of these project designs are flawed in the sense that their strength in one area important to design comes at the cost of severe weaknesses in other, equally important, areas. We elaborate this contention in the rest of the chapter. The many instances of the four project designs suggest that though their flaws may be avoidable in principle, they are difficult to avoid in practice. While the contention that frequently used project designs have severe flaws may sound pessimistic, the intention is otherwise. The aim of this chapter is (a) to increase the awareness among students and supervisors of the complex considerations involved in the design of projects and (b) to stimulate more reflective discussions of the pros and cons of different project designs by dismantling unrealistic expectations of devising a flawless project design.

In the following, we present the simplified design model from which the four project designs are derived (sec. 2), characterize the four project designs by analyzing their focus and limitations (secs. 3–6), propose a method for supporting student designers in thinking about the focus of their projects and in devising a project design (sec. 7), and discuss whether the limitations of the four project designs can be circumvented (sec. 8).

2 A Simplified Model of Design Projects

The literature contains a plethora of partly overlapping and partly inconsistent design models (e.g., Bødker, Kensing, and Simonsen, this vol.; Checkland 2000; Fallman 2008; Leonard-Barton 1988; Markus 2004). In this chapter, we adopt a simplified design model (fig. 2.1), adapted from Kensing and Munk-Madsen (1993). Our goal is not to

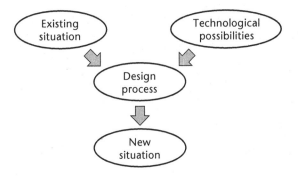

Figure 2.1
A simplified model of design projects.

propose a consensus about how to model design projects but simply to capture four basic elements that recur in many models. First, the *existing situation* must be understood. Users may already have this understanding, but designers need to experience the use situation, and the two groups of actors need relevant structures on the work, which can provide a common language for communication. Second, the *technological possibilities* must be explored. Designers need to maintain an overview of various technologies. Designers must also make relevant technologies available for users to experience, because such concrete experiences improve the users' ability to contribute creatively to the design process. Third, the *design process* must be organized and managed. The process of organization and management is complicated by the gradual and nonlinear way in which users and designers normally work out the desired match between the situation and the technological possibilities. Fourth, the *new situation* must be envisioned. Users as well as designers need abstract descriptions of design proposals to assign priorities and make decisions, but to better understand and more thoroughly assess proposed designs, they also need concrete experiences with prototypes and changes in work processes.

The new situation is an independent element because it involves a fundamental breaking away from the present understanding of how the users' tasks and the technological possibilities define the situation. The new situation is unknown at the outset and is only realized gradually. The cyclic nature of this gradual realization is fundamental to design processes, though not explicit in our simplified model. For this reason and because the cyclicity is important to the argument of this chapter, the simplified design model is supplemented with the task-artifact cycle (fig. 2.2). In the task-artifact cycle, designers respond to user requirements by building artifacts, which in turn present or deny possibilities to users (Carroll, Kellogg, and Rosson 1991). This process is nontrivial and inherently cyclic because users' and designers' understanding is situated (Haraway 1988). The users' understanding of their tasks is

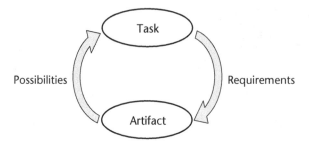

Figure 2.2
The task-artifact cycle.

determined by the artifacts they currently use, and at the same time, their under-standing of their artifacts is determined by the tasks for which they are using the artifacts. Likewise, designers' understanding of the technological possibilities is determined by their knowledge of tasks that need to be performed, and at the same time, their understanding of users' tasks is determined by the possibilities and restric-tions of the artifacts they currently know. Thus people's familiarity with certain artifacts and certain tasks shapes their understanding of what their tasks are and what technology has to offer. This understanding, in turn, constitutes a perspective that points to certain technological possibilities and makes people blind toward others (Naur 1965). The fundamentally important implication of such situated knowledge is that it is inherently difficult to transcend the current way of perceiving things and envision how tasks, users, and technology should interact in constituting the new situation.

3   The Analysis Project

The analysis project (fig. 2.3) takes the existing situation as its focal point and asks questions such as the following: Who are the stakeholders? What are they doing? Why are they doing it? How are they doing it? What is the problem? These questions call for understanding the users, their goals, tasks, present tools, and the broader context of use. In addition, the questions involve reaching an understanding of the users' experience both of the positive qualities of the use situation and of its negative aspects, such as inefficiencies, vulnerabilities to error, tediousness, and unappealingness. It is important to appreciate the positive qualities because they must be preserved—or changed very cautiously. In contrast, the negative aspects are important motivations for pursuing change and important starting points for the creative part of a design process. However, the positive and negative qualities of a use situation are often not readily apparent. What appears as a positive quality may, for example, be rendered

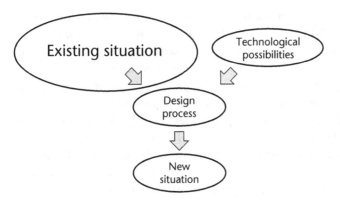

Figure 2.3
The analysis project.

obsolete by a new technology that removes some of the intermediate steps in a use process and thereby the need for the hitherto-appreciated tools for producing the input needed to complete these intermediate steps. Also, aspects perceived as negative by some stakeholders may be perceived as positive by others with different roles or responsibilities. Analyzing the existing situation involves reaching a balanced understanding of what must be preserved and what should be changed, that is, between tradition and transcendence (Ehn 1989).

The strength of an analysis project is the resulting rich understanding of the existing situation. Approaches that aim to reach such a rich understanding include science, technology, and society (STS) studies (e.g., Bijker, Hughes, and Pinch 1987), sense making (e.g., Weick 2001), and computer-supported cooperative work (Schmidt and Bannon 1992). However, reaching this understanding is often a project in itself, especially when the use situation is complex, the designers are new to the domain (as will often be the case with student designers), or both. For example, understanding the process through which patients receive medication at hospitals presupposes an understanding of, among other things, (a) the three subprocesses of ordering, administering, and giving medication; (b) the division of labor between physicians and nurses; (c) the documentation necessary to ensure that the right medication is given to the right patient at the right time; (d) the mundane practicalities that codetermine how the medication process is actually performed to get the work done; (e) the interrelations between the medication process and the other processes involved in treating the patient; and (f) the frequency with which physicians and nurses are interrupted during the medication process. To acquire this understanding, designers need to talk to physicians and nurses and, preferably, to observe them when they conduct the medication process. This takes time and effort.

Because reaching an understanding of the existing situation is often a project in itself, there is a considerable risk that the analysis project mainly accounts for the situation as is and pays cursory attention to needs for change and coherent ideas for satisfying such needs. This risk is exacerbated by the use of observation and (in situ) interviews as the main empirical methods in analysis projects. Observing the existing situation provides no input about alternative technological possibilities and thus little support for envisioning new situations that rethink user tasks and technological artifacts. Interviews have similar limitations, making it difficult for interviewees to formulate requirements that go beyond removing shortcomings in their current artifacts. Without a sustained focus on change during the analysis process, the acquired understanding of the situation as is will be unlikely to provide designers with sufficient information about the pertinent distinction between the elements of the use situation that must be preserved and those that should be changed, as this distinction evolves with each iteration of the task-artifact cycle.

4   The Construction Project

The construction project (fig. 2.4) focuses on the technological possibilities and provides answers to questions such as the following: How should the design's form reflect its function? What components are available as building blocks? How are any inputs transformed to outputs? Does it perform well? These questions call for understanding the available technologies, including their affordances, their look and feel, the extent to which their behavior can be configured or dynamically changed, and their openness toward integration with other technologies. But most importantly, the construction project calls for investigating the technological possibilities by actually constructing

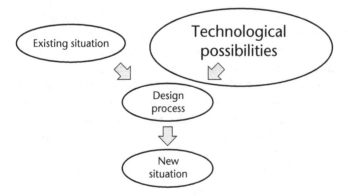

Figure 2.4
The construction project.

designs. By making hands-on experience with the technologies a driving element in the projects, one shifts the focus from principles to the application of principles and thereby to the complexity of handling the multiple practicalities that are abstracted away in principles. In the words of Schön (1983, 79), this complexity arises because the design situation "talks back," and it is handled by engaging in a "reflective conversation" with the situation. Construction is pivotal to this conversation because it is the construction of an initial design and the subsequent revisions of it that constitute the designer's moves in the conversation and thereby also constitute the material on which the situation talks back. The conversation becomes reflective when designers listen to the back talk and use it to form new appreciations of the situation and to refine their design. Conversely, the conversation remains unreflective if the designers merely apply principles without attending to the characteristics of the situation at hand.

The strength of the construction project is the reflective conversation that may ensue when constructing a design or a design prototype for use in a specified situation. Areas amenable to this type of project include architectural design, graphic design, industrial design, and IT design. However, the amount and quality of the back talk and reflection depend on the extent to which the use situation and its important details are impressed on the designers. When the designers are new to the use situation, the involved technologies, or both, it may be a project in itself to construct a design that matches even a simplistic use situation, thereby leaving little room for attending to the real complexity of the situation. For example, a project comprising the construction of an interface for flying a small, camera-equipped drone (unmanned aerial vehicle) by tilting a smartphone in three dimensions involves, among other things, developing a practical understanding of (a) the protocol for communicating with the drone, (b) the commands for operating the drone and reading its camera, (c) the protocol for communicating with the phone, (d) the command interfaces for accessing the phone's gyro that senses its tilting and for displaying a video stream on the phone, (e) the programming language used for developing apps and installing them on phones, and (f) the actual construction and testing of the app that reads the gyro, sends commands to the drone, receives the video stream from the drone, and shows it on the phone. To make room for addressing the technical challenges in this design, the use situation is virtually abstracted away, and back talk is reduced to the designers' own experience of the tilting interface.

Because it is often a project in itself to construct a design at even a prototype level of completion, there is considerable risk that construction projects become product-centric and dissociated from an understanding and appreciation of the use situation. This risk is exacerbated by the technical tools and skills necessary to construct actual designs but unhelpful when it comes to exploring the use situation. For example, constructing the app for maneuvering the drone creates little information about situations in which a tilt-controlled drone may be useful or appreciated. Such information is unlikely to emerge as a side effect of the construction activities. Construction projects predominantly study the artifact and technological possibilities, analogous to how analysis projects predominantly study the task and user requirements. Neither of these two project designs engages in a cyclic exploration of how requirements and possibilities mutually define each other, and both project designs therefore risk misunderstanding what users require, as well as what the technology has to offer.

5   The Process Project

The process project (fig. 2.5) focuses on the design process and asks how change is accomplished. This involves subquestions such as the following: What information is needed? How is it brought about, documented, and transformed into designs? How are designs evaluated and refined? How is the process managed? Are its outcomes reliable and valid? At an overall level, these questions call for knowledge about the organization of project activities into a linear or iterative process and the dual use of estimates to enforce plans and status information to enforce realism (Hertzum 2008). At a detail level, they call for knowledge about individual project activities, the methods available for performing them, and the pros and cons of the methods. The study of design processes is complicated by their situatedness. Processes, as prescribed in, for example, method handbooks and procedure manuals, are inherently underspecified. That is, their application to real-world situations involves a number of interpretations, steps, and prioritizations that are not specified but rather brought about by the local circumstances (Suchman 1987). The underspecified nature

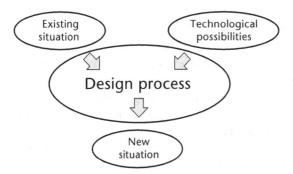

Figure 2.5
The process project.

of processes creates a tension between the process-as-prescribed and the process-as-practiced. This tension is central to process projects. The good process-as-prescribed provides guidance where needed but leaves sufficient freedom for the process-as-practiced to complement rather than contradict the prescription. At the same time, prescribed processes are intended to institute "best practices" and thereby to shape behavior to safeguard against error, produce outputs needed in other parts of the design process, comply with legal requirements to design documentation, or reduce quality variation through standardization.

The strength of the process project is the scrutiny and maturation of design processes. These processes include methods for work domain analysis (e.g., Vicente 1999), sketching (e.g., Greenberg et al. 2012), usability evaluation (e.g., Rubin and Chisnell 2008), and many other design processes. However, scrutinizing and maturing a design process is not easily integrated with an analysis, construction, or vision project because the design process becomes the end rather than remains a means. For example, investigating whether the process of thinking aloud affects how users in a usability test perform tasks involves, among other things, (a) knowledge of thinking aloud as originally prescribed by cognitive psychologists and as commonly practiced in the context of usability evaluation, (b) competence in conducting a thinking-aloud test, (c) knowledge of the aspects of the test procedure that may trigger thinking-aloud effects, (d) collection of data about these effects, (e) data about how users perform the tasks when not thinking out loud, and (f) analysis of any differences between the users who thought aloud and those who did not. In addition to introducing additional activities (e.g., activity e), the focus on the design process as an end also means that some otherwise similar activities grow in magnitude. For example, it is necessary with deeper background knowledge of thinking aloud.

Because it is often a project in itself to scrutinize the design process, or a part thereof, there is considerable risk that the process project loses sight of the design product. This risk is increased by the related risk of a dissociation between the process-as-prescribed and the process-as-practiced. For example, an overemphasis on the process-as-prescribed likely leads to processes that are too principled to be practically relevant, as when Carroll (1996), in his work on designing secure computer systems, states that "passwords to confidential information should be changed daily." In addition, the methods most useful to student designers may prescribe the design process in more step-by-step detail than the methods most useful to experienced design practitioners. The methods most useful to an experienced designer may instead provide a scaffolding that enables the designer to determine the right steps. This distinction between methods with scriptlike and maplike qualities (Schmidt 1999) further limits the possibilities of combining a process project with one of the three other project designs.

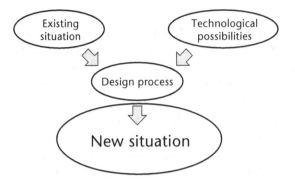

Figure 2.6
The vision project.

6   The Vision Project

The vision project (fig. 2.6) focuses on the new situation and aims to answer questions such as the following: What is the solution? Why is it desirable? How does it line up with a larger vision? What problems does it solve? How do we get there? These questions call for a coherent account of the envisioned new situation to show what the future may be like and expose the qualities of the vision. In so doing, the vision project seeks to short-circuit the task-artifact cycle by moving directly to the solution, thereby using the solution as a pivotal element in the design process rather than as its end point. However, a vision is normally not readily available, at least not in detail, but must be created. Even if a vision is available, it must be linked to user goals and technological possibilities to become convincing. This process of spelling out the vision is, according to many descriptions of design and creativity, most effective when the designers are knowledgeable about the current tasks and artifacts. For example, Petroski (1992, 22) asserts that "form follows failure" in the sense that the driver of design processes is the failure of existing designs to function properly. Also, more creative designs arise from carefully attending to constraints, whether they are imposed by the use situation, the technological possibilities, or the designers themselves (Stokes 2006). An important feature of targeting situation-defined and technology-defined constraints is that what initially appears an unwavering constraint may on closer scrutiny become more plastic.

The strength of the vision project is its coherent account of the new situation, not merely of a new technology. This account supports prospective users and other stakeholders in experiencing use, which adds context, meaning, and emotion to the technology. Methods for creating such visions include scenarios (Lindgren and Bandhold 2003), future search (Weisbord and Janoff 2007), and future workshops (Jungk and

Müllert 1987). However, an inspiring vision must strike a delicate balance to avoid both shortsightedness and getting lost in the degrees of freedom. This is often a project in itself. For example, a vision project about an electronic multikey that replaces all a person's keys with one device involves, among other things, that (a) the appealing reduction in the number of keys is not obtained at the cost of security; (b) the ease of using the multikey matches that of the keys it replaces; (c) a key owner can add a key to another person's multikey and subsequently revoke it; (d) the concept of keys may be extended to access cards, PIN codes, passwords, and so forth; (e) a unified security infrastructure is established across door keys, car keys, private keys, on-the-job keys, and so forth; and (f) many key producers adopt the system. In practice, it will only be possible to treat some of these topics in detail in any single student design project.

Because it is challenging to short-circuit the task-artifact cycle, there is considerable risk that the resulting vision will be unconvincingly linked to user goals and technological possibilities. An unconvincing vision appears to lack coherence, to make unrealistic assumptions, or simply to be vague. The vision may, for example, not handle existing constraints well, or it may presume widespread adoption of a single technological infrastructure across a large number of independent actors. If insufficiently linked to user goals, the vision may appear as a solution in search of a problem, indicating that the vision has failed in conveying a new situation, though it may have described a new technology. Alternatively, the vision may be convincingly linked to user goals and technological possibilities but be unconvincing in its short-termism. That is, it may lack vision. In this case, the scenarios or other methods have neither short-circuited the task-artifact cycle nor iteratively transcended the initial understanding of how tasks and artifacts codetermine each other.

7 The Four-Question Method

As a method for supporting student designers in forming groups, identifying a project focus, and devising a project design, this chapter proposes four project-design questions (fig. 2.7). Each question targets a different element of the design process (analysis, construction, process, and vision), and because the elements are interrelated, an answer to one question helps narrow down the possible answers to the other questions. In this way, the four questions offer four different entry points to the demanding process of devising a project focus and a project design.

A student designer may know neither what problem to work on in her next project nor what process to use, but she may have an interest in exploring the possibilities of growing plants without the use of soil, a technology known as hydroponics. That is, her starting point is a technological solution. From this starting point, she may, for example, go on to consider what problem hydroponics may solve, what kind of

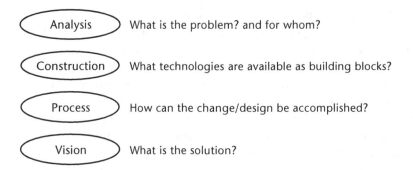

Figure 2.7
The four project-design questions.

empirical work she can do on this topic, and whether these analysis and process considerations appear interesting or her main interest is hydroponics as a vision. In the former case, she may proceed to think about the role she would want the empirical work to play in her project process. In the latter case, she may recognize that she, at present, does not have a good idea about how to work with the topic of hydroponics in her project.

The four questions serve the additional purpose of supporting the formation of groups by providing four dimensions along which students can state their interests and across which they can look for possibilities for collaboration. For example, a student with an interest in problems related to urbanization may discover that hydroponics provides a concrete way for him to work with urbanization by formulating a project about the problem of providing people in large, polluted cities with inexpensive, healthy food. His mainly analytic, problem-focused interest may or may not be compatible with the project designs envisaged by the other students interested in working with hydroponics. The question that a student designer feels most strongly about points toward a likely project design and also toward the main risk the student must consider in formulating a project. Thus the four questions may inform decisions about whether to team up with students who have a similar interest in a preferred project design or to seek out students who have complementary interests to avoid a risk that is perceived as too limiting.

The four questions may also be useful after the initial formative stage of a project. They may, for example, be used in discussions of whether the project focus has drifted or how it may need adjusting. The most important role of the four questions during the middle and late stages of a project may, however, be in helping student designers think of the flaws of project designs more as part and parcel of project work, that is, as normal, natural troubles (Garfinkel 1967), than as indications of bad project designs.

Project supervisors may play a role in promoting the use of the four questions as a vehicle for reflection on the consequences—both positive and negative—of the project design on the design solution.

8 Discussion

The four project designs discussed here do not exhaust the ways in which student design projects can be focused. A project design that may appear obvious is one that focuses evenly on all four basic elements in figure 2.1. Such a project design would avoid the shortcomings of the analysis, construction, process, and vision projects, but it is rare in practice, for several reasons. First, project designs that focus on a single basic element tend to require an effort that makes them full projects. Thus including all four elements in a student design project is likely to be unrealistic. Expecting all four elements appears a bit like expecting every research paper to include a formal theory, a survey, a laboratory experiment, and a field study to overcome the shortcomings of employing each of these research methods individually (McGrath 1981). Second, if a project focuses evenly on all four basic elements, it runs a considerable risk of attaining substandard performance on all four elements. In attempting to avoid this outcome, such a project design is under constant pressure to evolve into one of the four other project designs. Third, rather than focusing evenly on all four elements, a project may include all four elements but focus more on one than on the others. In such uneven projects, the analysis part, for example, has a strong foundation, whereas the other parts are more speculative. This imbalance will likely reinforce itself by directing more attention to the element that already receives most attention—to sharpen the project focus and clarify its contribution. Fourth, design is a cross-disciplinary area, at least in the sense that the four project designs call for different kinds of competences, considerations, and project deliverables. However, many supervisors of student design projects have their background in one discipline. Consequently, a supervisor may be more comfortable with one project design than with the others (e.g., a supervisor with a computer science background may be more comfortable with construction projects) and may therefore gravitate toward that project design rather than support students in balancing all four basic elements in their project designs.

The four project designs discussed here are defined by their main activity. Another way of defining project types is by distinguishing different areas to which design projects contribute. For example, Fallman (2008) distinguishes between projects that contribute to design practice with its focus on commercial and industrial considerations, to design studies with their focus on creating academic knowledge about design, and to design exploration with its focus on how design may be a voice in societal discussions about possible futures. Analogous to our argument, Fallman argues that the most interesting projects interrelate different positions rather than contribute to either design practice, design studies, or design exploration. The interrelations are interesting because they concern the dynamic and negotiated aspects of projects and point toward possible tensions or reinforcements. Thus bypassing the interrelations transmutes the design situation by making it less multifaceted, convoluted, and dynamic and, conversely, more orderly, linear, and artificial. This is contrary to the goal of project-based learning, which emphasizes "the connection of knowledge to the contexts of its application" (Barron et al. 1998, 272). Emphasizing that knowledge is situated implies that when a project design curtails the design situation, it also reduces the learning that student designers can gain from the project.

Interrelations between positions may be realized after the fact when looking back at a project, or they may be used proactively in planning and conducting a project. Major interrelations between the four project designs, defined by their focus on analysis, construction, process, or vision, are given in the simplified model of design projects (fig. 2.1) and in the task-artifact cycle (fig. 2.2). A project may, for example, aim to interrelate analysis and process to explore challenges in, and possible ways of working with, analysis throughout the process. In the next chapter, continuing our discussion of project designs, Nielsen and Andreasen make recommendations about how to foster and enhance learning from the collaborative activities of problem-based design projects.

Student designers may use the four-question method in thinking about the focus and project design of an individual project, but they may also use the four project designs in thinking about the series of projects that enters into their study program. One possibility is to focus on one basic element, such as the technological opportunities, in one project and on another in the next project, thereby devising a portfolio of projects that collectively cover all four basic elements. This strategy comes, however, at the cost of not experiencing how iterating among the elements leads to designs that transcend the existing situation and produce new ways for users, tasks, and technologies to interact. Another possibility is to create a personal profile in the series of projects by devising project designs that consistently give priority to a favored subset of the basic elements. This strategy builds on the rationale that most real design projects are staffed with groups of designers, each responsible for only part of the project.

To encourage project designs that comprise all four basic elements, supervisors and examiners need to acknowledge the required integration effort more than they criticize the flaws in the performance of the individual elements. In addition, supervisors need to provide models for student designers to follow. As an example, the method provided in chapter 4 of this book by Bødker, Kensing, and Simonsen may constitute a model for design projects in the area of information systems design, though with some risk of trivializing the technological possibilities. Alternatively, supervisors may support students in devising series of projects, in which the first project focuses on one basic element and provides input for the next project, which focuses on another basic element, and so forth. Such support could be educationally beneficial by providing for progressively more depth in the projects and for more coherence across study activities. In addition, it could be practically beneficial by rearing student designers' awareness of the importance of learning across projects, an activity that is associated with uncertainty in much practical design work (Hertzum 2008).

9 Conclusion

Design projects produce change by creating a new situation on the basis of input about the existing situation and the technological possibilities. Perceived in this way, design projects have four basic elements: the existing situation, the technological possibilities, the new situation, and the process through which the new situation is brought about. Each element contains complexly interrelated subelements and poses considerable challenges to the designer. This makes it even more challenging for student designers to handle competently the interrelations among the four elements. These interrelations, however, are fundamental to understanding the particularities and possibilities provided by the concrete situation and are thus central to situating the design successfully by emphasizing, de-emphasizing, and transforming these interrelations. Because the interrelations among the four basic elements are challenging to handle competently, project designs that focus predominantly on one of the basic elements are common but forgo important aspects of design:

• The analysis project focuses on the existing situation, aims to understand what the problem is, and risks becoming detached from change.
• The construction project focuses on the technological possibilities, aims to build something, and risks failing to appreciate the use situation.
• The process project focuses on the design process, aims to model how change is accomplished, and risks losing sight of the design product.
• The vision project focuses on the new situation, aims to explore where we want to go, and risks becoming an unconvincing extension of user goals or technological possibilities.

No matter which of these project designs the student chooses, the choice has serious limitations. Design students should be aware of this when they devise their project designs. This raises the question of whether the limitations can be circumvented by choosing a fifth project design. A project design that comprises all four basic elements is potentially highly rewarding but risks attaining substandard performance on all four elements. This risk creates a pressure toward evolving the project into one of the four other project designs.

References

Barron, Brigid J. S., Daniel L. Schwartz, Nancy J. Vye, Allison More, Anthony Petrosino, Linda Zech, John D. Bransford, and the Cognition and Technology Group at Vanderbilt. 1998. Doing with understanding: Lessons from research on problem- and project-based learning. *Journal of the Learning Sciences* 7 (3–4): 271–311.

Bijker, Wiebe E., Thomas P. Hughes, and Trevor Pinch, eds. 1987. *The Social Construction of Technological Systems: New Directions in the Sociology and History of Technology*. Cambridge, MA: MIT Press.

Carroll, John M. 1996. *Computer Security*, 3rd ed. Boston: Butterworth-Heinemann.

Carroll, John M., Wendy A. Kellogg, and Mary B. Rosson. 1991. The task-artifact cycle. In *Designing Interaction: Psychology at the Human-Computer Interface*, ed. John M. Carroll, 74–102. Cambridge: Cambridge University Press.

Checkland, Peter. 2000. Soft systems methodology: A thirty-year retrospective. *Systems Research and Behavioural Science* 17, Suppl. no. 1: S11–S58.

Ehn, Pelle. 1989. *Work-Oriented Design of Computer Artifacts*, 2nd ed. Stockholm: Arbetslivscentrum.

Fallman, Daniel. 2008. The interaction design research triangle of design practice, design studies, and design exploration. *Design Issues* 24 (3): 4–18.

Garfinkel, Harold. 1967. "Good" organizational reasons for "bad" clinic records. In *Studies in Ethnomethodology*, 186–207. Englewood Cliffs, NJ: Prentice Hall.

Greenberg, Saul, Sheelagh Carpendale, Nicolai Marquardt, and Bill Buxton. 2012. *Sketching User Experiences: The Workbook*. Waltham, MA: Morgan Kaufmann.

Haraway, Donna. 1988. Situated knowledges: The science question in feminism and the privilege of partial perspective. *Feminist Studies* 14 (3): 575–599.

Hertzum, Morten. 2008. On the process of software design: Sources of complexity and reasons for muddling through. In *Proceedings of the IFIP EIS 2007 Conference on Engineering Interactive Systems*, ed. Jan Gulliksen, Morten B. Harning, P. Palanque, G. C. van der Veer, and J. Wesson, 483–500. Berlin: Springer.

Jungk, Robert, and Norbert Müllert. 1987. *Future Workshops: How to Create Desirable Futures*. London: Institute for Social Inventions.

Kensing, Finn, and Andreas Munk-Madsen. 1993. PD: Structure in the toolbox. *Communications of the ACM* 36 (6): 78–85.

Leonard-Barton, Dorothy. 1988. Implementation as mutual adaptation of technology and organization. *Research Policy* 17 (5): 251–267.

Lindgren, Mats, and Hans Bandhold. 2003. *Scenario Planning: The Link between Future and Strategy.* New York: Palgrave Macmillan.

Markus, M. Lynne. 2004. Technochange management: Using IT to drive organizational change. *Journal of Information Technology* 19 (1): 4–20.

McGrath, Joseph E. 1981. Dilemmatics: The study of research choices and dilemmas. *American Behavioral Scientist* 25 (2): 179–210.

Naur, Peter. 1965. The place of programming in a world of problems, tools and people. In *Proceedings of the IFIP Congress 65,* vol. 1, ed. Wayne A. Kalenich, 195–199. Washington, DC: Spartan Books.

Petroski, Henry. 1992. *The Evolution of Useful Things: How Everyday Artifacts—from Forks and Pins to Paper Clips and Zippers—Came to Be as They Are.* New York: Vintage Books.

Rubin, Jeffrey, and Dana Chisnell. 2008. *Handbook of Usability Testing: How to Plan, Design, and Conduct Effective Tests,* 2nd ed. Indianapolis: Wiley.

Schmidt, Kjeld. 1999. Of maps and scripts: The status of formal constructs in cooperative work. *Information and Software Technology* 41 (6): 319–329.

Schmidt, Kjeld, and Liam Bannon. 1992. Taking CSCW seriously: Supporting articulation work. *Computer Supported Cooperative Work* 1 (1): 7–40.

Schön, Donald A. 1983. *The Reflective Practitioner: How Professionals Think in Action.* Aldershot, UK: Ashgate.

Simon, Herbert A. 1996. *The Sciences of the Artificial,* 3rd ed. Cambridge, MA: MIT Press.

Stokes, Patricia D. 2006. *Creativity from Constraints: The Psychology of Breakthrough.* New York: Springer.

Suchman, Lucy A. 1987. *Plans and Situated Action: The Problem of Human-Machine Interaction.* Cambridge: Cambridge University Press.

Vicente, Kim J. 1999. *Cognitive Work Analysis: Toward Safe, Productive, and Healthy Computer-Based Work.* Mahwah, NJ: Erlbaum.

Weick, Karl E. 2001. *Making Sense of the Organization.* Malden, MA: Blackwell.

Weisbord, Marvin, and Sandra Janoff. 2007. Future search: Common ground under complex conditions. In *The Change Handbook,* 2nd ed., ed. Peggy Holman, Tom Devane, and Steven Cady, 316–330. San Francisco: Berrett-Koehler.

3 Design and Co-Design of Project-Organized Studies

Jørgen Lerche Nielsen and Lars Birch Andreasen

What. The chapter contributes to discussions on design processes in relation to education, presenting different notions of design research and demonstrating how professors and students are involved together in designing innovative and constructive study processes that can help foster students' engagement, self-awareness, mutual evaluation, reflection, and critical and creative thinking. The case presented and analyzed is the master's program ICT and learning (MIL), where Roskilde University is partner in the cross-institutional collaboration behind the program.

Why. It is a challenge for the educational system to meet the new needs for competencies owing to the change from an industrial society to a knowledge-based society. The problem-based approach can be seen as an attempt to meet these challenges. Unlike a classic curriculum-oriented and teacher-steered model, project work is open-ended and directed at handling unknown and dynamic processes.

Where. Problem-based approaches are relevant for master's programs with a need for collaboration, flexibility, and implementation of technologies to overcome time, space, and geographical limitations, and for study programs, where students are involved in self-directed study practices, and where there is a need for continuing reflective processes of how to learn. In relation to the bachelor program in design, humanities, and technology at Roskilde University, it is relevant to reflect on designs for learning in relation to both experimental use and analytical dimensions of new technologies.

How. The methodological approach deals with developing designs for learning that involve students as co-designers through problem- and project-based learning. The approach can be applied by professors and students who collaboratively wish to develop their study programs. In the situated context of problem-based learning, we discuss how students can plan and continually redesign their project work, how a balance of verbal and written activity can be maintained, and how social media can support group processes.

1 Introduction

In this chapter, we show how design research can be related to the field of learning and how professors and students can design innovative and constructive study processes that can help meet competencies needed in a knowledge-based society. We discuss the tradition of designs for learning (Selander 2008) and the opposing tradition of instructional design. Furthermore, we try to show how the introduction and growth of information and communication technologies (ICT) within the last decade has set a new agenda for learning designs in schools and universities. We focus especially on problem- and project-based studies as they have developed in Denmark since the beginning of the 1970s. Our case will be the master's program in ICT and learning (MIL), where Roskilde and Aalborg universities are partners in the cross-institutional collaboration behind the program.

As an alternative to more curriculum-oriented teaching approaches, problem- and project-based learning has developed over the last decades into an institutionalized approach (Barron et al. 1998; Olesen and Jensen 1999; Kolmos, Fink, and Krogh 2004; Andreasen and Nielsen 2013). This approach focuses on exploring and working with problems as a didactic method. Problem-based learning (PBL) offered a new perspective to the existing teaching practice, a perspective where students, instead of only listening to professors lecturing, gained their own experiences through working with practical cases—scenarios, visual prompts, design briefs, puzzling phenomena, or other triggers, often based in real life—that may mobilize students to learn (Barrett and Moore 2011, 4). Frank and Barzilai (2006, 40) state that students who worked in a problem-based learning environment were likely to engage in processes of active learning and gain multidisciplinary knowledge, and note that "the PBL environment ... increased students' self-confidence, motivation to learn, creative abilities, and self-esteem."

In Denmark the approaches of problem- and project-based learning were developed at the universities of Roskilde and Aalborg, with an emphasis on collaboration and student-directed project work (Dirckinck-Holmfeld 2002; Kolmos, Fink, and Krogh 2004; Olesen and Jensen 1999). In relation to this approach, a central task, which we explore in this chapter, is how to develop designs for learning that may engage students in taking responsibility for their learning process. A challenge in this process is how teachers can help students to relate curriculum and theories to praxis. Thus the methodological approach that we introduce and discuss in this chapter is developing designs for learning that involves students as co-designers through problem- and project-based learning.

In relation to the MIL case, we have been involved as practitioners designing curricula and study sequences and, together with our students, designing frames for problem-based learning processes. This explorative endeavor covers both face-to-face learning environments (on-site) and networked learning environments (online). We will be examining how professors and students together are trying to create productive learning environments, and the implications of this for the professor-student relationship. Note that in this chapter we generally use the term *professor* to cover the positions of professor, associate professor, teacher, lecturer, assistant professor, and so on.

In relation to the bachelor program in design, humanities, and technology at Roskilde University, it is relevant to reflect on how study processes—in both experimental use and analytical dimensions of new technologies—can be designed and draw inspiration from the examples mentioned earlier.

2 Design-Based Research and Education

The term *design experiments* was first introduced in the field of education in articles by Ann Brown (1992) and Allan Collins (1992). Previously educational research in the United States to a high degree took place in controlled and fairly isolated environments, typically within laboratories, but since the early 1990s there has been lively debate on how "design-based research" or simply "design research" may have relevance for education and the understanding of learning processes. The central characteristics of using a design-based research approach in education will be as follows (Collins, Joseph, and Bielaczyc 2004, 16; Barab and Squire 2004):

• Approaching the study of learning phenomena situated in real-world settings through ethnographic methods rather than isolated laboratory studies.
• Producing new insights and theory through interventions in praxis.
• Conducting iterative processes, cycles of designing, implementing, analyzing, evaluating, and redesigning.
• Involving researchers as well as practitioners.
• Applying a pragmatic approach oriented toward improving the setting of the intervention.

New paradigms emerged with a greater focus on how learning and knowledge are created through the interaction and active participation of students in the learning processes. According to Barab and Squire (2004, 1), "Learning, cognition, knowing, and context are irreducibly co-constituted and cannot be treated as isolated entities or processes." Their argument is that a fuller understanding of how learning occurs should be reached in "messy" real-life circumstances, where study processes are explored situated in their social context. Within the last decade, special issues of educational journals have been published to examine this field, for example, *Educational Researcher* 32, no. 1 (2003), edited by Kelly and Bell; *Journal of the Learning Sciences* 13, no. 1 (2004), edited by Barab and Squire; *Educational Psychologist* 39, no. 4 (2004), edited by Sandoval and Bell; and *Journal of Computing in Higher Education* 16, no. 2 (2005), edited by MacKnight.

In Denmark the debate has taken quite another direction. Lab research within isolated controlled environments has been rare. Instead practice-oriented research focused on the specific situatedness has been conducted within schools and educational institutions and often in connection to efforts directed at reforming schools through practical experiments and developmental projects. More recently the term *design-based research* has been discussed in relation to education (Ejersbo et al. 2008; Christensen, Gynther, and Petersen 2012). In 2012 a special issue of the Danish online journal *Læring og Medier* (*Learning and Media* 5, no. 9 [2012], ed. Pedersen, Löfvall, Dalsgaard, and Bang) was dedicated to design-based research. The effort is to create a better understanding of the different processes connected to research and intervention in learning situations. By following the iterative processes of design-based research, researchers can carry out thorough investigations. Various kinds of data—ethnographic observations, recordings of logs, diary notes, online contributions, audio or video recordings, interviews, and quantitative data from surveys—may contribute to redefining the problems and proposing possible solutions and principles to address them. As data are reexamined and reflected on, new designs are created and implemented, producing a continuous cycle of design-reflection-design.

This iterative design method has similarities with the action research and the participatory design research traditions. Here also the common goal for practitioners and researchers is to achieve more satisfying and democratic practices. For the researcher or designer, the practitioners are valuable partners in identifying problems, developing solutions, helping to establish research questions, and supporting mutual learning (Robertson and Simonsen 2013), and there is a widespread tradition in the United States, Australia, the United Kingdom, and the Scandinavian countries of transforming the action research approach to action learning for the involved participants (Revans 1982; Kemmis and Wilkinson 1998).

3   Case Analysis: Design of Project Work

We turn now to the case of the MIL program and discuss how we as a team of professors have continually been working on designing and redesigning the educational program in interaction with the students.

3.1   The Master's Program in ICT and Learning (MIL)

The case that we discuss here comes from the Danish postgraduate master's program MIL, which is a part-time program. Most of the students are employed full-time or part-time while studying, and they come from all parts of the country. The MIL program was established in 2000 and is being offered as a joint program between four Danish universities.

The program builds on a networked learning structure and combines on-site seminars with online periods of course activities and project work. Pedagogically, the program builds on principles of student engagement in formulating research questions, investigating exemplary problems, and using interdisciplinary approaches. In their projects, the students study research problems from their own work practice, applying theories, concepts, and methods from the academic practice. Thus the master's program is a development of problem- and project-based learning, adapted to the virtual study environment.

The virtual learning environment used at MIL combines an e-learning platform with various open online facilities. The e-learning platform FirstClass contains asynchronous and synchronous communication and collaboration facilities, file sharing, individual mailboxes and profiles, a who-is-online facility, and virtual folders for student groups to save, share, and organize their contributions. In addition to these features, the students also use synchronous video meeting facilities (Adobe Connect, Google Hangout), peer-to-peer tools and Web 2.0 facilities (Skype, Messenger, Google Docs, Facebook, blogs), and tools to support project and course work (e.g., Camtasia for screen recording, Zotero for reference handling).

In the following, we present how MIL students in problem-based and project-organized studies work with their master's projects and act as co-designers of learning activities.

3.2 Developing Master's Projects

For MIL students, working with projects allows them to dive deeper into a problem they wish to clarify, thus supplementing their previous course activities.

At MIL the main part of the spring semester is dedicated to working with student-directed projects. At one of the preceding face-to-face seminars, the students have started a process of developing and negotiating which problems and research questions to focus on. A brainstorming event is organized, where proposals are lined up and students get a first idea of which themes could be relevant or possible and which groups could be formed. These initial discussions are followed by online dialogues during the following months, where students are continually presenting potential topics for projects and negotiating among them. Some students develop themes derived from courses and seminars in the previous semesters; others move into new areas. Taking part in a group is encouraged, but it is also possible for students to work individually on a project. Professors in the program are allocated as supervisors and facilitators for the projects.

Master's projects are often written by groups, where one of the members is an "insider" in relation to the case or organization being studied, while the other(s) are "outsiders" (Dirckinck-Holmfeld et al. 2008, 178). The insider will often have a deeper knowledge of the case and will be able to facilitate access to contacts, places, and so on. It may, however, be difficult to study practices you are involved in and to establish the view from a distance that is also necessary to study a case. As Alvesson states, "The challenge of ethnography, and of most qualitative work, is to be close and avoid closure" (2003, 190). For a group in this situation, the group members who are outsiders will be able to challenge understandings and pose critical questions. The possibilities of such collaboration in a master's project lie in the meeting of different perspectives, not by uncritically combining both but by constantly challenging the students' assumptions and interpretations of their material.

While creating papers for their project, the students are constantly reflecting on the processes they are engaged in. What insights do they achieve? What do they learn during the process? What can they eventually do otherwise next time in a similar situation? Speaking about the benefits of the group collaboration processes, a student explains that "we were not good in putting things down in writing, but on the other hand we were really good at talking and talking at our Skype meetings" (male student at MIL; our translation). It is a well-known challenge to establish a practice where groups not only talk and unfold ideas but also capture these ideas in writing. The process of writing may be hard work, but it often contributes to clarifying the students' ideas. This issue can be seen as a parallel to Wenger's (1998) discussion of the importance of the interplay between participation and reification, between the momentary process of generating ideas and the long stretch of forming products and results. Both processes are necessary parts of productive group collaboration.

Another challenge for groups is to establish and maintain an overview of decisions, materials, and texts produced during the process: "Like all other project groups who work 99 percent through mail or conferences in, e.g., FirstClass, we have in our group had difficulties in maintaining an overview of our work. I think we have been constrained by not having met face-to-face to clarify deadlines and other questions that needed to be decided" (student at MIL; our translation). This student points at some of the difficulties that may arise when working only asynchronously, in this case through e-mail and in Web conferences. A face-to-face meeting as suggested by the student might have eased the process, but a number of online Web 2.0 facilities are also available to make it easier for groups to create and share resources, connect to others, interact, and work collaboratively across time and space. The group might, for example, have gained a better overview by expanding the traditional asynchronous tools with storage facilities that allow revision control ("Where is the newest version of this chapter?") or easily manageable online spaces to share various kinds of materials, such as Dropbox or Google Drive. Moreover, the problem of decision making could be helped either through a Doodle (e.g., for small polls or decisions on dates) or through synchronous tools like Skype, Google Hangouts, or Adobe Connect that might facilitate their decision-making processes better than asynchronous tools.

As O'Reilly observes, Web 2.0 has made it possible for users of the Internet to engage in processes of "harnessing collective intelligence" by easing the conditions for collaboration, sharing, and active learning (O'Reilly 2007, 22). It is noteworthy how the relatively big changes of users' work practices that follow from working with Web 2.0 tools often seamlessly become an integrated part of the way of working.

When dealing with online project-organized learning activities, as in the MIL program and the bachelor program in design, humanities, and technology at Roskilde University, where students are engaged in analyzing complex matters and doing experimental and construction-based projects, the professor's main role is not solely as a lecturer or instructor but as a supervisor. As Kahiigi et al. suggest: "The teacher takes on a facilitator role while the students take ownership of their learning and personal development" (Kahiigi et al. 2008, 82). Some of the MIL students reflected on the relation between supervisor and students and the role of a teacher as a supervisor. One student indicated in retrospect that their group had made too little use of supervision. Another student pointed out the pitfalls of relying too much on supervision and advised not to turn on the "automatic pilot" when being supervised: "A supervisor meeting may cause a kind of tunnel vision, because you have a tendency to follow the guidelines from the supervision very strictly" (student at MIL; our translation). This highlights the reciprocity of the relationship between students and supervisor. As a supervisor, the professor may act as a coach, a mentor, and a discussion partner, that is, as one who supports as well as challenges the students in their project work.

A supervisor should not just give the students what they want but should instead stimulate the students to transgress their familiar abilities and enter new areas of activity. A supervisor can do this proactively in relation to the students' projects by showing possible ways for the students to go, but at the same time without taking too much responsibility. Thus a supervisor must strike a delicate balance between outwardly pushing and patiently waiting: "The ideal supervisor is a person that understands how 'to feed,' but also to hold back, in order for the expertise of the group to unfold" (student at MIL; our translation).

Based on our experiences teaching at the MIL program, we will point out that teaching online creates a need for technological as well as social awareness, where professors should be visible and accessible, in other words, mobilize telepresence. The challenge for the professor is to allow adequate space for students to operate and navigate, but at the same time provide clear criteria and standards to ensure students understand the tasks and activities. Especially in online activities, it is important to help the students stick to their work and hold on to their plans.

Through the problem- and project-based method of studying, students can thus actively participate in and design their own collaborative work processes. In the following sections, we point out some crucial aspects that students must deal with in this process.

4   Students Designing and Owning Their Project

In a problem- and project-based learning environment, it is important for participants to support one another in finding new ideas for relevant, challenging, and multifaceted problems to work with. The starting point of a student group's independent work on a project is to choose a topic or a problem that represents a challenge to them. This is similar to what the cultural anthropologist Michael Wesch (2012) underlines as the importance of supporting students' ability to wonder. The process of defining a problem involves questions such as the following: What are the meanings of this problem? Why should we try to solve it? How did it emerge? What could we aim to design, for what purpose, and for whose benefit? Working with questions like these can be a challenging but productive process (Hertzum, this vol.). Furthermore, it is interdisciplinary in that it may combine knowledge and ideas from different kinds of academic fields, as underlined by Olsen and Pedersen (2005).

Students participating in project groups should learn to combine the ability to plan ahead with the ability to improvise. In this combination of planning and acting, group decisions may deal with questions like what to do next, who should do what, and when in the process to undertake particular tasks. In this process, continuous redesign of the plans is a necessity. This is framed by Karl Weick's concept of "improvisational design," according to which tasks and surroundings are viewed as dynamic, complex processes, where activities can be planned only tentatively and through continuing iterations. It is therefore necessary for the participants—whether students, professors, or designers—to engage in dialogues and negotiations to reach strategies for action (Weick 2001, 57). This can be related to coping with the unknown and unexpected challenges confronting a student group. The collaborative processes of project work can be frustrating, but if the students do not become overwhelmed, those frustrations can also hold possibilities for new understandings and can thus be used as tools for learning.

In the process of reflecting on and clarifying their research question, students learn how to plan, manage, and evaluate projects. In this process, Schön's (1983, 1987) concept of "reflection-in-action," as well as "reflection-on-action," could be applied. Schön points to the ability of professionals to "think about what they are doing while doing it" (Schön 1983, 275). For students collaborating, it is crucial to be aware of what they are doing, and how they are interacting while they are doing it. Also, after meetings and in preparing for future meetings, it is important to reflect on what was going on last time: how can we, if necessary, do things in other ways, and what initiatives should we take in the future? Students' ways of dealing with the continuous evaluation of their situation and eventual redesign of their plans are central to their process. Do they stick firmly to agreements made earlier, or do they revise according to new needs?

The situation where students are designing and taking ownership of their own learning process has not always been the case within the field of education. To further elaborate the competing notions of education in play, we now discuss the development in educational paradigms, from the curriculum-oriented instructional design approach to a more learner-centered and dynamic approach.

5 From Instructional Design to Designs for Learning

A school of thought in the field of technology and education, which has influenced many educational approaches, is the paradigm of instructional design. Since the 1940s, the instructional design approach has focused on developing effective designs for instruction and teaching that are generally applicable for the teacher. Instructional design refers to the development and construction of educational systems of a fixed nature, which can easily be used by the instructor in any learning process. The course, its content, and its materials are standardized in the same way as the methodological conception of the course. We discuss in this section the approach of instructional design in contrast to the concept of designs for learning, which focus on how to design for learning processes that occur in situated contexts.

The concept of instructional design has its roots in behaviorism (focusing on external stimuli, observation of actions, and the ability to measure learning outcome) and in cognitivism (focusing on information processing and on instruction as transmission of information) in its view of learning activities (Harasim 2011, 41, 52). The original idea of instructional design can be said to reflect the surrounding environment of the industrial age, with its standardization and assembly lines. In relation to education, Staffan Selander describes this situation as a "world of prefabricated learning resources, formalized work and strict time-tables (lessons). The role of the teacher is to 'bring' knowledge to the student, and the student's role is to remember by heart and to learn specific skills" (Selander 2008, 14). The instructional design approach aims to transmit knowledge to the students as efficiently as possible. Karl Weick captures this situation with his architectural metaphor: "Organizational design modeled along the lines of architectural design is viewed as a bounded activity that occurs at a fixed point in time" (Weick 2001, 57). Plans that are made through this approach envision structures rather than processes. In a text directly related to education, Weick states that "preoccupation with rationalized, tidy, efficient, coordinated structures has blinded many practitioners as well as researchers to some of the attractive and unexpected properties of less rationalized and less tightly related clusters of events" (Weick 1976, 3), thereby pointing out the affordances of a more fluid approach, not bound by structures but following the situated processes as they evolve.

At the EdMedia World Conference on Educational Media and Technology in Denver, Colorado, in June 2012, where we participated, there was a lively discussion among some presenters—among them the Canadian online learning researcher Linda Harasim (Harasim et al. 1995; Harasim 2011)—on the perception of the term *instructional design*. Harasim viewed the term as a top-down approach, standardized, universalistic, and fixed, with a strict division between a professional instructional designer planning the course and the actual teachers conducting the activities of a class (Harasim 2011, 56). Other discussants, among them Tel Amiel and Thomas Reeves, pointed out that the instructional design paradigm has changed over the past twenty years, and today instructional designers also try to build a bridge to the practitioners in the classrooms and allow for customization and improved adaptability to the actual situation. The instructional design paradigm has therefore evolved into a broader understanding than originally.

Reigeluth (1999, 19) also talks of a paradigm shift in the theory of instructional design toward a "learning-focused" paradigm as a result of the need for communication, problem-solving, and collaboration skills in the modern information society. Reigeluth states that while the industrial age encouraged standardization, bureaucratic organization, and centralized control, the new era encourages customization. Reigeluth argues that this change will force instructional design to switch from a passive learning system based on instructor control to an active learning system, which will be learner centered. In the new paradigm, learners must be able to take initiative to guarantee their own learning experience. They will need to know that they can be autonomous, but must understand that they are also accountable for their learning, and a large amount of the learning responsibility is thereby shifted to the learner (19).

We acknowledge that the concept of instructional design has evolved. However, it still focuses more on the instructor's perspective than on the student as participant. And to focus on the learning that may unfold and the possible involvement of students as co-designers, we understand the paradigm of "designs for learning" to be more in line with a perspective supporting a problem- and project-based learning approach.

The paradigm of designs for learning focuses on the students' active learning processes and the creation of a learning environment that may foster dialogue, negotiation, sense making, and genuine collaboration among the participants. *Design* is both a noun and a verb, and therefore "designs for learning" refers as well to designing seen as a process and design seen as a product. Design is not only something you do before the practice. You design before, but you also design during, practice. The tradition of designs for learning thus builds on a constructivist view of learning, focusing on the mutual interaction between learners, teachers, and peers in developing knowledge. The specific designs for learning should aim at supporting a flexible and situational communicative setup and thus provide support for communicative actions, which is, as we have seen, crucial for project groups.

Regarding societal, organizational, and educational changes, we can apply Karl Weick's metaphors for organizational planning and learning, discussed earlier. Weick is skeptical about the common use of static architectural metaphors for organizational design and develops instead metaphors of improvisational theater as enabling designers to cope with emergent and unforeseen events (Weick 2001, 57ff). The design Weick aims to capture with the metaphor of improvisation is a pattern of interaction that is bottom-up and realized as a result of enacting "the unknown." This kind of "improvisational design" seems to capture many of the processes meeting us in a situated learning context, where many decisions by professors as well as students have to be made in the midst of actions and cannot be planned and decided beforehand.

The continuous consideration and negotiation of strategies is also framed by Suchman, who in her book *Plans and Situated Actions* puts forward a critique of the then-dominant cognitive science approach to technology design as it relied on an understanding of human activity where plans were directing actions. Suchman advocates an alternative view, where plans are seen not as directions but as potential resources for action, which need to be understood as they unfold in situ, and should be revised continuously according to the new situations (Suchman [1987] 2007; see also this vol., chap. 1).

A parallel can be made to the participatory design tradition, with its perspective of always looking forward to the shaping of future situations. Robertson and Simonsen define participatory design as "a process of investigating, understanding, reflecting upon, establishing, developing, and supporting mutual learning between multiple participants in collective 'reflection-in-action'" (Robertson and Simonsen 2013, 2). In this tradition there is an ongoing effort to deepen our understanding of how collaborative design processes can enable the participation of those who will in the future be affected by their results: "The participants typically undertake the two principal roles of users and designers where the designers strive to learn the realities of the users' situation while the users strive to articulate their desired aims and learn appropriate technological means to obtain them" (2). In problem- and project-organized studies, students similarly experience the realities of different roles, being as well learners and designers of learning situations. Working consciously with the perspectives of different roles can be valuable for students as well as professors. In educational settings like MIL and design, humanities, and technology, it is crucial to be able to think along new lines in designing and redesigning learning experiences through continuous didactic experiments and activities. Such reflections regarding design can help professors and students to plan, implement, and evaluate educational activities.

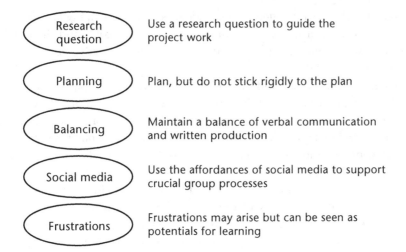

Figure 3.1
Learning from projects.

6 How to Learn from Projects?

Relating the insights from the MIL case to the discussions on design and education leads us to emphasize the following points, shown in figure 3.1 and elaborated hereafter in the text, regarding how to learn from project work.

• Use a research question to guide the project work.

The aim of the students' own development of a research question for their project work is that such a question should act as a guide for the direction of the research process. When decisions are to be made during the process, the group can consult their research question to decide what to do. In this process, the research question is not to be phrased once and for all but will need continuous evaluation and rephrasing.

• Plan, but do not stick rigidly to the plan.

Adapt plans continually to the specific situation, so that plans are not carried through without consideration but are used as resources for situated action.

• Maintain a balance of verbal communication and written production.

It is often difficult in a student group to handle the balance between, on the one hand, developing insights through verbal discussions and, on the other hand, maintaining and developing those insights further by producing written texts or constructing designs or artifacts.

• Use the affordances of social media to support crucial group processes.

Social media and Web 2.0 have made it easier to produce, publish, share, and take part in collaborations. These affordances represent considerable changes and improvements in users' work practice and offer students a wide variety of flexible tools to use in their project work.

• Frustrations may arise but can be seen as potentials for learning.

In the project work, difficulties may develop that can lead to frustrations and sometimes conflicts between group members. However, such frustrations often occur because the existing view of things is not fully adequate, and new understandings are about to be developed. In this situation, differences between group members should not be seen exclusively as negative but can be productive for the knowledge creation of the group. If used constructively, periods of frustration may thus be followed by breakthrough experiences: "We did it!"

Problem- and project-based learning can be seen as an active learning approach, characterized by multidisciplinarity. If successful, students may learn to collaborate, to plan their work processes, and to cope with unforeseen problems, thereby increasing the students' critical and creative thinking, self-esteem, and motivation to work.

7 Conclusion

In this chapter, we have shown how design research can be related to the field of learning and how professors and students can design innovative and constructive study processes that can help meet the new needs for competencies arising from the change from an industrial society to a knowledge-based society. We addressed the American debate regarding design research and education and compared the original type of research using more isolated and controlled environments (the tradition of instructional design) to researching learning processes in "messy" real-life situations (the tradition of design-based research in education). New paradigms have emerged, stressing the social dimensions of learning. Here a greater focus is on how learning and construction of knowledge are created through the interaction and active participation of students taking part in the learning processes.

A central focus of the chapter dealt with designing new and innovative learning processes within the tradition of problem- and project-based learning. Important here is to understand students not only as co-designers but as independently and collaboratively designing and having ownership of their own projects. In today's context of rapidly evolving new social media and active user involvement, problem- and project-based learning approaches gain new relevance in the interplay with new technological possibilities. Recognizing the specificity of situatedness is crucial. In complex and changing study settings, students must be able to engage in negotiations, and nothing can be taken for granted, as pointed out by Weick and Suchman.

Through the MIL case, we demonstrated how we as a team of professors have been continually working on designing and redesigning the educational program in interaction with the students. Processes involved in developing master's projects were demonstrated and discussed through articulations and reflections made by MIL students regarding collaboration with peer-students and regarding their relations and attitudes to teachers as supervisors.

Acknowledgments

The authors want to thank Ken Kempner, Professor of Education, Southern Oregon University, for valuable comments.

References

Alvesson, Mats. 2003. Methodology for close up studies: Struggling with closeness and closure. *Higher Education* 46 (2): 167–193.

Andreasen, Lars B., and Jørgen L. Nielsen. 2013. Dimensions of problem based learning: Dialogue and online collaboration in projects. *Journal of Problem Based Learning in Higher Education* 1 (1): 210–229.

Barab, Sasha A., and Kurt Squire. 2004. Design-based research: Putting a stake in the ground. *Journal of the Learning Sciences* 13 (1): 1–14.

Barrett, Terry, and Sarah Moore. 2011. *New Approaches to Problem-Based Learning: Revitalizing Your Practice in Higher Education*. New York: Routledge.

Barron, Brigid J. S., Daniel L. Schwartz, Nancy J. Vye, Allison Moore, Anthony Petrosino, Linda Zech, John D. Bransford, and the Cognition and Technology Group at Vanderbilt. 1998. Doing with understanding: Lessons from research on problem- and project-based learning. *Journal of the Learning Sciences* 7 (3–4): 271–311.

Brown, Ann L. 1992. Design experiments: Theoretical and methodological challenges in creating complex interventions in classroom settings. *Journal of the Learning Sciences* 2 (2): 141–178.

Christensen, Ove, Karsten Gynther, and Trine B. Petersen. 2012. Design-based research: Introduktion til en forskningsmetode i udvikling af nye E-læringskoncepter og didaktisk design medieret af digitale teknologier [Design based research: Introduction to a research methodology to develop new e-learning concepts and didactic design mediated by digital technologies]. *Læring & Medier* 5 (9): 1–20.

Collins, Allan. 1992. Toward a design science of education. In *New Directions in Educational Technology*, ed. E. Scanlon and T. O'Shea, 15–22. New York: Springer.

Collins, Allan, Diana Joseph, and Kate Bielaczyc. 2004. Design research: Theoretical and method-ological issues. *Journal of the Learning Sciences* 13 (1): 15–42.

Dirckinck-Holmfeld, Lone. 2002. Designing virtual learning environments based on problem ori-ented project pedagogy. In *Learning in Virtual Environments*, ed. Lone Dirckinck-Holmfeld and Bo Fibiger, 31–54. Frederiksberg: Samfundslitteratur.

Dirçkinck-Holmfeld, Lone, Torben Iversen, Ulla Konnerup, Merete Lindemann, Steener Oksb-jerre, Torben Pihler, Marianne Riis, and Dorte S. Schmidt. 2008. Når specialer gør en forskel: Om kollaborative arbejdsformer i virtuelle læremiljøer [When master's projects make a difference: Studying collaboratively in virtual learning environments]. In *Digitale medier og didaktisk design* [Digital media and didactic design], ed. Lars B. Andreasen, Bente Meyer, and Pernille Rattleff, 169–191. Copenhagen: Danish University of Education Press.

Ejersbo, Lisser R., Robin Engelhardt, Lisbeth Frølunde, Thorkild Hanghøj, Rikke Magnussen, and Morten Misfeldt. 2008. Balancing product design and theoretical insight. In *The Handbook of Design Research Methods in Education*, ed. A. E. Kelly, R. A. Lesh, and J. Y. Baek, 149–163. Mahwah, NJ: Erlbaum.

Frank, Moti, and Abigail Barzilai. 2006. Project-based technology: Instructional strategy for devel-oping technological literacy. *Journal of Technology Education* 18 (1): 39–53.

Harasim, Linda. 2011. *Learning Theory and Online Technology: How New Technologies Are Transform-ing Learning Opportunities*. New York: Routledge.

Harasim, Linda, Starr R. Hiltz, Lucio Teles, and Murray Turoff. 1995. *Learning Networks: A Field Guide to Teaching and Learning Online*. Cambridge, MA: MIT Press.

Kahiigi, Evelyn K., Love Ekenberg, Henrik Hansson, F. F. Tusubira, and Mats Danielson. 2008. Exploring the e-learning state of art. *Electronic Journal of e-Learning* 6 (2): 77–88.

Kemmis, Stephen, and Mervyn Wilkinson. 1998. Participatory action research and the study of practice. In *Action Research in Practice: Partnerships for Social Justice in Education*, ed. Bill Atweh, Stephen Kemmis, and Patricia Weeks, 21–36. London: Routledge.

Kensing, Finn, and Joan M. Greenbaum. 2013. Heritage: Having a say. In *Routledge International Hand-book of Participatory Design*, ed. Jesper Simonsen and Toni Robertson, 21–36. New York: Routledge.

Kolmos, Anette, Flemming Fink, and Lone Krogh, eds. 2004. *The Aalborg PBL Model: Progress, Diversity, and Challenges*. Aalborg: Aalborg University Press.

Nielsen, Jørgen L., and Lars B. Andreasen. 2013. Educational designs supporting student engage-ment through networked project studies. In *Increasing Student Engagement and Retention Using Mobile Applications: Smartphones, Skype, and Texting Technologies*, Cutting-Edge Technologies in Higher Education, vol. 6D, ed. Laura Wankel and Patrick Blessinger, 19–46. Bingley, UK: Emerald Publishing Group.

Nielsen, Jørgen L., and Oluf Danielsen. 2012. Problem-oriented project studies: The role of the teacher as supervisor for the study group in its learning processes. In *Exploring the Theory,*

Pedagogy, and Practice of Networked Learning, ed. Lone Dirckinck-Holmfeld, Vivien Hodgson, and David McConnell, 257–272. New York: Springer.

Olesen, Henning S., and Jens H. Jensen, eds. 1999. *Project Studies: A Late Modern University Reform?* Frederiksberg: Roskilde University Press.

Olsen, Poul B., and Kaare Pedersen. 2005. *Problem-Oriented Project Work: A Workbook*. Frederiksberg: Roskilde University Press.

O'Reilly, Tim. 2007. What is Web 2.0: Design patterns and business models for the next generation of software. *Communications and Strategies* 65: 17–37.

Reigeluth, Charles. 1999. What is instructional-design theory and how is it changing? In *Instructional-Design Theories and Models: A New Paradigm of Instructional Theory*, vol. 2, ed. Charles Reigeluth, 5–30. Mahwah, NJ: Erlbaum.

Revans, Reginald. 1982. *The Origins and Growth of Action Learning*. Brickley, UK: Chartwell-Bratt.

Robertson, Toni, and Jesper Simonsen. 2013. Participatory design: An introduction. In *Routledge International Handbook of Participatory Design*, ed. Jesper Simonsen and Toni Robertson, 1–17. London: Routledge.

Schön, Donald A. 1983. *The Reflective Practitioner*. New York: Basic Books.

Schön, Donald A. 1987. *Educating the Reflective Practitioner: Toward a New Design for Teaching and Learning in the Professions*. San Francisco: Jossey-Bass.

Selander, Staffan. 2008. Designs for learning—A theoretical perspective. *Designs for Learning* 1 (1): 10–22.

Suchman, Lucy. [1987] 2007. *Plans and Situated Actions: The Problem of Human-Machine Communication*, 2nd ed. New York: Cambridge University Press.

Weick, Karl E. 1976. Educational organizations as loosely coupled systems. *Administrative Science Quarterly* 21 (1): 1–19.

Weick, Karl E. 2001. *Making Sense of the Organization*. Malden, MA: Blackwell Business.

Wenger, Etienne. 1998. *Communities of Practice: Learning, Meaning, and Identity*. Cambridge: Cambridge University Press.

Wesch, Michael. 2012. The end of wonder in the age of whatever. Keynote speech presented at EdMedia: World Conference on Educational Media and Technology, Denver, Colorado, June 2012.

4 Investigating Situated Use of the MUST Method

Keld Bødker, Finn Kensing, and Jesper Simonsen

What. MUST is a design method that targets early IT design where future users are actively involved in the project. The textbooks about MUST have been used as part of the curriculum in many university courses, including at Roskilde University. The method has also been commercially applied by a large number of private companies and public organizations.

Why. IT design today takes place not only as an initial part of large IT development projects. Design projects often apply generic and configurable standard systems, and design activities may continue throughout organizational implementation and beyond.

Where. The challenges for participatory design arise because users are no longer only employees but also consumers, citizens, members of voluntary organizations, or the like, who may not be colocated with designers; so how can we ensure that users can have a say? And how do we organize design when design increasingly takes place as part of, or after, implementation—because the design product is increasingly made up of multiple generic systems, including smart phone apps, systems integrating data and functionality from existing systems, or systems dedicated to new ways of collaborating or coordinating across organizational or professional boundaries?

How. By investigating and reflecting on our experiences from two design projects outside the method's original application area, we derive lessons for how we situate the concepts, the principles, the organization of the design project, and the techniques and tools provided by MUST.

1 Introduction

MUST is a design method that targets early IT design where future users are actively involved in the design project. The textbooks about MUST have been used as part of the curriculum in many university courses, including at Roskilde University. The method has also been commercially applied by a large number of private companies and public organizations (Kensing 2000; Bødker, Kensing, and Simonsen 2011).

MUST is a method for participatory design firmly rooted in the Scandinavian tradition of information system development founded in the struggle for workplace democracy in Scandinavia. IT design today takes place not only as an initial part of large IT development projects; many design projects apply generic and highly configurable standard systems, and design activities may continue throughout organizational implementation and beyond. The methodological challenges can be summarized as follows (Bratteteig et al. 2012, 135–139):

• Users must be ensured a say in design when users and designers are not colocated.
• New technologies imply that design increasingly takes place as part of, or after, implementation.
• Users no longer share the commitments in relation to a shared workplace.

In this chapter, we want to investigate a question often posed to us by students and colleagues: How can we apply MUST outside its original domain? We intend to do this by critically examining two design projects in which we have been deeply involved ourselves. Both projects take place in contexts outside MUST's intended domain; the first is a design project to support communication and collaboration among health professionals and patients using ICD pacemakers, and the second is a design project on energy renovation of private houses. Based on these cases, we critically reflect on learning points in relation to answering the research question.

Research method-wise, we hereby adhere to Yin's multiple-case study approach (Yin 2009). Both cases involve one of the authors as a central actor, and the presentations in sections 3 and 4 represent accounts of the projects based on personal reflections and already published sources. From these cases, we intend to derive lessons learned regarding adapting the design method to the particular situations.

2   The MUST Method

The core idea behind MUST is to enable a participatory design approach responding to contemporary business needs and conditions for IT projects. Information technology has moved from supporting and automating well-structured tasks, typically within organizational boundaries like accounting, inventory control, and payroll, to supporting and informing less clearly defined activities of knowledgeable and often also quite powerful professionals, such as caseworkers or clinicians in direct contact with customers, citizens, or patients.

MUST includes a conceptual framework for the participatory design process, emphasizing the need for a thorough problem setting during the early stages of design that "reveals goals, defines problems, and indicates solutions" (Bødker, Kensing, and Simonsen 2004, 13). MUST is conceived as a "meta-method"; that is, in every design project, the participants have to design or situate the project using the method as a resource for action (Suchman 2007). MUST provides four types of resources for supporting designers in planning and conducting the project according to the particular situation:

• Well-defined concepts (seventeen in total) to help designers understand and frame the situation
• A particular perspective formulated as four design principles guiding the designers throughout the design project
• Suggestions for how to organize the design project in four phases
• A set of techniques and tools for specific activities (altogether sixteen techniques and related tools), including meta-guidelines to help in selecting and tailoring techniques or tools to specific purposes.

In the following, we briefly describe the four design principles, the project organization, and some of the core techniques and tools.

2.1 Four Participatory Design Principles

The objective of a design project in an organizational setting is to achieve sustainable change by introducing new IT systems. Visions play a central role in envisioning, outlining, and sketching future IT systems and their use. The result of a design project is one or more *coherent visions for change* in the company in question and in relation to its environment (principle 1). The claim for coherency is related to striking a balance between IT system(s), organization of work, and the qualifications that users need to perform their job with the help of the envisioned IT systems in the proposed work context. The method systematically relates its overall activities and results to such coherent visions for change.

The second principle, *genuine user participation*, calls for the active participation of organizational members (users) in the design project. In subscribing to both political and pragmatic arguments for participation, MUST acknowledges the challenges established by current business contexts:

• In large companies, not all employees can be involved in the design project; a design project thus has to rely on representation of users.
• Experienced users are hard to get involved because they are needed in daily operations.

In such circumstances, open criteria for participation are essential, as is anchoring the intermediary and end results from the design project among all interest groups. Further, mutual learning is essential for ensuring that all participants and their knowledge are genuinely accounted for. A framework for mutual learning functions as a guide to support different kinds of mutual learning situations (table 4.1).

Table 4.1
Six domains of knowledge (based on Kensing and Munk-Madsen 1993)

	Current practices	Practices with new technologies	Technological options
Abstract knowledge	Relevant descriptions	Visions and design proposals	Overview of technological options
Concrete experience	Concrete experience with current practices	Concrete experience using new technology	Concrete experience with technological options

We recommend iterating between abstract knowledge and concrete experience in many design activities, and a general movement from focusing on understanding current practices and technological options early in a design project to gradually shifting focus to deal with new practices.

Ethnographic techniques have come to play an important role in participatory design in getting access to concrete experience and other elements of tacit knowledge involved in work practices and the use of technology. Trying to overcome the classic say/do problem and its many dimensions in design projects by applying ethnographically inspired techniques is a vital part of the MUST method, manifested in principle 3, *firsthand experience with work practice*. Designers observe and participate in users' in situ practices to understand their current practices and their experience using early prototypes in worklike settings. Seeing firsthand how work—or another practice—is experienced as a social activity is different from reading descriptions, prescriptions, or visions. Firsthand experience brings a rich body of knowledge to any design project. Such insights can be used to challenge current understandings or early design visions, as well as to derive new designs.

The final principle, *anchoring visions*, involves ensuring that stakeholders understand and support the design project's goals, visions, and plans. The idea is that when the domain of the design project is large and complex, the project needs to ground findings and proposals in the larger group, encompassing the organization's employees as well as top management (Simonsen 2007). By openly presenting design ideas and proposals and testing critical assumptions and hypotheses, the project group not only establishes a sound foundation for critical decisions but also prepares the implementation.

2.2   Project Organization

MUST recommends organizing a design project in four phases. We use the term *phase* to denote a group of activities taking the design project from one decision point to the next. Thus the four phases support a stepwise decision process regarding the scope of the project, understanding the situation by in-depth analysis, and outlining visions by design-oriented activities (table 4.2).

Table 4.2
Focus of the four phases and associated decisions

Phase	Focus	Result	Decision
Initiation: project establishment	Scope of the design project	Project charter	Premise and scope of design project
In-line analysis: strategic alignment	Aligning the project's goals and company strategies	Strategic alignment report	Work domains to investigate
In-depth analysis: ethnographic analysis	Work practices in selected domains	Analysis report	Prioritizing goals and ideas for change
Innovation: vision development	Visions of IT and relation to work organization and qualifications	Design project report	Visions to realize, scope and order of successive implementation projects

We want to emphasize the successive decision process, not the phases. We recommend that designers start planning each phase by mapping the current situation, thereby identifying four prototypical situations with a distinct scope for each. In some rare situations, we may recommend skipping a phase altogether, reducing it to an activity in the following phase.

Further guidelines for situating the project suggest the focus of the various reports to support the upcoming decision: focusing on the project, the usage, and the technical dimension.

2.3 Techniques and Tools

MUST contains a toolbox of techniques and tools that each support specific activities in a design project. To help choose among the techniques and tools, designers are provided with a guide indicating appropriate techniques or tools for each knowledge domain in table 4.1 and for each principle.

We have illustrated how MUST is considered a toolbox for the designers in a specific project, not as a design recipe to be followed blindly. To a large extent, we have thus designed MUST to be *situated* in the specifics of a concrete design project. However, the method was developed for IT design projects in an organizational context, which accounts for only some of the contemporary design projects. Now we turn toward two projects outside this domain.

3 Empowered Patients and Better-Informed Clinicians

This case is about how we situated the MUST method for use in a design project to support communication and collaboration among health professionals and patients.

In Denmark, as well as internationally, there has been a trend toward involving patients more in their own treatment and care, and toward supporting professional communication across the sites where patients are treated. The national and regional IT strategies for the Danish health-care sector, as well as the IT strategy of the University Hospital in Copenhagen, mention that an effort should be made to give patients access to their own data.

Chronic patients have been in focus, as they take up a lot of time and economic resources in the health sector. Heart failure patients living with an implantable cardioverter-defibrillator (ICD) are one such group of patients. An ICD is an advanced pacemaker that can be implanted in patients who are at risk of sudden cardiac death owing to ventricular fibrillation. The ICD is designed to monitor the heart rhythm and to deliver electric shocks to restore the normal heart rhythm in case of arrhythmic events. The ICD also records data about detected arrhythmic events, as well as selected overall conditions of the body. In this way, ICD patients are not only carrying a monitoring device; it is also individually programmed to deliver the therapy (electric shock) when a certain level of ventricular fibrillation occurs. In the case described here, the implantation and the device follow-up (every three months) are performed by the University Hospital's Heart Center, and the patients also see a cardiologist at a local hospital every three months to have their medication checked.

For almost ten years, a telemedicine setup has been in place, and patients are now routinely included. It transfers data (an ICD reading) from a patient's device to the Heart Center. Here heart specialists interpret the data and decide if any actions need to be taken. For unproblematic device follow-ups (when nothing has to be done except sending a letter to the patients indicating that the device is working as planned), the telemedicine setup saves time for the Heart Center and also for patients, who now only have to go to the center once every other year. This setup has worked well in most situations, except that over the years, many patients have asked for more detailed information about the interpretation of the transmitted device data.

However, experience also shows that when patients are copresent when the device data are interpreted at the Heart Center, the heart specialists can collect further information from the patients. This information could, for example, be about their general well-being, the medication they take and how it works for them, and the circumstances under which events registered by the device took place. For problematic device follow-ups, such information is important for the specialists' interpretation of the transmitted data and for determining which actions should be taken to care for the patient. One consequence of the design rationale of telemedicine in general and for this IT setup in particular is that the patient is not available as a source of information. This means that the specialists have to use much time and effort to collect the data needed for providing the care that is necessary.

We now turn to a description of how some of the resources (key concepts, princi-ples, phases, tools, and techniques) of the MUST method were brought to bear in a design project with a group of IT designers, fifty ICD patients, and heart specialists from the Heart Center and Bispebjerg Hospital, a local hospital in Copenhagen.

Compared to earlier projects in which MUST has been applied, this project was special because the prospective users were not part of the same organization. They comprised health professionals at different hospitals, as well as chronic patients living at home. Further, while the health professionals could probably be required to use the system, this may or may not be the case when it comes to the patients. It turned out to be helpful to use the four phases suggested by MUST to structure the project from start to finish. Some of the selected tools and techniques are mentioned after a brief introduction to the application's main functions. Then in the subsequent sec-tions we discuss the degree to which we managed to realize MUST's four guiding principles.

After we conducted initial ethnographic studies in patients' homes and at the two hospitals, one of the design ideas that gradually evolved was myRecord, a personal health record kept and maintained by each patient. Some of the data are for the patient's personal use only; others are automatically made available to the heart specialists. The patient may decide to share other data with other clinicians and patients. MyRecord is a Web application that, to reduce integration problems, runs separately from the telemedicine system. Its purpose is to allow patients to take an active part in their own care and for patients and heart specialists to be better pre-pared for consultations, whether these take place in the clinic or via telemedicine. MyRecord has six main elements: (1) It provides the patient with a calendar for scheduled appointments. Before a scheduled face-to-face visit and an ICD reading through the telemedicine setup, the patient reports about his or her situation in (2) checkboxes for a set of symptoms defined by the cardiologists, and in a short free text in the patient's own words. The patient may also (3) monitor a set of self-defined parameters (e.g., in relation to diet, smoking, alcohol, etc.). Further, patients must (4) maintain a list of the medicine prescribed and taken, and keep track of any side effects. Finally, it is possible (5) to communicate with the Heart Center about the ICD readings and (6) to keep a diary. Note that the project did not include a redesign of the ICD and the associated software, since the company that supplies these parts was not interested in taking part in the project. That changed after the project ended, though.

MyRecord was iteratively designed based on observations and in situ interviews with heart specialists, focusing on which type of information they would normally ask for and use during face-to-face consultations. Further, the designers worked with patients in workshops and with patients experimenting with prototypes of myRecord at home, preparing for checkups at one of the hospitals. In the latter situations, the designers helped the patients use the prototype while analyzing which parts of the prototype worked, and which did not work, for the patient. Further, the designers introduced new features to collect initial feedback from the patients.

The designers then brought the prototype to the Heart Center and asked them to first go through the ICD follow-up procedure as they would normally do. When they had finished the procedure for each patient who had used the prototype, the designers asked the heart specialists to think aloud while going through what the patients had registered in the prototype. In this way, the patient was virtually present and able to contribute information needed by the specialists and other types of questions and information that the patient had found relevant. In about 20 percent of the cases, the heart specialists changed their mind or wanted to do something extra based on information provided by the patient through the system. Further, in potentially problematic cases, the designers encouraged the specialist using a recorder to send the response to the ICD reading to the patient. This feature was much appreciated by the patients and also, eventually, by the specialists, too.

3.1 Coherent Visions for Change

MyRecord and its use by patients and heart specialists was a coherent vision for change that guided the designers' work and their collaboration with patients and heart specialists. It was nurtured and challenged throughout the project by introducing and testing new ideas grounded in the ethnographic studies or stemming from interesting concepts found in the literature. The vision had two interlinked parts: a technical part in terms of functions, and an organizational part in terms of new ways to interact. But that would not lead to much change unless patients and heart specialists were to start acting differently with the help of the system. The designers kept refining the system until patients experienced the benefit of their own monitoring, and until heart specialists consulted the data entered by the patients to improve the quality and efficiency of their work. Finally, for the vision to materialize, both types of actors had to learn new skills to act differently.

3.2 Genuine User Participation

Genuine user participation relies on two rationales: a democratic ideal and the need for mutual learning. MUST was originally developed for in-house and contractual-bid types of projects. In such projects, it is possible to identify future users and have them participate if management and designers choose to do so. Instead this project was a product design type of project (Grudin 1991). Therefore the participating patients and specialists were not included to represent future users in a democratic sense; they could not be held responsible by any constituencies. The designers saw their input as representing the knowledge and interests of ICD patients and heart specialists. Further, the designers acknowledged that it was necessary to allow for mutual learning, and they included the aforementioned activities, tools, and techniques to make that happen.

3.3 Firsthand Experience with Work Practice

Firsthand experience was realized in two different ways. First, and in line with the recommendation of the MUST method, the designers began by conducting ethnographic studies focusing on actors, activities, information searched for and produced, and technologies and other artifacts involved in living the life of an ICD patient and working as a heart specialist. The designers interviewed patients, relatives, and heart specialists to understand better the rationales of their conduct. Second, the designers were present while patients and heart specialists were using the evolving prototypes. Also, they organized sessions in a way that allowed them to explore, experiment, and intervene in the daily practices of patients and specialists.

3.4 Anchoring Visions

Earlier we described how designers brought the prototype of myRecord to the patients' home and asked them to use it, and how the designers later took the prototype to the Heart Center for the specialists to work with. These examples show how the designers strove to anchor the vision with the future users as an integrated part of the design, experiment, and test activities.

The designers used the four phases to ensure an incremental decision-making process based on the materials produced in each phase. So to produce relevant groundings for the decisions, the designers iterated, within each phase, between analytic and design-oriented activities. However, the designers allowed themselves less-strict decision points than recommended by the MUST method. They did so because the project was both a research project, aiming for new knowledge, and a development project, aiming for a product within time and economic constraints.

Some of the prospective users were involved in different ways and with different intensity over a period of a year and a half. They participated out of interest and willingness to contribute to research, and they hoped that someday patients would benefit from the time they invested. This is again related to the difference in development context. There was no manager demanding that the users participate, or allowing them to use their working hours for the project. Therefore the designers had to strive for a fun and meaningful process to maintain a commitment to participation.

4 Energy Renovation and CO_2 Reduction Project

This case describes a private-home renovation project completely outside the application area of MUST. The case demonstrates how MUST's four principles can be situated in design projects that do not focus on IT. The project was not conducted as an IT-design project and did not specifically follow the phases or use any IT-related techniques and tools from the MUST method. The MUST principles were, however, an explicit concern during the project, as represented by one key designer, the owner, who is also a coauthor of this chapter.

Global climate changes caused by burning fossil fuels have led to a general concern about our society's energy consumption. A large part of energy consumption is due to heating and cooling the buildings we live and work in. The Nordic Council of Ministers established, as part of a joint Nordic vision to prepare for future independence from fossil fuels, the Nordic Energy Municipality initiative. This initiative focuses on sustainable energy, green growth, and energy-related climate work in the Nordic countries. The aim of the initiative was to recognize, in particular, municipalities that make an extraordinary effort to implement innovative energy and CO_2-reducing projects. The Danish municipality of Albertslund was, in 2011, named the Nordic Energy Municipality, based on the "Albertslund-concept of energy-effective renovation of houses" (Nordic Energy Municipality 2012).

The majority of the housing stock in Albertslund was built between 1968 and 1972, before the energy crises of the seventies. The municipality aimed for an overall 25 percent reduction in CO_2 emissions by energy renovation of the housing stock. Nine demonstration projects were completed to develop new standardized energy solutions in 2011 and 2012. These projects renovated energy-consuming houses built in the sixties and seventies into CO_2-friendly houses, meeting the new standards for low-energy houses (the so-called Building Regulation BR2015 standard).

One of the demonstration projects was a privately owned town house built in 1971. The project comprised the following features (see fig. 4.1):

• Exterior insulation of roof and walls mounted as a new shell on existing facades.
• Solar panels ensuring self-sufficiency in electricity.
• Electrical-grid-powered roof windows with rain sensors.
• Electricity-powered exterior awning blinds providing more daylight and fresh air while also preventing overheating during summertime.
• Air ventilation with heat recovery to maximize indoor climate as the renovation made the house completely airtight.
• Wireless centrally controlled heating thermostats allowing daytime and nighttime temperature drop when the occupants are away or asleep.
• Rainwater filter, draining rainwater from the roof back to the ground instead of to the sewer system to accommodate the increased flooding risks resulting from climate change.

4.1 Coherent Vision

The MUST principle of coherent visions for change includes a metaphor of sustainability that in the project became a key success factor regarding the economy.

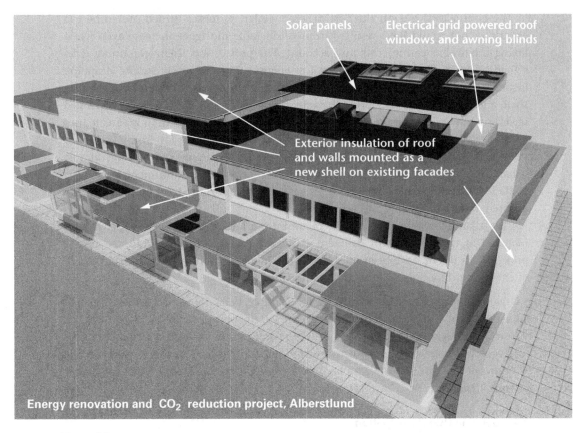

Figure 4.1
Model of the demonstration project made by Martin Rubow, Architect MAA, and Carl Galster, Architect MAA.

At the many public meetings where the architects presented their ideas, the residents repeatedly mentioned their concerns regarding the economy of the project. All houses in Albertslund are heated by a large district heating plant providing some of the cheapest heating costs in Denmark. Although the houses are poorly insulated and drafty, they are therefore relatively cheap to warm up. The architects and energy consultant were enthusiastic about the project and aimed for an ambitious energy renovation. This challenged a reasonable cost-benefit result that is sensible for a privately owned house. The resulting prototype house was to be designed as a standard solution to inspire future renovations throughout the neighborhood. However, no one could be forced to renovate his or her house; the owner of a private property solely decides on this investment. Thus a sustainable solution was contingent on being economically viable.

The contractors' bid on the first detailed design proposal turned out to be too expensive and would have resulted in a considerable mortgage increase even when taking the lower heating costs into account. The project was then profoundly redesigned, cutting all high-expense and low-energy-saving ideas, including dropping insulating the footing below ground level, aligning windows and doors with the new shell, and so on. Moreover, during the actual project, many new ideas were developed regarding how to further minimize costs, including blowing insulation granulate into prefabricated shells rather than attaching insulation batting and plastering a shell onto these afterward. The result is a renovation where the energy cost savings almost balance the investment. And taking the additional improved environmental, comfort-related, and aesthetic elements of the project into account, the investment is broadly assessed as both beneficial and attractive.

The balance between technology, organization, and qualifications, which is also included in the principle of coherent visions, was not explicitly addressed in the project. This might have been relevant, as the involved technologies do have consequences regarding organization and qualifications:

• Organizational consequences include, for example, behavioral change to airing, heat adjustment, and aligning electricity use with solar panels production.
• New qualifications are required to configure and use the advanced systems controlling ventilation, heating, and electrical windows and blinds. The user manual for the windows and blinds is, for example, ninety-eight pages long and written in a highly technical language.

4.2 Genuine User Participation

The MUST principle of genuine user participation, its political argument regarding the user's right to influence a design, and its related theory of mutual learning processes were realized during the renovation project in relation to the design of the roof construction of the house.

The architects' design ideas, drawings, and increasingly detailed plans of the project had been presented and discussed at several meetings with local authorities and at town hall meetings where the neighborhood residents were invited. The town houses are regulated by a restrictive district plan to maintain a uniform appearance, including a detailed list of the colors to be used for the buildings, style and size of windows, fences, extensions, and so on. The renovation had to be balanced in such a way that one renovated house among the others in a row did not look too different from the existing houses.

Any design that would differ too much from the existing regulations would require an alteration of the district plan, and this involves a complicated and time-consuming procedure, hearings among the local residents, and ultimately a new bill to be passed by the city council. Discussions involving the district plan usually spur great public

Figure 4.2
Design with roof overhang (left) and without (right). Model by Martin Rubow, Architect MAA, and Carl Galster, Architect MAA.

interest; this plan imposes many constraints that the residents need to be aware of when they maintain and change their houses.

Perhaps the most distinct feature of the architects' design ideas was to construct the new insulated roof with a large overhang (fig. 4.2). This overhang was intended to protect the facade and windows and to minimize solar radiation that caused the houses to overheat during summertime.

As a final step before the renovation could be initiated, the design had to be approved by the municipality's agency for construction work. The agency judged that all design ideas could pass through an exemption except the roof overhang, which would require an alteration of the district plan that the agency would not recommend to the city council. Therefore the agency asked the architects to redesign the project without a roof overhang.

The new design (roof without overhang) was discussed by the executive committee of the homeowners' association. The committee was extremely disappointed that the municipality had declined the former design. They objected to the decision, but the agency dismissed their protest. Then the committee brought the new design proposal to the neighborhood's annual general meeting. At the meeting, a motion was carried unanimously requiring the committee to insist on the original design solution. This public pressure forced the municipality's agency to acknowledge and initiate a change to the district plan to allow for an approval of the original design, including the large roof overhang.

The local democratic process and mutual learning involved in the participation of residents (users) and professionals (architects and local-authority experts) required that the residents learn about the design options of the project and that the professionals learn about a core interest of the residents. This interest was not driven by the designers' functional arguments for the roof overhang. Rather, it was the residents' interest in the aesthetic change—that the roof overhang actually represented a major change of the district plan. If a homeowner is to invest a considerable sum of money in renovating his house, he wants it to be visible that he has actually done so. The roof overhang was one of the most distinct changes indicating a modern and newly renovated house.

4.3 Firsthand Experience

In the MUST method, the principle of firsthand experience is originally intended for using ethnographically inspired techniques to access concrete experiences of work practices before the introduction of new technologies, as well as experiences of using early prototypes before full-scale implementation. In this project, the principle was applied with the latter intention in mind only.

Experiencing the newly renovated house proved to have a vital impact regarding the assessment of the different solutions and the dissemination of the renovation to other households (see also the next section, on the anchoring principle). There is a qualitative difference between looking at different models of the house (e.g., figs. 4.1 and 4.2) and considering calculations on energy savings versus entering and experiencing a full-size prototype house.

Hundreds of neighbors and other interested parties have visited the house at open-house arrangements. An immediate impression was meeting a house that looked like a newly built house (due to the new roof and new facades) and experiencing a highly perceptible change of the inflow of light inside the house (due to the new large roof windows). This considerable aesthetic improvement had no voice in the many discussions at public meetings held during the years before the project. Along with the owners' communicated experiences of an improved indoor climate without cold walls, drafts, and overheating on sunny days, and with constant fresh air and less dust without airing several times a day, experiencing the renovations firsthand will most likely provide many neighbors with the decisive motivating factor for making the investment.

4.4 Anchoring Visions

The MUST principle of anchoring visions includes attempting to gain wider support by openly presenting design ideas and proposals and testing critical assumptions and hypotheses. In the renovation project, the anchoring principle was specifically concerned with achieving a sustainable solution that would be both attractive and economically viable to households in the neighborhood, motivating them to invest in ambitious energy renovation.

The design strategy included completing the renovation while the house's occupants continued to live there. The insulation was done from outside, encasing the existing walls and roof with a new shell including 200 to 300 millimeters of insulation. The project was designed in modules (each with a separate energy-savings calculation) to be completed in separate phases and at levels of ambition concurrent with the owner's desires and economic capability; a household could, for example, start with a new insulated roof (when the roof needed maintenance anyway) and then later insulate the walls.

One major design approach to minimize costs was to attach the new insulated roof on top of the existing roof, thereby also closing the ventilation of the existing roof. This necessitated many technical considerations to ensure that the new vapor barrier would not later cause moisture and mold. Albertslund is widely known for a major construction scandal in the 1970s, when many of the prefabricated constructions with flat roofs (a new construction approach at the time) resulted in severe and costly moisture and mold damage. Construction experts approved the final solution, but many residents were concerned about whether it would actually work out. To test the hypotheses underlying the roof solution, wireless readable humidity sensors were placed in the roof construction. In this way, the validity of the roof construction solution and possible risks of moisture damage could be monitored.

After the renovation was completed, a number of logging devices (measuring district heating consumption, room temperatures, electricity consumption and production, ventilation volume, etc.) were installed to test the assumed energy reduction and cost savings related to different technologies implemented in the project. The data from these loggings aim at measuring the solar panel electricity production compared to the concurrent electricity consumption, efficiency of the ventilation with heat recovery versus traditional ventilation, savings resulting from daytime and nighttime temperature drop regulation, and so on. Consequently the calculated (assumed) savings can be supplemented by actual values measured from each different energy solution.

The principle of anchoring visions was of great relevance in the renovation project to establish support and motivation for the residents to invest in energy and CO_2 reduction in their private households. This was approached by taking the residents' economic concerns seriously, testing and documenting economic and technical assumptions and hypotheses, and implementing a full-size demonstration project where aesthetic, economic, technical, and indoor climate aspects could be experienced and evaluated.

5   Lessons Learned

In sections 3 and 4, we described how the MUST method has been applied in two projects outside its original use domain. This is an important message in its own right: it has been possible to situate the method by using its guidelines to tailor, or design, the project to the specifics of each situation.

Based on the experience from the two projects, we propose a model of the MUST method to be used in design projects, as depicted in figure 4.3.

More specifically, we derive the following lessons with regard to the method's resources:

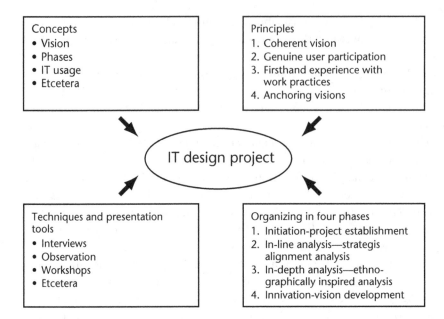

Figure 4.3
Four types of resources for design when using the MUST method.

• Concepts: Designers using MUST outside the original application domain will have to add concepts and definitions from that domain. For example, in the energy renovation project, concepts of energy consumption in housing, political initiatives to minimize CO_2 reduction, and the administrative procedures for approving construction projects were central.

• Principles: The two cases have demonstrated that the principles can be situated while maintaining their validity, as shown, for example, by the description on anchoring visions in the energy renovation project.

• Project organization: The MUST textbooks already contain some guidelines for adjustments to the recommend phases. The two cases have demonstrated further options: to start early with ethnographic studies and to combine ethnographic field visits with design experiments (visions, mock-ups, and prototypes).

• Techniques and tools: There is already room in the MUST textbooks for including other suitable techniques and tools that designers have experience with. As indicated by Simonsen and Friberg (chap. 6, this vol.), techniques from MUST have also been demonstrated to be applicable in other contexts.

The basic finding that MUST could be applied to design projects outside its intended use domain is—in our reading—due to the general understanding of a textbook method as a resource for action by an informed project group, not as a cookbook with finished recipes. This is supported by how the method is presented as consisting of four basic types of resources, as depicted in figure 4.3.

From the health-care case, we more specifically learned that it was possible to use the MUST method in a combined research and product development project, with users participating on behalf of themselves only—not as representing a larger group. From the CO_2 reduction project, we learned that the core principles were relevant to a high degree and could be supported by a pool of techniques.

Finally, we also learned that risk management is embedded in the method. In the project management literature, risk management is traditionally a project manager's task; the approach in MUST is to make it a design project issue, as in Boehm's spiral model (Boehm 1986). Positioning the design project in relation to (company) strategies and other ongoing projects (in the initiation and in-line analysis phases) contributes to managing the relations across design projects and with established strategies. And setting the scope and extent of activities in each phase, by positioning the current project in one of four prototypical situations within the project group by two-by-two matrices, incorporates an evaluation of the risks when deciding on the scope of the activities.

6 Conclusion

Participatory design has moved into many different areas, as witnessed, for example, by recent accounts by Trigg and Ishimaru (2013), Braa and Sahay (2013), and Balka (2013).

Based on the cases and experiences presented in this chapter, we see MUST as a suitable support for projects across the traditional terrain. We see the four guiding principles as the most stable elements of the method across different contexts of use. This conclusion is based not only on the two cases presented here but also on other projects we have been involved in (Bødker, Kensing, and Simonsen 2011). Further, we know from colleagues who use the textbooks in their teaching that students have used the four resources in a great variety of contexts.

Combining the lessons learned in this chapter and our experience from teaching (Bødker, Kensing, and Simonsen 2011), we can offer some general advice if you are about to start on your first participatory design project using MUST:

• Situate the four principles to the situation at hand.
• Use the four phases as a way to structure the process.
• Select a few of the techniques that allow for the degree of participation that, from a pragmatic standpoint, it is possible to bring to bear.

Enjoy.

References

Balka, Ellen. 2013. ACTION for health: Influencing technology design, practice, and policy through participatory design. In *Routledge International Handbook of Participatory Design*, ed. Jesper Simonsen and Toni Robertson, 257–280. New York: Routledge.

Bødker, Keld, Finn Kensing, and Jesper Simonsen. 2004. *Participatory IT Design: Designing for Business and Workplace Realities*. Cambridge, MA: MIT Press.

Bødker, Keld, Finn Kensing, and Jesper Simonsen. 2011. Participatory design in information systems development. In *Reframing Humans and Information Systems*, ed. H. Isomäki and S. Pekkola, 115–134. London: Springer.

Boehm, Barry H. 1986. A spiral model of software development and enhancement. *ACM SIGSOFT Software Engineering Notes* 11 (4): 14–24.

Braa, Jørn, and Sundeep Sahay. 2013. Health information systems programme: Participatory design within the HISP network. In *Routledge International Handbook of Participatory Design*, ed. Jesper Simonsen and Toni Robertson, 235–256. New York: Routledge.

Bratteteig, Tone, Keld Bødker, Yvonne Dittrich, Preben Mogensen, and Jesper Simonsen. 2012. Methods: Organising principles and general guidelines for participatory design. In *Routledge International Handbook of Participatory Design*, ed. Jesper Simonsen and Toni Robertson, 117–144. New York: Routledge.

Grudin, Jonathan. 1991. Interactive systems: Bridging the gaps between developers and users. *IEEE Computer* 24 (4): 59–69.

Kensing, Finn. 2000. Participatory design in a commercial context: A conceptual framework. In *PDC 2000: Proceedings of the Participatory Design Conference*, ed. Todd Cherkasky, Joan Greenbaum, Peter Mambrey, and Jens K. Pors, 116–126. Palo Alto, CA: CPSR.

Kensing, Finn, and Andreas Munk-Madsen. 1993. PD: Structure in the toolbox. *Communications of the ACM* 36 (6): 78–84.

Nordic Energy Municipality. 2012. Nordic Council of Ministers' description of the Nordic Energy Municipality project award. http://www.nordicenergymunicipality.org.

Simonsen, Jesper. 2007. Involving top management in IT projects: Aligning business needs and IT solutions with the problem mapping technique. *Communications of the ACM* 50 (8): 53–58.

Suchman, Lucy A. 2007. *Human-Machine Reconfigurations: Plans and Situated Action*. 2nd ed. New York: Cambridge University Press.

Trigg, Randy, and Karen Ishimaru. 2013. Integrating participatory design into everyday work at the Global Fund for Women. In *Routledge International Handbook of Participatory Design*, ed. Jesper Simonsen and Toni Robertson, 213–234. New York: Routledge.

Yin, Robert K. 2009. *Case Study Research: Design and Methods*, 4th ed. Thousand Oaks, CA: Sage.

5 Soft Design Science Methodology

Jan Pries-Heje, John Venable, and Richard Baskerville

What. This chapter proposes and evaluates a soft systems approach to design science research. The approach consists of seven activities starting with the specific problem and ending with a constructed, but also generalized, design solution. The proposed methodology is evaluated by applying it retrospectively to a published case on improving organizational implementation.

Why. Soft Design Science Methodology (SDSM) provides a much-needed new approach to develop new ways to improve human organizations, especially with consideration for social aspects, through the activities of design, development, instantiation, evaluation, and evolution of any kind of sociotechnological artifact.

Where. SDSM can be used for any design science process where a new sociotechnical artifact is developed as part of designing and constructing a solution for improving a problematic human situation.

How. SDSM merges a common design science research process (design, build, and evaluate a new artifact) with iterative soft systems methodology. SDSM takes an iterative approach to situated learning, development of situated knowledge, and situated action as a means for both improving a specific situation and generating generalized knowledge about problems and new and useful ways to solve those problems. The SDSM cycle begins with real-world situated learning about a specific problem; continues with generalizing about the problem, using design thinking to develop a generalized design, as well as a specific, situated design; evaluates the designs ex ante; and evaluates the new sociotechnical solution ex post through constructing and operating the situated sociotechnical artifact.

1 Introduction

Design Science Research (DSR) is a research paradigm relevant to applied disciplines. DSR research attempts to develop and evaluate a new technology or technologies to address practical problems or goals.

However, DSR in information systems (IS) has placed heavy emphasis on the design of new technical artifacts (such as IS) while largely ignoring sociotechnical aspects of IS and their integration into organizations and society. Moreover, methods in DSR also face challenges in balancing the rigor of science on the one hand with the creativity of design on the other.

The purpose of this chapter is to propose, develop, and evaluate a Soft Design Science Methodology (SDSM) to address these issues. We draw inspiration from Soft Systems Methodology (SSM; Checkland 1981; Checkland and Scholes 1990), which addresses issues of problem analysis and the sociotechnical nature of information systems. SSM also relies on systems thinking, which is allied with design thinking and develops its own perspective on system design within a sociotechnical context.

We first review and very briefly summarize the major relevant DSR methodological work before developing a design and rationale for SDSM in the subsequent section. Following that, we evaluate the proposed SDSM by analyzing insights and improvements resulting from the post hoc application of SDSM to a published case study, contrasting the results from the design-oriented action research method that was applied. Finally, we discuss and draw conclusions from the analysis.

2   Extant Design Science Research Methodologies

Methodology in DSR has generally begun emerging in the literature in the past few years. The early seminal works in information systems DSR have been concerned mainly with its relevance in the philosophy of science, the nature of theory in DSR, and criteria for evaluating DSR. The overall view of methodology in these early seminal works is a simplistic iterative build-evaluate method.

Some prominent works that do elaborate a research methodology in more detail include the following: Nunamaker, Chen, and Purdin (1991) propose a linear methodological process for DSR, which has five activities: construct a conceptual framework, develop a system architecture, analyze and design the system, build the (prototype) system, and observe and evaluate the system.

Vaishnavi and Kuechler (2013) also propose an essentially linear process model that includes five activities in "the design cycle": awareness of problem, suggestion, development, evaluation, and conclusion. Importantly, they identify that the suggestion activity involves abductive reasoning.

Peffers et al. (2008) provide the most comprehensive model of activities in a DSR methodology. They propose a six stage process model: identify problem and motivate, define objectives of a solution, design and development, demonstration, evaluation, and communication.

Sein and colleagues (2011) developed the Action Design Research (ADR) methodology, in which they merge DSR with action research (AR). The methodology has four stages: (1) problem formulation; (2) building, intervention, and evaluation, which tightly couples these three activities; (3) reflection and learning; and (4) formalization of learning. ADR emphasizes the development of generalized theory and well-crafted iteration.

Such DSR methods offer careful attention to rigor in their scientific aspects and provide latitude for creative design (e.g., a suggestion stage) but give little guidance on design (with the exception of Vaishnavi and Kuechler's note on abductive reasoning at the suggestion stage). They also provide little guidance on coping with social aspects of information systems, such as accommodating differing goals, organizational change, and quality of working life. Future DSR methods should provide better balance both between socio-organizational and technical issues and between science and design, that is, where science occurs in the context of design, as well as vice versa.

3   Inspirations for a New Design Science Research Methodology

Our goal is to better support design creativity as a key part of situated learning and practice while still retaining invention of new sociotechnical artifacts in a new DSR method. SDSM builds on Soft Systems Methodology (SSM) concepts because of its more extensive latitude for human factors in systems and room for design thinking. The next two subsections review SSM and design thinking concepts that inspire the SDSM adaptation.

3.1   Soft Systems Methodology (SSM)

Soft Systems Methodology (SSM) (Checkland 1981; Checkland and Scholes 1990; Checkland and Holwell 1998) is a prominent systems science approach to sociotechnical problems. Its systems science and systems thinking make it effective for developing systems (including information systems) that succeed in difficult social organizational settings. Most importantly for our purposes, the approach distinguishes thinking in an abstract systems world from thinking in the real world. See the representation of the seven-stage model of SSM in figure 5.1 (Checkland 1981).

The older seven-stage model of SSM shown in figure 5.1 is anchored to the notion of a planned transition across a boundary distinguishing thinking in the real world from thinking in an abstract world. Stages 1 and 2 explore and structure a problematic situation within the real-world frame of thinking, but in ways that stakeholders can understand them. Stages 3 and 4 shift across the boundary to system thinking (using systems concepts and system-thinking-inspired techniques) to develop a model of an idealized solution. Stages 5 through 7 ground the idealized solution back in the real world by considering practical aspects of feasibility in whether the idealized solution addresses the problem (stage 5), whether making changes will work within the existing social system (stage 6), and carrying out those changes (stage 7). Iteration and

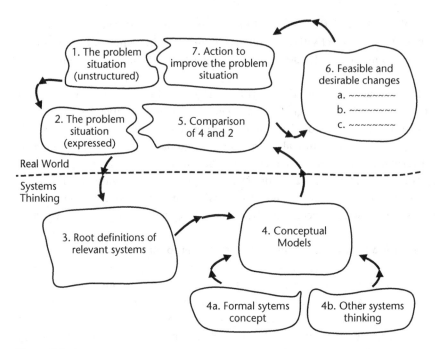

Figure 5.1
Soft Systems Methodology (inspired by Checkland 1981).

evaluation are key parts of SSM, as shown by two backward links that support them: the link from stage 5 back to stage 2 and the link from stage 7 back to stage 1 (both shown with a dovetail fit between the stages), which form two possible (optional) opportunities for iteration. Iteration through stages 2–5 allows refinement of design decisions by grounding them back in the real world. Iteration to repeat all stages (1–7) may be taken to assess situations where solution implementation has either introduced new problems or made insufficient improvement.

3.2 Design Thinking

Design thinking is the specific design-oriented cognitive activities that design science researchers use when designing. Design thinking has found its way into business and other real-world endeavors through its close relationship to systems thinking. Because design ideas must ultimately be executed in the practical production of artifacts, successful design thinking incorporates systems thinking. Recasting the abstract world as design thinking would enable an SSM-like approach that supports design thinking.

Design thinking is more creative and disorderly in its reasoning, critically negotiating between science, technology, and aesthetics. It is intuitive in its nature, abductive in its reasoning, exploratory in its learning strategy, and futuristic in its validity. Design thinking is not a problem-solving process but a creative and phenomenological process that can be set against ill-structured or wicked problems.

Importantly, design thinking improves when designers act as reflective practitioners rather than technical rationalists. Such reflection is supported by moving between situated knowledge, learning, and action to reflect on generic principles and designs and how they interact with the specific design at hand. It typically also involves iteration as new ideas are explored and tried out. Thus design thinking actually fits very well with both DSR and SSM.

4   Soft Design Science Methodology (SDSM)

Because of the similarities we have described, modeling a DSR method after SSM is an appealing exercise. For example, iteration can easily be conceptualized as distinguishing between thinking in the real world and thinking in the abstract systems world, with the distinction placed after the design and before the construction of the new solution artifact. Here the search for the design solution and the evaluation of the design solution are activities that take place in the abstract world of design thinking. Artifact construction and its evaluation are activities that take place in the real world of the social system into which the artifact becomes situated.

Soft Design Science Methodology (SDSM), as we have formulated it, can be elaborated by expressing the DSR activities in the basic two-world framework inhabited by SSM activities (see also fig. 5.3 toward the end of the chapter). SDSM has seven activities, which we describe here. Further details are illustrated in the example application in section 5.

4.1   Learn about Specific Problem

The researcher (designer/scientist) becomes aware (through an assignment or discovery) of a specific problem and begins learning about the problem. Learning usually includes lengthy and in-depth exploring and sharing of the stakeholders' points of view. Some tools can be useful here, such as CATWOE criteria (Checkland 1981), Critical Systems Heuristics (Ulrich 1983, 1987, 2002), Rich Pictures (Checkland 1981), and Cognitive Maps (Ackermann and Eden 2001; Eden and Ackermann 2001; Eden 1988). This real-world learning work is dominated by analytical thinking where one follows a series of clearly defined steps or activities.

4.2   Inspire and Create the Problem and General Requirements

In learning about the specific problem, the researcher finds inspiration for broader understanding of a general class of problems that the problem at hand may represent. This problem understanding can be articulated as general requirements embodied by such a class of problems. As this is largely a creative and imaginative process, the process has moved into the domain of design thinking.

The researcher needs to imagine how other situations are similar or different and whether the specific situation being considered can fruitfully be generalized by removing constraints from the problem space. This mode of design thinking, like systems thinking, is abstract. However, its centralization of creative thought means that the search for a problem class will iterate with the search for a solution class. This aspect of design thinking makes it operate well with "wicked problems," that is, problems that must be redefined in terms of their solutions (Martin 2010).

4.3 Intuit and Abduce the General Solution

A general solution design (a class of solutions) for the general problem will begin to emerge in the design thinking taking place in activity 2.

Such general solutions are often necessarily the product of intuition and abductive reasoning. As the thinking moves in the general solution space, it is characterized by two important features (Martin 2010).

One of these features is explorational learning strategies. Such learning strategies operate in contrast to exploitational learning strategies and aim resources toward achieving invention and innovation (March 1991).

Another important feature is the willingness to validate knowledge in the future. The validity of this design knowledge is necessarily unknown at this point; thus in SDSM, design science is anchored to a future validity rather than known reliability (Martin 2010).

The creative and explorational thinking will interact with the conceptualization of the general problem. This interaction between solution formulation and problem formulation is especially characteristic for wicked problems, where solution choices tend to define the problem boundaries.

4.4 Ex Ante Evaluation (General)

As a general solution becomes more articulated, it will drive a rearticulation of the general problem. Thus the articulation of the general problem and general solution are interactive. This interaction manifests the continuous evaluation of the general design before any real-world instantiation is considered.

This interactive evaluation process is characterized as ex ante because it occurs before any artifact outcomes intended by the general design have been instantiated. In design science terms, activities 2, 3, and 4 ultimately embody a disciplined process of design theorizing that embodies a set of hypothesized relationships between a set of meta-requirements and a meta-solution design.

4.5 Design Specific Solution for Specific Problem

Once the researcher settles on the general requirements (activity 2) and the general solution (activity 3), possibly after some iterations based on ex ante evaluation of the generalized design (activity 4), the process moves back to real-world thinking to search for the specific design solution for the exact problem at hand.

This task is largely an analytical search for a workable set of the feasible elements available for constructing the solution. This specific design solution adapts the general and abstract design solution to the exact real-world problem at hand. This activity replicates the task that the eventual users of the general solution design will have to undertake when implementing the general design for specific organizational situations.

4.6 Ex Ante Evaluation (Specific)

We then bring the specific solution for the specific problem back to the real world. That is, we evaluate it against the reality where we originally learned about the specific problem (activity 1).

4.7 Construct Specific Solution

An instance of the specific solution is constructed and deployed, and the outcome is assessed in terms of the fit between the specific problem and the specific solution. Like SSM, SDSM is likely to be used where solutions are regarded as emergent and tentative, as is the case with iterative development and prototyping. The construction of the solution will itself drive further understanding of the specific real-world problem.

4.8 Ex Post Evaluation

Because the constructed solution may be tentative in many cases, its articulation can lead to rearticulation of the specific real-world problem. The evaluation of the constructed (articulated) solution may drive rearticulation of the problem and vice versa. This evaluation and rearticulation embody the ex post evaluation approach common in many design science research methods. Ex post evaluation occurs once the design is instantiated. Learning continues through both the construction and the evaluation.

If the outcome of the SDSM evaluation is deemed satisfactory and successful, the research may conclude. If the outcome is not satisfactory, another SDSM cycle (as shown by the way activities 8 and 1 link to each other in fig. 5.3) may then begin, and cycles may continue until the specific problem is resolved. Once the problem is resolved, the design thinking will have been validated along with the problem solved.

4.9 Summing Up SDSM

SDSM is similar to other forms of design science because it operates with generalized forms of requirements (meta-requirements) and general solutions (meta-designs) (Walls, Widmeyer, and El Sawy 1992). By designing with a class of problems and solutions, the generalizations are similar to explanatory design theories (Baskerville and

Pries-Heje 2010). Such design theories are expressed in the relationship between the general requirements and the general solutions. Like other forms of DSR, it recognizes two stages of evaluation.

SDSM differs from many other forms of design science because it incorporates the sociotechnical assumptions of SSM into its real-world thinking about the problem and the solution space. SDSM is most distinctive in its incorporation of design thinking into the design theorizing process. The application of design thinking as the primary mode of abstract thinking in the research process is an interesting advance. It is interesting because, like the use of design thinking in management, it accepts disorderly modes of thought, like creativity, intuition, and inspiration as key processes. This acceptance blurs somewhat the lines between science and art. The outcomes remain highly scientific, because any successful design tenets have been reasoned abductively and ultimately validated in an ex post evaluation. However, the outcomes are also artfully derived through the abstract inspiration and imagination of designer/researchers.

SDSM is similar to other forms of SSM because it carefully iterates real-world activities and abstract-world activities and manages the movement across these lines. Careful attention is paid to both the social and the technical aspects of the real world. Learning is retained as an important anchor in formulating solutions and designs. The holistic fit between solutions and problems is carefully measured and evaluated.

SDSM differs from SSM in many ways. It elaborates SSM because of its prominent use of design thinking and design theorizing in the abstract parts of the process. In the abstract world, this means that the deductive, analytical nature of systems thinking is supplemented with the creative and intuitive nature of design thinking. Much more care is given to articulating and evaluating solution designs in the abstract world. These differences represent a substantial shift (but not a complete departure) from the systems perspective of SSM to the science perspective of DSR, while at the same time allowing the subjective and artistic perspective of design thinking to flourish in the process.

5 SSM in Action: An Analytic Evaluation

Before a proposed research methodology such as SDSM is given a live evaluation in field trials, evidence should be required to provide indications of its likelihood for developing a successful design outcome and significant research discoveries. Hence we apply SDSM constructs in evaluating a completed DSR example. The purpose of this application is to evaluate how that research might have been improved (or at least done differently) with SDSM. Such an evaluation will provide prospective researchers with good indications of potential outcomes.

We selected a DSR project conducted with a large commercial bank that studied diffusion and adoption of IT. This case was selected for several reasons. The details of the original study have been published elsewhere (Pries-Heje and Tryde 2001). We had access to background material, participants, and experience from the original case. This case used a design-oriented action research approach that makes it a candidate for consideration as improvement research, an early example of a design science type of study. Finally, as an action research case, it also enables us to distinguish how the design science orientation of SDSM would differ from (or improve) an action research study. The contrast between SDSM and action research also provides insights into the contrasts between action research and design science in general.

The case involves Danske Bank, a large European bank with more than twenty thousand employees. The bank operates a large IT division, Danske Data, which develops applications for banking and insurance. Primarily applications are meant to run on a mainframe, but some applications are for Internet banking, client-server environments, and PCs. Danske Data mainframe systems are up and running twenty-four hours a day, and every day nine million transactions are carried out from eleven thousand workstations. The developers typically have IT educations at a bachelor level or come from a background in banking. Recently more and more employees with a master's degree have been hired.

For the purposes of evaluating the research in terms of SDSM, we will discuss the evaluation of the events with an SDSM perspective at the end of each activity (the following subsections).

5.1   SDSM Activity 1: Learn about Specific Problem

From a combined Capability Maturity Model (Paulk et al. 1995) and Bootstrap (Kuvaja et al. 1994) assessment where the development capabilities of the organization were assessed, it became clear that many products and processes developed by the IT department were not diffused and adopted as intended. The assessment report asked: "Why are so many products and procedures well described but not used?" Further, the assessment report suggested that Danske Bank should analyze diffusion and adoption, which was subsequently done.

Insightful people from all parts of the organization, including project managers, line managers, and people from the methodology department, agreed to be part of a task force. In two workshops, the task force diagnosed the diffusion and adoption problem. The cause of the inadequate diffusion and adoption was narrowed down to a number of issues. The problem specified was expressed as a specific set of requirements:

1. It is a requirement to ensure diffusion and adoption of products and processes from IT projects in Danske Bank.
2. It is a requirement that the individual project ensures that its new product will be used as expected when it has been completed.

Evaluation of Activity 1   The initial learning about the problem is common to both action research and design science projects. The basic problem situation is defined clearly in such pragmatic research approaches.

This activity was well thought through and carefully executed through the use of participative workshops. The specific requirements appear explicit and valid. Nothing new could have been added here by using SDSM.

5.2   SDSM Activity 2: Inspire and Create the General Problem and the General Requirements

As the undertaking at Danske Bank was part of an externally funded research project called the Centre for Software Process Improvement, numerous attempts were made to clarify and specify the general problem (cf. Pries-Heje and Tryde 2001). However, there was no formalized explicit translation of the specific requirements into a general problem statement about a class of problems. After studying the problem, the researchers in situ consulted the literature on diffusion and adoption and found inspiration for a framework approach. The framework approach offers a process for organizational implementation of IT innovations (described hereafter). This approach embodies the theory-driven nature of action research and implies that the general problem with IT innovation diffusion was perceived to be disorganized and incomplete innovation implementation processes.

Evaluation of Activity 2   Generalization of the problem was not explicitly addressed in the research project. It is an obvious assumption, similar to a "Toulminian warrant" that modifies the translation of the specific requirements to the general requirements (Toulmin 1958). A clearly and explicitly stated generalized problem would have improved the logical basis for the solution and might possibly have modified the requirements, if this general problem statement had been made explicit. More generalized statements (not specific to Danske Bank) would be the following:

1. It is a requirement to ensure diffusion and adoption of products and processes from IT projects in general.
2. It is a requirement that individual projects ensure that the things they produce are used as expected.

So here SDSM would have put an early emphasis on the meta-level of the problem(s). That could definitely have been beneficial.

5.3   SDSM Activity 3: Intuit and Abduce the General Solution

The research project had an explicit and rigorous search process for available components of the general solution. This search process involved additional workshops and the development of a sub-task force. To answer the specific problems, the infrastructure of the project was changed from a twelve-person task force to a smaller sub-task force group of three (one being an author of this chapter), each working half of their available time. The process unfolded as a second workshop one month later, which identified a number of solutions to the problems.

The sub-task force, while studying the organization's successes and failures in the first workshop, realized that attempts to ensure diffusion by adding additional activities at the end of the project often fail. The group reasoned that starting such attempts early in the project would have an effect on the product itself. The major component for such a solution could be a framework to be used in a one-day workshop for projects focusing on diffusion and adoption right after the requirements to a given product had been defined.

The evidence that such a one-day workshop was promising was an earlier (unusual) successful diffusion effort. This effort included an analysis workshop to bring customers and developers together for agreement on scope and requirements. It also meant that projects within Danske Bank were familiar with the one-day facilitated workshop concept.

Three further exploration search strategies can be easily identified in the case:

1. Hold an innovation diffusion planning meeting in a workshop format.
2. Hold the workshop early in the project process.
3. Follow a clear framework for the workshop.

Finally, a focus on the future was completely lacking in the case. The whole process improvement initiative was building on the classic plan-do-check-act so-called quality circle, where considering the future is never really in the picture.

Evaluation of Activity 3 The search process for components of the general solution is evident in the research reports. A lot of time and effort was put into this specific search activity. Many alternative (candidate) components were identified that ended up not being used as part of the specific solution. The components that were drawn into the solution include the workshop format, the framework, and the early timing for the workshop.

As stated earlier, there was also no consideration of the solution of the general, rather than the specific, problem at Danske Bank. Consideration for generality in activity 3 of SDSM might have guided the researchers to allow for different organizational settings. For example, in some other settings, some solution components might operate successfully, and some not. In this way, SDSM would have guided the researchers to further consider the degree to which the general requirements were unnecessarily specific to the immediate problem. Clearly, the specific solution is appropriate for Danske Bank, but the generality of the research results could have been improved by SDSM.

While the general solution involved the use of three exploration search strategies, there was no explicit search for the best components of the solution. Compared with SDSM, the descriptions of the research show rapid progression from the specific problem description toward a specific solution. The use of SDSM would have drawn more research resources into consideration for expressing the general problem and the general solution.

5.4 SDSM Activity 4: Ex Ante Evaluation

In most forms of action research, what compares to the ex ante evaluation is left as an implication of action planning. As the action plan is constructed, gaps or mismatches will grow more obvious. The main comparison stage is made in evaluating the outcome of the implementation of the planned action (i.e., post hoc). The research study at hand is not particularly different. Although it may not have been explicit, it is likely that the researchers were constantly comparing the problem and the general nature of the proposed solution as a routine part of the continued development of the solution.

Evaluation of Activity 4 If considered from a SDSM perspective, the terms of the specific problem and the terms of the general requirements surface as comparable. See table 5.1.

Specific problem 1 (ensure diffusion) and general requirement 1 (diffusion workshop) do align the general solution with the specific problem. Likewise specific problem 2 (project products) and general requirement 2 (early project timing) also align a general solution with the specific problem. The unmatched third requirement seems sensible as a measure to ensure the workability of the other two requirements.

5.5 SDSM Activity 5: Design Specific Solution for Specific Problem

The specific solution that was designed had three phases, called analysis, design, and planning, each covering two stages as shown in figure 5.2.

Table 5.1
Comparison of the specific problem and the general requirements

Specific problem from activity 1	General requirements from activity 2
1. It is a requirement to ensure diffusion and adoption of products and processes from IT projects in Danske Bank. 2. It is a requirement that the individual project ensures that its new product will be used as expected when it has been completed.	1. Hold an innovation diffusion planning meeting in a workshop format. 2. Hold the workshop early in the project process. 3. Follow a clear framework for the workshop (specifics to be determined).

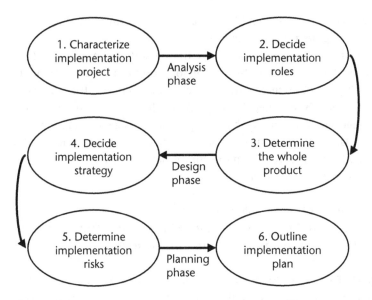

Figure 5.2
The example-specific solution.

Evaluation of Activity 5   There is no reason to believe that the design would have been different using SDSM. It is in fact quite generalized in the sense that none of the six activities are specific to Danske Bank.

5.6   SDSM Activity 6: Ex Ante Evaluation
A number of iterations and three ex post evaluations appear to have been conducted, but we found no evidence of an ex ante evaluation.

Evaluation of Activity 6   The search process for components of the specific solution is mentioned in the research reports but is not well defined. The overall process included early workshops and later library work and inspiration by the smaller research team. The components of the specific solution appear to have arisen mostly from this latter, unstructured part of the study. We learned from the study reports why the components were selected and how they should operate, but it appears that little attention was given to exactly how the literature search and selection process were conducted. For example, the reports do not clarify what components were considered and rejected or what the criteria were for the selection process. Following SDSM would have led the researchers to consider the search processes more carefully and pay closer attention to the component selection criteria. It is likely that a broader search could have produced more workable components, and these components might have been more carefully described and expressed. The solution would likely have been improved by this attention to detail and the development of more diversity.

Because of the action research framework, rather than a soft DSR approach, it is difficult to distinguish the development of the specific solution from the development of the general solution. To a certain degree, the only clear distinction is that the specific solution, the framework, is specified in more detail. Indeed, it is hard to say whether the more detailed process framework developed earlier is general (applicable broadly, not just within Danske Bank) or tuned specifically to Danske Bank. The details of the general requirements might have been more appropriately considered at activity 2, then matched to the specific requirements here.

5.7   SDSM Activity 7: Construct Specific Solution

The researchers clearly designed the specific solution (which could be interpreted as an instance of a general solution) and deployed it in bank projects.

Evaluation of Activity 7   There is no doubt that the knowledge we have today, ten years later, on diffusion and adoption, as well as the way the organization (Danske Bank) developed, would have made the specific solution look different. However, at the time, SDSM would not have added anything to the specifics.

5.8   SDSM Activity 8: Ex Post Evaluation

Since this was a design-oriented action research project, the solution was improved over five iterations. Each iteration included an evaluation that by our definition is ex post, as it happened after the construction of the specific solution. The initial deployment in a real Danske Bank project resulted in a number of adjustments, and further adjustments occurred after a second iteration in two other projects workshops. After the third iteration, the framework and the workshop had evolved into a form that was acceptable for internal projects. A fourth and a fifth iteration were carried out a year later to adapt the framework to external projects—meaning projects involving customers from the bank or outside the bank. In this way, the specific problem was changed and improved four times, illustrating the cyclical, iterative nature of design science.

Evaluation of Activity 8   Both action research and SDSM are iterative approaches to research. Each involves a number of phases. The research report is not clear about the nature of the adjustments that proceeded from the iterations. Indeed, it is possible that aspects of the reported solution are those that resulted from the refinements of several iterations, rather than results of an initial solution search. In terms of reporting length, the researchers are probably reporting the final framework, not the initial one. However, the report does suggest that adjustments were directed to the specific solution, and it is not clear that the general problem or general requirements were revisited. It could be obvious that the general solution was working, and the extra effort to reexamine the abstractions was simply unnecessary. In other words, the iterations may simply have been through activities 1, 7, and 8, instead of activities 1 through 8. SDSM might have improved the research process by adding emphasis to the need to constantly reexpress the specific problem after the need for adjustments arose, and to reevaluate the general problem, its requirements, and its relationship to the specific problems.

6 Analysis and Discussion of SDSM and the Evaluation

The review of a published DSR study, which used a design-oriented action research case, developed a number of key insights about the similarities and differences between the two approaches. With a focus on possible improvements in the research study that might have proceeded from the use of SDSM, we have developed evidence of its probable success as a methodology in a future research study. The analysis has identified similarities, ambiguous differences, probable improvements, and possible disadvantages.

6.1 Similarities
The design-oriented action research study examined in this chapter shares some clear similarities with SDSM. Consistent with the Soft Design Science ideals, the action research project seemed to approach problem definition with an aim to clarity and specificity. Explicit, valid, and specific requirements are an ideal in both approaches. The design-oriented action research DSR project also engaged in a prominent and documented solution search process. There was also a good match between the specific problem and the general requirements generated in the action research study. This match is also an ideal for SDSM. The iterative nature of the action research project was also appropriate for SDSM.

6.2 Ambiguous Differences
The action research study also differed from SDSM in several ways. However, it is not clear that all differences are improvements. For example, the design-oriented action research study did not clearly distinguish the various stages of solution development, as would have been expected with SDSM. As a result, the distinction between the general requirements and the specific solution could have been clearer. While this is a difference between SDSR and the project studied, it may be that the quest for a seamless, specific solution, without identifying a general problem and solution, would be appropriate in some research settings (e.g., where time is of the essence), and other settings (e.g., where an ideal, high-quality, or optimal solution is critical) might benefit from the distinctions.

6.3 Probable Improvements

Some differences would very likely have improved the study outcomes if SDSM had informed the research approach. In shifting to design thinking, an explicit investigation into the general problem was missing from the action research study. SDSM would involve more careful explication of the general problem, and this additional detail could have changed or improved the direction of the research. Also, by expressly using imperative statements and declarative logic, SDSM would have promoted more structure in the search process for both the general requirements and the specific solutions. Particularly at the general requirements level, it is quite possible that by using SDSM the researchers may have gained clearer insights into the generality of the solution addressed by the requirements. At the specific search level, the added structure may have enabled the research to discover more alternative components for the specific solution. SDSM might also have improved the action research project by constantly reviewing the specific and general representations of the problem and solution spaces. This comparison could detect shifts in underlying constructs that might otherwise have been missed in the action research project.

6.4 Possible Disadvantages

A third type of difference offers insight into how the use of SDSM to inform the action research study might indeed have degraded its processes and outcomes. It is clear from the SDSM evaluation of the action research study that more structures are incorporated in the more elaborate methodology. While offering rigor, this additional structure could also weigh down researchers with additional complexity in their tasks.

7 Conclusion

This chapter has proposed a Soft Design Science Methodology (SDSM), as shown in figure 5.3, which incorporates aspects of Soft Systems Methodology and other related methods into a DSR process. SDSM is a situated methodology in that the application of the methodology will produce different solutions in different situations. The chapter analyzes a hypothetical application of SDSM to a published DSR study that used design-oriented action research. The analysis identified similarities and differences, including probable improvements and some possible disadvantages.

An important benefit of using SDSM will possibly be improved outcomes from DSR in terms of improved adoption. If researchers using this method carefully consider the stakeholders and their interests (activity 1), carefully generalize from a specific problem (activities 2–3), and carefully recheck the generalized solution artifact against the original problem (activities 6 and 8), the applicability of the solution artifact is much more likely to fit well and be adopted.

Furthermore, testing the solution artifact iteratively can give excellent ideas for correct fit in subsequent iterations of the solution artifact. The experience of

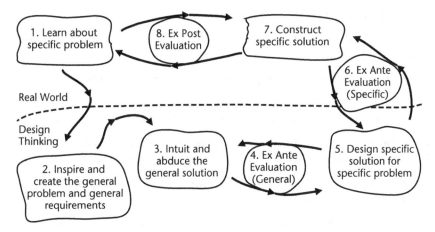

Figure 5.3
Soft Design Science Methodology.

transferring the technology during evaluation iterations can also indicate areas that need to be addressed in subsequent implementations in other contexts for other stakeholders.

Overall the potential improvements enumerated here provide a positive indication of the potential value of using SDSM. The limiting and thereby harder-to-come-to-terms-with implication is that all methodologies have inherent limitations that make them inescapably partial and biased toward some situations and solutions at the expense of others. In that sense, we have to admit that our background in information systems may have led us to design SDSM in a way that makes it suitable primarily in the IS discipline and limits its applicability to other applied disciplines and their practice of DSR, although we foresee no specific problems with applying SDSM in other disciplines than IS.

References

Ackermann, Frank, and Colin Eden. 2001. SODA—Journey making and mapping in practice. In *Rational Analysis for a Problematic World Revisited*, ed. Jonathan Rosenhead and John Mingers, 43–60. Chichester: John Wiley.

Baskerville, Richard, and Jan Pries-Heje. 2010. Explanatory design theory. *Business and Information Systems Engineering* 2 (5): 271–282.

Bousbaci, Rabah. 2008. "Models of man" in design thinking: The "bounded rationality" episode. *Design Issues* 24 (4): 38–52.

Brown, Tim. 2008. Design thinking. *Harvard Business Review* 86 (6): 84–93.

Checkland, Peter. 1981. *Systems Thinking, Systems Practice*. Chichester: John Wiley.

Checkland, Peter, and Sue Holwell. 1998. *Information, Systems, and Information Systems: Making Sense of the Field*. Chichester: John Wiley.

Checkland, Peter, and Ji Scholes. 1990. *Soft Systems Methodology in Practice*. Chichester: John Wiley.

Eden, Colin. 1988. Cognitive mapping. *European Journal of Operational Research* 36 (1): 1–13.

Eden, Colin, and Frank Ackermann. 2001. SODA—The principles. In *Rational Analysis for a Problematic World Revisited*, ed. J. Rosenhead and J. Mingers, 21–42. Chichester: J. Wiley.

Gregor, Shirley, and David Jones. 2007. The anatomy of a design theory. *Journal of the Association for Information Systems* 8 (5): 312–335.

Hall, Peter. 2009. Disorderly reasoning in information design. *Journal of the American Society for Information Science and Technology* 60 (9): 1877.

Hevner, Alan R., Salvatore T. March, Jinsoo Park, and Sudha Ram. 2004. Design science in information systems research. *Management Information Systems Quarterly* 28 (1): 75–105.

Iivari, Juhani. 2007. A paradigmatic analysis of information systems as a design science. *Scandinavian Journal of Information Systems* 19 (2): 39–63.

Kuvaja, Pasi, Jouni Similä, Lech Krzanik, Adriana Bicego, Samuli Saukkonen, and Günter Koch. 1994. *Software Process Assessment and Improvement: The Bootstrap Approach*. Oxford: Blackwell.

March, James G. 1991. Exploration and exploitation in organizational learning. *Organization Science* 2 (1): 71–87.

March, Salvatore T., and Gerald F. Smith. 1995. Design and natural science research on information technology. *Decision Support Systems* 15 (4): 251–266.

Martin, Roger. 2010. Design thinking: Achieving insights via the "knowledge funnel." *Strategy and Leadership* 38 (2): 37.

Nunamaker, Jay F., Jr., Minder Chen, and Titus D. M. Purdin. 1991. Systems development in information systems research. *Journal of Management Information Systems* 7 (3): 89–106.

Paulk, Mark C., Charles Weber, Bill Curtis, and Mary Beth Chrissis. 1995. *The Capability Maturity Model: Guidelines for Improving the Software Process*. Reading, MA: Addison-Wesley.

Peffers, Ken, Tuure Tuunanen, Marcus A. Rothenberger, and Samir Chatterjee. 2008. A design science research methodology for information systems research. *Journal of Management Information Systems* 24 (3): 45–77.

Pries-Heje, Jan, and Susanne Tryde. 2001. Diffusion and adoption of IT products and processes in a Danish bank. Paper presented at the IFIP TC8 WG 8.6 Fourth Working Conference on Diffusing Software Product and Process Innovations, Banff, Canada.

Schön, Donald. 1983. *The Reflective Practitioner: How Professionals Think in Action*. New York: Basic.

Sein, Maung K., Ola Henfridsson, Sandeep Purao, Matti Rossi, and Robert Lindgren. 2011. Action design research. *Management Information Systems Quarterly* 35 (1): 37–56.

Toulmin, Stephen. 1958. *The Uses of Argument*. Cambridge: Cambridge University Press.

Ulrich, Werner. 1983. *Critical Heuristics of Social Planning: A New Approach to Practical Philosophy*. Bern: Paul Hapt.

Ulrich, Werner. 1987. Critical heuristics of social systems design. *European Journal of Operational Research* 31: 276–283.

Ulrich, Werner. 2002. Critical systems heuristics. In *The Informed Student Guide to Management Science*, ed. H. G. Daellenbach and R. L. Flood. London: Thomson Learning.

Vaishnavi, Vijay, and William Kuechler. 2013. Design research in information systems. IS World, http://desrist.org/design-research-in-information-systems/.

Walls, Joseph G., George R. Widmeyer, and Omar A. El Sawy. 1992. Building an information system design theory for vigilant EIS. *Information Systems Research* 3 (1): 36–59.

Wynne, Martin. 2004. Evaluation in the arts and humanities data service. *Vine* 34 (4): 196–200.

II Methods for Collaborative Processes

6 Collective Analysis of Qualitative Data

Jesper Simonsen and Karin Friberg

What. Many students and practitioners do not know how to systematically process qualitative data once it is gathered—at least not as a collective effort. This chapter presents two workshop techniques, affinity diagramming and diagnostic mapping, that support collective analysis of large amounts of qualitative data. Affinity diagramming is used to make collective analysis and interpretations of qualitative data to identify core problems that need to be addressed in the design process. Diagnostic mapping supports collective interpretation and description of these problems and how to intervene in them. We explain the techniques through a case where they were used to analyze why a new electronic medical record system introduced life-threatening situations for patients.

Why. Collective analyses offer all participants a voice, visualize their contributions, combine different actors' perspectives, and anchor the result of the interpretation to the participating actors. Combining the techniques is a powerful way to analyze and intervene in situations before or after the introduction of new technologies.

Where. The techniques are general tools that might be widely applied in different domains. In particular, collective analysis can be used to identify, understand, and act on complex design problems that emerge, for example, after the introduction of new technologies. Such problems might be hard to clarify, and the basis for the analysis often involves large amounts of unstructured qualitative data, for example, from numerous interviews.

How. Affinity diagrams visualize "core categories" from the body of data. Diagnostic mapping visualizes problems, their causes, and their consequences, along with any ideas for solutions. Both techniques are used in workshop form where the participants jointly analyze, discuss, and interpret the empirical material visualized by pads of adhesive notes.

1 Introduction

Academic work often includes analysis of large amounts of unstructured and qualitative data. Consider the situation where a student group or a research team at a university has conducted a number of interviews: How does the project group make a systematic analysis of the resulting interview material, such as audio recordings, transcripts, personal notes, and thoughts? In some situations, they might do so simply by having a meeting where the participants from the project group meet and discuss what each of them believes to be important contributions from the interviews. But then the individual participants risk approaching the discussion solely from their own interpretation and perspective of the data, promoting their own ideas, agendas, and interests, and perhaps ignoring or misunderstanding others' ideas and input. In this case, maybe only by chance will general insights emerge as a result of what the project group is collectively able to interpret and conclude.

This chapter offers a systematic method for conducting a collective analysis of qualitative data. The main point is to facilitate a collective process of interpretation (versus an individual interpretation process). The collective interpretation process includes an initial inductive collective analysis of the data material based on grounded theory (Glaser and Strauss 1967), and a subsequent abductive collective process supporting an innovative and design-oriented intervention for change. The collective interpretation process is supported by the affinity diagramming technique (Brassard 1989), and the abductive collective process is facilitated by the diagnostic mapping technique (Lanzara and Mathiassen 1985).

The combined use of the two techniques has been part of the curriculum at a university design course taught by one of the authors for more than a decade. The experience from the course has shown that the students are able to apply the techniques quickly and independently while also conducting high-quality collective analysis. Using the techniques for the first time typically provides the students with a great "aha" experience.

We begin by outlining the background and the main ideas behind affinity diagramming and diagnostic mapping. Then we describe a case, analyzing a complex, problematic situation involving a new electronic medical record (EMR) system. The system was introduced to obtain a safer medication procedure. After the implementation, the designers undertook a questionnaire survey to learn about the user experience. To their astonishment, one-third of the respondents reported that the medication procedure had become less safe, sometimes leading to life-threatening situations. This raised an immediate design problem: Why is the new EMR-supported medication process not experienced as being unequivocally safer? The case describes how large amounts of qualitative data were gathered and analyzed by affinity diagramming and diagnostic mapping to investigate why the system introduced life-threatening situations for patients. The chapter then gives a concrete hands-on suggestion for how collective analysis can be applied in student projects. Finally, we close with a summarizing conclusion.

2 Background

The affinity diagramming technique has Japanese origins, was originally described by Brassard (1989), and has been widely used in design methods, including contextual design (Beyer and Holtzblatt 1998, 154ff.) and the MUST method (Bødker, Kensing, and Simonsen, this vol.; Bødker, Kensing, and Simonsen 2004, 253).

Affinity diagramming is theoretically rooted in grounded theory. Grounded theory was developed by Glaser and Strauss (Glaser and Strauss 1967; Glaser 1992) as a strategy for analyzing qualitative data. The theory is "grounded," meaning that it includes descriptions and explanations made through an analysis of empirical data—that is, it is grounded in this data: "Grounded theory is derived from data and then illustrated by characteristic examples of data" (Glaser and Strauss 1967, 5).

Grounded theory forms an inductive process where numerous single observations from the data are analyzed in a bottom-up approach to form more general conclusions. The theory analyzes qualitative data from, for example, transcripts or elaborated summaries of interviews. First, this data is coded; that is, key points of interest in the data are marked, for example, by underlining a word or text passage in an interview transcript. Second, through a process of constant comparison of codes, low-level categories emerge from the data as groups of codes of similar content (Glaser and Strauss 1967, 36). Third, low-level categories might evolve into high-level categories or core categories (Glaser 1992, 75). High-level categories can, for example, identify a problematic situation that is described and elaborated through all the associated codes. The goal of grounded theory is "the generation of theory around a core category [that explains the] patterns of behavior" that are relevant or problematic (75).

Affinity diagramming helps to create an overview over large amounts of data through an inductive process as described by grounded theory: "Building an affinity is inductive reasoning at its purest. To put up one note, then for everyone to look for other notes that seem to go with it" (Brassard 1989, 30). The starting point is a number of isolated statements (codes) written on pads of adhesive notes. The adhesive notes are distributed and grouped on a board (fig. 6.1). The statements (codes) on the notes are interpreted and assessed to clarify and determine which group (category) an adhesive note might belong to. This principle of "making the data talk" is central to grounded theory and affinity diagramming: the point is to enable categories to emerge as part of the process of analyzing and comparing of the data, rather than analyzing data based on predefined categories or hypotheses (Glaser and Strauss 1967, 36; Glaser 1992, 39). The result is an affinity diagram outlining low-level and high-level categories. Affinity diagramming is a workshop technique offering a resource for situated action (Suchman 2007). The technique's core aspect is that it is data driven, that is, driven by the empirical data at hand. The technique stipulates how to work with these

Figure 6.1
An affinity diagram workshop.

data, while the actual workshop processes, as well as the results, depend totally on the available qualitative data.

The problem-mapping technique can be used to analyze problems that have been identified in the affinity diagram. Problem mapping supports an abductive reasoning: a process of suggesting and stating hypotheses explaining problems, as well as suggesting possible ways to solve them. The technique was originally described by Lanzara and Mathiassen (1985), has been applied to information technology design methods (Andersen et al. 1990, 136ff.; Bødker, Kensing, and Simonsen 2004, 277ff.), used to support the principle of "anchoring visions" (see Bødker, Kensing, and Simonsen, this vol.), and used to engage top management in design projects (Simonsen 2007). Diagnostic mapping is used to analyze (diagnose) problematic situations. When it is combined with affinity diagramming, the technique takes a starting point in problems identified in the affinity diagram as core categories. For each of these problems, the technique enables a

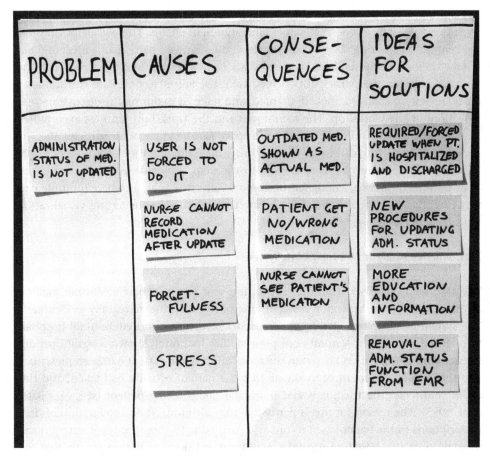

Figure 6.2
A diagnostic map. The diagnosed problem is further described in section 3.1.

structuring of arguments, explaining their causes, consequences, and ideas for solutions. The argument chains are built using adhesive notes from the affinity diagram (when appropriate), as well as new added statements (hypotheses) not directly evident in the data (fig. 6.2). The aim of diagnostic mapping is to generate ideas for how to solve problems. The technique pursues the explanation of problems and how to intervene in them. In this way, the technique supplements an inductive grounded-theory-based analysis with an abductive and design-oriented intervention. Just like affinity diagramming, diagnostic mapping constitutes a resource for situated action (Suchman 2007). The technique's core aspect is that it involves stakeholders. The technique offers an agenda and a visualization tool for the workshop, while the processes, as well as the results, depend totally on reflections and discussions raised by the participants.

Common to both affinity diagramming and diagnostic mapping is the use of adhesive notes to visualize codes, categories, and argument chains. These visualizations are the central tools during the workshops where the involved participants meet and use the techniques. The visualizations work as an agenda-setting tool through which the dialogue between the participants is mediated: the adhesive notes are continuously made, reviewed, changed, moved, pointed, and referred to during the discussions and reflections at the workshop. The techniques and the workshop form (as exemplified and described in the following sections) a space for the voice of all participants. The grouping of codes into categories in the affinity diagram, and the structuring of explanations and argument chains in the diagnostic map, are made as a collective effort. Thus both techniques are designed to support collective analysis where multiple participants share interpretations and mediate their discussions using the visualization tools depicted in figures 6.1 and 6.2.

3   Collective Analysis of a New EMR System

The case study involved the implementation and use of a new electronic medical record (EMR) system in Region Zealand, one of five health-care regions in Denmark. The system was implemented to obtain a safer medication procedure in all hospitals throughout the region. A number of prior studies had often shown a significant difference ("noncompliance") between the medication that a patient had been prescribed and the kind and amount of medicine that the patient actually had taken, and this could counteract the treatment and harm the safety of the patient (see, e.g., Bates et al. 1995). The reason for this is partly due to multipronged documentation of drug prescriptions in the paper-based record and partly due to absent or inconsistent documentation of the actual drug intake. Multipronged documentation means that the same prescription is recorded several times at different places in the record, for example, documented both in the nursing record and in the physician record specific to a single ward. Examples of errors resulting from the use of the EMR system are described by Hertzum (2010).

Political pressure was applied to increase the documentation and control of the medication process. EMR systems are expected to eliminate (or drastically reduce) medication errors by providing a technological platform that ensures single-stranded documentation and an accurate alignment of the patient's prescriptions and actual intake (Bates et al. 2003).

The Zealand region was the first to complete a large-scale implementation of EMR. The system was implemented during 2003 and 2004, accompanied by a thorough and systematic introduction and training of the clinical staff (which in 2004 involved twenty-one man-years). In April 2004 the system had about 2,500 users, and they had passed one million medical transactions from more than 20,000 patients. The hospitals in the region handle about 50,000 hospitalizations and 300,000 outpatient treatments every year.

After the implementation, the people in charge of the project (referred to hereafter as "the project group") undertook a questionnaire survey to learn about the user experience during the implementation period and when using the system on a daily basis. Participation in the survey was anonymous, and 377 users responded, including 115 physicians and 220 nurses representing the main users of the EMR system. The response rate was low, most probably because the survey, with its 127 fixed-response questions, took approximately forty-five minutes to complete. Nevertheless the result of the survey included more than 2,200 optional free-text comments, 700 from physicians, 1,300 from nurses, and 200 from others.

It came as a surprise to the project group that the clinicians did not experience the new medication practice as being unequivocally safe: one-third of the respondents reported, to the contrary, that the medication procedure had become less safe and sometimes led to life-threatening situations. The immediate design problem in question was: Why is the new EMR-supported medication process not experienced as being unequivocally safer?

While the survey identified a severe design problem, it gave no immediate answer as to *why* this problem had emerged. The many optional comments entered by the clinicians indicated a high desire to explain in their own words how they had experienced problems using the system. Some of the reasons for the design problem may have been explained in these comments. The project group did not know how to deal with all these "unstructured" qualitative statements, and they asked two researchers (the authors of this chapter) to analyze the statements and look for possible reasons for the problem.

In addition, the project group decided to conduct focus group interviews with clinicians to let them reflect on, discuss, and elaborate on their experiences using the system. Four focus group interviews were conducted with ten chief physicians, nine specialist registrars and residents, and seven nurses respectively, as well as one with a mixed group of seven physicians and nurses. One of the authors of this chapter participated in the interviews. Before the interviews, she had visited a medical ward to observe how the nurses administrated the medicine and how physicians used the system during their ward rounds. The focus interviews were audio-recorded and transcribed in "a more formal, written style" (Kvale 1996, 170), focusing on passages related to the safety issue.

3.1 Using Affinity Diagramming

All the survey statements were printed with a relatively high font size and cut into individual paper notes, each representing one statement. Using a large font size allowed multiple participants to more easily get an overview of the notes when

Figure 6.3
The process of making the affinity diagram.

arranged on a table or wall. A primary sorting of the notes reduced the number to approximately 250 different-type statements as a result of sorting out identical (or almost identical) statements and statements that were clearly not related to the safety issue. The selected survey statements and selected statements from the interview were then subjected to constant comparison using the affinity diagramming technique.

The statements were taken one by one, briefly discussed and interpreted by the researchers, and then attached to a wall. To begin with, each statement was compared to all the statements on the wall to assess if it pointed toward one or another of them, and in this way, groups of statements quickly began to form. A headline for a group was written on colored adhesive notes (fig. 6.3). After about one-third of the statements had been placed on the wall, the process shifted toward an assessment of which group a new statement belonged to. Sometimes a statement could be related to more than one group, and this triggered a discussion of how to interpret groups of statements. The groups in the affinity diagram developed during the process, and some groups formed groups with subgroups (high-level categories with associated low-level categories).

The affinity diagram identified four problems:

1. Administration status is not updated.
2. Medication status is not updated.
3. Medical procedures are circumvented.
4. Medical documentation is multipronged.

It is noteworthy that the affinity diagramming identified four general problematic situations in using the new electronic medical system, and no new problematic situations arose later in the case. We describe and explain the first three problems in section 3.3, "Results of the Analysis." We do not touch further on the fourth category in this chapter; this problem addressed the system's failure to obtain a single-stranded documentation, that is, where a given medication is recorded once only in the system.

3.2 Using Diagnostic Mapping

Diagnostic mapping was used to analyze the relationship between the problems of using EMR, their causes, the negative consequences, and possible solutions. The starting point for the mapping session was the problems identified in the affinity diagram.

The researchers made a first version of the diagnostic maps and then used them during a workshop with the project group where the maps were presented, discussed, revised, and elaborated. Problem situations were mapped through diagnostic maps related to the use of the system's administration status, medicine status, and circumvented procedures. The resulting diagnostic maps reflected the researchers' and project group participants' collective analysis and interpretation of the problematic situations, and they were subsequently used by the project group to initiate actions to remedy the problems.

The maps were made with adhesive notes attached to flip-over papers that could easily be moved around and revised (see fig. 6.2, representing a map diagnosing the problem "administration status is not updated"). Affinity diagram notes formed part of the input to the map representing this problem. However, there is not a one-to-one relation between notes on the diagnostic map and the affinity diagram. Some notes from the affinity diagram may fit into the map, while the participants, based on their interpretation of the situation, construct others. This was typically the case for notes relating to "causes" and "ideas for solutions."

The ideas for solutions in the maps comprised changes to the technology and clinical procedures, as well as education and information related to the EMR system. Figure 6.4 shows one immediate action taken after the workshop: informing the clinicians at the emergency departments by drawing attention to the possible risk induced by the EMR system. Readers interested in the efforts and experiences in trying to remedy the problems are referred to Granlien, Hertzum, and Gudmundsen (2008) and Granlien and Hertzum (2012).

3.3 Results of the Analysis

Why did the clinicians not experience the new EMR-supported medication process as being unequivocally safer? While the clinicians do agree that the system solves some medication errors and inexpediencies, they also point out that new, potentially

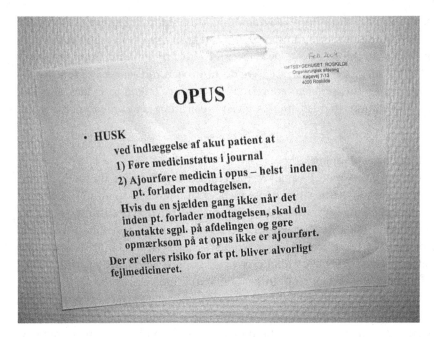

Figure 6.4
The attention sign at an emergency department, warning the clinicians about a potentially dangerous situation with the EMR system (text in Danish). The sign was made immediately after the diagnostic mapping workshop and reads as follows: "REMEMBER when hospitalizing an acute patient to (1) set the medicine status in the patient record; (2) update the medicine in the system—preferably before the patient leaves the emergency department [and is transferred to another ward]. If occasionally you are not able to make it before the patient is transferred, you must contact the nurse at the receiving ward and call attention to the fact that the system is not updated. Otherwise there is a risk that the patient will have seriously inappropriate medication."

dangerous situations emerge. Common to these situations is incorrect use of the system (i.e., incorrect according to the formal medication procedure), resulting in erroneous data in the system, again leading to dangerous situations that are difficult to detect, predict, and prevent.

The new EMR system led to critical medication situations deeply embedded within the complex organization and practice of using the technology. The system entailed a more detailed and less flexible documentation practice. The system enforced workflows that previously were also mandatory but easy to circumvent. Laborious new procedures introduced by the system were sometimes forgotten, omitted, or circumvented to "get the job done" in a busy situation, while other stricter and mandatory procedures were either deliberately opposed or omitted owing to confusion about the division of responsibilities among the clinicians.

We now describe the aforementioned three problem situations arising from the use of the system's administration status, the medicine status, and the related circumvented medical procedures.

The first situation concerns the introduction of a new procedure in updating the drug administration status (indicating who is administrating the patient's drug). This procedure aims to reduce medication errors, but it introduces new error situations if not used consistently by all clinicians. The administration status provides the clinician with a functionality to explicitly decide who should administer the patient's different types of medicine during and after being hospitalized. The medicine should, among other things, be given the status of either none, partial, or full self-administration, referring to how much the patient is in control of taking the medicine. This did not always work as intended, as described by a physician in a focus group interview:

We discharged the patient from our ward to the outpatient clinic. Treating a patient on an outpatient basis means that the patient, in principle, is in charge of the medicine, and the administration status in the system must be set to "self-administration." The patient then gets worse and is admitted once again to our ward as an emergency patient. The physician receiving the patient looks into the medical system and notices all the ordinated medicine—that's okay, that's what the patient should have. But he overlooks a tiny little box with a check mark, which means that the status of the administration is set to "full self-administration" [see fig. 6.5]. So the patient is

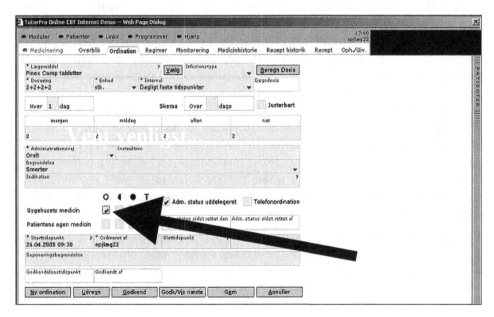

Figure 6.5
Screen dump from the system with arrow pointing to checkbox with administration status.

hospitalized, but without any medicine prescribed [by the hospital]. The nurse checks whether the patient should have any medicine and cannot see any prescriptions [that she is in charge of—because the patient himself is responsible for taking this]. The error is realized three days later when the patient suffers from an accumulated and severe epileptic seizure. You might claim that this is a human error—that it is not an error in the system—but it really imposes a factor of uncertainty.

The second situation describes how some physicians resist complying with an enforced procedure related to the "medicine status." It concerns a well-known clinical procedure as described by the Danish National Board of Health: that the physician in charge of a patient must be responsible for the complete drug portfolio of that patient. This procedure aims at, among other things, avoiding the risk of drug interactions, where different drugs change the impact of one another. While this has always been a general rule of attention for the physician, the implementation of the system required the physician to set the medicine status, thereby explicitly recording who and when made this judgment for a given patient:

I never touch the medicine status—because I work in a psychiatry ward and then [if I touch the medicine status] I become responsible for all the somatic medicine ordinated too. And I don't know anything about that. (focus group interview)

If the physician does not set the medicine status, the EMR has failed to resolve a problem that was equally present before its introduction, but in addition, new problems might occur, as illustrated in the third situation.

The third situation illustrates that the enforced workflow implies that a correct marking of the administrative and medical status is sometimes forgotten. Before a patient is discharged from the hospital, the physician should assess the medicine status and decide which medication is no longer relevant (and mark this as "discontinued"') and which medication the patient should continue to take (and mark this as "full self-administration"). However, when the physician marks a drug as "full self-administration," the nurse is no longer allowed to mark that the medication has been given. And sometimes the nurse gives the patient medication just before the patient is discharged. This enforces a procedure where the physician must await any remaining medication before setting the status—and thus this was often forgotten, as illustrated in the following story:

What they do is actually right [waiting to set the status until after the patient is discharged] because otherwise the nurse is prevented from doing anything when discharging the patient. So they postpone it, and this initiates the problem at a subsequent hospitalization. They skip it because it bothers us right now, and then we forget to set it [afterward]. (diagnostic mapping workshop)

A patient was hospitalized at the anesthesia ward and was then discharged ... without any change recorded on the medicine status. Then [several months later] the patient was hospitalized in our ward, and I noticed that the patient was ordinated ten different intravenous drugs. I discontinued all of it. (focus group interview)

These problems arose owing to the new reconfigurations of existing procedures, organization, and clinical work practices that took place. These reconfigurations aim at making the clinicians comply with new technologies in the EMR system, as well as the new medication procedures imposed and facilitated by the system. Such intrinsic and complex relationships between information technologies and work practices are far from an exception and have been found in other empirical investigations within the health-care domain (e.g., Berg 1999; Berg, Aarts, and van der Lei 2003).

4   Hands-On Guidelines for Collective Analysis

How can a university student group approach a collective analysis of their qualitative data? In this section, we present some concrete hands-on guidelines to begin such an analysis. An illustrative overview is given in figure 6.6.

A starting point for using the affinity diagramming technique could be that the student group had conducted a number of interviews. For the sake of this example, let us picture a situation where you participate in a group with three other fellow students. Your group has conducted five interviews where two or three students together met the interviewees. Each interview was audio-recorded. After each interview, one of the students who participated in the interview listened through the audio recording and made a transcription (Kvale 1996, 170) (e.g., five to ten pages for an interview). The resulting five transcripts were distributed to all of you, and you now make your individual preparation for a joint affinity diagramming workshop.

Your preparation comprises your individual interpretation of the interviews. You start by making a printout of all five interview transcripts and sequentially marking them with a number and your initials. You now read them and mark all words, phrases, and short passages where you observe something of special interest to you (e.g., using a highlighter or felt-tip pen). Then you go through all the markings and make, for each of them, a relevant headline on an adhesive note with a large pen. The headline on each adhesive note should be readable from a distance when the group meets and looks at the affinity diagram. On each adhesive note, you also make a small referential comment in the lower-right-hand corner with your initials, number of the interview, and the page number where the passage that the note refers to (e.g., "AJ, int. 3, p. 5"). In this way, you can consult the interview transcription printout and see the context for the specific code on each of the adhesive notes.

When your group meets for the affinity diagramming workshop, all of you should bring your annotated interview printouts and your pile of adhesive notes. During the workshop, your collective analysis is initiated based on each of your individual interpretations. If it's your first time making an affinity diagram, you might experience the significant, and positive, difference from how you have worked with qualitative material beforehand, or, as the inventor of affinity diagramming might put it: "Breakthrough in traditional concepts is needed. When the only solutions are old solutions, try an Affinity to expand the team's thinking" (Brassard 1989, 18).

You go through the interviews one by one. As the group member who conducted the interview, you carefully review all your observations one by one. You take each adhesive note, put it on the whiteboard or wall in front of you, and explain briefly what this code is about and why you chose it. The others might ask clarifying questions. Then, in turn, the other group participants go through their observations and stick their notes on the wall near to similar notes and categories that emerge during the process. At the same time, you will also be considering headlines for the emerging categories, noted on new adhesive notes and placed above the group of notes they belong to.

When all of you have gone through all your notes, you will have an affinity diagram structured in categories. You may also have a number of notes that do not belong to any specific category; these notes can be grouped together in a group headlined "the fridge." The fridge can help you concentrate on the notes you find interesting while not having a sense that you are ignoring other notes, since they are preserved in the fridge, and you can return to them later, if needed. The categories might form the sections of a subsequent report. Writing this report may be distributed among you, so each of you makes a draft of some of the categories. The notes for each category constitute the headwords to consider. If you question the meaning or context of a headword, you can use its reference to return to the interview summary to which it belongs.

Diagnostic mapping is a relevant technique after one or more affinity diagrams have been made. You can use the technique to establish an overview and joint understanding of a problematic situation while also noting possible courses of action for solving the situation. It allows your group and others with whom you collaborate to express and solidify your statements, interpretations, and ideas for solutions regarding a situation that you want to improve. Diagnostic mapping can help you to visualize your argument chains that explain how you interpret a problem and how it might be solved. The map supports you in explicating your abductive hypotheses and candidates (guesses) of explanations so that they can be collectively reviewed. Two typical situations using diagnostic mapping could be as follows:

• As a follow-up to the affinity diagramming of your interviews. The affinity diagram might reveal a number of problematic situations you would like to investigate further. This may involve mapping such situations in collaboration with the interviewees or others with whom you collaborate.

• As a tool for your project group for outlining and establishing an overview of the total volume of problems, needs, and solution proposals that your project has revealed so far—for instance, to assist you in a prioritization (Bødker, Kensing, and Simonsen 2004, 278f).

As with affinity diagramming, the mapping is done in a joint workshop where you engage in a process of collectively analyzing the problematic situations. In preparing the workshop, you should agree on what problematic situations you want to analyze. And just as with affinity diagramming, you should make an individual interpretation of these problematic situations by outlining your own diagnostic maps before conducting the workshop. The individual preparation is important for both techniques: if you skip the individual work, this might outweigh what is gained by working collectively.

The mapping is done on a wall or on big sheets of paper on the wall with four (empty) columns: Problem, Causes, Consequences, and Ideas for Solutions. Using sheets of paper from a flip-over helps you make a map that you can easily move and take with you. Each problematic situation that is being studied provides the title of one map.

Start by listing the possible interpretations of the problematic situation, that is, problem candidates in the left-hand column. Write down all the suggestions in the problems column as short statements that fit into the adhesive notes. Let the group member who suggested the problem propose the wording. You may help define the problem, but it is not very helpful if you merely reinterpret or rephrase the problem. Use adhesive notes as in affinity diagramming so that it is easy to move a suggestion to a different spot on the map. Often something that is initially perceived as a problem later turns out to constitute a cause or a consequence.

Next, take up the problems one by one and outline the causes, consequences, and potential solutions for each. It might help to ask questions like the following:

• What is causing the problem? What are the conditions and reasons behind the problem?
• What are the most negative consequences of the problem—those we are unwilling to accept? What consequences and additional problems does the original problem entail?
• What potential solutions to the problem can we come up with? What do we imagine would eliminate or remedy the problem?

Codes from the affinity diagrams might form some of the candidates for input to the diagnostic map, but more often the affinity diagram forms a basis for making the diagnostic map rather than any kind of one-to-one transfer of adhesive notes from the diagram to the map. In our experience, the qualitative data from interviews and other sources often form observable input to the problems and consequences columns, while the participants making the map interpret and suggest most of the input to the causes and ideas for the solutions column. Reviews of diagnostic maps made together with a partner thus often challenge the hypotheses of causes and provide new candidates for interventions (see, e.g., Simonsen 2007).

If a problem has few consequences or no suggested unacceptable consequences, the problem may be superficial—that is, the interpretation of the problematic situation is irrelevant. If, on closer consideration, the consequences of a problem are found to be bearable, the problem probably does not warrant further study.

It may be hard to distinguish among problems, consequences, and causes. The consequences of a problem are perhaps seen as constituting problems in themselves. If a consequence of a problem is regarded as a significant separate problem, we recommend putting it down on the list as a new problem.

Diagnostic mapping is an effective technique for the project group to discuss and agree on how to interpret and intervene in problematic situations. It is equally effective to bring your analysis to your collaborating partners, just as the researchers brought their diagnostic maps to the project group in the case of the EMR system described earlier. We generally advise that you make a diagnostic map on your own that you present and revise together with your partner (see Simonsen 2007 for an elaborated example for how to do this). If you have a trustful relationship with your partner(s), you might also consider making the diagnostic map together from scratch.

5 Conclusion

This chapter has presented a method as a resource for situated action, specifically oriented toward facing large amounts of qualitative data; the objective is to traverse the empirical data and distill the relevant issues and problems as part of a design process. The two presented techniques cannot direct any exact pathway to follow, but they can form a concrete resource for the project group to embark on in a collective analysis of the qualitative data.

In the case presented, the qualitative data came from two sources: (1) free-text comments from a survey originally designed to make an overall evaluation of the EMR system, its use, and the implementation process; and (2) transcriptions from focus group interviews where clinicians reflected on their experiences using the system. The techniques might be used with qualitative data from other sources too, for example, from observations or from collections of documents. We explained how the data were initially analyzed through an inductive and grounded-theory-inspired approach using affinity diagramming as a simple yet effective technique to manage large qualitative data material. The affinity diagramming process identified, characterized, and generalized the problems. The affinity diagramming was followed by the diagnostic mapping technique. This technique undertakes an abductive approach by forming hypothetical explanations to the problems from the affinity diagram, as well as suggesting possible interventions that might solve the problems. Both techniques are based on making

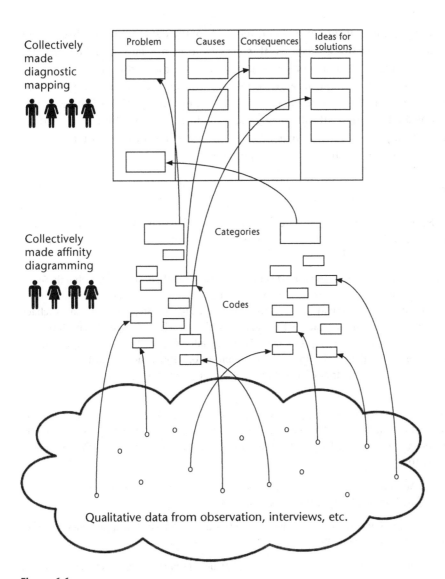

Figure 6.6

Collective analysis of qualitative data by combining affinity diagramming and diagnostic mapping. Codes are made from the qualitative data forming input to the affinity diagram, where the codes are grouped in categories. Categories identifying problems form initial input to diagnostic maps, where problems are explained and solutions suggested. The map is constructed by the participants, drawing on their interpretation and hypotheses. Codes might form part of the input to the diagnostic maps.

the data and the participating actors' interpretations of the data highly visible by using adhesive notes. During the workshops, this visualization mediates and supports the collective discussions and reflections taking place among the participants.

Thus we have demonstrated how to combine techniques to manage a process of descriptive analysis and proactive intervention activities. An overview of the problem was accomplished through affinity diagrams, and diagnostic mapping was used to facilitate workshops aimed at problem solving and devising ideas for interventions. This collective analysis is summarized in figure 6.6.

References

Andersen, Niels Erik, Finn Kensing, Jette Lundin, Lars Mathiassen, Andreas Munk-Madsen, Monika Rasbech, and Pål Sørgaard. 1990. *Professional Systems Development: Experience, Ideas, and Action.* New York: Prentice Hall.

Bates, D. W., J. David Cullen, Nan Laird, Laura A. Petersen, Stephen D. Small, Deborah Servi, Glenn Laffel, Bobbie J. Sweitzer, Brian F. Shea, Robert Hallisey, Martha Vander Vliet, Roberta Nemeskal, Lucian L. Leape, David Bates, Patricia Hojnowski-Diaz, Stephen Petrycki, Michael Cotugno, Heather Patterson, Mairead Hickey, Sharon Kleefield, Jeffrey Cooper, Ellen Kinneally, Harold J. Demonaco, Margaret Dempsey Clapp, Theresa Gallivan, Jeanette Ives, Kathy Porter, B. Taylor Thompson, J. Richard Hackman, and Amy Edmondson. 1995. Incidence of adverse drug events and potential adverse drug events: Implications for prevention. *Journal of the American Medical Association* 274 (1): 29–34.

Bates, D. W., G. J. Kuperman, S. Wang, T. Gandhi, A. Kittler, L. Volk, C. Spurr, R. Khorasani, M. Tanasijevic, and B. Middleton. 2003. Ten commandments for effective clinical decision support: Making the practice of evidence-based medicine a reality. *Journal of the American Medical Informatics Association* 10 (6): 523–530.

Berg, M. 1999. Accumulating and coordinating: Occasions for information technologies in medical work. *Computer Supported Cooperative Work* 8 (4): 373–401.

Berg, M., J. Aarts, and J. van der Lei. 2003. ICT in health care: Sociotechnical approaches. *Methods of Information in Medicine* 42 (4): 297–301.

Beyer, Hugh, and Karen Holtzblatt. 1998. *Contextual Design: Defining Customer-Centered Systems.* San Francisco: Morgan Kaufmann.

Bødker, Keld, Finn Kensing, and Jesper Simonsen. 2004. *Participatory IT Design: Designing for Business and Workplace Realities.* Cambridge, MA: MIT Press.

Brassard, Michael. 1989. *The Memory Jogger Plus: Featuring the Seven Management and Planning Tools.* Methuen, MA: GOAL/QPC.

Glaser, B. 1992. *Basics of Grounded Theory Analysis: Emergence vs. Forcing.* Mill Valley, CA: Sociology Press.

Glaser, Barney G., and Anselm L. Strauss. 1967. *The Discovery of Grounded Theory: Strategies for Qualitative Research*. New York: Aldine de Gruyter.

Granlien, M. F., M. Hertzum, and J. Gudmundsen. 2008. The gap between actual and mandated use of an electronic medication record three years after deployment. In *MIE2008: Proceedings of the XXIst International Congress of the European Federation for Medical Informatics*, ed. S. K. Andersen, G. O. Klein, S. Schulz, J. Arts, and M. C. Mazzoleni, 419–424. Göteborg, Sweden, May 25–28.

Granlien, Maren Sander, and Morten Hertzum. 2012. Barriers to the adoption and use of an electronic medication record. *Electronic Journal of Information Systems Evaluation* 15 (2): 216–227.

Hertzum, Morten. 2010. Breakdowns in collaborative information seeking: A study of the medication process. *Information Processing and Management* 46 (6): 646–655.

Kvale, Steinar. 1996. *Interviews: An Introduction to Qualitative Research Writing*. Thousand Oaks, CA: Sage Publications.

Lanzara, Giovan Francesco, and Lars Mathiassen. 1985. Mapping situations within a system development project. *Information and Management* 8 (1): 3–20.

Simonsen, Jesper. 2007. Involving top management in IT projects: Aligning business needs and IT solutions with the problem mapping technique. *Communications of the ACM* 50 (8): 53–58.

Suchman, Lucy A. 2007. *Human-Machine Reconfigurations: Plans and Situated Action*, 2nd ed. Cambridge: Cambridge University Press.

7 Wheel of Rituals in Design

Henriette Christrup

What. In this chapter, we present methods that can be used to create states of consciousness and spheres that promote situated action in a collaborative design process. The concrete approach is to use a wheel with four rituals, called the Wheel of Rituals. We develop a position based on theory with inspiration from performance theory, sociology, psychology, and neuroscience to understand design processes as fields of emotional tension that can be handled by means of rituals. The Wheel of Rituals is associated with guiding principles for promoting synergy in the process between the creative development of content and the mutual relationships between participants. In the case, a project group from Roskilde University design a performance event with user involvement. Otto C. Scharmer's phase model in Theory U is used together with the Wheel of Rituals.

Why. Collaborative design processes are influenced by the emotions experienced by the participants. We approach the design process as a spiral movement into the unknown—the external and internal worlds—associated with feelings such as happiness, anger, fear, interest, and anxiety. When pressure is experienced in the design field, emotional tension can lead to destructive interactions: the ego roulette rolls. Rituals can create states for creative progress.

Where. The Wheel of Rituals can be used in situated action in numerous design domains, contexts, and situations; only ethical challenges set the limits. This chapter focuses on its use in collaborative design process.

How. The Wheel of Rituals uses equipment such as colored lights, music, computerized measurement of heart rhythms, posters, balloons. The wheel can be linked with numerous design methods and models. The rituals can be used by design groups, with or without a facilitator, paying extra attention to ethical challenges associated with altered states of consciousness.

1 Introduction

The intention of this chapter is to inspire the reader to use and develop rituals in design processes. The Wheel of Rituals can be seen as a resource for situated action

(Suchman 2007), to create states that are favorable in collaborative creative processes. In a situated design practice, the wheel can be used together with a repertoire of methods in reflection in action processes (Schön 1983).

An impression of one of the rituals will illustrate my intentions. The ritual *Embracing Pink Coherence* creates a favorable state for a design process: the feeling of being embraced, free, and connected. Bathed in pink light with music playing, the group follows a ball on a heart rhythm computer program. Thus the group members breathe synchronously and reach a state of balance: coherence.

Using the wheel together with a model for directing attention can have considerable influence on a design process, because it takes place in a powerful emotional field—a journey into the unknown: "What is not but could be," as the Nobel Prize winner Herbert Simon (1969) so elegantly defined design. Among other things, the design process involves states of tension with fear and curiosity about meeting the unknown future in the external world, and anxiety and joy about the meeting unknown internal depths from which the creative source arises. In short, design is an explosive field.

In the next section, I present a theory-based point of view for understanding processes and creating favorable states in this field. I describe the types of ritual and present the design of the Wheel of Rituals, using one of the rituals as an illustration. Then follows a case, in which the wheel and the model of attention directions are used in a collaborative design process. A project group from Performance Design at Roskilde University design a performance event in collaboration with thirteen- to fifteen-year-olds, with me as adviser. Work on all four rituals in the wheel is linked to Scharmer's Theory U, with five phases for a creative process, which the project group follows (Scharmer 2007). The last part of the chapter contains reflections on the use and further development of the rituals, including a review of ethical challenges. The final conclusion is supported by a model with the essence of the theory and methods for understanding and influencing design processes.

2   Understanding and Influencing Design Processes

Through many years' work as teacher and consultant on handling groups, I have developed a theoretical approach to understanding obstacles and possibilities for optimal development of the relationships and content of creative processes—as well as methods that can be used in practice (Christrup 2008, 2010). The essence of this approach, which forms the basis for the Wheel of Rituals, takes some inspiration from creativity research: that positive emotions make the range of thought-action options broader in the present moment while building up personal resources that facilitate the management of difficulties in the future (Fredrickson 2009).

However, the design process as a journey into the unknown takes place under pressures that can create negative emotions and lead to destructive interactions. From stress research, I have found inspiration from the six types of pressure that give most people some type of discomfort: (1) pressure of time, (2) contradictory communication, (3) impossibility of building up expectations, (4) missing expected outcome, (5) being evaluated while performing task, and (6) choosing among many possibilities (Christrup 2010).

The meeting with the unknown can be understood in terms of these pressures: it is difficult to choose (6), because there can be contradictory communication on an epistemological level (2), while at the same time it is impossible to build up clear expectations to the result of one's actions (3), and if you do so, the expected outcome may not materialize (4). From childhood we have developed ego reactions as protection, to avoid the experience of unpleasant chaotic states of tension with fear and anger in pressed situations: (1) moralize, (2) manipulate, (3) self-assertion, (4) self-control with arrogance, (5) withdrawal to the inner universe, (6) suspiciously defending, (7) planning, (8) blaming, (9) "falling asleep" (Almaas 1998). In the design process as a journey into the unknown, there is a considerable risk that an automatic, negatively charged ego reaction results in someone else getting the feeling of being hit—and then the ego roulette of destructive interactions rolls (Christrup 2010). There is also a risk that ego reactions cannot handle the pressure—and this can cause feelings of anxiety. Anxiety may also be provoked by overstepping the ego's limits for contact with inner depths in a creative process. Fear is embedded in all forms of anxiety, and in practice it is this idea that I work with.

This theoretical approach created earlier—and its associated models, methods, and equipment—are followed throughout this chapter, but the focus is on my latest experiment with a design group, which resulted in the creation of the Wheel of Rituals with four rituals (Christrup 2010).

By using the wheel in situated action, individuals and groups can get contact with embodied emotional states, become aware of and contain emotional tensions, and create states of consciousness that promote synergy between the development in the design process's content and the mutual relationships of the participants. To promote this synergy process, I have, inspired by Hart and Scharmer, defined three guiding principles—"guiding stars"—for direction of attention (Hart 2013; Scharmer 2007):

1. Attention in relation to the world outside: sense clearly and be surprised; drop judgments.
2. Attention in relation to oneself: feel your body or get contact with inner depths, including layers of the psyche that create images.
3. Empathy created by sensing attention directed to the person in the external world, and to your own bodily feelings—a neuro-affective resonance space where the other person feels seen, heard, and understood.

The competences in these principles are innate, so the challenge is to recapture them as a starting point for development, together with recapturing the free flow of energy through the body, a competence that is also innate.

An important starting point for practicing and developing these competences is to create clarity and fix their basis in intention and basic values: what does life call you to do? With this anchoring, fear of the unknown is transformed and self-esteem developed through action, if the individual and the group have contact with this fear (Harris 2010).

Figure 7.1 illustrates the design process as a life-expanding movement into the unknown; anchored in intention with basic values (the anchor), synergy between relationships and content is created in the interaction with the guiding principles, or "guiding stars." The topmost arrow indicates principle 1, attention to the world outside, and the bottommost arrow indicates principle 2, attention to oneself. The central star symbolizes empathy, which expedites attention to both the internal and external universe.

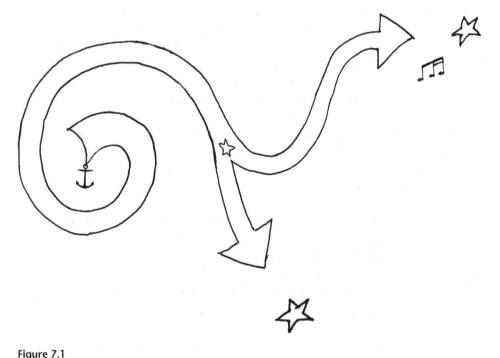

Figure 7.1
Spiral movement into the unknown, anchored in intention and basic values. Topmost arrow to guiding star (1) and notes symbolizing design of event. Downward arrow to guiding star (2). At split in spiral, guiding star (3).

By coupling the four rituals of the wheel with the model of figure 7.1 in situated action, it has proved possible to create states in the design process that creativity research shows promote the process.

3   The Wheel of Rituals

A ritual can be defined as an action that is thought significant for achieving a state and rhythm for an individual—or a group, who feel themselves connected through the ritual (Dissanayake 2000).

There are two main types of rituals (Turner 1982). The first entails a liminal transformative capacity with lasting changes of consciousness and possibly of state. Lutheran church weddings are an example. The ritual consists of a series of sequences, such as the introit and the prayer before the transition implied by the proclamation "I declare that you are man and wife, for God and humanity." Thereafter follow more sequences, such as the Lord's Prayer, blessing, and recession.

The other type can be characterized by a transportation: a temporary change in the state of consciousness, with a return to the usual state. An example is a lullaby. Here it is the mother's rocking of the child, voice, text, and the melody's rhythmic structure and underlying beat that cause a transportation from wakeful to sleeping state, after which the child returns to the wakeful state in the morning. It can, however, be imagined that repeated use of the lullaby ritual can affect the child's development: the attachment between mother and child can be strengthened, and peaceful sleep affects the child's development positively. Rituals in the wheel can be characterized by transportation, but with possible transformations leading to permanent change and development through continual use, as with the lullaby.

Four rituals are placed in the wheel (fig. 7.2): *Expanding Play Balloon* with great enthusiasm in the top right-hand field; *Embracing Pink Coherence* with appreciation, inner peace and clarity, and an impression of feeling oneself embraced, free, and connected on the right on the horizontal mid-axis; *Embracing Blue Ocean Fish* with an egoless state and contact with inner depths in wakeful relaxation on the way out of a normal conscious state in the bottom right-hand field; and *Exploring Fear—Pin It Up* in the top left field. In the bottom left-hand field is the symbol for sadness, for which there is no ritual yet.

The horizontal axis indicates how emotions are experienced: a conscious feeling, positive to the right and negative to the left. The vertical axis shows the strength of this emotion. A specific pattern in the heart rhythm corresponds to each individual ritual. This rhythm is controlled by the autonomic nervous system, which has two branches: sympathetic, which dominates emotions with high intensity–high arousal (top of vertical axis); and parasympathetic, which dominates at low intensity–low arousal (bottom of vertical axis). The axes and the placement of the coherence state

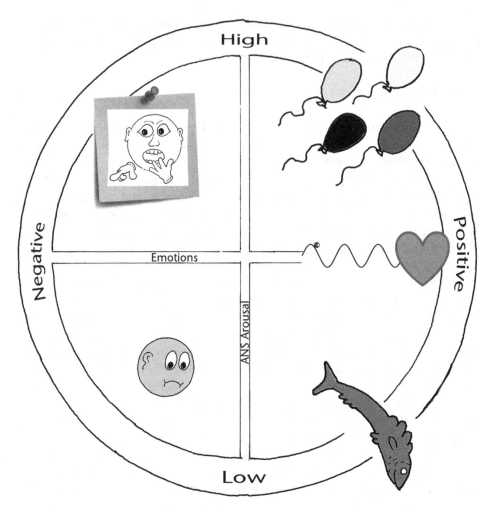

Figure 7.2
Wheel of Rituals. The horizontal axis shows emotions: positive on the right, negative on the left. The vertical axis shows their energy levels. Four rituals clockwise from top right: *Expanding Play Balloon, Embracing Pink Coherence, Embracing Blue Ocean Fish, Exploring Fear—Pin It Up.*

are from a model by HeartMath Institute (McCraty et al. 2006). To help explain the wheel, I will describe the ritual of *Embracing Pink Coherence*.

Coherence is a state with positive emotions and can facilitate the process toward guiding principles 1, attention to the world outside, and 3, empathy. On a psychological level, this state is "associated with reduced perceptions of stress, sustained positive affect, and a high degree of mental clarity and emotional stability" (McCraty et al. 2006, 10).

Physiologically, the coherence state is characterized by a heart rhythm pattern like a harmonic sine curve, which reflects an optimal state of physiological balance between the two branches of the autonomic nervous system. This state also includes "increased heart-brain synchronization, increased vascular resonance, and entrainment between diverse physiological oscillatory systems" (McCraty et al. 2006, 10).

The ritual uses a lamp with pink light, which has a soothing effect, and music designed to achieve the state. In this space, participants follow with their eyes a little ball's movement up (5 sec.) and down (5 sec.) in a sine wave on a HeartMath computer program, and they breathe in time with the ball's movement (McCraty et al. 2006). After a while, the participants turn their attention to principle 3, flow of energy within the body, with the feeling "I like myself." With light, music, and synchronized heartbeats, the participants can attain the feeling of being embraced, free, and connected. The ritual is used as a basic ritual, where the coherence state achieved is a good basis for changing to the other rituals.

The wheel is used together with the spiral model with guiding principles, in which the wheel has particular significance for creativity based on deeper internal sources. The development of the spiral model has been partly inspired by the book *Theory U: Leading from the Future as It Emerges*, by the German American sociologist Otto C. Scharmer at MIT. Scharmer's intention is to contribute to transformations in the external world, persons, and relations, and he points out: "The development of new collective presencing practices is one of the most urgent and important undertakings of the years to come" (Scharmer 2007, 189). The word *presencing* is created from *sensing* and *presence*. It denotes a creative presence with an opening to deep internal sources from which images and ideas in generative streams can be crystallized in visions and sketches for the most potential future. The wheel can be regarded as a response to Scharmer's assertion.

4   A Case

We follow a project group from Performance Design at Roskilde University who are designing a performance event. Through projects and other activities, the program aims for students to develop theoretical positions and methods for designing, organizing, managing, and evaluating performances and cultural events. The performance event contains elements from three styles of music—hip-hop dance, free style hip-hop

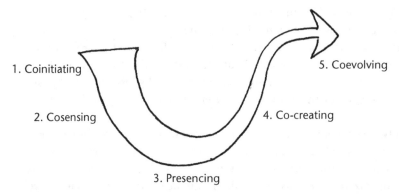

Figure 7.3
Scharmer's Theory U with five phases: coinitiating, cosensing, presencing, co-creating, coevolving.

battle rap, and dancehall rap—and an important intention of the project is user involvement and empowerment. The process follows Scharmer's Theory U with five phases, as shown in figure 7.3.

4.1   Coinitiating

Build common intent—stop and listen to others and to what life calls you to.

—Otto C. Scharmer, *Theory U*

In a corner in the basement of a library, I am sitting as adviser with nine performance design students and an employee of an organization that has proposed an event project that the group has agreed to. But several of the students are now in doubt: will the project be dominated by applying to funding agencies, so that the aim of creating something that can have a deeper meaning for themselves and others cannot be realized? They want to say no. Thus the big group will have to be split up and two new projects created. It is difficult to create a space with a positive atmosphere for this process. I read the space with inspiration from researchers—among others Gernot Böhme—who theoretically and empirically work with space and atmosphere as embodied experiences of awareness. The materials and artifacts of the room do not contribute to a positive emotional tuning of body and mind, and each participant is a contributor to the atmosphere, whether or not she is conscious of her state, because the participants can detect and thus be affected by one another's physical emotional display (Christrup 2010).

The basement and its interior contribute to producing a sad, gray mood. But through the ritual *Embracing Pink Coherence* with soothing pink light and music, we created a pleasant sphere and breathed in time with the rolling ball on the sine curve of the HeartMath program, focused our attention on the body's rhythm, and tried to experience "I like myself." Then we could feel embraced and free in a positive mood, which turned out to be propitious for the difficult decisions.

Five of the students chose a project proposed by a cultural organization with associated actors: in collaboration with thirteen- to fifteen-year-olds from a socially challenged area, they would design and execute a performance event for young people called "Life in the Dark." The students' intention was—by establishing an equal-footed relationship with the young people—to develop self-confidence and creative ability for everyone involved.

At two supervision meetings with the students, we used the ritual *Embracing Pink Coherence* to clarify their intentions through dialogue, focusing on principle 3, empathy. This process resulted in their being willing to listen and emphatically understand the young people's musical preferences while at the same time making it possible for them to have new music experiences. Together they would create a fantastic event, but the most important result was that the young people would feel they were being listened to and understood.

In two meetings with the young people, the project group worked as reflecting practitioners, based on these intentions (Schön 1983). First each of the young people chose a clip on YouTube from a concert or music video that they considered great. The intention was to realize a process inspired by principles 1 and 3, the guiding stars in the model. To train these states, the students made a listening exercise for the young people. Some of the students in the project group used the ritual *Embracing Pink Coherence* to control their nervousness.

4.2 Cosensing

Observe, observe, observe—go to the places of most potential and listen with your mind and heart wide open.

—Otto C. Scharmer, *Theory U*

In this phase, the first guiding principle, to sense attentively without previous evaluations, and the third, empathic dialogue, are of vital significance. Allow yourself to be surprised and disturbed; open up for inspiration to create a unique event; have a dialogue about your experiences. So the students and the young people went to a concert together. Their intention was to release attentiveness by using all senses without habitual judgments. This turned out to be hard in practice; preconceived opinions about what is good and bad music dominated the experience.

4.3 Presencing

Connect to the source of inspiration, and will—go to the place of silence and allow the inner knowing to emerge.

—Otto C. Scharmer, *Theory U*

Surprisingly, and without planning it, the project group got to work on this phase at a workshop where I was responsible for the process. The agreement was that the project group should be trained at the workshop to handle the imminent concept development process for the young people. The students were frustrated when they arrived at the workshop: they had followed the wishes of the cultural organization and other actors in the field to extend the event to include not one but three genres, in a hall with room for three times as many as planned, but still in eleven days' time, as agreed. The group felt obliged to develop the concepts at once, without the participation of the young people, but with their acceptance that it was necessary owing to the time pressure.

To handle the students' frustrations and feeling of pressure, and to create instead a sphere where we felt ourselves embraced, free, and connected, we started with the familiar ritual *Embracing Pink Coherence*. Then we worked with the fear ritual *Exploring Fear—Pin It Up* from the top left-hand field. Each participant wrote her fear on a poster and pinned it on the wall. Then we worked actively with this fear, for example, "not to have a check on the process" and "overstep one's own limits." The fears were transformed by action. A contributing factor was the powerful drawings with life-enhancing movement, which each student had produced in advance and hung on the wall (Christrup 2010).

As the aim was to create a secure atmosphere for creative activity, the students also had the possibility of stopping the process if they experienced pressure. On the wall we hung a large poster showing the six previously mentioned types of pressure. Next to it was a poster of ego roulette, showing which reactions can come into play under pressure. We also needed to improve awareness of overstepping zones of untouchability (Christrup 2010).

Then the creative process could begin. Each individual could select from the many images one through which they could express their basic idea with the process—for example, the image with water and a lighthouse indicated that they could turn the ship and get it safely into land.

We could now start to produce ideas, using inspiration from the concert research with the young people. From *Embracing Pink Coherence* we created a state change via the ritual *Expanding Play Balloon* with high energy, enthusiasm, and laughter (the ritual was developed by Camilla Duus, a student; see Christrup 2010). To electronic cello music with an intense rhythm, each participant blows up a balloon and lets it float up. By their combined efforts, the group must keep the balloons floating in the air. Then each must grab a balloon, write his or her event idea on it, release it and again keep the balloons floating, and finally grab a balloon and freely associate from the idea written on it. The group's energy was transformed; they bubbled with ideas, which were noted on posters: rituals when changing genre, audience as co-creators of the space, visuals during concert, breach of genre, senses into play, physical contact, light/

darkness, smell/taste, diversity, intimate space, fun. It was amazing to experience the group's transformation process, and they wrote in their project report that the ritual created liveliness, commitment, and delight—and gave renewed energy.

The challenge was now to create a more unifying idea—to follow principle 2 and make contact with deep internal sources in a presencing phase. This involves a complete release of control: in an egoless state to open up for an emergent stream from the internal source so as to create the highest future possibility. This is a state that can be associated with fear of releasing control and anxiety about overstepping the boundary to the unknown in one's own inner depths. I therefore chose the ritual *Embracing Blue Ocean Fish*. To research-based blue ocean music "Waves," which can facilitate changed states of consciousness (Eje 2006), I guided the group from the *Embracing Pink Coherence* state to breathe even more slowly and deeply while immersing themselves in delightfully warm blue water, where they should imagine swimming freely like a fish in the ocean and visualize an idea. Through this ritual, four of the five saw the vision of the space. They swam down into deeper layers of consciousness without fear or anxiety: "I was swimming in a bright sea and could see everything clearly—it was transparent—and I turned into a mermaid who swam with the current into the hall [where the event was to be held] and saw it was divided into small, intimate spaces with colors, such as orange and red." Another said, "I could notice that I felt myself free inside—I've also done this at yoga—but I didn't think I could get into this state in a group when we were under such pressure—I was really surprised." A third said, "I saw the room with audience interaction. Everything we had talked about in connection with *Expanding Play Balloon* got to hang together—and I could see the room before my eyes when I started to draw it afterwards."

One by one, the students sketched their visions on large posters and added descriptions: for example, division into smaller spaces with rituals when moving from one to another. In the project report, they wrote: "It was really fantastic to experience this presentation. Before we started the workshop, none of us had any idea of how we should put the event together. Now we stood there and in turn drew the space and verbalized the concept. In terms of Scharmer's ideas, we succeeded in going directly from the Presencing phase to Co-creating, where we started to create new ideas and prototypes of the final concept."

4.4 Co-Creating

Prototype the new—in living examples to explore the future by doing.

—Otto C. Scharmer, *Theory U*

At the meeting with the young people two days after the workshop, the students presented the concept for the event in the form of a drawing—a first prototype—and together they researched the new locality for the event. In this field of tension between the concept on paper and the huge space in reality, the concept now had to be filled out together with the young people.

In this situation, the students dared to use the ritual *Expanding Play Balloon* together with the young people, using balloons on which the five senses were inscribed one by one. The result of this process was that together they created two rituals for the event. The first involved sudden darkness and stopping the music. Then only the sense of taste would be available by licking a lollipop. The second involved a surprising change to bright lighting and sounds from the next space where the young people were to draw on the audience with luminous pens. One young fellow remarked that it was fun to push the balloon and grab it—in that way, he generated more ideas and got into a good mood because he was together with happy people.

4.5 Coevolving

Embody the new in ecosystems—that facilitate seeing and acting from the whole.
—Otto C. Scharmer, *Theory U*

In reality the event did not quite go as planned; for example, the room dividers were not set up, so that the rituals just described, which the students and young people had created as elements of the event—such as using the sense of taste in the dark—could not be realized. This is a story of negotiations in a complex field, where the student group negotiated with many actors associated with the cultural organization and made decisions about who does what—but where the expected action never took place.

The students analyzed the situation, taking inspiration from the ego roulette, a model that focuses on ego reactions created in the past, which in the present contribute to destructive interactions. The student group acknowledged that they had adapted themselves, showed consideration, and used a lot of energy in blaming the other actors. They could have taken responsibility for creating clarity and trying creatively to play with various ideas and impressions during negotiation, avoiding agreeing on something no one wanted or believed in—and discovering that one could agree on something everyone believed in, or else that there was a dangerous conflict (Harvey 1988). The possible conflict and the fear of rejection mean that people do not dare to express their deep intentions.

In spite of this process, the young people were happy to have created an event, and they learned something about collaboration and had fun.

5   Reflections on the Use and Development of the Wheel of Rituals

My intention is to inspire people to use the wheel as a resource for situated action: to use the four rituals and create new ones. Theory-based reflections beginning with the following four questions can be a useful fulcrum for this process: Where and how can the wheel be used? Can a project group of students use the wheel without a facilitator? Which ethical challenges should one be especially attentive to? How to continue development of the wheel?

5.1   Where and How Can the Wheel of Rituals Be Used?

The aim is for the wheel to be usable in all situations anywhere in the world, independently of time and space. Only questions of ethics associated with limits to intimacy and zones of untouchability set limitations.

In a group interview, the student group gave a highly positive evaluation of the use of the wheel in "Life in the Dark." One of them, for example, said: "I have never before in my life been to a meeting where one was so frustrated at the start, and where the process had been so pleasant—and I was even more surprised about how well all the rituals and exercises worked—we got that out of it for our project with the young people…and it gave us a feeling of release when we went back to our fear posters: we had got over it."

I use the wheel individually or collectively every day—and here I focus on my competence at turning the wheel in collaborative design processes. Basically it is a question of being able to make qualified choices of rituals when under pressure, to achieve favorable states. This requires self-regulation, which involves contact with embodied emotional states, and being able to contain and transform them. The best way to get into a state of balance that makes it possible to turn the wheel competently is, paradoxically enough, the rituals *Embracing Pink Coherence* and *Exploring Fear—Pin It Up*. The mental guideline for my continual development of competence to use the wheel's different rituals can, to use the Danish therapist Susan Hart's terms, be called *empathic, vitalizing, positive harmonization* in a group where there is an intention of equality with asymmetrical responsibility for handling the process (Hart 2013). I have to take the responsibility for creating a pattern in my own heart rhythm that is favorable for the group process; under all circumstances, my heart's electromagnetic field affects people within a radius of three meters (McCraty et al. 2006). The aim is to create a neuro-affective resonance space for synergy between the development of the design process's content and the mutual relationships of the participants.

5.2   Can a Project Group of Students Use the Wheel of Rituals?

Embracing Pink Coherence uses the computer program HeartMath, which can be purchased through www.hearthmath.com. HeartMath contains various programs, including the one with the rolling ball, which can be used with an ear sensor so that one can see on the screen whether the person achieves coherence. The best-known program is for continuous measurement of heart rhythm and its pattern. Via an ear sensor connected to the computer, one can see on the screen the pulse rate, heart rhythm pattern, and power spectrum (a bar chart showing the activity in the sympathetic and parasympathetic systems). A light signal and sound give feedback on whether coherence is achieved.

Experience from advising project groups at Roskilde University who have worked with music projects, shows that the students themselves can use these programs without guidance. And with the HeartMath program, they can experiment with the effects of light and music while registering heart rhythm patterns and power spectra.

There are no problems in performing the ritual *Exploring Fear—Pin It Up*; it only requires posters and pencils. The ritual *Expanding Play Balloon* can likewise be used without previous guidance, as it requires only balloons and music.

It is more uncertain whether the ritual *Embracing Blue Ocean Fish* can be used by a group of students to get contact with the creative source in deep layers of consciousness. There can be individual differences in how much fear and anxiety are associated with releasing the controlling ego and crossing the boundary to the inner depths. Scharmer stresses that it can be difficult to create this state in a group. It arises more easily spontaneously in individuals in modified states of consciousness. My dialogue with the project group for "Life in the Dark" indicates that it is advantageous to let the ritual *Embracing Pink Coherence* come immediately before it, and the students stressed the significance of the music for being able to let go and swim freely like a fish in the depths. A solution to the problems of creating this state collectively can be to work with a considered choice of alternation between individual and collective processes (Christrup 2010).

5.3   Which Ethical Challenges Must One Be Especially Attentive To?

It is important to recognize that in a group there can be big differences in the reaction to meeting the unknown—both in the design process and in the use of rituals—from the neophile, who is almost hooked on the dopamine kick, to the neophobe, who has fear and anxiety about the unknown (Gallagher 2012).

It is therefore important to be especially attentive to two ethical questions: Is it defensible to work with internal states in the current situation? Who is going to see or hear the material in this process?

In *Embracing Pink Coherence*, it must be made clear that it is optional to use the ear sensor that will show the state of coherence and heart rhythm pattern, whether or not the measurement is shown to the group.

In *Exploring Fear—Pin It Up*, each individual has the possibility of making a conscious choice: what will I show of myself in this context? I have not experienced participants who opt out of this ritual, but in large groups there is a choice as to whether the poster should be anonymous or not.

The greatest ethical challenge is associated with the ritual *Embracing Blue Ocean Fish*. The innovation researcher Lotte Darsøe (2011) points out that participants in the presencing phase can get into deep water (in the existential sense), and therefore thinks one should not work with this state in a teaching context. I have tried to minimize the risk through my work with the feeling of *Embracing* via pink light, music, and blue water when we work with our attention focused on guiding principle 2, for example, via contact with inner depths. The risk is that participants get contact with states of emotional tension that can be hard to encompass—such as something painful that provokes tears. So far no situations have arisen that I or the participants consider ethically irresponsible.

For the second ethical question—who is going to see or hear the material in this process—a general mental guideline for situated action can be that the more knowledge you have of a person's inner depths, the more effectively you can strike at him (Christrup 2008).

It is a question of trust (Luhmann 1979). Many interactions involve risks. B demonstrates trust in A if he dares openly to make the first move in relation to A, who can observe something that B himself cannot observe, and A has the freedom to choose his position in relation to this observation. But A is subject to the same conditions. Thus there is a double uncertainty in the situation—double contingency—where demonstrating trust in a situation with inherent uncertainty consists in daring openly to make the first move—to dare to be yourself and thus to show confidence that the other party will not reject you for what you are. Thus the anchoring point is mutual acceptance of the other's freedom.

The ethical challenge can be changed but not solved by letting the person recover the customary ego control and consciously choose what she wants to convey in the group. However, this turning to ego control can reduce the significance of the ritual, because the conscious reflection can inhibit the creative process.

In relation to the foregoing ethical challenges, it is difficult to define clear rules for handling experiences of pressure, and even with precautions, discomfort cannot be avoided—the experience of pressure with a risk of a disapproving assessment from the group. Creating a common awareness of the possibilities for (1) stopping the process, (2) leaving the space, and (3) helping one another with things that are difficult is crucial for reducing fear in the space.

Risks connected with accessing deeper layers of consciousness must be held up against the fact that interactions in design spaces where rituals are not used are not risk free. For example, participants may play ego roulette, where it requires a lot of emotional work for the individual to repair the feeling of being hit when the ego roulette rolls.

5.4   How to Continue Development of the Wheel of Rituals?

The rituals that we used in the workshop were first systematized into the Wheel of Rituals afterward, which contributes to greater security and freedom for situated action. The process of creating the wheel has been influenced by interesting challenges and inspirations from performance art, science, and the practical handling of design processes. An exciting challenge awaits me and other interested persons in further developing the rituals that are already in the wheel, and in designing new ones. Examples of the process associated with creating the wheel are given hereafter, followed by the students' further development of the rituals. My intention is to stimulate the reader's desire to creatively modify and create new rituals.

Embracing Pink Coherence was created starting from my basic abilities to use the HeartMath programs and knowledge of the research associated with them. The significance of colored light for creating the intended atmosphere and states stood out clearly when I was in Danmarks Radio's shiny, fascinating, high-ceilinged concert hall, where a project group for which I was adviser was designing a lounge. The choice of orange and red light from the ceiling contributed to an atmosphere that I later called "Embracing Space." My choice of pink light draws on research, which shows that pink has a soothing effect. The choice of music is primarily works designed to create the intended somatically based emotional states, based on research on measuring the frequency of brain waves and patterns in heart rhythm.

Embracing Blue Ocean Fish takes its inspiration, among other things, from the director David Lynch. Using meditation, Lynch gets himself into a state of joy for "catching big fish." This means diving into the Self—into the deep ocean and consciousness inside him—and thus intuitively to see the solution, when emotions and intellect play together in a sublime manner (Lynch 2006). For a publication, I produced a fascinating color picture of a beautiful fish in a blue sea to illustrate the essence of this. I had the picture with me when, a couple of weeks later, I somewhat by chance experienced the installation *Aquarium* by Carsten Höller at the New Museum in New York. In a space with stroboscopic light, which brings the museum visitor into a changed alpha wave state of consciousness with deep wakeful relaxation, one can lie down on a bench and put one's head into an aquarium, where fish speed past the spectator's eyes (Carrion-Murayari 2011; Wiley 2011).

During my course in creative leadership, a student added a sequence to *Exploring Fear—Pin It Up*. All twenty-two participants were supposed to bring with them a picture as a symbol of courage to overcome fear. This process ended in a bonfire being lit outside, and most of the pictures being burned. Another student has developed an installation for *Embracing Pink Coherence*: In five seconds, a clear glass ball is gradually transformed into a beautiful purple ball by being illuminated by a projector—and at the same time the participants breathe in. Then the color disappears over five seconds as the participants breathe out. This gives a fantastic feeling of the change between expanding and letting go.

I myself intend to contribute to creating an interactive installation for *Embracing Blue Ocean Fish* so that the group can create the intended collective state through feedback on emotional states.

My aims for developing the Wheel of Rituals also go in the opposite direction: drop using equipment, so that the rituals can be used anywhere, maybe even daily, and thus contribute to transformation: inspired by brain research, to create new neural traces. A challenge is to design rituals that individuals or groups are enthusiastic about using, perhaps with miniature symbols or artifacts.

I finish by summarizing the points in the process that have had most significance for the creation of the wheel, as inspiration for other creators of rituals:

• Investigation of one's own and others' experiences in performance spaces
• Artists' and designers' reports on creative processes and scientific investigation of these processes
• Literature studies and dialogue with experts on scientific evidence for the effect of spaces and artifacts
• Scientific and communicative insight into the seven universal emotions
• Theoretical and empirical methods from scientific fields, primarily psychology, neuroscience, performance theory, and sociology

6   Conclusion

The challenge in situated action is to choose the individual rituals at the right moment to achieve states that are advantageous in the collaborative design process. For the time being, the wheel comprises four rituals: *Expanding Play Balloon, Embracing Pink Coherence, Embracing Blue Ocean Fish, Exploring Fear—Pin It Up*.

The design process is considered as emotional states in movement in the unknown—in both the external and internal worlds—with three guiding principles. These principles indicate the directions of attention that can create synergy between the design process's content, the mutual relationships of the participants, and the individual's recapturing and development of innate competences. The design process as a movement in the unknown is inextricably connected with the experience of pressure and states of tension that can lead to destructive interactions: the ego roulette rolls. Through the collective use of the rituals, each individual participant gets contact with emotions, becomes conscious of and encompasses emotional states, and creates new states that are advantageous for the group's situated action.

Competent use of the wheel can be perceived on the basis of the essence of creativity research: the positive emotions affect the creative process favorably—and recognized fear can be transformed through action, which also contributes to developing self-esteem, if the actions are rooted in intentional basic values. Using the individual rituals in the optimal order and at the right moment is regarded as empathic, vitalizing, positive harmonization.

Figure 7.4 shows the wheel, where the spiral movement toward the three principles—the guiding stars—is anchored in the wheel's right-hand side with the positive

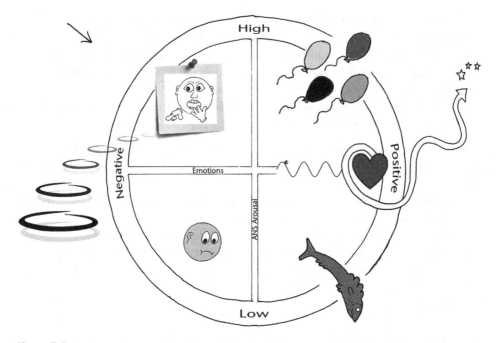

Figure 7.4
Wheel of Rituals in design field with guiding stars on the right and pressure (arrow) and ego roulette on the left.

emotions. The arrow as a symbol of pressure that can result in negative emotions and ego roulette interactions is placed outside the wheel's left-hand side with the negative emotions.

Using the wheel in the project case "Life in the Dark," together with the spiral model's guiding principles and increased awareness of pressure and ego roulette, has affected the design process extremely favorably. The most significant experience was that the students, freed of anxiety and fear, got contact with, and could design on the basis of, their deep inner creative sources. In close connection with this, future possibilities for the use and development of the wheel—for example, in a project group at the university—were sketched, and attention was drawn to the ethical challenges that using the wheel involves.

Acknowledgments

Dialogues on the text: Josephine Christrup, Hanne Dankert, Tilde Mardahl, Ida Toldbod. Model design and rights: Henriette Christrup. Illustrations: Lars Trier. Model construction and graphics: Mads Folmer. Translation: Robin Sharp.

References

Almaas, Hameed Ali. 1998. *Facets of Unity*. Berkeley, CA: Diamond Books.

Carrion-Murayari, Gary. 2012. Entertainment. In *Carsten Höller: Experience*, ed. Gary Carrion-Murayari and Niki Columbus, 93–95. New York: Skira Rizzoli and New Museum.

Christrup, Henriette. 2008. On sense and sensibility in performative processes. In *Creating Experiences in the Experience Economy*, ed. Jon Sundbo and Per Darmer, 203–231. Cheltenham: Edward Elgar.

Christrup, Henriette. 2010. Joyful, collective design processes. In *Design Research: Synergies from Interdisciplinary Perspectives*, ed. Jesper Simonsen, Jørgen Ole Bærenholdt, Monika Büscher, and John D. Scheuer, 156–171. Oxford: Routledge.

Darsøe, Lotte. 2011. *Innovationspædagogik* [Innovation pedagogics]. Copenhagen: Samfundslitteratur.

Dissanayake, Ellen. 2000. *Art and Intimacy*. London: University of Washington Press.

Eje, Niels. 2006. *Musicure, 6. Waves*. Copenhagen: Gefion Records.

Fredrickson, Barbara L. 2009. *Positivity*. New York: Crown.

Gallagher, Winifred. 2012. *New: Understanding Our Need for Novelty and Change*. New York: Penguin.

Harris, Russ. 2010. *The Confidence Gap: From Fear to Freedom*. Australia: Penguin Group.

Hart, Susan. 2013. Den fødte leder [The born leader]. In *Ledelse mellem Hjerne og Hjerte*, ed. Susan Hart and Henrik Hvilshøj, 29–54. Copenhagen: Hans Reitzels.

Harvey, Jerry B. 1988. The Abilene paradox: The management of agreement. In *The Abilene Paradox*. San Francisco: Jossey-Bass.

Luhmann, Niklas. 1979. *Trust and Power*. Chichester: Wiley.

Lynch, David. 2006. *Catching the Big Fish*. New York: Penguin Group.

McCraty, Rollin, Mike Atkinson, Dana Tomasino, and Raymond Trevor Bradley. 2006. *The Coherent Heart*. Boulder Creek: Institute of HeartMath.

Scharmer, C. O. 2007. *Theory U: Leading from the Future as It Emerges*. Cambridge, MA: SoL.

Scharmer, C. O. 2008. Addressing the blind spot of our time. An executive summary of *Theory U: Leading from the Future as it Emerges*, by Otto Scharmer. http://www.ottoscharmer.com/publications/summaries.php.

Schön, Donald A. 1983. *The Reflective Practitioner: How Professionals Think in Action*. New York: Basic Books.

Simon, Herbert A. 1969. *The Sciences of the Artificial*. Cambridge, MA: MIT Press.

Suchman, Lucy. 2007. *Human-Machine Reconfigurations: Plans and Situated Actions*, 2nd ed. Cambridge: Cambridge University Press.

Turner, Victor. 1982. *From Ritual to Theatre: The Human Seriousness of Play*. New York: Performing Arts Publications.

Wiley, Chris Flicker. 2011. *Carsten Höller: Experience*. Ed. Gary Carrion-Murayari and Niki Columbus. New York: Skira Rizzoli and New Museum.

8 Making and Playing with Customer Journeys

Sune Gudiksen and Connie Svabo

What. This chapter engages with customer journeys as a design method for use in service-based experience design. The method is illustrated by presenting two specific participatory design journey tools—Journey Touchpoints and Pinball Customer Flow—each of them applied in collaborative design activities.

Why. Understanding and exploring experiences as journeys, and supporting this understanding with tangible and playable tools, is necessary because conventional user experience design too often focuses on singular touchpoints instead of building an understanding of a temporally more comprehensive route of experiences where various physical, social, and object interactions may interrelate.

Where. The journey tools are unfolded in relation to cultural leisure-time service experience design (museum visits, pop-up marketing for a house, amusement park, and food festival). The journey tool is used in facilitated collaborative concept development workshops and is a way to engage participants in tangible and playable design activities within experience design.

How. Customer journeys are tools that help participants imagine and develop multiple points of connection, interaction, and exchange between users and experience designs.

1 Introduction

In service-based experience design there is a significant focus on considering the whole service experience as a run of different inputs, with each input having an impact on the overall experience that the customer, visitor, or user remembers and tells about. In service design especially two terms are used to describe this: "customer journey" and "touchpoints" (Løvlie et al. 2008). Furthermore, it is common to work with different temporal divisions, for instance, "before, during, and after."

The metaphor of a journey seems relevant: to journey is to engage with something in the passing, traveling from one place to another (Svabo and Shanks 2014). Customer journey tools have the central advantage of assuming a point of view that is temporally extended and takes into consideration that for customers, "experience" is a series of interactions with various features of a service experience design. Literature on service and experience design does acknowledge the nonlinear and nonstandardized aspects of journeys, where each customer is seen to go through a unique combination of different touchpoints. However, service and experience design *tools* tend to miss out on central elements in this journey understanding. Linear paper templates do not take into account the dynamics of the touchpoints, the in-betweens, and the relations between them. Furthermore, the tools typically have no tangible or playable elements. An example of this is Stickdorn and Schneider's "poster template," which is based on visualization alone and does not have tangibility through kinetic materials or changeability through game bricks and game mechanics (Stickdorn and Schneider 2010).

To contribute to the further development of customer journey tools, we turn to participatory design tools and techniques. This field of research has been particularly good at taking user experiences and perspectives into consideration.

Participatory design has roots in Scandinavia and has traditionally been related to the empowerment of employees when ICTs were introduced in work settings, but recently an effort has been made to reach a wider design studies audience (Simonsen and Robertson 2012).

A central feature of participatory design is the use of mock-ups, and recent studies in participatory design illustrate how tangibility through prototyping can lead to fruitful discussions on future scenarios in interaction design and business model development (Hornecker and Buur 2007; Eriksen 2012; Gudiksen et al. 2014).

This chapter focuses on how participatory design tools and techniques can make a service and experience design tool like the customer journey more flexible, dynamic, tangible, and playable. First, we describe the development in experience design and relate it to participatory design principles and tools. Second, we describe two journey touchpoint tools with a point of departure in participatory design activities from four workshops. Third, we discuss the tools' abilities and effects and provide suggestions about how service-based experience design and participatory design can benefit from each other, as well as proposing a future example of what a journey tool could look like and how we may conceive the concept of a journey in relation to the tool.

2 Background

This chapter is based on participatory design workshops in which we engage participants in trying out new collaborative approaches. As design researchers, we work with organizations or businesses to propose a new course of action to help their community improve its work practices. The research relates to what Frayling has called research-through-design. We record the design activities on video, transcribe conversations, and study actions using interaction analysis (Jordan and Henderson 1995). In this way, we can communicate the results, and by comparing incidents across the sessions, we are able to explain how the design tool kits scaffold the discussion of new design initiatives. Workshops typically last a half or one day and consist of consecutive co-design activities with a mix of participants such as organizational representatives, stakeholders, employees, consultants, and students. From different workshops, we have selected two tools, each with two cases for demonstration in this chapter, as they show a potential to move discussions on journeys in an innovative direction.

3   Service-Based Experience Design Journeys

Experience design can be traced to several parallel areas of application. The orientation toward experience in service design has strong roots in management and marketing and the operational side of businesses. The concept of customer experience from marketing is related mostly to social interactions between staff and customers (Shaw 2002, 2004), and also brand strategy or management (Schmitt 1999; Smilansky 2009), but an orientation toward experience is also present in product design (Desmet et al. 2011; McDonagh et al. 2002; Koskinen 2003), in the design of digital media and human-computer interaction (McCarthy and Wright 2004; Shedroff 2001; Unger and Chandler 2012, and in spatial design (Riewoldt 2002; Klingmann 2007). The big difference between service experience design and other areas of application is whether one designs for a single interaction with one product, object, or digital device or for a series of events, cues, interactions, or touchpoints, and how these may influence each other. For example, being in an amusement park leads to several interactions from the fun roller coaster to the interaction with the different staff workers or the digital interaction in the fun house or cinema. The same goes for the museum visit: purchasing tickets, experience the museum theme via digital media, the exhibition, restaurant queuing, souvenir shopping in the gift shop, or getting a parking ticket upon departure. The experience design begins from the moment a customer gets in contact with the organization (it is clear to see the marketing roots here) and until the customer withdraws from contact. An experience design thus can be considered a circular, never-ending journey (or so some companies may wish).

Customer journey tools make it possible to address the spatiotemporal and interactional dynamics of an experience design. This implies considering aspects like queuing and easy-access food and restrooms in the overall experience journey instead of envisioning only singular touchpoints. An example is Disney's way of ensuring that standing in a queue is not boring by initiating fireworks scenes. The design perspective may shift from zooming in on a single touchpoint and zooming out to consider the whole journey.

Carbone and Haeckel (1994) argue that the role of the service provider, producer, or designer is to orchestrate cues, and Pine and Gilmore (1999) use the term *staging* to envision what experience offering firms should do in order to cater to customer needs. However, recent experience research has provided counterpositions to the purely producer-staged interactions, for example by blurring the division between producer and consumer with Toffler's (1981) concept of the "prosumer," and ideas like co-creation and self-steering journeys (Prahalad and Ramasvamy 2004; Boswijk et al. 2007). As a further contribution to this growing orientation toward the active role of customers , it is interesting to turn to participatory design as a resource for working with user experiences.

4 Participatory Design and Tools

The participatory design community has in general been more concerned with the *how* of design than the *what*, that is, the content of the design (Bannon and Ehn 2012). Participatory design is used to deal with different participants and to open up work processes.

In the 1990s, participatory designers started to experiment with different tools and techniques. Some designers used visual materials to assist the participants in telling about experiences, while others suggested game-inspired tools (Muller 1993; Sjögren and Ehn 1991). The intention was to bridge the gap between separate knowledge domains, for example, the programmer and the workers or employees who were going to use a technology.

From the beginning, participatory design focused on involving users in design processes. In the 1970s, the rationale behind this inclusion was that it was the workers who were going to use the technology afterward, so their point of view mattered. This is still the fundamental principle in participatory design, but in contemporary participatory design practices, it varies who the users are, since they may be everyone who potentially plays a role in operating the design—from the end user to the janitor or manager.

Participatory design implies recognizing that design will always be completed in use by end users, employers, suppliers, and partners (Balka and Kahnamoui 2004). Another key issue is that designing is a social process that involves agreement making and rule making (Habraken and Gross 1988).

In relation to service and experience design, it is important to involve both the representatives from the different staff sectors and the customers or end users in the co-design process, as many of the touchpoints will probably be social interactions between staff and customer. By including employees, potential end users, and other stakeholders, an ownership and togetherness is established, as well as intrinsic motivation for the ones who are part of the operating phase afterward.

4.1 Tools

In the process of involving users in design, a wide range of tools may be used. Tools for dialogue have long been a part of participatory design and have evolved in many directions since the shift from system descriptions to mock-ups and prototyping by paper sketching or 3-D mock-ups (Bjögvinsson et al. 2012).

Several researchers suggest using generative tools to enable nondesigners to express thoughts and feelings about scenarios (Sanders 2002; Sanders and Stappers 2008; Brandt et al. 2012). Generative tools are tools for creating or making, and their power is that they facilitate imaginative hands-on activity. Sanders (2002) argues that "generative methods are a new language that enables all the stakeholders to contribute directly to the development of products, goods and services." Recently generative tools have been used to open up discussions on partnerships in business and in general to consider other aspects of future scenarios (Gudiksen et al. 2014). Buur and colleagues focus on tangible manipulation, by which they mean material representations with distinct tactile qualities to support or elicit scenario generation (Hornecker and Buur 2006; Buur and Mitchell 2011). Bødker (2000) identifies three uses for scenarios: (1) to present and situate solutions, (2) to illustrate alternative solutions, and (3) to identify potential problems. She argues further that the purpose is continuous reflection and action in line with Schönian reflective practice (Schön 1983, 1987). Essentially scenarios are stories about people and their activities (Carroll 2004).

A related participatory design method is the use of design games. Habraken and colleagues were perhaps the first to use game aspects as part of the design process (Habraken and Gross 1988), and several studies show that design games successfully establish a good basis for mutual learning (Ehn 1988; Brandt 2006). What differentiate games from other tools are especially the rules and procedures used in the activities, called game mechanics and inspired by video game design (Schell 2008). Good game mechanics can elicit radical new scenarios. Brandt et al. (2008) argue that design games create discussion of an "as-if-world." Furthermore, the use of concept design games (Brandt 2006; Habraken and Gross 1988) creates a safe space for improvisation of alternative scenarios before choosing a certain path to follow.

If we use the insights from research on generative tools, scenarios, and design games, what we search for in a journey tool is its ability to encapsulate the following aspects:

• Accessing and addressing user perspectives
• Flexible, easy changeable journeys
• Tangible and dynamic materials
• Game mechanics to enable "as-if-journey-scenarios"

In the following, we describe two journey tools, which facilitators can use in a workshop setting to develop an understanding of customer journeys and to elicit discussions on different scenarios. The two tools are Journey Touchpoints and Pinball Customer Flow. They are both collaborative tools to be introduced by a facilitator. Compared to earlier versions of customer journeys, these tools are designed to offer interactions, which involve tangibility as well as visuality. The idea is that the hands-on qualities of the tools inspire user creativity and imagination of alternative or future scenarios.

The goal of activities and tools such as these is to contribute to an overarching goal of innovation in experience and service design. We present the tools in some detail to support the design, planning, and execution of workshop processes, but we urge that the tools be combined and situated appropriately. The instructions for how to use the tools should not be perceived as rigid. A tool-making process relies on several situated elements such as the overall theme (in this case customer journeys) the specific design cases, the participants' professional expertise, and the local place. An understanding of situatedness relates to Suchman's suggestion that plans should be seen as resources for action, rather than as prescriptions (1987, 2007, 72), as well as to Haraway's point that knowledge is always partial and for this reason situated and potentially subject to negotiation (Haraway 1988, 589).

Before going into analysis, we begin by providing a figure (fig. 8.1) that clarifies the relations between tools and cases.

5 Journey Touchpoints

For this participatory design activity, customer journeys are made tangible and playable by allowing participants to move around touchpoints as they envision use scenarios. The tool is developed by one of the authors of this chapter, Sune Gudiksen, and has been facilitated by him in the following two cases.

5.1 Geological Museum

The first one was a museum case about making new experiences. As the world-famous geological site Stevns Klint is a candidate for UNESCO World Heritage status, the museum seeks to redefine the experience site, indoors as well as outdoors. A potential future exhibition, the outdoor area of the coastline and cliff, and mobile-based digital mediation are some of the many different touchpoints. The participants in the workshop activity were the museum clients and employers, as well as a few researchers. In this case the workshop activity facilitated by Gudiksen was one element of a more comprehensive experience design project carried out by the other author of this chapter, Connie Svabo.

5.2 New Nordic Home

The second case, New Nordic Home, was a new Danish initiative on a sustainable stacking house with the idea of making the house a promotion channel in itself by

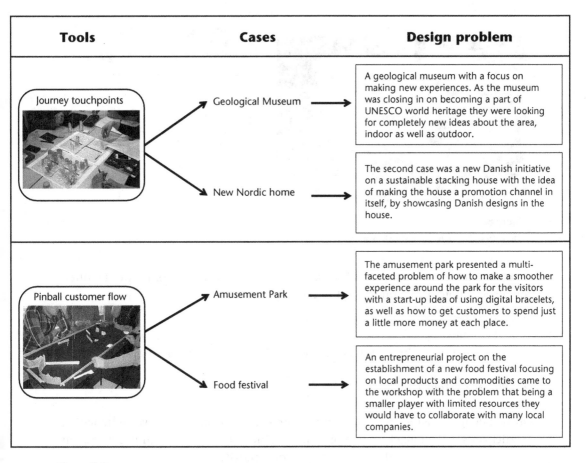

Tools	Cases	Design problem
Journey touchpoints	Geological Museum	A geological museum with a focus on making new experiences. As the museum was closing in on becoming a part of UNESCO world heritage they were looking for completely new ideas about the area, indoor as well as outdoor.
	New Nordic home	The second case was a new Danish initiative on a sustainable stacking house with the idea of making the house a promotion channel in itself, by showcasing Danish designs in the house.
Pinball customer flow	Amusement Park	The amusement park presented a multi-faceted problem of how to make a smoother experience around the park for the visitors with a start-up idea of using digital bracelets, as well as how to get customers to spend just a little more money at each place.
	Food festival	An entrepreneurial project on the establishment of a new food festival focusing on local products and commodities came to the workshop with the problem that being a smaller player with limited resources they would have to collaborate with many local companies.

Figure 8.1
Overview of tools, related cases, and design problems.

showcasing Danish designs in the house. The case owner emphasized that he thought it was innovative to see the house both as a unique product and as a promotion channel for other products. The participants besides the case owner were design students and a few researchers.

5.3 Setup
The tool consists of a paper-based "playing field" with a number of round circles printed on it, corresponding to a number of touchpoints (fig. 8.2). Two lines on the paper mark a division of the journey into the phases before, during, and after the experience, though some circles transcend these lines to illustrate that the divisions might not be so sharp. Small plastic shot glasses are used as game bricks, which mark

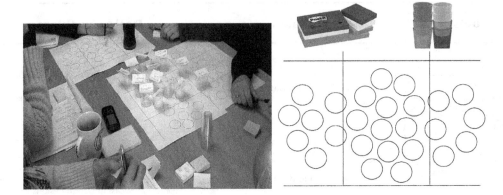

Figure 8.2
The tool kit for the glass journey activity.

a touchpoint. Each touchpoint/shot glass is explained with a title or keyword written on a sticky note placed on top of the glass.

• Shot glasses
• Sticky notes
• The playing field with customer journeys divided into before, during, and after

6   Pinball Customer Flow

In this design activity, customer journeys are made tangible and playable by letting participants build a mock-up of a pinball machine. The tool is used in two cases, but not the same ones as in the journey touchpoint activity.

The tool is developed by SPIRE, a center for participatory innovation, and has been used in a joint workshop facilitated by Gudiksen and SPIRE (for an amusement park), and later in a workshop for a food festival, facilitated by Gudiksen.

6.1   Amusement Park
The amusement park presented a multifaceted problem of how to make a smoother experience around the park for the visitors with an initial idea of using digital bracelets, as well as how to get customers to spend a little more money at each place. Besides a manager and marketer from the amusement park, the participants were consultants, researchers and students.

6.2   Food Festival
An entrepreneurial project on the establishment of a new food festival focusing on local products and commodities came to the workshop with the problem that, being

a smaller player with limited resources, they would have to collaborate with many local companies and rely on volunteers to create a unique festival experience. The two founders were present, along with consultants and students.

6.3   Setup

We introduced the metaphor of a pinball game, balls running down a table, and then asked the participants to build up the field with the value offerings or touchpoints in the park or at the festival (setup is illustrated in fig. 8.3). Two wooden lists were placed at each side, and the first thing the participants had to do was to figure out the ending points (e.g., "higher purchase" and "usual purchase" below). Few rules were made, and participants instead discussed them under way.

- Balls
- Fixed wooden lists on each side
- Different soft, bendable materials like cardboard and foam
- Sticky tape

7   Playing with Restructuring

In this section, we look at how well the two tools performed in evoking new journey scenarios.

7.1   Journey Touchpoints

In the museum case, participants first identified and discussed touchpoints by taking a shot glass and writing a name for each touchpoint they could recall, identify, or imagine. Criteria such as placement, significance, or relevance were continuously mentioned. During the activity, it was clear that the glasses with the sticky notes allowed everyone to propose a touchpoint because of the familiarity and the easy accessibility of the materials at hand. The way this was done was simply by writing a touchpoint heading or title on a sticky note, putting it on top of a small plastic glass, and placing the glass on the piece of paper that represented the journey (fig. 8.4). The ease of use (that it was accessible for all participants) is a typical example of what has often been pointed out as one of the key elements of a generative tool: allowing every participant to propose new elements.

Participant A, *holding a touchpoint in her hand*: What do you think of this one? Is that it?
Participant B: I think we have covered that.
(A silent participant C slips in a touchpoint she has just written, and participant A sees it.)
Participant A: Hey, yes, that's a good one.
(They all start to discuss the newly identified touchpoint.)

For participant C, the tool becomes a way to have a say in the discussion and at the same time allows for new ideas to emerge based on physical reasoning (as when a

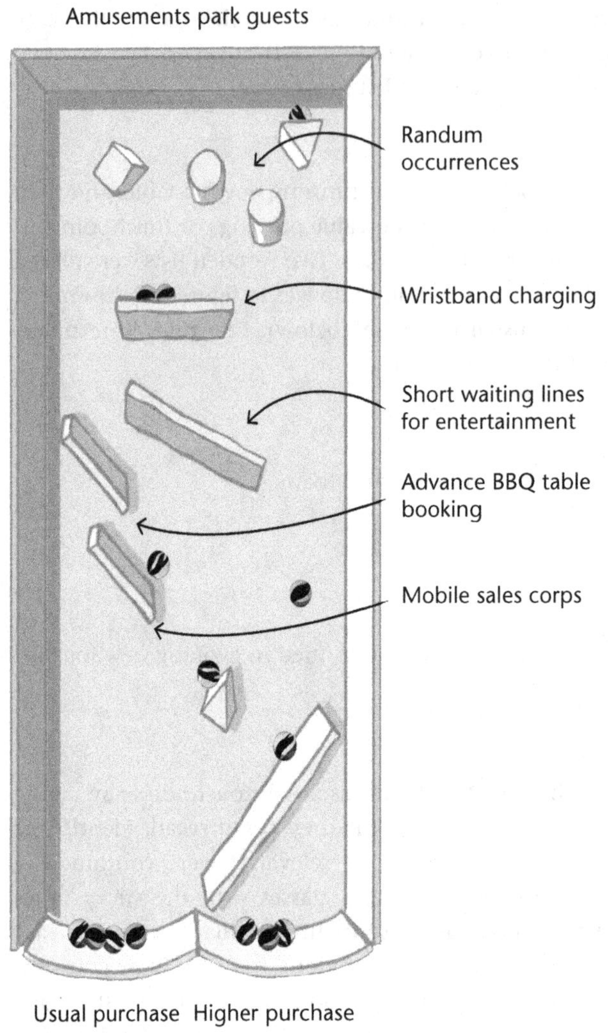

Amusements park guests

Randum
occurrences

Wristband charging

Short waiting lines
for entertainment

Advance BBQ table
booking

Mobile sales corps

Usual purchase Higher purchase

Figure 8.3
An example of the playing field in the pinball activity (the amusement park case).

Figure 8.4
The customer journey start-up process (left) and, later on in the process, the stacking of touchpoints (right).

child reasons in playing with different toys; Piaget 1962). The plastic-cup-supported sticky note in this example can be said to "speak up for the speaker." The participant does not use words to communicate her contribution but communicates via the materiality of the cup + note = touchpoint. This little assemblage in one moment "speaks for" the participant, and she then "speaks for it" when all participants discuss the newly identified touchpoint.

In the New Nordic Home case, the participants started out in a similar manner, discussing touchpoints and their placement, although they were more focused on brainstorming and threw in touchpoints at a rapid pace. At some point they started stacking the touchpoints, giving the activity a new dimension (the stacking to the right in fig. 8.4).

7.2 Pinball Customer Flow

The pinball activity followed the same start-up pattern in both the amusement park case and the food festival case. The strong metaphor of a pinball game led all participants to take part in the activities with highly engaged discussions and enjoyment. The participants discussed elements to add to the play, sometimes by talking and then adding a material, and sometimes the other way around by simply experimenting with materials and then giving the object a meaning similar to the touchpoint activity. The pinball activity also had another level. After making the playing field, they released the balls often with random, surprising effects (e.g., balls got stuck behind materials; not enough balls went the anticipated way; barriers, helpers, or obstacles in the field behaved in unexpected ways), all which led to what Schön (1987, 1992) calls the "surprising backtalk" of the material. After initial laughs because of the surprising effects, the participants started to respond by restructuring the playing field by removing and adding materials or by changing the placement or material attributes.

Figure 8.5
Balls stuck at a barrier in the amusement park (left) and a broken bowl in the food festival (right).

In one experiment in the amusement park group, many balls got stuck on the "short waiting lines" barrier, placed perpendicular to the slope direction. This triggered a discussion of which way it ought to be angled, and thus what effect ride waiting time may have on purchase (fig. 8.5).

Participant A: This one has to turn, doesn't it?
Participant B: Can't we imagine that it should be angled this way (*toward "higher purchase"*), because if people are bored, then they buy more?
Participant C: Yes, that's absolutely right.
Participant A: It could point in both directions; we could split it in two parts (*picks up the barrier, intending to split it*).
Participant C: No, wait—let's put it precisely here (*in the middle of the slope, angled slightly toward "higher purchase"*).

In the beginning of the pinball activity, the participants discussed how to make a realistic setup of the situation, or they worked toward a realistic picture either based on own initiatives or because of the tool. For example, in an incident in the Food Festival workshop, a large portion of the balls ended up in the "right" ending bowl for the participants, but as they discussed the seemingly fantastic result, the bowl was "overloaded" and started to break loose (fig. 8.5, right picture).

(The participants prepare a test run and let go of the balls.)
Participant A: Yeaaahhhii (*rejoicing the successful outcome*).
Participant B: We just missed a few. This one was on the way down there. The table seems a bit skewed.
(Container breaks loose; balls drop to the floor. Participants try to stop the catastrophic incident.)
Participant C: Maybe we were too confident—it was too easy. This seems to be more our situation, losing the customers on the floor.
Participant D: Let's try to move in new helpers that could provide a stronger safety net.
(They continue discussing and experimenting.)

The use of cardboard and foam materials gives the plasticity needed to evoke surprises on ball tryouts. It is similar to Star's (1989) boundary objects, "which are both plastic enough to adapt to local needs and constraints of the several parties employing them, yet robust enough to maintain a common identity across sites."

Letting the balls go can be compared to rolling dice in board games or games of chance. In this case, it functions as a way to knock the participants out of habitual thinking and enable new perspectives followed by action. In the amusement park case, it took a while before they made the first test run, so we encouraged them to take one by saying in a polite way, "Do you have to build it all before testing?" This way of moving a discussion ahead is an example of the way the tool plays together with the facilitator in searching for new questions.

The pinball game functions as a partial representation or a mock-up that initially illustrates journey patterns, but when the balls roll, the structure is challenged and restructured, so that the activity continuously involves journey scenario building and testing.

8   Playing with User Perspectives

In this section, we examine the way user perspectives entered discussions in the different activities.

8.1   Journey Touchpoints

In the Stevns Klint geology museum case, premade personae from a previous workshop entered discussions after a first round of journey thinking, giving the journey an explicitly user-centered point of view. Working with personae is a way of thinking about and working with user scenarios that both contributes to conceptual development and assists communications. Participants viewed the journey according to chosen personae, for example, an elderly couple hiking in the area or a family with children. The persona perspective led to a reiterating process of identification of touchpoints related to each of the persona (fig. 8.6).

While the perspectives of the various personae were shared through descriptions and pictures, interpretation of descriptions in relation to the touchpoints still occurred.

(Participant A holds up a persona description of a family with children.)
Participant A: They want to be guided, right?
Participant B: Do they?
Participant C: Yes.
Participant A: They want to be guided in their visit—in accordance with their priorities (*reads aloud description*).

Through the dialogue snippet, we can see that participant A reads aloud lines from the description and uses it as justification for changing a touchpoint. The tangibility

Figure 8.6
Discussing touchpoints based on interpretation of persona perspectives (the museum case).

and easy movement of glasses make it more painless or appealing to change the journeys based on the persona perspectives. The colors of the sticky notes make it possible to ascribe a touchpoint to a specific persona.

In the New Nordic Home stacking house case, there were no premade personae. Here the journeys were made according to agreements around the table and based on positive conflicts, although participants took user perspectives several times during the activity. In participatory design, it is often noted that participants not directly related to the service or experience design case quickly position themselves with a users' point of view. Sometimes they refer to themselves as having tried a similar experience, or they talk on behalf of a larger segment of users. This guides the discussion toward conflicts on producer-view versus user-view as an important element of refuting points of view before taking actions.

Participant A: What do you think when going into the house? What comes to your mind?
Participant B: It's a pop-up house. Besides the Danish designs, we would like it to be a Danish-inspired atmosphere and welcoming.

8.2   Pinball Customer Flow

In the pinball activity, several participants took the user perspective, but more interestingly it allowed for changing perspectives—the manager taking the user perspective and the other way around.

(Participants holding different materials ready to swap in.)
Participant A: A queue with the ice cream shop will always be a challenge.
Participant B: But if we take waiting time at amusements, it might be another parameter?
Participant C: Is it waiting time in general?
Participant B: But it depends. We have two perspectives. One is when we measure during one day, another is if we measure returning visitors. (*Stands with a barrier, looking at the others to see if they agree or approve it to enter the playing field.*)
Participant D: It is good enough to have in the middle.

This is a typical discussion aimed at agreeing on which kinds of materials and meanings should be part of the playing field. Participant B takes the users' point of view and after discussions is allowed by the other participants to set up a barrier.

The pinball activity differed significantly from the journey touchpoint activity in another way, as the balls represented the users or revenue streams but were all alike, which meant that the user perspective was addressed only by the participants, not through the tool. Here the balls can be seen as a flow of customers and how the case owners can take them into account when setting up the different barriers, helpers, or touchpoints.

When surprises occur during the test runs, it reminds the participants that we cannot always predict what users will do; it is not simply a chain of causation.

9   Discussion

In the discussion, we look back on the design tool criteria we established beforehand, comparing and discussing the two journey tools to compare our intentions with the outcome.

9.1   On Tangibility, Playability, and Scenarios

The journey touchpoint had a simple setup with few materials in play, but the tactile elements of the glasses and the movability it gave to the journeys worked well, as it encouraged changes when persona descriptions or user perspectives entered the discussions. The sticky note colors made it possible to distinguish between different journeys, allowing multiple journey scenarios to exist simultaneously, especially in the museum case with the premade personae. In the house case, participants did not visually represent different journeys. This would seem to be a major strength in using personae. It would be interesting to develop personae and turn them into playable figures, standing paper personae, or dolls, which has been done in interesting ways in other projects (Jakobsen 2012; Halse et al. 2010). They would probably work well along with the touchpoint glasses. Experiments on replacing the glasses with materials that have more attributes would also be worth a try, and writing directly on the glasses could prove to have a better aesthetic quality. In Bødker's scenario divisions, discussions were mostly on (1) presenting and situating solutions and (3) identifying potential problems or touchpoints to deal with. It was only when supported by a second activity, such as the personae description, that customer journey discussions led to a more concentrated focus on (2) alternative scenarios.

The pinball activity, on the other hand, was particularly successful for trying out various alternative scenarios. The balls are a highly dynamic material to work with, and the activity is well suited to finish off a workshop day where other aspects of a business or innovation case have already been discussed. The game mechanic of randomness has a large effect on how the participants give new meaning to materials in the playing field. The dynamic qualities of the balls make it difficult to trace back the different scenarios the participants discussed and worked through. Video may be used to record the sessions and subsequent presentations, and such documentation may help participants remember the steps they have gone through.

The playful and open character of the activities engages participants. Gamelike playing boards focus dialogue and provide shared objects of activity (Svabo 2009).

9.2 On Assessing and Addressing User Perspectives

In the activities, we identified three ways that user perspectives entered the discussions.

(1) Addressing user perspectives explicitly: In the Stevns Klint journey touchpoint activity, premade personae made it possible to rapidly engage with and develop different journey paths. Combining personae and customer journeys thus is desirable. It is crucial, however, to give space to refining persona descriptions along the way during the process. Introducing premade personae needs a tool, or a facilitator can encourage discussions where personae and journey descriptions evolve together based on new understandings and insights generated during workshops.

(2) Working with user perspectives in an intuitive manner: In both tools, participants who were not directly related to the case took the user perspectives. They would either argue on behalf of a larger group or relate their own experiences in similar situations. The conflicts and discussions between case owner and other participants often led to new things to consider. Compared with the premade personae, it can sometimes be a problem if the self-referential participant dominates conclusions, but most of the time the user perspectives in these activities ensure empathic considerations that would not necessarily be present in non-participatory design activities.

(3) Seeing users as a flow of people: The pinball activity focuses not on a single group of people but on general ways to persuade, lead, or help customers. Here persona or segment thinking is somewhat suspended, and instead the flow of people is at play. This introduces an interesting new dimension of volume into the design work in a way that complements other types of tools very well.

10 Implications for Service-Based Experience Design and Participatory Design Practice

In this chapter, we have combined a tool—the customer journey—from the emerging fields of service and experience design with well-established participatory design tools. The design fields can benefit from each other. With the example of the customer journey tool, service and experience design can do the following:

• Move away from linear, fixed journey tools to dynamic, changeable journey tools with many user perspectives in play.

• Through participatory design tools such as Journey Touchpoints and Pinball Customer Flow, it becomes possible to open up the process; gather many views of competing alternatives; and then decide on which road to choose from the available scenarios.

• Open up the design process by including users, as well as employees and other stakeholders. When looking at a full service experience, social context between staff and customers is as important as all the other touchpoints, so a mutual understanding of new initiatives through co-design activities leads to a good operating advantage.

While service and experience design can learn from participatory design, the same holds true the other way around:

• Tackling service and experience design with participatory design tools expands the domain of participatory design and research.

• Participatory design tools or games that are in line with trends like customer journeys, co-creation, and open innovation can unfold new participatory design principles, which may be useful in traditional participatory design areas as well.

Customer journeys are a useful method if combined with a participatory design setting and the design principles of participatory design. One can see the multiple customer journeys as a snake continuously trying to bite its own tail to elicit circular,

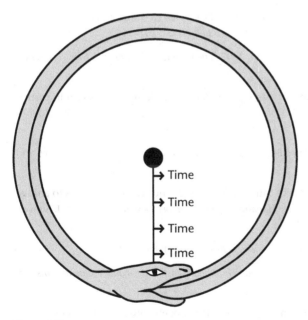

Figure 8.7
The Ouroboros of customer journeys.

ongoing journeys. In Greek this symbol is called an *Ouroboros* in the sense of something constantly re-creating itself; in this case it could be the touchpoints as well as the customers. We expect future customer journey tool experiments to reveal whether a ring- or spiral-like game board (like the one in fig. 8.7), in combination with various tangible game pieces, is a better way of grasping and working with never-ending customer journeys.

Acknowledgments

We would like to thank Invio, the Danish innovation network for knowledge-based experience economy, as well as Region Zealand, for supporting and financing these activities. Furthermore, we thank the case owners, consultants, researchers, and students who participated in the design activities.

References

Balka, E., and N. Kahnamoui. 2004. Technology trouble? Talk to us: Findings from an ethnographic field study. http://dl.acm.org/citation.cfm?id=1011896.

Bannon, Liam, and Pelle Ehn. 2012. Design matters in participatory design. In *Routledge Handbook of Participatory Design*, vol. 37, ed. J. Simonsen and T. Robertson. New York: Routledge.

Bjögvinsson, Erling, Pelle Ehn, and Per-Anders Hillgren. 2012. Design things and design thinking: Contemporary participatory design challenges. *Design Issues* 28 (3): 101–116.

Boswijk, Albert, Thomas Thijssen, and Ed Peelen. 2007. *The Experience Economy: A New Perspective*. Boston: Pearson Education.

Brandt, Eva. 2006. Designing exploratory design games: A framework for participation in participatory design? Paper presented at Ninth Conference on Participatory Design: Expanding Boundaries in Design.

Brandt, Eva, Jörn Messeter, and Thomas Binder. 2008. Formatting design dialogues: Games and participation. *CoDesign* 4 (1): 51–64.

Brandt, Eva, Thomas Binder, and Elizabeth Sanders. 2012. Tools and techniques: Ways to engage telling, making and enacting. In *Routledge Handbook of Participatory Design*, vol. 37, ed. J. Simonsen and T. Robertson. New York: Routledge.

Brown, Tim. 2008. Design thinking. *Harvard Business Review* 86 (6): 84.

Brown, Tim. 2009. *Change by Design: How Design Thinking Transforms Organizations and Inspires Innovation*. New York: HarperBusiness.

Buur, Jacob, and Sune Gudiksen. 2012. Innovating business models with pinball designs. In *Proceedings of the DMI 2012 International Research Conference*. Boston, MA, August 8–9.

Buur, Jacob, and Henry Larsen. 2010. The quality of conversations in participatory innovation. *CoDesign* 6 (3): 121–138.

Buur, Jacob, and Ben Matthews. 2008. Participatory innovation. *International Journal of Innovation Management* 12 (3): 255–273.

Buur, Jacob, and Robb Mitchell. 2011. The business modeling lab. Participatory Innovation Conference 2011.

Bødker, Susanne, Pelle Ehn, Dan Sjögren, and Yngve Sundblad. 2000. Co-operative design—Perspectives on 20 years with "the Scandinavian IT Design Model." http://zaphod.mindlab.umd.edu:16080/mediawiki-1.15.1/images/5/5d/4-Utopia.pdf.

Carbone, Lewis, and Stephan Haeckel. 1994. Engineering customer experiences. *Marketing Management* 3 (3): 8–19.

Carbone, Lewis, and Stephan Haeckel. 2000. Engineering customer experiences. White Paper Series. White Plains, NY: IBM Advanced Business Institute.

Carroll, Jennie. 2004. Completing design in use: Closing the appropriation cycle. In *Proceedings of the 13th European Conference on Information Systems*, ed. Timo Leimo, Timo Saarinen, and Stefan Klein, 337–347.

Clarke, Adele. 2004. Situational analyses: Grounded theory mapping after the postmodern turn. *Symbolic Interaction* 26 (4): 553–576.

Cooper, Alan, R. Reimann, and D. Cronin. 2012. *About Face 3: The Essentials of Interaction Design*. New York: John Wiley & Sons.

Creswell, John W. 2006. *Qualitative Inquiry and Research Design: Choosing among Five Approaches*. Thousand Oaks, CA: Sage.

Desmet, Pieter M. A., and H. Schifferstein, eds. 2011. *From Floating Wheelchairs to Mobile Car Parks: Selected Work from TU Delft: A Collection of 35 Experience-Driven Design Projects*. The Hague: Eleven International Publishing.

Ehn, Pelle. 1988. Work-oriented design of computer artifacts. Umeå University.

Ehn, Pelle, and Dan Sjøgren. 1991. From system descriptions to scripts for action. *Design at Work: Cooperative Design of Computer Systems*: 241–268.

Ehn, Pelle, and R. Badham. 2002. Participatory design and the collective designer. In *PDC 02 Proceedings of the Participatory Design Conference*, ed. T. Binder, J. Gregory, and I. Wagner. Malmo, Sweden, June 23–25.

Eriksen, Mette Agger. 2012. Material matters in co-designing: Formatting and staging with participating materials in co-design projects, events, and situations. Faculty of Culture and Society, Malmö University.

Greenbaum, Joan, and Daria Loi. 2012. Participation, the camel, and the elephant of design: An introduction. *CoDesign* 8 (2–3): 81–85.

Gudiksen, Sune, Søren Poulsen, and Jacob Buur. 2014. Making business models. *CoDesign*.

Habraken, N. J., and M. D. Gross. 1988. Concept design games. *Design Studies* 9 (3): 150–158.

Halse, Joachim, Eva Brandt, Brendan Clark, and Thomas Binder. 2010. *Rehearsing the Future*. Copenhagen: Danish Design School Press.

Haraway, Donna. 1988. Situated knowledges: The science question in feminism and the privilege of partial perspective. *Feminist Studies* 14 (3): 575–599.

Hornecker, E., and Jacob Buur. 2006. Getting a grip on tangible interaction: A framework on physical space and social interaction. Paper presented at the SIGCHI Conference on Human Factors in Computing Systems.

Jakobsen, Christina. 2012. Towards doll-based design: Framework, guidelines, and research potentials. In *Proceedings of the 7th Nordic Conference on Human-Computer Interaction: Making Sense through Design*.

Jordan, Brigitte, and Austin Henderson. 1995. Interaction analysis: Foundations and practice. *Journal of the Learning Sciences* 4 (1): 39–103.

Klingmann, Anna. 2007. *Brandscapes: Architecture in the Experience Economy*. Cambridge, MA: MIT Press.

Koskinen, Ilpo, and Katja Battarbee. 2003. Introduction to user experience and empathic design. In *Empathic Design: User Experience in Product Design*, ed. I. Koskinen, K. Battarbee, and T. Mattelmäki, 37–50. Helsinki: IT Press.

Løvlie, Lavrans, Chris Downs, and Ben Reason. 2008. Bottom-line experiences: Measuring the value of design in service. *Design Management Review* 19 (1): 73–79.

McCarthy, John, and Peter Wright. 2004. Technology as experience. *Interactions* 11 (5): 42–43.

McDonagh, Deana, Paul Hekkert, Jeroen van Erp, and Diane Gyi. 2002. *Design and Emotion*. Boca Raton, FL: CRC Press.

Muller, Michael J, and Sarah Kuhn. 1993. Participatory design. *Communications of the ACM* 36 (6): 24–28.

Nachmanovitch, Stephen. 1990. *Free Play: Improvisation in Life and Art*. New York: J. P. Tarcher.

Piaget, Jean. 1962. *Play, Dreams, and Imitation*, vol. 24. New York: Norton.

Prahalad, C. K., and V. Ramaswamy. 2004. Co-creating unique value with customers. *Strategy and Leadership* 32 (3): 4–9.

Sanders, Elizabeth. 2002. From user-centered to participatory design approaches. *Design and the Social Sciences: Making Connections*, ed. J. Frascara, 1–8. London: Taylor & Francis.

Sanders, Elizabeth, Eva Brandt, and Thomas Binder. 2010. A framework for organizing the tools and techniques of participatory design. Paper presented at the Eleventh Biennial Participatory Design Conference.

Sanders, Elizabeth, and Pieter Stappers. 2008. Co-creation and the new landscapes of design. *CoDesign* 4 (1): 5–18.

Schell, Jesse. 2008. *The Art of Game Design: A Book of Lenses*. Burlington, MA: Morgan Kaufmann.

Schmitt, Bernd. 1999. Experiential marketing. *Journal of Marketing Management* 15 (1–3): 53–67.

Schön, Donald. 1983. *The Reflective Practitioner: How Professionals Think in Action*. New York: Basic Books.

Schön, Donald. 1987. *Educating the Reflective Practitioner*. San Francisco: Jossey-Bass.

Schön, Donald A. 1992. Designing as reflective conversation with the materials of a design situation. *Knowledge-Based Systems* 5 (1): 3–14.

Shaw, Colin. 2004. *Revolutionize Your Customer Experience*. Basingstoke: Palgrave Macmillan.

Shaw, Colin, and John Ivens. 2002. *Building Great Customer Experiences*. Basingstoke: Palgrave Macmillan.

Shedroff, Nathan. 2001. *Experience Design*. Indianapolis: New Riders.

Smilansky, Shaz. 2009. *Experiential Marketing: A Practical Guide to Interactive Brand Experiences*. London: Kogan Page.

Simonsen, Jesper, and Toni Robertson, eds. 2012. *Routledge Handbook of Participatory Design*. New York: Routledge.

Star, Susan. 1989. The structure of ill-structured solutions: Boundary objects and heterogeneous distributed problem solving. *Distributed Artificial Intelligence* 2: 37–54.

Stickdorn, Marc, and Jakob Schneider. 2010. *This Is Service Design Thinking: Basics—Tools—Cases*. Amsterdam: BIS Publishers.

Suchman, L. A. 1987. *Plans and Situated Actions: The Problem of Human-Machine Communication*. Cambridge: Cambridge University Press.

Suchman, L. A. 2007. *Human-Machine Reconfigurations: Plans and Situated Action*, 2nd ed. Cambridge: Cambridge University Press.

Svabo, Connie. 2009. Materiality in a practice-based approach. *Learning Organization* 16 (5): 360–370.

Svabo, Connie, and Michael Shanks. 2014. Experience as excursion: A note towards a metaphysics of design thinking. In *Designing Experience: Positions and Approaches*, ed. Peter Benz. London: Bloomsbury Academic.

Toffler, A., W. Longul, and H. Forbes. 1981. *The Third Wave*. New York: Bantam Books New York.

Unger, Russ, and Carolyn Chandler. 2012. *A Project Guide to Ux Design: For User Experience Designers in the Field or in the Making*. Indianapolis: New Riders.

9 Reflexive Learning through Visual Methods

Lisbeth Frølunde

What. This chapter concerns how visual methods and visual materials can support visually oriented, collaborative, and creative learning processes in education. The focus is on facilitation (guiding, teaching) with visual methods in learning processes that are designerly or involve design. Visual methods are exemplified through two university classroom cases about collaborative idea generation processes. The visual methods and materials in the cases are photo elicitation using photo cards, and modeling with LEGO Serious Play sets.

Why. The goal is to encourage the reader, whether student or professional, to facilitate with visual methods in a critical, reflective, and experimental way. The chapter offers recommendations for facilitating with visual methods to support playful, emergent designerly processes. The chapter also has a critical, situated perspective.

Where. This chapter offers case vignettes that refer to design-oriented workshops where student groups generate ideas, such as for a campaign. The cases are set at Roskilde University.

How. There are recommendations on how to facilitate workshops and develop your own practice as a reflexive facilitator. Some of the typical facilitation challenges are discussed, including supporting difficult group collaborative processes (such as dealing with interpersonal tensions). You will gain an understanding about how and why to work with visual methods and how to develop a dynamic, reflexive facilitation practice. The chapter contains recommendations on four aspects that can develop facilitation: being attentive to situatedness, differences, challenges, and nurturing reflexivity. Theoretical perspectives on facilitating with visual methods are discussed using pragmatic and dialogic approaches. A summary of facilitation stages is presented through a generic model (PASIR).

1 Introduction

This chapter explores how visual methods and visual materials and artifacts can be facilitated to support playfulness, creativity, and knowledge production through visuals and potentially lead to a rich range of design ideas in a group. Perhaps the reader has tried to participate in visually oriented group design processes, for instance, making mind maps of ideas, sketching portraits of would-be customers as part of a game, storyboarding an advertisement as a team exercise, or the like. Visual and game-inspired methods in design workshops have roots in fields such as architecture, film, and design education but are becoming popular in, for instance, IT development, engineering, marketing, and organizational learning (Casakin 2007; Coyne, Snodgrass, and Martin 1994). Prominent design firms like IDEO have developed and spread methods for exploring visual, empathic design processes with end users (Brown 2008; Moggridge 2006). As this book testifies, using design games and other collaborative design methods in interdisciplinary teams aligns with Scandinavian participatory design traditions.

This chapter offers the reader a critical look at the values and challenges of visual methods and an appreciation of visuals (images) as a complex phenomenon. The author and contributing colleagues are group facilitators and university teachers and have experimented with a wide spectrum of visual methods and visual artifacts used for the purpose of learning about design (such as idea generation), as well as for other purposes, such as strategic thinking and self-development. Visual methods (or any methods) are always situated. Facilitation involves learning from concrete, situated experience and continuously reflecting on how methods suit a particular context.

The chapter is organized as follows. Section 2 outlines a reflexive facilitation approach based on dialogic and pragmatic learning theory and explores why visual methods are so challenging to use. Section 3 introduces two well-known visual methods, photo elicitation and modeling, with accompanying case vignettes. The cases exemplify how university students participate in idea generation within design-related group projects. The cases explore the situated integration of materials and facilitation approaches: a photo card set used for photo elicitation, and LEGO blocks used with the LEGO Serious Play approach to modeling ideas. Section 4 discusses facilitation challenges and the generic facilitation model PASIR. The chapter concludes with recommendations for developing four aspects of facilitation practice with visual methods, namely, situatedness, differences, challenges and reflexivity.

1.1 Challenges and Potentials

The rising popularity of visual methods is sometimes presented with a goal of improving our everyday creativity and innovative capacities, perhaps propelled by the extensive use of visual methods within IT-oriented business development in Silicon Valley (Gray, Brown, and Macanufo 2010; Duarte 2010; Roam 2008) and IDEO (Brown 2008). Dan Roam offers persuasive arguments for a holistic design orientation, contending that visual methods work by capitalizing on visual thinking processes, offering ways to "quickly look at problems, more intuitively understand them, more confidently address them, and more rapidly convey to others what we've discovered" (Roam 2008, 3). Roam refers to how simple sketches, such as those drawn on the back of a napkin, function as ways to look and focus, to model, and to explain complex ideas in any work-related collaboration.

In essence, designerly education and designerly thinking are about learning visual thinking, and what can be called constructive or concrete thinking, which differs from the kind of analytical thinking or reasoning usually offered by the sciences and the humanities (Cross 2007). Cross points out that the designerly way of thinking is about making *constructive* responses to practical problems, issues, and situations. It is about imagining how something might be, which involves thinking about the design problem in new and different terms from a currently known design solution. Designing is called a wicked problem (a term introduced by Rittel) (Coyne 2005; Møller and Tollestrup 2013), meaning complex, ill-structured problems in need of redefinition and resolution over time, such as designing a new mass transit system or getting young people to exercise more. To approach such wicked problems, Coyne suggests that we need to be able to make *new connections* and conceptual leaps—or "think outside the box"—and visualization aids in idea generation.

Visual methods are often described as potentially opening up new connections and enhancing group communication. However, the visual unfolds in the preexisting conditions and can be said to amplify whatever tensions exist. Visual methods are challenging to facilitate because of the emergent qualities of visuals and their surprising complexity. Students (and others) have extremely different responses to visuals (such as fears of revealing too much, or being wrong, etc.). While visual methods can be useful in designerly educational contexts and many other contexts, the key is facilitation. As demonstrated in the cases, many kinds of tensions and discomforts accompany the use of creative visual methods. This chapter offers no recipes—but does offer recommendations to aid the reader, whether you are a prospective facilitator, teacher, student, or professional, in assembling a repertoire of visual methods.

1.2   A Critical Approach

This chapter offers a critical as well as a normative approach. The popularity of visual methods in handbooks is often oriented to exercises, methods, and techniques and becomes normative. The risk is that applying visual methods becomes too generalized and implicitly "good." To avoid exaggerating the claims about visual methods, this chapter offers a critical, situated perspective.

Using visual methods is embedded in complex situations, where there are entangled aspects (roles, institutions, materials) that interplay. The rising popularity of visual methods and rhetoric about play, creativity, and innovation (Banaji and Burn 2007) risks inflating the claims of visual methods. The education researcher David Buckingham (2009) warns that a somewhat uncritical and celebratory approach has spread along with the popularity of creative methods, including LEGO Serious Play. This risk of simplifying the complexity of visuals as a phenomenon for inquiry is not new (Latour 1990).

Concerns within design education about the influence of business-oriented mantras on innovation and creativity are rising. The design field is being pushed toward designing "experiences" and services, a sustainable future, and ingenious businesses ideas (Salamon 2006; Brown 2008; Martin 2009). The design educator Salomon cautions about the ideals formerly belonging to the private business sector, such as accountability, spreading to design training, because it increases "pressure on design to further articulate itself as a technical science and a 'hard' machine of production, rather than as an aesthetic, philosophical or social capacity" (Salamon 2006, 37). This pressure can weaken the delightful, emergent, creative core of design. It is important to preserve the designerly way of thinking as a social, creative capacity—its unpredictable, playful, emergent, and rather unaccountable characteristics.

2   Theories about Facilitation with Visual Methods

This section introduces a combined pragmatic and dialogic approach to learning theory, with attention to the challenges of facilitation. Key notions are reflective learning, inertia, and tensions in relation to facilitation.

2.1   Facilitation as a Learning Process

"Facilitation" is a word with relation to the Latin *facilis*, or "easy to do," such as helping to make learning easier. The commonsense understanding of the facilitator role includes being responsible for designing the overall instruction (including the structure, or framework, often called the scaffolding [Tabak 2004]). A facilitator develops a way of asking questions, guiding, or coaching a group toward a given learning purpose. Becoming a facilitator, I believe, involves reflecting on the role and one's own practice: questioning what and why, as well as how, to facilitate learning toward a particular situated purpose. In educational contexts, a facilitator may also be teacher or researcher, which entails broader areas of responsibility. In business contexts, a facilitator is typically an external consultant facilitating short-term workshops or seminars. Any facilitator is inevitably confronted with having to define and adjust his or her approach according to the situatedness of contexts.

I want to assure the reader that it is rewarding, fascinating, and challenging to facilitate learning processes and support emergent designerly thinking. Being open to challenges with a critical approach helps us to gain insight and develop our unique practice. Continuous evaluation of our own experiences and facilitation philosophy supports our growth. Learning facilitation goes beyond using any particular tool or method. It involves questioning our ways of relating to others, our comfort levels, core beliefs, and values. Through reflexivity we may develop our understandings of the challenges that students (and others) face, such as fears about participating the "wrong way" in creative visual workshops.

The pragmatic and dialogic approach to facilitation presented in this section underpins the use of visual methods and can be termed *reflexive*. It is a blend of pragmatic and dialogic theories inspired by the key thinkers John Dewey, M. M. Bakhtin, and others. The two approaches are reviewed and form the backdrop for the generic PASIR model (sec. 4).

2.2   A Pragmatic Approach

A Deweyan pragmatic approach involves an integration of abstract *thinking* about experience and *doing*, or the hands-on experience with materials in a situated practice (Dewey 1923). Reflexivity refers to reflecting on one's own practice but involves more than just examining materials, methods, and our own experience (Dewey 1938). A pragmatic, critical *reflexive* approach to learning, teaching, and facilitating involves considering the situated, such as the organizational setting and the interrelatedness of all aspects in our whole complex social world (Mitchell 2008; Dixon 1999).

Dewey calls reflective thinking troublesome because "it involves overcoming the inertia that inclines one to accept suggestions at their face value; it involves willingness to endure a condition of mental unrest and disturbance" (Dewey 1910, 13). Overcoming inertia involves, for instance, exploring an idea as part of an inquiry process and staying open and reflecting while developing ideas. Facilitation involves guiding and encouraging participants to, in a sense, overcome inertia and to be a bit disturbed. Through an exploration of ideas and materials, participants may get into a playful state; see Christrup's chapter in this volume. Dewey (1938) suggests that a teacher (and by extension a facilitator) has a responsibility to help learners set a strong purpose for their learning and to guide them toward their own path or their quest to meet that purpose.

Pragmatists such as David Kolb (1984) and Donald Schön (1983) have explored reflective practice further. Schön studied the development of ideas, for example, among architects, who exemplify what he termed "reflective practitioners," and distinguished between reflection-in-action and reflection-on-action. Schön (1983) discusses how designing buildings involves architects making models and reflection *in* (or through doing) the design actions; architects also review and present their models and drawings for critique and reflection *on* the design actions (in collaboration with others). Reflection is often explained as a cyclic pattern of experience that integrates an iterative "thinking–doing" processes. The pragmatic approach has been applied to organizational learning where the intentional use of learning processes at the individual, group, and system level is seen as contributing to the continuous cycle of transformation in organizations (Dixon 1999).

Mark Johnson and others propose that experiential, embodied correlations between several domains or concepts (e.g., "design is a journey") are basic to our abstract thinking ability (Johnson 2007). A *designerly way of thinking* echoes the pragmatic understanding of learning processes as a unity of abstract designerly thinking and playful processes of doing.

2.3   A Dialogic Approach

A neo-Bakhtinian dialogic approach to facilitation and visual phenomena pays attention to shifting, socially constructed understandings of texts. (I apply a contemporary expanded text notion of multimedia text, which includes the relations between words, sounds, images, and interactive narrative elements, for example, in online or off-line games.) Texts are in dialogue, interrelated and evolving; and interpretations are in flux, situated and open (Bakhtin 1981). Therefore when we engage with visuals in an ongoing process of dialogue and discovery, for instance, during idea generation processes, meanings are seen as coproduced dialogically. The dialogic interplay involves tensions between different, often opposing voices (not literal voices, but the way that various meanings emerge and relate) (Phillips 2011). Tensions between meanings and people are seen as dynamic, fluid, and relational constructions rather than static, clearly delineated entities.

Louise Phillips (2011) suggests that this interrelational dialogic perspective involves recognizing the necessity of difference as a dynamic force in a group. Difference may become problematic in a group basically when tensions are *not* allowed to emerge. Phillips argues that dialogues oscillate (shift) between the centrifugal tendency (opening up for plural and different voices) and the centripetal tendency (closing down, or a unity of voices). The complex oscillation also refers to how different voices and interests can meet in unforeseen ways through visuals, such as how images act as helpers (or as "anchors") for opening the plurality of meanings (Hee Pedersen 2008).

From a normative perspective, the dialogic and pragmatic perspectives emphasize, in different ways, that we can expect tensions and our own and others' discomfort to emerge in learning processes. A dialogic approach to facilitation involves respectfully exploring how dialogues oscillate between centrifugal and centripetal tendencies in a group. Dissent, differences and tensions are seen as valuable for promoting change and idea development and learning.

3   Applying Visual Methods

This section presents visual methods with a focus on applying two overarching methods. Visual methods are shaped by the theory, methodology, and philosophy behind the facilitation approach. The visual methods presented in the cases are not meant as static or exclusive; visual methods are often used together and mixed with other creative methods. A workshop with visual methods and materials obviously uses multiple means or modes of expression (such as spoken dialogue or gesturing) and a wide range of materials (such as predesigned game elements or cards, basic art materials, sticky notes, and much more, as described throughout this book).

Designing scaffolds or structures for learning overlaps with many terms for establishing play, story, or game worlds and "game rules" in group work. In the book *Gamestorming*, the authors offer what they call "design principles" that may be helpful for a facilitator who wants to develop his or her own versions of their collaborative game exercises based on the "underlying mechanics or architecture of games" (Gray, Brown, and Macanufo 2010, xvi).

Visual methods can aid both in capturing complexity and in discovering simple solutions. The two cases in this chapter on photo elicitation and modeling demonstrate different ways to open for ideas, stimulate dialogue about ideas, and connect various patterns of ideas, thereby potentially improving design results. The methods have commonalities in terms of working with visualization of ideas and generating ideas through associations and analogies (such as metaphors). The specific visual methods are introduced in sections 3.1 and 3.2 and are presented through case vignettes that exemplify challenges facing the facilitator. The challenges are harnessed for discussion on a more general level in section 4.

It is beyond this chapter's scope to give an overview or compare the rich traditions of visual methods. Various academic publications offer overviews of visual methods (Rose 2011; Jewitt and van Leeuwen 2001) and include approaches relevant for understanding designerly thinking (Simonsen et al. 2010; Simonsen and Robertson 2012; Møller and Tollestrup 2013; Moggridge 2006). Selected handbooks (Roam 2008; Gray, Brown, and Macanufo 2010) and accompanying websites also offer overviews.

3.1   Photo Elicitation

Using photos in fieldwork or in an interview situation to elicit or evoke responses is a seemingly easy way to stimulate design ideas, associations, metaphors, stories, and memories. The photo-elicitation method relies on the participants taking their own photos (or video, photo diaries, multimedia artifacts) and can also rely on the use of premade photo sets or the like. Photo-elicitation has many roots. The visual anthropologists Malcolm and John Collier (1986/1996) have been influential in promoting photography and other image-based research methods. Photo-elicitation is used extensively in participatory interaction design, such as the design-driven research method developed by Bill Gaver called Cultural Probes, intended to uncover people's values and activities (Moggridge 2006).

Photos elicit a wealth of information, feelings, and memories owing to the photographic medium's particularly evocative form of representation. When people talk about the many meanings of an image, it can bring up extremely personal histories and emotions (Hee Pedersen 2008; Harper 2002; Mitchell 2008; Keats 2009). The use of photo elicitation is an adaptable, fluid method that is powerful for stimulating associations and memories. Humans can be said to exchange cultural and deeply emotional histories through opening up for images and our associated meanings and stories (Mitchell 2008; Banks 2001). A common alternative to using premade materials (such as photo cards) is to incorporate the participants' own photos for elicitation. Using their own photos in relation to design reportedly provides more detailed answers because more personal meanings and narratives unfold about the photos (Carter and Mankoff 2005). (See discussion in sec. 4.)

The photo case exemplifies the challenges of facilitating interpersonal tensions that emerge in a student group during their negotiation about making a collective design idea. Differences and tensions emerge in this group as they progress from working with individual ideas to forming a collective model. The case demonstrates photo elicitation using premade photographic images on cards and other materials in a classroom group exercise.

The sixty photo cards used are prototypes for the currently available "Pick a Picture" set, which resemble playing cards. Most of the photos are by Kim Sandholdt. Kim is also a facilitator and teacher (and documented the case for research). The case involves one student group (ages 22–50) in a course on project management in a master's program at Roskilde University in 2010. The students were in an introductory session that revolved around solving a design problem about campaigns. The design problem given to the student group was to generate ideas and design solutions for a campaign regarding young people's lack of exercise. The design problem was framed by a review of information, including statistics on young people's exercise habits and health implications.

Kim created an instructional scaffold for group work that combines his photo card set with Dan Roam's visual brainstorming exercises that focus on the "six W's" (who/what, how much, when, where, what, why) or "problem clumps" to visualize problems and solutions (Roam 2008). Kim laid out four activity phases for group design work on problems and solutions as follows.

(1) Each student in the group reflects on the design problem and selects two to four images (from the photo card set) that illustrate their individual reflections. Large paper sheets lie on tables with two drawn squares (one called "problems" and one called "solutions") intended for the placement of photo cards.

(2) The students present each of their chosen images, ideas, and associations about their selected image. All selected images are thereby placed on the table.

(3) The students look for possible correlations of meanings and structures among the various images on the table. They move cards around and talk about the meanings in relation to addressing the design problem.

(4) The group constructs a collective model, an abstract concept that shows a few of the correlations based on their discussion. In this fourth phase, the group is offered other materials, such as glue, string, knives, and foam core for building the model(s).

The student group in this case has four members: Anders, Birthe, Carla, and Dorthe (pseudonyms). The group's design process experiences a sort of breakdown in phase 4 because they are struggling to decide on a collective model. It exemplifies the difficulty of progressing from individual ideas to a single collective design idea.

At the start of phase 4, Birthe has turned to Kim to ask for guidance, saying that they are "far apart" within the group. Kim reiterates that the goal is to create a single collective model that can accommodate the many perspectives in a group. He suggests that the group could try to express (arrange and show) their different perspectives and ideas on a tray (a tray being a piece of foam core cut to A4 size) and subsequently try "playing ideas out" against each other to find a new collective solution.

Kim's suggestion about playing out differences is taken up partially. The group reviews their individual cards and selects a few more. This generates further associations in the group; Birthe says, "It's all about perspective," while pointing (see figs. 9.1 and 9.2) to what she calls the "target card" (the image resembles a bull's-eye or shooting target). Dorthe suggests that the target card can be placed in the middle of the collective model on the table. After some heated discussion, the other two in the group agree, but Anders expresses frustration with how fast the others "make

Figure 9.1
Birthe points to the target card.

Figure 9.2
Close-up of the target card.

decisions." Carla negotiates with Anders about using different, multiple meanings as a central idea that belongs in the center.

During the process of deciding on a collective design idea, the group combines meanings about having multiple perspectives with campaign ideas. After the target card is placed in the physical center of their model, the group ascribes more abstract meanings to the card. The students combine notions of multiple perspectives as being determined by where you stand (concretely, standpoint determines point of view). Their final collective model is explained later as showing the central value of "positioning oneself in the point of view of young people" to look at what sorts of exercise young people enjoy.

Kim faces a common facilitation challenge of guiding a group when tensions hinder the collective idea generation and decision-making processes. Birthe asks him to intervene at a critical point (in phase 4) when the group is struggling to progress from an individual to a collective level. Kim guides them toward playing out their different meanings and ideas in the group. In this way, he pushes the group members to rebuild and clarify their individual ideas. The group slows down and takes a step back. They renegotiate a central, collective idea as a center and later build multiple ideas on boards around their "center."

The case shows the complexity of tensions (including interpersonal ones) that arise in a group situation where different voices and interests meet. The tensions emerge in unforeseen ways in relation to how different students respond to the whole situation. Individuals (such as Andreas) disagree about how the group progresses, and possibly feel pressured to adopt the dominant ideas.

The student group in this case is situated in a new learning situation with unfamiliar people, materials, and methods. As Hee Pedersen (2008) discusses, images and visual methods can help the exploration of plural meanings. Yet such an exploration oscillates between opening up for diverse meanings and closing, constricting and uniting meanings. The oscillation is being "pushed" by the facilitator and the scaffolding, for example, by designing a final phase for a collective idea, which closes down certain voices. The situated tensions, such as the interpersonal tensions and differences between ideas within a group, are in a synergistic relation with all other aspects, including the methods and materials.

Kim facilitates using differences as a way to proceed in the group work by suggesting that they play out differences. In this manner, he scaffolds a return to individual ideas to recollect ideas for the collective idea during the last phase of this design process. The photo case shows how facilitation can support the difficult progression from individual to collective group work by reopening different, dissenting ideas and voices.

3.2 Modeling

The traditions of modeling (and mapping) relate in a commonsense way to design, since illustrating ideas, building physical models, and drawing maps are essential for thinking about design. Modeling involves looking at and selecting information, for instance, which factors to include for understanding bicycle patterns in Copenhagen: the population density, bicycle paths, topography, and so on. Models of all kinds can show affinities, relations, and networks (Eriksen 2009; Møller and Tollestrup 2013). Visual models can be created two- or three-dimensionally, be rough or detailed, concrete or abstract (including mind maps), and can readily be combined with other visual methods.

Modeling can represent different situated factors, whether the relationships involve human or nonhuman actors (objects, places, events, etc.). Models can be used to simulate changes, for instance, visualizing how changes in one part of a system influence the whole. Models can be drawn, sculpted, or visualized with software.

The following case shows modeling with LEGO Serious Play (LSP), a commercial facilitation approach that uses a set of LEGO bricks as modular building material. The case stems from a two-hour session using the LSP method on the given topic idea generation. The situated setup is complex; some aspects are illustrated as rings in figure

9.3. It involved eighteen students (ages 22–50) who attended a master's-level course on research methodology and creativity in communication studies at Roskilde University. The course included critical evaluation of different methods for facilitating creative thinking. The LSP session lasted one afternoon.

The theoretical inspiration for LSP includes cognitive and pragmatic learning theories, as explained in the "open-source manual" (Kristiansen and Rasmussen 2010). LSP was conceived for training staff communication and improving business development and strategy. Creating metaphors through building and sharing is key in the approach, involving processual "spiral" stages comparable to Kolb's reflection cycle. Design researchers, including Eriksen (2009) and Møller and Tollestrup (2013), have conducted design research experiments with LSP and find it useful for harnessing wide-ranging ideas and creating collaborative ideas. The LSP approach has been criticized for highlighting individual creativity and downplaying the social context, including power issues in a group, organization, or institution (Buckingham 2009; Andersen 2009).

The LSP case exemplifies the challenges of facilitating tensions with focus on the way different relations, roles, and materials are enacted in a classroom context. This LSP session included a research purpose that also affects the relations in the classroom. The case demonstrates how tensions are amplified and used pedagogically through a reflexive setup. It highlights facilitating a turbulent creative process and how this is handled (by facilitator and teacher) through reflection. The case also exemplifies how metaphors emerge about one specific idea generation model.

The reflexive setup in the classroom involves me as facilitator of the LSP session. (I am trained and certified as an LSP facilitator.) Six students are volunteer participants (shown in the innermost, first circle in fig. 9.3). The remaining twelve students in the class are assigned roles as observers of the session (the second circle in fig. 9.3). The rest of the rings indicate a few layers of the situatedness around the session. The teacher Christina Hee Pedersen codeveloped the session and led a subsequent meta-reflection round. (The facilitator and teacher are marked "X" in fig. 9.3.)

The LSP session has three iterations of the basic LSP three-phase approach. First, the students build a "bridge" and share stories about their bridge as a warm-up. Second, they build their own idea generation models; the phases of this iteration are explained below.

(1) The challenge (design problem): I ask the students to build an individual model about a good idea generation experience they have had in a group, based on a prior experience.

(2) Building: the students build a model representing ideas and reflections on the topic of idea generation.

(3) Sharing: the students share the meanings of models through the stories that they assign to their own models.

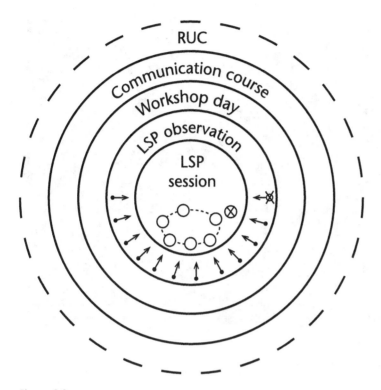

Figure 9.3
The situated setup for the LSP session within the course.

In the third LSP iteration, the students are asked to combine models as a collective "landscape" model. This course setup included an additional meta-reflection round for joint evaluation.

The LSP case demonstrates oscillating tensions (centripetal and centrifugal movements). I highlight the tensions involving two of the six students in the LSP group (Emma and Frida) and their models. Emma is interrupted (by me) while telling a long, rather winding story during the sharing phase about the individual idea generation models. I ask her to "stick with the model" (a common request in LSP). During the meta-reflection round, Christina brings up how she felt tensions emerging while Emma was sharing her individual idea generation model. Emma responds that she did feel interrupted and "wrong." It also becomes apparent that Emma is not well prepared for LSP (e.g., has not read the handouts and was distracted during introductions, although she volunteered as participant). In hindsight, my interruption of Emma creates a centrifugal movement with distance to me as facilitator during the session. The reflexive setup with student observers and teacher amplifies the tensions, but it also aids in creating a forum for reflection and closure.

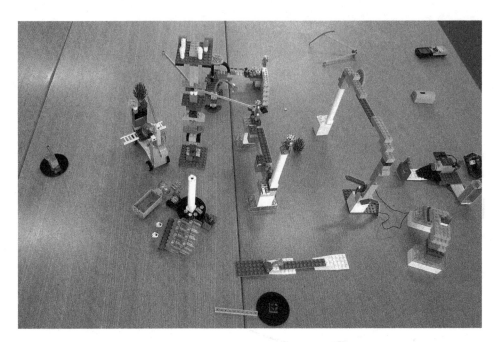

Figure 9.4
LSP landscape with Frida's idea generation model (far left).

A centripetal movement (toward unity, harmony) occurs in relation to the multiple meanings ascribed to Frida's model, which unites the group as they build and share their collective landscape (figs. 9.4 and 9.5). Frida has associated her individual model with "fantasy and fairy tales" and "how communication in words and images in children's literature stimulates the imagination" and "opens a sort of port from reality to fantasy." Others add different meanings to Frida's model when it is in the collective landscape. For instance, Frida's model is described as "hermaphroditic," mutable, simple, and representing "the fantastic flow" of idea generation. Frida's model is also called "a miniature that shows the sum of the whole," referring to the collective landscape, and becomes the "destination of a creative journey." This journey is enacted (with laughter) by flying models above the table, whereby Frida's model is placed as the final destination for idea generation (fig. 9.4).

The LSP case vignette exemplifies how tensions in a group oscillate and become amplified through the reflexive setup used in this session. Several aspects about timing and roles in the session contribute to the tensions. One aspect of timing relates to the short exchanges or dialogues, such as the way I interrupted Emma. Her reaction to being interrupted also seemed to be a reaction to the role of an external, unfamiliar facilitator. Facilitation involves the timekeeper role, which is difficult, since it involves

Figure 9.5
Close-up of Frida's idea generation model.

interrupting and thereby closing down voices. Another aspect of timekeeping is establishing the overall timing and tempo (pace) of a session. Half of the students in the LSP group reported feeling "rushed" through the phases of building and sharing stories. They also said that it took a while to "get used to" the materials and the alternating phases of building and sharing stories.

Facilitation is a continuous learning process, and I certainly learned about being clear and gentle when interrupting. I appreciate the educational value of a meta-reflection round after a session because it opens up for discussion of tensions. It thereby enables reflection on tensions and closure. It was beneficial to coteach with Christina, because she is better able to reflect on the LSP session in her roles as observer and familiar teacher and can leverage her long experience with developing "reflexive setups" (Hee Pedersen 2008).

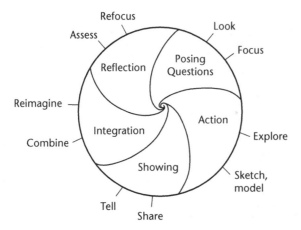

Figure 9.6
The cyclical generic facilitation model PASIR with five stages.

4   Discussion of Facilitation Challenges

This final section discusses facilitation challenges and offers recommendations for a reflexive facilitation approach. The generic facilitation model PASIR collates the processes as stages with reference to the pragmatic and dialogic theoretical approaches and visual methods presented earlier.

4.1   A Generic Facilitation Model

PASIR (fig. 9.6) is an acronym for *posing questions, action (designing), showing, integration, reflection*. The highly simplified cyclical process of idea development in PASIR starts with posing questions and revolves in a clockwise direction.

In correlation to the pragmatic ideas about ongoing cycles of reflection, the five PASIR stages are not linear in practice. Much design literature points out (and the cases in this chapter confirm) that designerly learning processes are often messy and chaotic. The stages are lined up in my description here for the sake of clarity.

An initial facilitation stage in PASIR is to begin by *posing questions*, or deciding on a design-oriented problem in a group. The group gets or chooses a problem or challenge and has to decide on how to look at the problem. The second stage, *action (designing)*, involves the group in generating and exploring the preliminary ideas about the problem through warm-up activities such as selecting photo cards, building models, or sketching to stimulate visual ideas on an individual basis. The third stage is *showing*, storytelling and associating with one another's ideas and sketches. Through presenting ideas and getting feedback, more ideas are generated. The fourth stage is the difficult *integration*, whereby a group explores ideas and thereby tries to combine and reimagine ideas as collective ideas. Some ideas lose, others win, and conflicts often emerge about decision making. Integration activities are often chaotic because they involve prioritizing ideas. The fifth and final stage is *reflection*, which involves reflecting on the emergent meaning-making process and tying the ends toward closure and a design solution. The last stage involves assessing the first stage and the design problem in terms of what was achieved. It can lead to a refocusing and preparation for posing new, different questions and taking another cycle of design actions. Reflection can be extensive, as exemplified in the situated setup for the LSP session.

4.2   Recommendations

This is a final discussion about the complex and contextual practice of facilitation. Four aspects are reviewed and recommended for further reflection by the reader. Despite the risks of making normative claims, I suggest that the four aspects can develop facilitation practice when applying visual methods.

• Consider the *situatedness* of methods when you plan a workshop. What are the possible tensions in the overall context? What are the most relevant methods and materials? Numerous factors can contribute to the tensions and discomforts that may arise in a group as a whole. Discomforts can arise from fears of being evaluated as "wrong," or a lack of clarity about the purpose, emotional reactions, and so on. Be prepared to adjust plans to the situation.

• Fertilize *differences* among group participants. How can facilitation encourage individuals to contribute their different ideas? Facilitation methods (such as LSP) are based on giving equal time and space to each participant in a group. Therefore all participants, all voices (across status), in principle get equal time to share ideas. A facilitator sometimes interrupts to manage time or with an intention to refocus, but doing so can cause tensions. Establishing explicit frames for sharing is helpful. Facilitation is a fine balance between acknowledging different contributions, giving equal time, and progressing toward closure. Fertilizing group differences is fruitful for idea generation, and prospects for embarking on a robust design process can actually be enhanced by working with differences (Simonsen et al. 2010).

• Adapt to *challenges* such as the emergent meanings and tensions in an ethical way. How can fleeting emergent ideas and interpersonal tensions be facilitated? For instance, metaphors shift in the cases: a multiperspectival approach to designing a campaign emerges from the target photo card in the photo case; a hermaphroditic, mutable end destination of the idea generation creative journey emerges from Frida's idea generation model in the LSP case. Adapting to interpersonal tensions is a general challenge for facilitators. As the photo case demonstrates, Kim adapts in situ to help a group progress from static positions, and facilitates their path or quest and helps counteract what Dewey (1910) calls inertia. I recommend acknowledging that the facilitator role includes both "shaking things up" and also being respectful. A primary ethical concern is informing and protecting everyone, including ensuring that workshop participants get a thorough introduction (which contributed to the tensions with Emma).

• Nurture *reflexivity* about your own facilitation practice. How can a reflexive facilitator assemble a repertoire of visual methods? Keeping a learning journal of facilitation efforts is helpful for grounding experience. It is important to explore specific and concrete actions. Thereby we learn from the situated experience. Training reflexivity as a facilitator (and researcher, teacher, etc.) can be boosted through collegial supervision and feedback (such as reflexive setups). Facilitation practice develops through acknowledging our own and others' tensions, comforts, and discomforts. Through nurturing our own facilitation practice, the field evolves, and we are better able to spread the enjoyment of working with creative design processes.

A final recommendation is (1) stay open for tensions in facilitation, (2) dare to explore difficulties and "mistakes" in a learning journal, and (3) nourish your critical reflexivity with colleagues, because collaborative learning generates deeper insights.

Acknowledgments

This chapter is a result of ongoing collaborative teaching and research practice. Colleagues Kim Sandholdt and Christina Hee Pedersen have contributed greatly with inspiring discussions and casework about facilitation. Thanks to participating students. Special thanks to editor Jesper Simonsen.

References

Andersen, Niels Åkerstrøm. 2009. *Power at Play: The Relationships between Play, Work, and Governance*. Basingstoke: Palgrave Macmillan.

Bakhtin, M. M. 1981. *The Dialogic Imagination: Four Essays*. Ed. Michael Holquist. Austin: University of Texas Press.

Banaji, Shakuntala, and Andrew Burn. 2007. Creativity through a rhetorical lens: Implications for schooling, literacy, and media education. *Literacy* 41 (2): 62–70.

Banks, Marcus. 2001. *Visual Methods in Social Research*. London: SAGE.

Brown, Tim. 2008. Design thinking. *Harvard Business Review* 86 (6): 84–92.

Buckingham, D. 2009. Creative visual methods in media research: Possibilities, problems, and proposals. *Media Culture and Society* 31 (4): 633–652.

Carter, Scott and Mankoff, Jennifer. 2005. When participants do the capturing: The role of media in diary studies. Human-Computer Interaction Institute, Carnegie Mellon University. Conference Proceeding Paper 123. http://repository.cmu.edu/hcii/123.

Casakin, Hernan Pablo. 2007. Metaphors in design problem solving: Implications for creativity. *International Journal of Design* 1 (2): 21–33.

Collier, John Jr., and Malcolm Collier. 1986/1996. *Visual Anthropology: Photography as a Research Method*. Albuquerque: University of New Mexico Press.

Coyne, Richard. 2005. Wicked problems revisited. *Design Studies* 26 (1): 5–17.

Coyne, Richard, Adrian Snodgrass, and David Martin. 1994. Metaphors in the design studio. *Journal of Architectural Education* 48 (2): 113–125.

Cross, Nigel. 2007. *Designerly Ways of Knowing*. London: Birkhäuser.

Dewey, John. 1910. *How We Think*. Lexington, MA: D. C. Heath.

Dewey, John. 1923. *Art as Experience*. New York: Capricorn Books.

Dewey, John. 1938. *Experience and Education: Touchstone*. New York: Simon & Schuster.

Dixon, Nancy. 1999. *The Organizational Learning Cycle: How Can We Learn Collectively*. 2nd ed. Aldershot: Gower.

Duarte, Nancy. 2010. *Resonate: Present Visual Stories That Transform Audiences*. Hoboken, NJ: Wiley.

Eriksen, Mette Agger. 2009. Engaging design materials, formats, and framings in specific situated co-designing: A micro-material perspective. In *Nordes 2009: Engaging Artifacts*, 1–10. http://www.nordes.org/opj/index.php/n13/issue/view/9.

Gray, Dave, Sunni Brown, and James Macanufo. 2010. *Gamestorming: A Playbook for Innovators, Rulebreakers, and Changemakers*. Sebastopol, CA: O'Reilly Media.

Harper, Douglas. 2002. Talking about pictures: A case for photo elicitation. *Visual Studies* 17 (1): 13–26.

Hee Pedersen, Christina. 2008. Anchors of meaning—helpers of dialogue: The use of images in production of relations and meaning. *International Journal of Qualitative Studies in Education* 21 (1): 35–47.

Jewitt, Carey, and Theo van Leeuwen, eds. 2001. *The Handbook of Visual Analysis*. London: Sage.

Johnson, Mark. 2007. *The Meaning of the Body: Aesthetics of Human Understanding*. Chicago: University of Chicago Press.

Keats, Patrice A. 2009. Multiple text analysis in narrative research: Visual, written, and spoken stories of experience. *Qualitative Research* 9 (2): 181–195.

Kolb, David A. 1984. *Experiential Learning: Experience as the Source of Learning and Development*. Englewood Cliffs, NJ: Prentice Hall.

Kristiansen, Per, and Robert Rasmussen. 2010. Open-source: Introduction to LEGO Serious Play. http://seriousplaypro.com.

Latour, Bruno. 1990. Visualisation and cognition: Drawing things together. http://www.bruno. latour.fr.

Martin, Roger. 2009. *The Design of Business: Why Design Thinking Is the Next Competitive Advantage.* Boston: Harvard Business Press.

Mitchell, Claudia. 2008. Getting the picture and changing the picture: Visual methodologies and educational research in South Africa. *South African Journal of Education* 28: 365–383.

Moggridge, Bill. 2006. *Designing Interactions.* Cambridge, MA: MIT Press.

Møller, Louise, and Christian Tollestrup. 2013. *Creating Shared Understanding in Product Development Teams: How to "Build the Beginning."* London: Springer.

Phillips, Louise Jane. 2011. *The Promise of Dialogue: The Dialogic Turn in the Production and Communication of Knowledge.* Amsterdam: John Benjamins.

Roam, Dan. 2008. *The Back of the Napkin: Solving Problems and Selling Ideas with Pictures.* New York: Portfolio.

Rose, Gillian. 2011. *Visual Methodologies: An Introduction to Researching with Visual Materials.* 3rd ed. London: Sage.

Salamon, Karen Lisa Goldschmidt. 2006. The business of beauty? Educating tomorrow's designer. In *Cumulus Conference on Future Design and Innovation, 23–25 September 2005*, ed. Yrjö Sotamaa, 34–41. Copenhagen: University of Art and Design Helsinki.

Schön, Donald. 1983. *The Reflective Practitioner: How Professionals Think in Action.* New York: Basic Books.

Simonsen, Jesper, Jørgen Ole Bærenholdt, Monica Büscher, and Jon Damm Scheuer, eds. 2010. *Design Research: Synergies from Interdisciplinary Perspectives.* London: Routledge.

Simonsen, Jesper, and Toni Robertson, eds. 2012. *Routledge International Handbook of Participatory Design.* Abingdon, NY: Routledge (Taylor & Francis).

Tabak, Iris. 2004. Synergy: A complement to emerging patterns of distributed scaffolding. *Journal of the Learning Sciences* 13 (3): 305–335.

10   Urban Co-Creation

Martin Severin Frandsen and Lene Pfeiffer Petersen

What.   Urban Co-creation is a participatory design method for use in urban pedagogy developed by the organization Supertanker. The method consists of a set of guidelines, tools, and techniques through which school pupils can develop and realize an urban design in a collaborative process with inhabitants and organizations in their neighborhood. The use of the method is exemplified in a case study where youths from a disadvantaged neighborhood in the suburbs of Copenhagen designed and co-constructed colorful and imaginative dustbins to handle problems with local littering.

Why.   Becoming an urban citizen and a full participant in urban life requires the development of particular skills and capabilities. The most effective way to develop these skills is through experiential and situated learning where learners participate in real-world activities in the urban environment. Through Urban Co-creation, school pupils learn about the urban environment by being involved in a collaborative process of urban design and construction. The process educates not only the pupils but also their communities, who learn how children and youths can contribute to local problem solving and development.

Where.   The method is intended for use in schools and educational institutions in urban neighborhoods. The most effective learning takes place in situations where the educational activities are linked to real-world practices in the neighborhood, such as community development, local environmental work, or local urban development.

How.   Drawing on an exploration and mapping of local issues, the pupils develop ideas and problem solutions, which are presented and publicized at a local exhibition. The best ideas are further developed into small-scale prototypes, and one or more prototypes are realized in 1:1. The realized designs are celebrated at an inauguration followed by an evaluation of their use and functionality when put into practice.

1   Introduction

This chapter illustrates how participatory design methods can be used to educate and empower urban inhabitants. In recent years on an international level we have seen a growing interest in the power of design and art as tools to improve participation and civic engagement of children, youths, and adults alike. Renewed practices and theories of urban pedagogy are taking form through collaborations between designers, architects, artists, community activists, and academic researchers working across traditional disciplinary boundaries. Uniting the different practitioners of urban pedagogy is a commitment to empowering others through educational programs focused on equipping people with the tools and awareness to allow them to take on urban issues themselves. Participatory design as a form of urban pedagogy is thus concerned with developing the skills and capabilities required in participating in the design and production of the urban environment.

In section 2, we introduce the field of urban pedagogy by tracing its historical roots and highlighting some contemporary examples. We pay particular attention to how a new generation of urban educators is using design methods as pedagogical tools and to how urban pedagogy is practiced as a form of experiential education and situated learning. Section 3 exemplifies the use of Urban Co-creation, the design method we present in this chapter. Through a case study from a disadvantaged neighborhood in the suburbs of Copenhagen, we explore in more detail the potentials of using design methods in urban pedagogy. The case study tells the story of a design process led by the group Supertanker, where youths from a local school designed and constructed colorful and imaginative dustbins to handle problems with local littering. The project succeeded in creating an increased local awareness of waste management and reducing the amount of litter in the neighborhood. The most important but less tangible product of the design process was, however, the skills and capabilities acquired by the youths, and the mutual learning produced between all the involved participants in the local community.

In section 4, we present the Urban Co-creation method in general terms and introduce the overall guidelines, the specific phases in the design process, and the tools and techniques that can be used. To conclude, we show a figure that in visual form captures the main ingredients of the presented design method, and we sum up the main potentials of using design methods in urban pedagogy exemplified in the chapter.

2   Urban Pedagogy

Urban pedagogy can be defined as the educational practice concerned with equipping people for life in an urban environment. Echoing a long heritage in urban sociology,

Stephen Dobson argues that to live in an urban environment requires the development of particular intellectual, social, and bodily skills (Dobson 2006, 100). One must learn to live in the midst of strangers, to adapt to quickly shifting situations and new environments, and to work together with unfamiliar others to solve problems and create change.

Practitioners of urban pedagogy often start from the premise that these things are best learned from experience and through practical involvement in the social activities that shape the urban environment. In contrast to more traditional forms of education, a key characteristic in urban pedagogy is that the educational efforts move from the institutional setting of the school to the public life of the street and the community.

Pedagogy is moved from the formal, institutionalized space of the classroom with fixed and stable teacher-pupil roles to the street and the community expressed in the life of the street, where many other shifting significant others can be figures of identification and the source of mimetic inspiration. (Dobson 2006, 103)

Educational activities that take place in the urban environment can take many different forms. Typically urban pedagogy combines explorations and field trips into the urban environment with practical involvement and participation in local urban design and community planning projects.

2.1 Historical Roots

Although the concept may be new, the practice of an early form of urban pedagogy can be traced back to the educational experiments in the Hull House settlement in Chicago that was founded in 1889 by Jane Addams and Ellen Gates Starr. Located in an immigrant neighborhood in the Near West Side, Hull House was a center for civic and community life. The residents in the social settlement, mostly women with a middle-class background who chose to live among the urban poor, engaged in a wide range of philanthropic and educational activities and worked to investigate and improve the conditions in the industrial districts of Chicago. An important part of the educational activities of Hull House was helping the recently arrived immigrants—Bohemians, Italians, Poles, Russians, Greeks, and Arabs, mostly with a peasant background—to adjust to the unfamiliar surroundings and life of a large city (Addams 2002).

In her recollections of her first twenty years in Hull House, Jane Addams recalls how the residents of the settlement were overwhelmed by how isolated many of the immigrants were. She recalls how an Italian woman was surprised when she saw red roses at one of the receptions at Hull House. The woman, who had lived in Chicago for six years, would not for an instant believe that the roses had been grown in America, and believed that they must have been brought fresh all the way from Italy.

During all that time, of course, the woman had lived within ten blocks of a florist's window; she had not been more than a five-cent car ride away from the public parks; but she had never dreamed of faring forth for herself, and no one had taken her. Her conception of America had been the untidy street in which she lived and had made her long struggle to adapt herself to American ways. (Addams 1911, 110–111)

A key issue for urban pedagogy, the isolation of urban inhabitants in segregated enclaves of the city and the need to develop their knowledge and capabilities as users of the larger urban area surrounding them, was thus already being addressed in the early settlement work at Hull House.

Another important element in urban pedagogy that can be traced back to the social settlements was, in Dobson's words, the ability "to identify, understand and interpret urban experiences" (Dobson 2006, 100). An important part of the educational efforts undertaken by the residents at Hull House was the cultivation of what the sociologist C. W. Mills has termed the "sociological imagination" (Mills 1959/2000). Cultivating a sociological imagination meant developing the ability to perceive how the personal and local troubles that the newfound urban inhabitants experienced in their neighborhood in the Near West Side of Chicago related to the larger public issues of the city of Chicago as a whole. As an example, Addams mentions how the inhabitants learned that a local problem with unpaved streets was related to the larger politics of the city, and the issue had to be addressed at that level.

A settlement constantly endeavors to make its neighborhood realize that it belongs to the city as a whole, and can only improve as the city improves. We, at Hull House, have undertaken to pave the streets of our ward only to find that we must agitate for an ordinance, that repaving shall be done from a general fund before we can hope to have our streets properly paved. (Addams, 1899, 52)

Some of the first efforts at developing, through educational activities, a kind of urban citizenship similar to what the French urban philosopher Henri Lefebvre would later advocate for as "the right to the city" were thus already undertaken in the early days of the American settlement movement.

The right to the city ... should modify, concretize and make more practical the rights of the citizen as an urban dweller (*citadin*) and user of multiple services. It would affirm, on the one hand, the right of the users to make known their ideas on the space and time of their activities in the urban area; it would also cover the right to the use of the centre, a privileged place, instead of being stuck and dispersed into ghettos (for workers, immigrants, the "marginal" and even for the "privileged"). (Lefebvre, cited in Kofman and Lebas 1996, 34)

2.2 Design Methods in Urban Pedagogy

Moving forward to present times, in recent decades we have seen a revitalization of urban pedagogy on an international level as a new generation of educators and activists have taken urban pedagogy to new places and in new directions. A characteristic feature of the renewed urban pedagogy is that it is practiced in transdisciplinary collaborations between artists, architects, designers, community organizers, and academic researchers, often based in independent civil society organizations outside formal educational institutions. Many of these contemporary practitioners of urban pedagogy use participatory design methods as part of their pedagogical methodology and integrate them in creative ways with practices developed in other disciplines. Design methods can, for example, be combined with the psychogeography invented by the situationist art movement, relational or social art practices, ethnographic methods from the social sciences, or organizing methods from community development (Bourriaud 2002; DiSalvo et al. 2008; Pinder 2008; Awan, Schneider, and Till 2011).

A prominent example is the Center for Urban Pedagogy (CUP), a nonprofit organization based in Brooklyn, New York. Their work consists of using design methods and artistic practices to create awareness and engagement in the city. They believe that greater understanding of "how the city works" plays a vital role in engaging citizens in issues in their community. CUP's projects are always based on the lived experiences of the people of the city. CUP works with local students and community groups in investigating the city through simple and somewhat naive questions that arise when using the city, for example: Where does the electricity come from? Why are there no supermarkets in inner New York? Where is the federal government? The results of the research are then conveyed via design and art methods into understandable, illustrative, and fun materials such as maps, newspapers, videos, and so on, that can be used to educate other members of the community. The following two examples illustrate CUP's methodology and use of design.

Bodegas Down Bronx: In trying to understand the system of grocery sales in their local community, young people from a high school in the Bronx investigate the widespread phenomena of local grocery shops called *bodegas*. The bodegas are small businesses selling mainly snacks, alcohol, cigarettes, and a limited grocery selection. The shops are vital to the supply of groceries in the Bronx and are an integral part of the everyday life of the area and of the students involved. CUP and the students head out to explore why their area holds so many bodegas and no supermarkets. They interview their local bodega owners, market analysts, and experts and learn about supply chains and market strategies. They examine the bodegas' product range and consumer habits and the consequences of the grocery structure of the Bronx on public health. Afterward CUP and the students use design methods to create a fun and educational folder that conveys the knowledge and understanding the students have acquired about their local urban area (CUP 2013a).

The Internet Is Serious Business: The Internet Is Serious Business is a project that strives to understand how the Internet works and is distributed in New York City. Young people from a local high school and CUP set out to the city to investigate the issue, asking questions such as: How does the Internet work? Why is the Internet so slow? Who owns the Internet? These questions come from the students themselves based on their own experience of using the Internet. They interview experts and large and small suppliers and have a firsthand look at the large wire network under the city. The whole process is documented and afterward presented in an educational video that tells the story of the Internet though the eyes of an alien from outer space. The straightforward narration of the video and the simple illustrations help create awareness of complex issues of ownership, politics, and regulation in a legible and fun way (CUP 2013b).

Other contemporary examples of urban pedagogy from around the world are Asiye eTafuleni in South Africa, Arif Hassan in Pakistan, Ankur in India, and Supertanker in Copenhagen, Denmark, to which we will return in the case study. Uniting all these cases is the decision "to invest agency in empowering others through various educational programs focused on equipping people with the tools and awareness to allow them to take on spatial issues themselves" (Awan, Schneider, and Till 2011, 48).

2.3 Experiential Education and Situated Learning

Practitioners of urban pedagogy draw mainly on the two pedagogical traditions and methodologies of experiential education and critical pedagogy (Dobson 2006, 102–103; Awan, Schneider, and Till 2011, 45–48). Common to both methodologies is a concern with "the preparation of individuals to participate in a democratic society" and the development of "critical thinking, self-motivated, problem-solving individuals who participate actively in their communities" (Itin 1999, 94).

Proponents of experiential education mostly refer to the pragmatist philosopher John Dewey as the founder of this tradition (Itin 1999; Illeris 2010). Dewey conceived of experience as a transaction between an individual or a group of individuals and their physical and social environment. Experience is the process where we act on our surroundings and undergo the consequences of our actions.

On the active hand, experience is *trying*—a meaning which is made explicit in the connected term experiment. On the passive, it is *undergoing*. When we experience something we act upon it, we do something with it; then we suffer or undergo the consequences. (Dewey 1966, 139)

Practitioners of experiential education thus start from the premise that the most effective way, and possibly the only way, to learn about something is by trying to change it. We learn when we discover the relation between what we do and what happens in consequence.

To "learn from experience" is to make a backward and forward connection between what we do to things and what we enjoy or suffer from things in consequence. Under such conditions, doing becomes a trying; an experiment with the world to find out what it is like; the undergoing becomes instruction—discovery of the connection of things. (Dewey 1966, 140)

Urban pedagogy as experiential education is thus a learning process that takes place through interactions and transactions with the urban environment. Pupils learn about the urban environment by trying to change it. Hence when pupils are involved in real-world design projects in the urban environment, it becomes an experiment with the city to find out what it is like—or, to use the phrase of CUP, to find out "how the city works."

As Itin points out, however, the transactions taking place in experiential education are not only those between the pupils and, in this case, the urban environment but also those between teacher and student. Not only the students but also the teacher learns something from the process.

In a transactive model, the teacher brings information to the process, but so does the student. Teachers and students not only interact, but they exchange knowledge. Students learn from teachers, and teachers learn from students. (Itin 1999, 95)

Moreover, a characteristic feature of urban pedagogy is that it is not always entirely clear who are the educators and who are the students. As Dobson remarks, the answers to the questions "who does the educating in an urban pedagogy?" and "who are the pupils in such a pedagogy?" are not necessarily obvious (Dobson 2006, 110). When pedagogy is moved from the classroom with fixed and stable teacher-pupil roles to the street and the community, many others can assume the role of educators: local residents who convey their experiences from their life in the community, practitioners in local community development organizations, people in local businesses and local institutions, and so forth.

In such cases, the learning that takes places in urban pedagogy becomes situated in a double sense. It is not only situated in the urban environment but also situated in what Jean Lave and Etienne Wenger would term local communities of practice. Like proponents of experiential education, Lave and Wenger question the belief that effective learning can occur in institutions such as many schools that are separated from real-world social practice. In their theory of situated learning, they instead argue that successful learning takes place through what they term legitimate peripheral participation in communities of practice. As a legitimate peripheral participant, the learner performs parts of the real-world activities of the community of practice and moves from initially simple to more complex tasks through observing and learning from the more skilled participants. For Lave and Wenger, legitimate peripheral participation is thus akin to apprenticeship (Lave and Wenger 1991).

As we have mentioned, in urban pedagogy it is not entirely obvious who are the educators or who are the pupils—or, in the terms of Lave and Wenger, who are the apprentices and who are the skilled participants. In some cases, the pupils themselves can become teachers or local experts as they convey their experiences and the results of their investigations to other members of the community, as illustrated in the CUP examples. Furthermore, when children and youths are involved in collaborative and real-world design processes in their communities, the outcome of the process is sometimes not only the situated learning of the pupils. It can also be an educative process for the community, whose members can learn how children and youths can contribute to local problem solving and development.

To explore in more detail the learning potentials in involving children and youths in collaborative local urban design processes, the next section presents a case study from a disadvantaged neighborhood in the suburbs of Copenhagen.

3   From "Troublemakers" to Problem Solvers

We now turn to a case study of urban pedagogy to more fully illustrate how design methods can be used in an educational urban context. The case tells a story of how youths from a local school designed and constructed colorful and imaginative dustbins to handle problems with local littering. The project succeeded in creating an increased local awareness of waste management and reducing the amount of litter in the neighborhood. An equally important but less tangible by-product of the design process was the skills and capabilities acquired by the participating youths and the social learning and change in social relations it produced in the neighborhood. By giving young people the opportunity to work as designers, the process contributed to a shift from the image of the youths as "troublemakers" to a positive image of collaborative problem solvers. The case study is based on interviews with the designer Anders Hagedorn, ethnographic field observations, and documentation from the community development project.

3.1   A Disadvantaged Neighborhood

The neighborhood of Charlotteager is located in the former industrial town of Hedehusene, today mostly a residential suburb to Copenhagen. Charlotteager consists of three nonprofit housing associations that were built in three successive stages from the early 1970s to the mid-1980s. In 2007 a new five-year experimental community development project was undertaken in the neighborhood. Having recently had only modest success in engaging a broader spectrum of local residents, and here in particular local youths, in the development of the community, the lead partners behind the new project wanted to try out a more asset-based and participatory approach. The project was initially a partnership between the three housing associations and the municipality of Høje-Taastrup. To introduce and test new participatory methods, Supertanker, an interdisciplinary group of urbanists based in Copenhagen (Brandt, Frandsen, and Larsen 2008), was subsequently brought in. For Supertanker, the new community development project was an opportunity to test ideas of using design processes as catalysts for social interaction and change.

From the interdisciplinary Supertanker group, the designer Anders Hagedorn, together with the artist Martin Rosenkreutz Madsen, were put in charge of the effort to engage the local youths in the development of the neighborhood. Through his daily work in Charlotteager, Hagedorn learned that many local youths were viewed as "troublemakers" who did not contribute positively to the community. This view included a broad group of young people, most of whom were not guilty of anything but minor incivilities and occasionally noisy behavior. For Hagedorn, it was thus crucial that the effort to engage the local youths would address and work with some of the perceptions in the neighborhood that cast many of the adolescents in a bad light. As he had already learned, and as would become more obvious as the collaboration with the local youths progressed, the youths were often just as worried about the issues of the community as were the other older residents.

3.2 Designing Dustbins

The educational design project was organized in close collaboration with the local public school, as well as the local youth club. The design process started in February 2009 and ran for approximately three months. It was organized as an integrated part of the curriculum of a class of eighth-grade pupils.

The first stage consisted in mapping and identifying the issues and development potentials in the neighborhood as seen from the perspective of the pupils (fig. 10.1). After the mapping, the pupils brainstormed and developed a range of ideas and suggestions for solutions to the identified problems, which were visualized and further elaborated in sketches (fig. 10.1).

The results of the mapping and development of ideas were presented at the school in an exhibition open to all residents in Charlotteager (fig. 10.1). On the basis of the feedback and response to the exhibited ideas, two projects were chosen for realization. One of the ideas was to design and produce new dustbins to handle a problem with littering in the neighborhood. This idea was chosen because it both was feasible and could help solve a problem that concerned the entire neighborhood and not just the youths themselves.

To create as much possible ownership and at the same time the highest learning outcome, it was essential for Hagedorn that the pupils were involved in all the stages of the design process from idea to construction. After the exhibition, the different design ideas were further elaborated, first in sketches and later in small-scale prototypes in the form of cardboard models (fig. 10.1). A fundamental design idea was to create some spectacular and creative designs that could bring a playful element to the use of dustbins.

With the small-scale prototypes, the basic designs of the dustbins were ready, and the production stage could begin. This meant that the design process was now taken outside the school and neighborhood setting. To begin with, Hagedorn took the

Figure 10.1
Mapping, developing ideas, exhibiting, and prototyping. Photos: Anders Hagedorn and Farokh
Berenjgani. Collage: Henrique Figueira.

students to a junkyard, where they found old barrels and other metal waste that could be reused as material for dustbins (fig. 10.2). Then the process continued at a production school in the nearby town of Roskilde, where the pupils learned to forge dustbins out of the found recycled objects (fig. 10.2). Back at the school and in the neighborhood, the dustbins were then painted and decorated with stencils.

During the production stage, the group of individuals and organizations involved in the participatory process gradually expanded. To help the pupils forge the bins, the group enlisted the services of a local blacksmith, who would become a permanent collaborator in the community development project. The same thing happened with a teacher from the production school who later became involved in several other activities in the neighborhood.

In addition to the eighth-grade class, other youths from the neighborhood also became involved. The sketches and small models of the bins were exhibited at the local youth club, and members of the club contributed by spray painting and making stencils to decorate the bins (fig. 10.2). Furthermore, in a more random manner and outside the auspices of school and club, several other children and youths who happened to pass by while the bins were being decorated and installed in the neighborhood were invited to participate. For Hagedorn, an important element in the process was the methodological rule that everyone who showed an interest and wanted to participate could become part of the process. With this openness, the design and production process was able to include and give many groups from the neighborhood a share in the project.

In addition to the neighborhood children and youths, the design process also involved the caretakers and tenant boards of the housing associations. Collaboration with the caretakers was important because they were the ones responsible for emptying the dustbins once they were put into service. The caretakers' feedback about the functionality and the location of the dustbins was therefore needed. The question of the maintenance and location of the dustbins was also discussed at a meeting between the pupils and the tenant boards, who had the formal role of approving and supporting the project financially. The design process thus provided an occasion for the youths to become acquainted with and learn about the tenant democracy in the housing associations where they lived, and for the board to see the youths acting in a new and unaccustomed situation.

Furthermore, the broad local ownership of the dustbin project was promoted because the whole process was continually documented and communicated by the local newspaper and on the housing associations' own TV channel, where residents could view short films on the process and continuously keep themselves informed about the ongoing work. Residents who did not participate directly in the project could thus have the story of the dustbin design process conveyed, and get a positive image of the youths as people who were concerned with waste problems and contributed positively to resolving them.

Figure 10.2
Co-constructing, inaugurating, and testing. Photos: Anders Hagedorn and Farokh Berenjgani. Collage: Henrique Figueira.

Finally, an additional element that contributed to community ownership was the inauguration of the dustbins. In addition to a large group of pupils from different classes and age groups in the school, teachers, parents, residents, youth club workers, representatives from the tenant boards, caretakers, children and nursery nurses from local day care institutions, active citizens in Hedehusene, and the local press participated (fig. 10.2). The inauguration thus also helped convey a positive image of the local youths and at the same time an image of a community cooperating in solving problems.

3.3   Products of the Design Process

Looking back and reflecting on the design process, Supertanker learned an important lesson that the essential thing was not so much the specific product the design process created but the changes the process triggered in the neighborhood. One of the by-products of the process was the creation of a range of new and collaborative social relations in the local area that were to endure for the remaining three years of the community development project. Another by-product was the knowledge on design processes and democratic collaboration the project created among the youths. In this process, both the youths' own sense of self and the surrounding community's image of them changed. Part of the learning process consisted in the pupils being allowed to try out new and unfamiliar situations that might challenge their perception of their abilities and skills. The project was an opportunity for students to experience themselves in new situations and challenge their own, but also their teachers', perceptions of their abilities and talents.

To sum up, the overall picture of the design process shows that it created, besides the concrete rubbish bins, a range of new and enduring social relations of collaboration in the neighborhood and extending to the surrounding towns. In addition, the project produced new experiences and changed self-perceptions among the participating youths, fostering a more positive outward image. The process also generally spawned an increased awareness of waste management in the area, and the caretakers reported less littering in a subsequent period. Finally, the project created and communicated a story of the local neighborhood as a collaborative community.

4   Urban Co-Creation

Now we present the Urban Co-creation method exemplified in the case study in more general terms. The method has been developed by Supertanker (including Frandsen, one of the coauthors of this chapter) on the basis of a number of experimentations and collaborations with schools in the Copenhagen region. In short, Urban Co-creation is a participatory design method where local school pupils develop and realize an urban design together with inhabitants and organizations in their neighborhood.

University students who are interested in learning how to create participatory urban design projects with children and youths can use the method to find inspiration on how to conduct their own experiments with urban pedagogy. As going through all the phases of the design process in the case study took about three months, we recommend that university students consider focusing on two or three of the phases in the design process, depending on the situation at hand. In the following, we present the overall guidelines for the method, the specific phases in the design process, and some of the tools and techniques that can be used in the different phases.

Following Dewey, we understand methods as working hypotheses, guiding ideas, or plans of action that "are formed in one situation and are then transferred as 'programmes of behavior' to other situations as tools of reflection, analysis and anticipation" (Miettinen 2000, 69). As Bratteteig et al. (2012) point out, a method must always be tailored and adapted to the unique problematic situation one is confronting. Also following Bratteteig et al., we distinguish between methods as general guidelines for how to carry out the design process and tools and techniques as the more specific instruments and "ways of doing" that can be applied in the design process (118–119).

Another important feature of methods in participatory design is, as Simonsen and Robertson points out, that "what is being designed is both the technological product or artifact and the process that enables different participants to engage in designing this product" (Simonsen and Robertson 2012, 8–9). Participatory design thus has "a strong focus on the 'how' of designing, i.e., a focus on the process of designing and the particular participatory practices that different processes can enable." Consequently participatory design includes tools and techniques "that enable the participants in the design process to propose, represent, interrogate and reflect on different aspects of the developing design continually throughout that process" (9).

4.1 Overall Guidelines

The overall purpose of using the Urban Co-creation method is to create and facilitate an experiential and situated learning process for schoolchildren and youths where they develop new skills and learn about the urban environment through trying to change it. The most effective learning takes place when the pupils work to solve real-life problems in their neighborhoods and cities in collaboration with local residents and organizations.

To motivate and engage the interest of the pupils, the starting point for the design process should be the experiences and problematic situations that the pupils are familiar with from their own everyday life in the neighborhood, as in the cases discussed earlier: problems with maintaining and cleaning streets and public space, difficulties with finding and accessing shops and stores, a slow Internet connection in the neighborhood, and so forth. Furthermore, an important initial task is to identify the local residents, organizations, businesses, and institutions that are affected by, and have an interest in, the chosen problem or possess knowledge, skills, or resources that can be useful in the design process.

4.2   Phases, Tools, and Techniques

After an initial phase of preparation, the method takes the pupils through six phases or steps. Drawing on an exploration and mapping of local issues and opportunities, the pupils develop ideas and problem solutions, which are presented and publicized at a local exhibition. The best ideas are further developed into small-scale prototypes, and one or more prototypes are realized in 1:1 in collaboration with local residents and organizations. The realized designs are celebrated at an inauguration followed by an evaluation of their use and functionality when put into practice. A variety of tools and techniques, such as mapping, sketching, development of ideas, prototyping, and so on, can be applied in the different stages and steps of the design process.

Exploring and mapping. In the first phase of the design process, the pupils set out to explore and investigate the problem and area at hand, using techniques such as observing, taking notes, photographing, and interviewing. The information gathered through these explorations is used to create maps that give an overview of the situation of an area as it is seen from different perspectives. Mapping is thus used to gather information about both pupils' own experiences of living in an area and the experiences of others. At the same time, mapping an area is also a way of pointing out the challenges or problems of a place and therefore the starting point for identifying possible ways of improvement and generating ideas and problem solutions. In that way, mapping is a tool that can help foster relevant ideas for development that are based on the actual context of an area and not detached from the genuine circumstances (Wates 2000, 76–77).

Developing ideas. The purpose of the second phase is to develop ideas based on the knowledge and understanding of the problem or area in question produced through the first phase. In this phase, techniques like brainstorming and sketching are used to stimulate imagination, to explore ideas and visions, and to communicate them in an accessible and nontechnical language. Sketching is used as a way of concretizing ideas and thoughts by turning them into visualizations. In this way, thoughts get tangible form and expression and make it possible for people involved in the process to visualize possible end results. Sketching, however, mostly functions as a means to open up and create ideas rather than a way to develop exact solutions (Brandt, Binder, and Sanders 2012, 164–170; Bratteteig et al. 2012, 128–131).

Exhibiting and selecting ideas. In the third phase, the developed ideas and sketches are put on public display at an exhibition. The exhibition serves as a tool to create awareness about the project or design process. The exhibition also functions as a form of evaluation and thereby helps develop the ideas further by involving other parties and listening to their views. Letting people vote about which ideas they prefer is used as a tool for choosing which ideas to realize and to create local legitimacy and ownership. Exhibiting ideas also requires the ideas to be presented in an educational and illustrative way, forcing participants and designers to concretize and focus the information (Wates 2000, 70–73).

Prototyping and co-constructing. In the fourth phase, the ideas and problem solutions are given physical shape and materialized into first prototypes before being realized through co-construction. Prototyping serves different means. First, it can be seen as a way of testing a product in small scale and giving room for adjustments before constructing the final product. Prototyping is a way of considering different proposals for design solution in relation to their consequences and other proposed solutions. Second, with a prototype it becomes easier for the parties involved to understand and consider the consequences of one or more design proposals and problem solutions. Prototypes are therefore a way of concretizing and embodying nonfigurative ideas and discussions. Furthermore, having a tangible artifact makes collective exploration possible and assists further in creating a common language for different parties in the process.

Next, the construction of the final product is a good opportunity to involve new local residents and organizations and to explore the local area anew. Finding materials and facilities for construction can be a vehicle for learning about the physical infrastructure of the city and for exploring the city as a space of production. Having pupils and local residents construct actual objects in collaboration is at the same time a way of creating a space for building new relations and creating mutual learning through sharing a concrete experience of corealization (Brandt, Binder, and Sanders 2012, 155; Bratteteig et al. 2012, 133).

Inaugurating and publicizing. The fifth phase is the celebration of the finished product in the form of a public ritual. An inauguration functions as a social ritual that, through a mutual celebration of human achievement, enforces and strengthens the social relations that have been created in the collaborative process. The public inauguration, combined with publicity in local newspapers and other media, at the same time creates further awareness of the issue or problem in question, thereby more or less temporarily bringing a public into being (Marres 2005).

Testing and evaluating. The sixth and final phase in the design and learning process is the testing and evaluation of the functionality of the finished urban design and the problem solution once put into practice. As urban design products and artifacts are intended for use in a public space as public goods, the testing and evaluation of an urban design thus involves the involvement and the engagement of a larger public of users to decide whether a problem or an issue has been dealt with successfully. The most important part of the evaluation, however, concerns the learning outcome produced by the process. This can be explored through collective and retrospective reflection among the pupils and through interviews with other participants in the design process.

5   Conclusion

In this chapter, we have explored the potentials of using participatory design methods in urban pedagogy through illustrative examples and a more detailed case study. We have presented a method intended for use in schools and educational institutions in urban neighborhoods where school pupils learn about the urban environment by being involved in a collaborative process of urban design and co-construction together with local residents and organizations. The primary purpose of the method is to empower and educate children and youths through an experiential and situated learning process. However, when used effectively, the method educates not only the pupils but also their communities, who learn how children and youths can contribute to local problem solving and development.

The six phases in the Urban Co-creation method are illustrated in figure 10.3. Although the design process follows a logical progression and succession of steps, note that the phases cannot be absolutely distinguished from each other and overlap in many ways. Spontaneous ideas and suggestions for problem solutions often arise

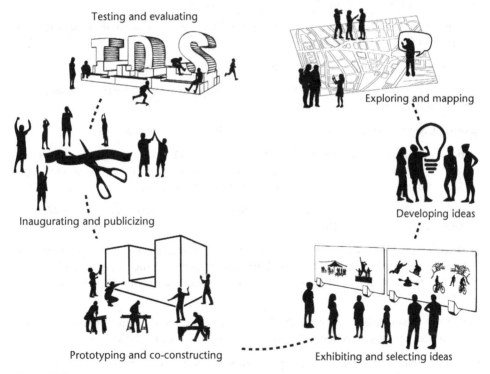

Figure 10.3
The six phases of the Urban Co-creation method. Illustrations: Henrique Figueira.

during the phase of exploring and mapping, but they are not explored systematically in this phase. Early prototypes are sometimes already made in the phase of idea development, but again they are not systematically developed before the prototyping phase. Furthermore, the phases in the design process are to a different degree situated in the urban environment and in local communities of practice. Idea development may, for example, take place entirely inside the classroom. Meanwhile the phases of exploring and mapping and of prototyping and co-construction will typically alternate between workshop sessions in the classroom and situated activities such as explorations of the urban environment and on-site collaborations with local residents and organizations. The purpose of the classroom workshop sessions is to allow the pupils to reflect on their urban experiences, to develop new ideas and problem solutions, and to prepare for new explorations and activities outside the school premises.

References

Addams, Jane. [1893] 2002. The objective value of a social settlement. In *The Jane Addams Reader*, ed. Jean Bethke Elshtain, 29–45. New York: Basic Books.

Addams, Jane. 1899. A function of the social settlement. *Annals of the American Academy of Political and Social Science* 13: 33–55.

Addams, Jane. 1911. *Twenty Years at Hull-House*. New York: Macmillan.

Awan, Nishat, Tatjana Schneider, and Jeremy Till. 2011. *Spatial Agency: Other Ways of Doing Architecture*. New York: Routledge.

Bourriaud, Nicolas. 2002. *Relational Aesthetics*. Dijon, France: Les Presses du Réel.

Brandt, Eva, Thomas Binder, and Elisabeth B.-N. Sanders. 2012. Tools and techniques: Ways to engage telling, making, and enacting. In *Routledge International Handbook of Participatory Design*, ed. Jesper Simonsen and Toni Robertson, 145–181. New York: Routledge.

Brandt, J., M. Frandsen, and J. L. Larsen. 2008. Supertanker: In search of urbanity. *Architectural Research Quarterly* 12 (2): 173–181.

Bratteteig, Tone, Keld Bødker, Yvonne Dittrich, Preben Holst Jørgensen, and Jesper Simonsen. 2012. Methods: Organizing principles and general guidelines for participatory design. In *Handbook of Participatory Design*, ed. Jesper Simonsen and Toni Robertson, 117–144. New York: Routledge.

Center for Urban Pedagogy (CUP). 2013a. Bodega Down Bronx. http://welcometocup.org/Projects/UrbanInvestigations/BodegaDownBronx (accessed August 13, 2013).

Center for Urban Pedagogy (CUP). 2013b. The Internet is serious business. http://welcometocup.org/Projects/UrbanInvestigations/TheInternetIsSeriousBusiness (accessed August 13, 2013).

Dewey, John. 1966. *Democracy and Education: An Introduction to the Philosophy of Education*. New York: Free Press.

DiSalvo, Carl, Illah Nourbakhsh, David Holstius, Ayca Akin, and Marti Louw. 2008. The Neighborhood Networks projects: A case study of critical engagement and creative expression though participatory design. In *Proceedings of the Tenth Anniversary Conference on Participatory Design*, ed. Jesper Simonsen, Toni Robinson, and David Hakken, 41–50. Indianapolis: Indiana University Press.

Dobson, Stephen. 2006. Urban pedagogy: A proposal for the twenty-first century. *London Review of Education* 4 (2): 99–114.

Illeris, Knud. 2010. Erfaringspædagogik og projektarbejde. In *Pædagogiske teorier*, 4th ed., ed. Niels Jørgen Bisgaard and Jens Rasmussen, 148–166. Værløse: Billesø and Baltzer.

Itin, Christian M. 1999. Reasserting the philosophy of experiential education as a vehicle for change in the 21st century. *Journal of Experiential Education* 22 (2): 91–98.

Kofman, Eleonore, and Elizabeth Lebas. 1996. Lost in transposition: Time, space, and the city. In *Writings on Cities*, by Henri Lefebvre, trans. and ed. Eleonore Kofman and Elizabeth Lebas, 3–60. Oxford: Blackwell.

Lave, Jean, and Etienne Wenger. 1991. *Situated Learning: Legitimate Peripheral Participation*. Cambridge: Cambridge University Press.

Marres, Noortje. 2005. Issues spark a public into being: A key but often forgotten point of the Lippman-Dewey debate. In *Makings Things Public: Atmospheres of Democracy*, ed. Bruno Latour and Peter Weibel, 208–217. Cambridge, MA: MIT Press.

Miettinen, Reijo. 2000. The concept of experiential learning and John Dewey's theory of reflective thought and action. *International Journal of Lifelong Education* 19 (1): 54–72.

Mills, C. Wright. 1959/2000. *The Sociological Imagination*, 40th anniv. ed. New York: Oxford University Press.

Pinder, David. 2008. Interventions: Art, politics, and pedagogy. *International Journal of Urban and Regional Research* 32 (3): 730–736.

Simonsen, Jesper, and Toni Robertson, eds. 2012. *Routledge International Handbook of Participatory Design*. New York: Routledge.

Wates, Nick. 2000. *The Community Planning Handbook: How People Can Shape Their Cities, Towns, and Villages in Any Part of the World*. London: Earthscan.

III Methods for Aesthetic Experiences

11 Emergent Urban Spaces

Kristine Samson

What. This chapter reconsiders the role of the designer as a singular mastermind by sketching out a design method on how to work with the existing urban environment at hand. Departing from an aesthetic materialism and a participatory approach, the chapter proposes a situated method for spatial urban design. In recent culture-led practices of spatial design, the designers do not only seek to create aesthetic experiences based on their own ideas. Rather, they design urban spaces with a situated, collective, and aesthetic approach in the way users and existing resources are engaged. These design practices illustrate how aesthetic judgment is not reduced to the skill of an artistic mastermind alone; rather, it must be understood as a dispersed, participatory process unfolded in the context of the urban space intended for transformation.

Why. While many European and Western societies call for a rethinking of urban design, culture-led urban transformation and temporary spaces have become more frequent. By arguing that master planning and the universality of design must be modified to accommodate social, economic, and cultural challenges in the city, this chapter suggests that the discipline of durable architecture and design can learn from the informal, temporal, and situated approaches in recent spatial design.

Where. The methods presented here will be applicable to urban design, event design, experience design, spatial design, place making, participatory planning, and temporary spaces such as concert venues, art exhibitions in public spaces, and festival design. Situated spatial methods might potentially be applicable in the discipline of architecture.

How. As situated spatial design practices often tend to integrate potential users in the design process, the three cases will focus on how to involve users and engaging with the urban environment by means of aesthetic spatial experimentation. The three cases will serve as inspiration for developing five principles for assembling urban spaces as a situated design practice.

1   Introduction

Designing a public space has increasingly become a complex act involving citizens, users, stakeholders, and commercial interests. Whereas urban design traditionally belonged to the discipline of designers and architects alone, today we witness a diverse range of cultural activists, planners, artists, and nonprofessionals who redesign and re-create urban environments. Today the found city, opportunistic tactics, and the emergent and participatory process of the everyday are being broadly celebrated (Cuff and Sherman 2011; Stickells 2011; Chase, Crawford, and Kaliski 2005; Amin 2008). As we shall see, these spatial designs are often created in collectives.

Recently we have witnessed an analytical focus on the notion of "urban assemblages," in which the social and the material complexities of the city are taken into consideration (Farías and Bender 2010; Thrift 2008). In this theoretical framework, urban spaces are seen as messy configurations of social acts, material layouts, flows, and everyday rhythms. These analytic perspectives have had a major impact on the disciplines of urban studies, architecture, and cultural studies. However, a methodological design approach taking its point of departure in assemblage theory (Latour 2005; Bennett 2010; Farías and Bender 2010; Deleuze and Guattari 1987) would allow designers to design urban spaces with spatial complexity as the starting point. By asking how the citizens react to the aesthetic and material environments in the city, and how people inhabit urban space in their everyday life, designers and cultural planners could draw from the vast sociomaterial resources in urban space.

When the São Paulo–based collective Muda designed a temporary intervention in downtown São Paulo, they chose to leave the office and to situate themselves in the unruly yet seductive spaces of the city. As I will illustrate, situated design processes taking place in the urban spaces intended for transformation often tend to involve people and unfold potentials from the enclosing environment. This kind of situated practice changes the roles in the design process and the hierarchy between user and designer, material and form. For instance, the users become participating designers in the process, whereas the designer assimilates the role of the project leader. The urban planner in top-down planning, who formerly took the first steps, may end up being the supportive provider of the funding. In that sense, hierarchies in the design process are reversed or transformed into collaborative processes where diverse cultures and social groups renegotiate the sense of public space in the city (Amin 2008). More important, situated design challenges our understanding of what design is, and how and by whom design is practiced. Urban design must increasingly be understood as situated design processes and becomings of urban space rather than a top-down plan imposed on the city (Samson 2010).

Let us briefly look back at how urban design has conventionally been practiced. The planning of Copenhagen's infrastructure is an example of architectural design as object design. The Finger Plan, designed by the architect Steen Eiler Rasmussen in 1945, was meant as a structuring plan enabling the growth of Copenhagen in the future. Five "fingers" providing train connections to the center of Copenhagen allowed the city to expand in five directions, giving citizens quick access to recreational green space in between the fingers. The plan is a great example of modernist master planning where a single mastermind succeeded in creating a universal plan followed by thousands of people, while also setting the frame for future urban development.

However, not all kinds of master planning are as successful as the Finger Plan. One of the major limitations of master planning is the lack of participation from users and citizens. Today, despite good intentions in relation to social sustainability, well-known architectural offices like OMA, MVRPD, and BIG fail to include users in the design process. Instead, it is the mastermind and signature of the star architect that sells the projects. Almere City Center outside Amsterdam, Ørestad in Copenhagen, and the Olympic cities in London and Rio de Janeiro are recent examples of master planning where the citizens had no influence, and where the architectural design was imposed on urban matter without any sensibility of existing urban qualities. In that perspective, master planning remains a top-down way of designing, neglecting the complexities and aesthetic potentials in existing urban environments.

As an alternative to the discipline of architecture, I suggest we look into the participatory, situated cultural practices happening today. First, these emerging initiatives must be seen in relation to the socioeconomic changes happening in many Western cities. After the financial crisis in 2008, and the fact that most European cities are shrinking in population, redesign, experience design, and culture-led transformation projects have become more frequent (Oswalt, Overmeyer, and Misselwitz 2013). Moreover, the relocation of production in postindustrial societies, where the industrial production is directed to low-wage-income countries, has meant an increase of empty factories and industrial zones—sites now used for temporary use, cultural activities, and smaller service productions. Not only cultural activists but also strategic planners increasingly see the potential in creating temporary spaces for cultural activities to attract future users and redevelop former industrial zones for recreational use. Santral in Istanbul, the Carlsberg City in Copenhagen, and NDSM Wharf in Amsterdam are but a few examples of how culture, events, and temporary spaces become means for transforming former industrial sites into thriving, living neighborhoods. Thus cultural grassroots and urban planners alike see the potential in temporary architecture and culture as catalysts for urban transformation (Fabian and Samson 2014).

Culture-led urban development is also sustained by the idea that urban planning is a creative process involving the sensory landscapes of cities (Landry 2006). Public space becomes ludic as various games and playful activities take place in public

(Stevens 2007, Kristiansen this vol., chap. 13). At the same time, exhibitions and art installations move from the white-cube spaces of the museum into urban spaces where they are renegotiated by the people as part of the consumption of spaces and places. Festivals taking place in old factories, in the streets, and on former viaducts and bridges are all examples of how the well-designed infrastructure of the modernist city is being reused for experiences and events.

These culture-led initiatives include new ways of use based on sensory and aesthetic experiences of the environment. And they open up alternative and artistic ways of collaboration in cross-disciplinary teams. Thus culture-led urban design initiatives require another kind of knowledge; cultural and historical knowledge of the site and a sense of place are just as important as the mathematical and physical knowledge of the engineer and the construction designer. Therefore knowledge is often established across various disciplines with a renewed focus on aesthetic judgment, a sense of place, and knowledge of the city in its historical, cultural, and social context. In that sense, it calls for a situated knowledge (Haraway 1988) that allows partial and embodied knowledge to serve as the point of departure for research and design.

The art critic and curator Claire Doherty notes that recent culture and art practices share an interest in *situations*, as they prioritize affective moments and aesthetic experiences of space rather than their functionality. Situations are multidisciplinary, as they "are displayed by a complex network of artworks, projects, events, interventions, happenings, small gestures and spectacular intrusions over time" (Doherty 2009, 13).

Artists seem increasingly to work situated in the urban space, where the design takes place by collecting and reassembling the potentials at hand. They choreograph space with the spatial qualities at hand. Compared to the architect and urban planner, artists operate on neither a formal nor a strategic level; rather, they are mapping urban territories in the situation, proposing ad hoc solutions, and often reusing existing materials. The result is often lucrative in terms of how people and nonprofessionals are engaged, how the local community contributes, and how the design is carried out through participatory, situated, and material practices. Thus I call for a situated design method by drawing from current design practices. Based on three contemporary cases, I propose five design principles to follow when designing emergent urban spaces.

2 Cases

2.1 Designing the High Line

The High Line is an elevated park in the Meatpacking District of Chelsea, New York. It is an urban reuse of the old elevated industrial railway on the West Side of Manhattan funded by local citizens and arts and creative institutions. The High Line was redesigned as a public park by Diller Scofidio + Renfro in collaboration with the landscape architect James Corner of Field Operations. The design of the High Line can be seen as a project that signals a transformation of the industrial city to the postindustrial—one that emphasizes aesthetic experiences and recreational value.

Originally the High Line was an industrial railway track established for better transportation to and from the Meatpacking District—an infrastructural enhancement of the productive and functionalistic city. As part of New York's economic and productive infrastructure, the High Line was affected by the financial crisis of the 1930s. In the 1980s, it was abandoned for a decade and became forgotten. The redevelopment and redesign emerged out of that lack of interest. From the abandoned industrial tracks, a new sensory urban landscape emerged, and with it new and aesthetic potentials for experiencing the city from a sensuous perspective (fig. 11.1). Instead of designing a completely new park, architect Joshua David and artist Robert Hammond saw the potential to develop a park dense with experiences—and out of the aesthetic ruins of a forgotten industrial society. Inspired by the art photographer Joel Sternfeld's photographs of the High Line, his framings of the wild grass, the rusty surfaces, and the decaying storefronts, David and Hammond founded Friends of the High Line in 1992. The aim of this nonprofit organization was to raise money for a redevelopment of the old infrastructure into a public park.

With its great views of the surrounding city, and with the existing industrial decay from the old warehouses in the Meatpacking District, the space became known for its characteristic materiality and aesthetics—telling the history of urban gentrification and the process of slaughter, meat production, decay, and the formalization of the informal (Hannah 2004). By means of a visual campaign in collaboration with Fuji in 2002, and by engaging local design and art institutions such as the Kitchen and fashion designer Diane von Furstenberg, the High Line soon became world famous and portrayed in fashion and design magazines. Thus the sensory and aesthetic urban landscape, and the visual distribution of it, served as the framework for announcing an architecture competition. In that sense, the design process was partly initiated by David and Hammond, and partly the material and aesthetic agency of the site played a noteworthy role as images of the site were distributed worldwide.

When landscape architects Field Operations and performance architects DS+R won the design competition, they focused on the specific characteristics of the urban landscape to underline its existing materiality and aesthetics. In the final design, great views down Tenth Avenue, a paint roller tag from REUS COST on a building facade (fig. 11.2), and the dense atmosphere of materiality of the former slaughterhouses were kept intact or sustained by the design. In that sense, the designers succeeded in integrating history, culture, and materiality with the aesthetic qualities in their design solution. The role of the architect and landscape designer was in this case to *reassemble* existing spatial qualities in a new, inventive, and thought-provoking way.

Furthermore, the material aesthetics of the site informed the design process: the spurs from the former railway turned into paths, the industrial warehouses into

Figures 11.1 and 11.2
The everyday rhythms in the Meatpacking District, amazing views over the rooftops in Manhattan, and a street art roller by the notorious street artists REUS COST are examples of aesthetic qualities being integrated in the design.

choreographed spaces. However, the design solution was developed in the architect's office and carried out through a construction phase where the public was not allowed to enter the site. In that perspective, the design process cannot be described as participatory as such. Although a wide range of sponsors, investors, photographers, artists, and designers were involved during the first phases of the process, the design was still carried out behind closed doors in the offices of DS+R and Field Operations—the main signatures. While the design process was situated in terms of how the final design solution integrated the surrounding urban landscape and elaborated on the cultural history of the site, it was not situated as a participatory process in the neighborhood. Field Operations did not invite the people from the neighborhood to grow their own plants on the rail track as part of the landscape design, nor did the local people in the neighborhood have any influence on the design decisions of DS+R. In that sense, the design was only situated aesthetically and materially in urban space.

2.2 Designing the LAK Festival

The second case is the making of the LAK festival, a sound art festival for Nordic sound art that took place in the summer of 2012 in Amager, Copenhagen. Compared to the design process of the High Line, the spatial festival design is closer to a grassroots initiative, as the initiators, Sif Madsen and Katrine Møllebæk, work with bottom-up tactics integrating people along the process. However, the design of the festival venue also shares some characteristics with the High Line process because it involved a wide range of actors, in particular the material affects and atmospheres present at the site.

The concept of the LAK festival was to take sound art from its institutional settings—the museum and art gallery—and place it in the rough urban settings at Prag's Boulevard 43. The place is a former lacquer factory, now used as a workshop for young creatives. With its rusty materiality, disused industrial objects, abandoned machines, and chemical traces on the wall, the factory and the surrounding environment became the inspiration for the festival design.

Whereas Madsen and Møllebæk were responsible for the spatial design of the venue, they engaged two curators to assemble the sound installations suitable for the raw industrial environment. The process quickly accumulated several more people, from the curators, to an architect, to a lighting designer, to people working or living at the site. In that sense, creating the LAK festival became a *do-it-together* project, where people renting a workshop space at Prag's Boulevard became contributors to the festival design.

For Madsen and Møllebæk, it was important that the outdoor facilities and public hangout zone were integrated with the exhibition space. A young architect who was working at the site in a shipping container offered his help. Simply by reorganizing four shipping containers and adding a few chairs, the architect created a territory out of found objects (figs. 11.3 and 11.4). Reassembled from found materials into a new

Figures 11.3 and 11.4
The designers of the LAK festival created an environment out of found objects at the site, while visitors engaged with their bodies and senses. Figure 11.3 by LAK. Photo: Hanne Budtz Jørgensen.

organization, but with no clear borderline to the rest of the area, the spatial rearrangement turned out to be one of the most affective features in the festival design.

When visitors came to the opening, it was clear that the aesthetic experience was not only to listen to the sound art installations but also to discover the sounds in the urban environment. Thus the design of the containers, the urban garden, and the highly differentiated spaces inside the lacquer factory broke with the neutrality of the white-cube gallery.

By listening to the containers and objects scattered around the site, visitors expanded the spatial design by directing their intentions to other aesthetic qualities around them. Although the architect initially saw potential in the rusty containers, not all the old industrial machines and objects on the site were intentionally included in his composition. One of the containers was used for a site-specific artwork, *Metal on Metal on Metal*, in which a metallic sound came out of the container (fig. 11.3). However, as the visitors could not clearly distinguish artistic objects from regular objects on the site, they intuitively engaged with each surface and its materiality to test whether sounds were attached, or whether an artwork could possibly be hidden in it. During the festival, several people pointed out that they had become aware of everyday sounds and the aesthetic qualities of everyday objects. In that way, unintended meanings occurred out of the environment as visitors discovered its vibrant qualities, even in the objects and spaces not being used as part of the sound exhibition.

Due to the diffuse and somewhat unfinished environment, the festival design gained a strong aesthetic affectivity: intuitively the visitors had to sense the environment by discovering the heterogeneous spaces within the festival venue with their senses. Visitors even had to decide what was art and what was part of the urban environment. No clear boundaries were found in the design.

In that sense, the open and inclusive design process of the LAK festival was dispersed and included the engagement of the visitor. By not drawing a clear line between the sound objects on display and the sensory and affective qualities of the environment, the experience became dispersed within the material surroundings. Visitors coproduced the environment by engaging with and discovering its many potentials. The open scenography of the urban environment at Prag's acted on participants in the event. Thus the environment had an impact on how visitors experienced and sensed the art installations. The environment enacted and performed specific relations between the somewhat hidden artworks and the festival visitors.

2.3   Reassembling São Paulo

The final case is a DIY initiative that will illustrate a more participatory and situated approach where the role of the designer is dispersed and shared with various actors. The design object is Muda Coletivo's *Bolha Imobiliaria* (Inflammable Bubble), an inflammable structure that was set up at Minhocao on Sunday, December 16, 2012, as part of the urban movement Preliminares, which involved interventions in downtown São Paulo (fig. 11.5). This section focuses not on the intervention itself but on the process of making it.

From the conception of the idea, the *Bolha Imobiliaria* was meant to be a collective design intervention. Muda Coletivo is a young São Paulo–based collective. Because of cultural politics in Brazil, most young artists and designers work in loosely organized networks, as each project depends on collaboration with the right stakeholders to get funded. Thus Muda Coletivo changes with each project, making each design project situated and unique from the beginning. In this case, Muda took part in the urban movement Preliminares. Their spatial design consisted of an intervention on the Minhocao, a highway cutting through downtown São Paulo. For Muda, it was important to question market-driven urban development and to reclaim urban spaces by means of design. Thus the intervention was both a kind of protest campaign and a temporary design illustrating the possibility of other kinds of human-scale spaces in the city. From that background, the idea of the *Bolha Imobiliaria* was conceived: an inflammable structure made out of reused plastic bags. As most architects in São Paulo are developing architecture and design on market-driven premises, it was obvious for Muda to break with existing architectural practices. Thus the design had to be developed out of people's own desire and engagement, taking the existing urban condition as a point of departure. The intervention was further limited because it had no funding. These constraints initiated the collaboration with Misterio Basurama, a design office working with reuse of urban waste. Though Basurama had expertise in working with reused materials, it did not have access to them. So a third collaborator was introduced: Basurama knew of the recycling collective Coletivo Glicério, in the neighborhood of Liberdade.

Under a vast network of interconnected highways, Joao Batista, a former homeless person, had started to collect and reuse urban waste. Due to his organizational talents, JB had successfully established a recycling station where people in Liberdade could exchange objects and materials. To get access to the materials for the design, Muda and Misterio Basurama got involved with Coletivo and decided to produce the design in the recycling station. Despite having no professional training as a designer, JB had a specialized knowledge of the different sorts of plastic and their potentials for reuse. During the week of construction, people from the Preliminares movement were invited to participate in the design process. However, only a few dared to go, as the place was difficult to access and was considered unsafe territory among the middle class and young creatives in Preliminares. So Muda and Basurama had to rely on the workforce connected to Coletivo Glicério: homeless and poor people from the neighborhood who depended on the gift economy and the exchange of goods in JB's collective. Thus, in collaborating with the people in the Coletivo Glicério, it became obvious for Muda that they were not only designing temporary architecture—they were also designing a political commentary on gentrification and the use of public space. The everyday practice of exchanging labor and found materials was a way for the people in the Liberdade neighborhood to survive. Participation in these informal processes for Muda and Basurama became a political act where the design process was both the design of an object but also a way of doing design directed otherwise. By their situated design practice, they drew attention to how the homeless and the poor are neglected when market-driven interests govern urban development, and how urban waste accumulates in megacities because of the consumption of the rich.

Thus, from several perspectives, Muda's construction of *Bolha Imobiliaria* was a design processes situated in the city (fig. 11.6). It was a situated practice (1) in the way it was constructed through a collective process integrating local people, (2) in the way it took place as a site-specific process in a neglected space reusing urban waste, and (3) in the sense that the process included discursive issues of urban development, meaning that the design process became entangled with the complex sociopolitical situation in São Paulo.

In that regard, the process illustrates a reassembling of the city—socially, mentally, methodologically, and aesthetically. For instance, the locals enabled the designers to see aesthetic and functional values in otherwise neglected materials. In that sense, the production of the temporary structure established temporary spaces of collaboration in a city normally governed by economic growth and capital interests. Thus the process indicates that spatial designs are not strictly about the design of a design object; rather, spatial design can be understood as acts establishing relations between people in the process of making it. For instance, the few middle-class people who came to Coletivo Glicério's space under the highway were inevitably confronted with an urban reality quite different from their own.

Design here becomes a situated act engaging people and materialities in and through the situation: by choosing the recycling station Coletivo Glicério underneath a highway in São Paulo's slum, the designers chose to reuse resources from existing urban spaces. By reusing urban waste for the structure, they transformed the existing urban assemblage in a specific and original way. And they involved and engaged different social groups and people along the way. On that basis, it becomes an example of co-creative practices emerging from specific urban situations: though the making of the *Bolha Imobiliaria* was initially a collaboration between Misterio Basurama and Muda Coletivo, out of necessity it became a dispersed act involving not merely Coletivo Glicério and the people in Liberdade but also the found materials and the site-specific qualities at hand. Thus the design practice of Muda Coletivo is a situated practice, as it engages resources from a broad spectrum of sociomaterial spaces.

Figures 11.5 and 11.6
Designing *Bolha Imobiliaria* is a design process that takes place with the city as the material and
social stage.

3   Three Kinds of Situated Performances

While the three cases we have discussed have radically different contexts, they share specific elements with one another. These similarities are instructive for the definition of a situated and sociomaterial design methodology in which various actors perform through the changing situations in the design process. The anthropologist and performance theorist Barbara Kirshenblatt-Gimblett (2008) has noted that artistic activities such as festivals and events "are themselves architectural in the sense that performance (broadly conceived) gives form to space." This broad definition of performance may help us to understand the processes taking place between the urban environment, the designer, and participant user.

However, it is important to stress that when we regard design processes as a collective of performances, design objects, design processes, and users, we cannot regard them as separate entities. Rather, they perform together in situations where they relate in temporary formations.

3.1   The Performance of the Environment

In all three cases, the qualities and materials are actively used in the design process. Both in the High Line design process and in the making of the LAK festival, the urban environment performed an aesthetic role in the process. The places initiated the design process as bodily, visual, affective qualities, for instance, when the organizers behind LAK saw the potential in using the sociomaterial setting of Prag's Boulevard 43 for introducing sound art in public space (fig. 11.7).

The performance of the milieu covers social, cultural, and material qualities already present at Prag's Boulevard. The organizers mention the "messiness" of the place: that it had great potential because it was unfinished and not yet designed. Furthermore, the unpredictability relating to the people working and living there was mentioned as characterizing the milieu.

Anne Marie Mol has argued that things can enact and perform: "like (human) subjects, (natural) objects are framed as parts of events that occur and plays that are staged. If an object is real, this is because it is part of a practice. It is a reality enacted" (Mol 2002, 44). In other words, performance can also take place though the performativity of natural objects or spatial affectivity. For instance, the orange container during LAK had a certain performativity (understood as agency) on the visitors. The outdoor space engaged the visitors in several ways. People were leaning against the container, listening to it and perceiving its qualities. After discovering the sounds of the container, they wanted to discover whether other objects might have sounds attached to them too. As enactments between visitors and sound, the containers did not present something intentionally designed; thus they had a powerful effect on the visitors wanting to explore the site. The same can be said about the High Line. The

Figure 11.7
Design is an assembly of social and material components from the urban environment.

materiality and the urban landscape affected Robert Hammond and Joshua David. The spatial qualities that emerged over time drew the attention of the neighborhood and inspired the photographer Joel Sternberg to visualize the landscape and to call attention to the aesthetics and materiality of the urban landscape. These visualizations gave rise to the funding for the project.

3.2 The Performance of the Designer

If urban environments have the capacity to perform and to affect the designer to initiate the design process, then what is the performance of the designer? Broadly speaking, we could say that the designer follows the material flows of the environment. In the design of the LAK festival, the process accumulated more and more people, from the curators, to the architect, to the lighting designer, to people working and living in the site, to the visitors participating in the festival. Thus the design intention was gradually distributed to more and more people. Obstacles occurred during the design process, for instance, when some of the daily users of Prag's Boulevard 43 intervened in the festival construction through everyday use. Instead of prohibiting interference, however, Madsen and Møllebæk allowed the users to influence the festival design.

By situating the design problem in urban space, the designers succeeded in reassembling social and technical skills that already existed in the urban environment. In that sense, the designer is no longer the rational planner working in the office or in the laboratory. Rather, she intervenes in urban space by distributing the act to other collectives, situations, and the material potentials inherent in the environment. In other words, she transforms urban space by giving attention to formerly unseen qualities and forgotten meanings, and by letting the environment unfold its potentials.

In the two cases we have discussed, we can see a clear distinction from the design practice of master planning and formal urban design. In master planning, when the plan is drawn up and accepted by the stakeholders, professionals such as engineers and craftspeople finish the design according to the plan. The design is implemented in a construction phase where the site is closed to the public. In the case of the LAK festival, instead of closing down the process, the project leaders allowed people to contribute. This resulted in curious people working at Prag's Boulevard to come up with spontaneous ideas and to become part of the design process. Because the project leaders were not able to close the site down before the opening of the festival, the material and social everyday practices and routines influenced the design of the festival. In the final festival design, this meant an extraordinary sense of being part of an already existing community with a material and cultural history.

Designers and event makers also choreograph social and cultural interactions. In the words of Mol, we can say that the designer allows daily acts to be staged. In that sense, the role of the designer is basically to situate the design in the urban environment. A situated design method thus implies that the designers are able to open up inherent potentials in the environment.

3.3   The Performance of the Participant

The borderline between participant and designer is fluid. The many daily visitors at the High Line share their photos and experiences on social media such as Flickr and Facebook. In that sense, they continuously participate in and perform the spatial practices of the High Line.

In the LAK festival case, the participants' influence on the design was even more obvious. People occupying offices on Prag's Boulevard engaged with the design process, contributing their knowledge. Visitors to the festival participated in the design process by engaging with the different tableaus or by discovering new places and spatial qualities at the site. In a similar way, the trash collectors Coletivo Glicério contributed to the aesthetic design of *Bolha Imobiliaria*, becoming co-designers rather than participants.

In all three cases, the design process was prolonged after the opening of the design as people engaged with it by taking photos, sharing their experiences, and thereby contributing to the design and its future users. Participation is here closely related to the aesthetics and material affectivity of the design: if people feel engaged and affected, they share and distribute the aesthetic experience with others. Thus user participation is related to the unfinished explorative aesthetics of the environment, for instance, when users have the chance to discover and unfold a site's qualities themselves without feeling that they are fulfilling the intentions of the designer. Here we see a clear difference between aesthetic experience design and functional design. Whereas design would normally be associated with functionality or affordance of the object, aesthetic spatial design allows a wide range of aesthetic experiences. Thus the design of aesthetic experiences calls for openness, risk taking, and awareness of potentiality in the situation.

Finally, this leads me to define five design principles on how to act situatedly and according to the situation.

4   Design Principles for Assembling Urban Design

4.1   Situate

First, the designer will have to situate herself in the urban environment. To situate oneself means to take local and specific constraints into consideration. These include material and spatial constraints, social and cultural capacities, and possible conflicts. Second, the act of designing must take into consideration specific situations in the city. These include affective atmospheres, local people with specific knowledge and capacities, and objects and materials being reused and recomposed in the design process. The method calls for action in situ. The designer must allow the design to be produced as a plateau. "The plateau is always in the middle, not at the beginning or the end," observe Deleuze and Guattari (1987, 21). Similar to the plateau, design is a process taking place in the middle of things, in the urban environment and in the already existing sociocultural processes. Like recent art practices, designs occur as temporary assemblages and situations (Doherty 2009).

4.2   Collect

When the designer is situated discursively and bodily at the site of design production, she collects what is at hand and reassembles materials in new compositions. Anything goes: from waste to amazing viewpoints and haptic surfaces, abandoned objects and local people, anything with aesthetic and productive value may be reassembled. In that sense, designing means reassembling space in new ways. Whereas traditional approaches to spatial design develop a design object, situated design practices are closer to the notion of assemblies or assemblages, where aesthetic qualities and social resources are collected from diverse milieus. The designer is here a nomad, collecting already existing materials and capacities within the urban environment. As noted by

Deleuze and Guattari, "the primary determination of nomads is to occupy and hold smooth space" (1987, 410). Here design becomes a collection spatial expressions, materials, and social capacities in the urban environment.

4.3   Assemble

Assemblages are constituted when social and material actors relate (Farías and Bender 2010), for instance, when Coletivo Glicério and Muda Coletivo collected garbage with the help of the people in the neighborhood. As noted by the political theorist Jane Bennett, "assemblages are ad hoc groupings of diverse elements, of vibrant materials of all sorts" (Bennett 2010, 24). If urban design, in accordance with Bennett, can be redefined as ad hoc groupings of diverse elements, it also points to the fact that the design practice is no longer in the hands of the designer alone; rather, it emerges in situations informed by the social and material urban environment. The act of designing is thus to establish such ad hoc groupings of vibrant materials, to recompose the social and the material in affective urban assemblages.

4.4   Distribute

When urban materials and people are reassembled, design must be understood as a collection distributed to a broad group of people, including spectators, users, and participants. To distribute can be understood as a way to share and to communicate the design to an audience in an urban environment, a neighborhood. The LAK festival design illustrates that the visitors become participants and co-creators at the same time by contributing their ideas, discovering unseen potentials, sharing their private experiences in public, and distributing their experiences across various media, such as by filming or taking photos.

4.5   Disperse

When the design is distributed to an audience that engages with the design, the designer should allow the design to disperse into the urban environment. This implies that the users disperse the design by sharing pictures and posting experiences via social media, thus allowing the parts of the spatial design to be reused in other venues, in other sociospatial and material assemblages.

Design as an act of dispersing thus means to separate it from a single discipline into a broader environment. Holert (2011, 51) understands design as a "distributed agency," not an object or a work of art with a single author and signature. In his words, "Design could become a discipline of un-disciplinary moves and motions and turn itself into a practice of possibility and an articulation of becoming" (51). Here design is understood not as an object but as an emerging process taking place between a wide range of sociomaterial components.

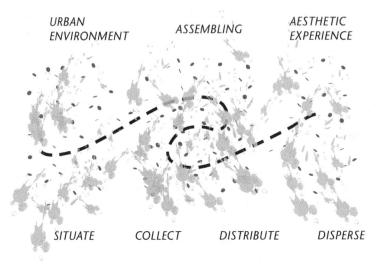

Figure 11.8
Design as assembling: *situate, collect, assemble, distribute, disperse.*

4.6 Redefining the Designer

To sum up, my proposed method points to a situated practice where the design not only engages the users but also allows them to contribute to the design process. The participant thus gains an important role by connecting the designer with the aesthetic potentialities in the urban environment. The Fuji campaign gave the designers ideas of the affective qualities of the urban landscape around the High Line; the homeless and people from the neighborhood taught the designers about the usability of urban waste, and visitors at the LAK festival discovered hidden spaces and objects at the festival venue. Each of these examples questions the role of the designer as the universal mastermind who has expert knowledge of spatial qualities and aesthetics. Rather, the designer is the artisan surrendering to the city by following its flow of matter; she is the one working with "intuition in action" (Deleuze and Guattari 1987, 409), an intuition oriented toward site-specific values, urban materiality, and "the material traits of expression constituting affects" (408). User-citizens and visitors also contribute with specific knowledge on the city throughout the design process.

The role of the designer suddenly disperses into various roles: she is no longer the one conceiving the design as an aesthetic object; rather, the existing material and social flows of the environment intervene in the process, informing the final design. Furthermore, the design process not only occurs between the designer and the material site but covers how users and visitors engage with the assemblages taking shape. For instance, the visitors to the LAK festival explored the containers, thus prolonging the design by interacting with it. Design, then, becomes a temporary constellation of the material environment, connecting designer, users, and environment.

5 Conclusion

The aim of this chapter was to suggest a situated method for spatial design. In the three case studies, we saw how designers, artists, and users work with existing materials and found objects, and how they create, shape, enact, distort, and reorganize socio-materials in collaborative processes.

Design practices were carried out with partial perspectives from a specific, embedded position in urban spaces. In that sense, the design participated in already ongoing processes in the city.

From the way the three cases follow material flows in the urban environment, we can deduce five principles for creating spatial design with an emphasis on aesthetic experiences. The principles may be followed simultaneously but take specific and partial situations into consideration: as a method, reassembling urban space differs from a rationalistic universal design perspective as we know it in master planning and architecture. Rather, these principles take into consideration the partial interests of the designer and the spatial constraints and materiality of the city. The existing urban assemblages may inform design processes. By assembling urban space, the designer intervenes in and reconfigures real-world situations. Thus the design method also breaks with relativism and social constructivism. Despite being partial, the design is neither a subjective conception in the mind of the designer nor a mere functional object; in the examples, a design emerges from the social and material complexity in the urban environment. Last, the proposed method suggests that we cannot regard users as passive consumers of experience products; rather, the method allows design research to rethink the hierarchy and linear relation between users, participants, spatial design, and designer.

References

Amin, Ash. 2008. Collective culture and urban public space. *City* 12 (1): 131–147.

Bennett, Janet. 2010. *Vibrant Matter: A Political Ecology of Things*. Durham, NC: Duke University Press.

Chase, J. L., M. Crawford, and J. Kaliski. 2005. *Everyday Urbanism*. New York: Monacelli Press.

Cuff, Dana, and Roger Sherman. 2011. *Fast-Forward Urbanism: Rethinking Architecture's Engagement with the City*. New York: Princeton Architectural Press.

Deleuze, Gilles, and Félix Guattari. 1987. *A Thousand Plateaus*. Minneapolis: University of Minnesota Press.

Doherty, Claire. 2009. *Situation: Documents of Contemporary Art*. Cambridge, MA: MIT Press.

Fabian, Louise, and Kristine Samson. 2014. Do-it-yourself as do-it-together. *Journal of Urbanism*.

Farías, Ignacio, and Thomas Bender. 2010. *Urban Assemblages: How Actor-Network Theory Changes Urban Studies*. London: Routledge.

Hannah, Dorita. 2004. Butcher's white: Where art meets the meat market. In *Eating Architecture*, ed. Jamie Horwitz and Paulette Singley. Cambridge, MA: MIT Press.

Haraway, Donna. 1988. Situated knowledges: The science question in feminism and the privilege of partial perspective. *Feminist Studies* 14 (3): 575–599.

Holert, Tom. 2011. *Distributed Agency: Design's Potentiality*. Civic City Cahier 3. London: Bedford Press.

Kirshenblatt-Gimblett, Barbara. 2008. Performing the city: Reflections on the Urban Vernacular. In *Everyday Urbanism*, ed. John L. Chase, Margaret Crawford, and John Kaliski. New York: Monacelli Press.

Landry, Charles. 2006. *The Art of City-Making*. London: Earthscan.

Latour, Bruno. 2005. *Reassembling the Social: An Introduction to Actor-Network-Theory*. Oxford: Oxford University Press.

Mol, Annemarie. 2002. *The Body Multiple: Ontology in Medical Practices of Medicine*. Durham, NC: Duke University Press.

Oswalt, Philipp, Klaus Overmeyer, and Philipp Misselwitz. 2013. *Urban Catalyst: The Power of Temporary Use*. Berlin: Dom Publishers.

Samson, Kristine. 2010. The becoming of urban space. In *Design Research*, ed. Jesper Simonsen, Jørgen O. Bærenholdt, Monika Büscher, and John D. Scheuer. London: Routledge.

Stevens, Quintin. 2007. *The Ludic City*. New York: Routledge.

Stickells, Lee. 2011. The right to the city: Rethinking architecture's social significance. *Architectural Theory Review* 16 (3): 213–227.

Thrift, N. 2008. *Non-representational Theory: Space, Politics, Affect*. London: Routledge.

12   Portable Audio Design

Sanne Krogh Groth

What.   The chapter presents a methodological approach to be applied in the early process of producing portable audio design such as audio walks and audio guides. The approach focuses especially on the relationship to specific spaces, and how an awareness of the relationship between the space and the production can be part of the design process. Such awareness entails several approaches: the necessity of paying attention to the specific genre; a grasping of the complex relationship between space, time, the actual, and the virtual; and an excavation of the specific space's soundscape by approaching it both intuitively and systematically. The method is presented along with three cases.

Why.   The methodological approach takes its point of departure in the field of sound studies and sound art, in which the imaginary and the actual have been investigated since the 1950s. If we bring such methods and theories into the field of design, a focus on sensorial aspects can be added the process to finally lead to an audio production that not only narrates the actual through the virtual but also blurs the distinction.

Where.   The chapter highlights audio guides and audio walks, but the approach can also be of inspiration to those working with site-specific graphical and video productions. The final products can be presented within online and physical institutional contexts.

How.   The approach will particularly focus on the tension between the virtual and the actual, taking a point of departure in a discussion of time and space. The term *situated* is here used as the adjacent to the "objective" paradigm within science, as discussed by Haraway (1991). Such an approach is here discussed in the context of postwar avant-garde movements "advancing the real and the imaginary hand-in-hand" (e.g., Debecque-Michel 1999).

1   Introduction

With newer digital playback technologies such as iPods, iPhones, and Android telephones, with the high-quality recording equipment that is now within the layman's economic reach, and with access to intuitive editing software, the possibilities of sound production have changed from being reserved for professionals to now be within reach for anyone who wishes to use them. Concurrently with these technological expansions, the interest in expressing oneself and communicating via auditory media has grown. So has the creativity in the production and use of these media, where we find audio walks and audio guides among some of the most interesting (e.g., Rawes 2008; Fisher 2004). Common for these formats is that they are designed to be performed through headphones, and that they to various degrees relate to a specific space auditorily, visually, and socially.

My purpose in this chapter is to develop a methodological approach that can both heighten awareness of, and deal with the complex relationship between, what is here named the actual (the chosen concrete location) and the virtual (the audio production). I do this to establish a solid ground to design and produce portable audio design that to various degrees blends and negotiates time and space. The approach therefore particularly focuses on the tension between the virtual and the actual.

To develop the methodological approach, I bring in various theories and examples to suggest and reflect on how best to define and construct an audio production that is situated in time and space. This I do by a careful introduction to the following:

• The matter of genre: audio walk or audio guide?
• The sonic envelope and the grasping of complexity
• Intuitive listening to actual soundscapes
• Tools to analyze actual and compose virtual soundscapes

These steps lead to an investigation of the actual soundscape to construct a virtual soundscape that blends with a specific space.

Aesthetics, dramaturgy, and implementation are also important in the overall production process, but since the context of this anthology is an excavation of the situated, my focus here will also be on this. The term *situated* is here used as the opposite of the "objective" paradigm within science, as discussed by Haraway (1991), who states: "'Objects' do not preexist as such. Objects are boundary projects. But boundaries shift from within; boundaries are very tricky. What boundaries provisionally contain remains generative, productive of meanings and bodies. Siting (sighting) boundaries is a risky practice" (201). This leads me to issues and discussions within the postwar avant-garde movements that also focus on diffuse borders between and the "advancing [of] the real and the imaginary hand-in-hand" (Debecque-Michel 1999), with the Situationist International movement as the most radical when it came to using art for political and revolutionary means.

My approach in this chapter differs from the majority of previous writings within the field of sound production, which are mainly written by practitioners (e.g., Brown

2010; Sonnenschein 2001). As a musicologist, my background is mainly theoretical, and I therefore draw on my knowledge of theories on sound, aesthetics, and history. At the same time, the present work has also been developed in close relation with my teaching of larger and smaller groups of students in the program on performance design, CBIT (Department of Communication, Business, and Information Technology), at Roskilde University, which has included practical as well as theoretical dimensions.

The method is developed for portable audio design—audio guides and audio walks—but can also be of inspiration when working with situated graphical and video production for portable devices.

2   Defining the Subject Matter: Audio Guide or Audio Walk?

Before starting producing the audio file, it is important to consider whether the result will end up as either an *audio walk* or an *audio guide*. Although the two types of audio productions at first glance might appear almost identical, we find essential differences between them. This is illustrated by the following two examples from which essential characteristics are drawn. The characteristics appear later in a table, which can be used as a guideline and overview when deciding whether the production is to become an audio walk or an audio guide.

My two cases are both accessed as downloads for smartphones, and both relate to specific locations. Where they differ is in their way of relating to the chosen location, which finally results in different ways of engaging with time and space. The two cases are introduced by focusing on:

1. Actual space and time (the location the production is designed to take place in)
2. Virtual space and time (the constructed audio production sounding through headphones)

2.1   Audio Walk: *Mit Vesterbro* (My Vesterbro)
My first example, *Mit Vesterbro* (My Vesterbro), was developed by a group of candidate students at Roskilde University in 2011.[1] *Mit Vesterbro* is an hour-long site-specific audio walk produced in relation to the annual literature festival *Kbh Læser* (Copenhagen Reads). The students proposed the project to the festival themselves, and the proposal was accepted if the audio walk would also include literature. The students' intention was to portray Vesterbro both as it once was and as what it has become. The festival's requirement was met by combining readings of fiction taking place at Vesterbro and interviews with selected citizens of Vesterbro (representing the everyday of Vesterbro today), recordings of a live tour guide (speaking about the past), and voice-overs with additional information (both about the past and presence).

The audio walk was downloaded from a website made by the students (www.mit-vesterbro.dk) with a link from the official festival site (www.kbhlaeser.dk). In addition to this, it was also promoted on postcards, which were handed out at the festival opening. Both the Web site and the postcard showed a map with the tour marked, which would support the guidelines in the actual production.

Actual Space and Time   Vesterbro is a part of Copenhagen, which during the past fifteen to twenty years of gentrification has encompassed Copenhagen's red light district, drugs, pubs, hipster cafés, cheap student apartments, and more expensive apartments rented by, for example, families with children. Copenhagen's central station, heavily trafficked streets, and more quiet parallel streets and parks characterize the area. These different areas result in an overall soundscape that includes both diffuse noisy areas and so-called quieter areas that allow a more detailed soundscape to appear (e.g., sound from apartments, stores, birds, and pedestrians). The area is not large, only about four square kilometers, and it is possible to walk from one end to the other in less than an hour. Vesterbro's population is 35,000 citizens.

The audio walk was designed to last forty-four minutes as a real-time walk beginning at the central station, going through one of the two main streets (Istedgade), through a park (Skydebanehaven), on to quieter streets (such as Westend), and ending up at a larger central square (Enghaveplads).

The production was connected to the sites the visitor passed by, by referring concretely either to the surroundings' present functions or to the inhabited histories of the various places. It also entailed parts with music, which had the function of transportation, but also had the side effect of leaving space for the visitor to walk and reflect without new information being added.

Virtual Space and Time   The overall production consists of various elements all in one way or another concerning the actual surroundings at Vesterbro. In describing the production, it makes sense to divide it into three levels: (1) narrator, (2) narration, and (3) reflection. Each level is characterized by being presented in an individual setting of a space and presenting an individual time or timing.

1. Narrator: A voice guiding the tour and reading from selected books. Environmental sounds such as footsteps and street noise are added to this layer of the production, so that the narrator is placed in the same space as the listener. The experience of the narrator as being in the same space as the listener enhances the perception of the experienced present.

2. Narration: Interviews and recordings of live city guide. The interviews are also located in concrete spaces, but these spaces are not part of the listener's environment. Instead the listener is introduced to imagined physical spaces that represent what the

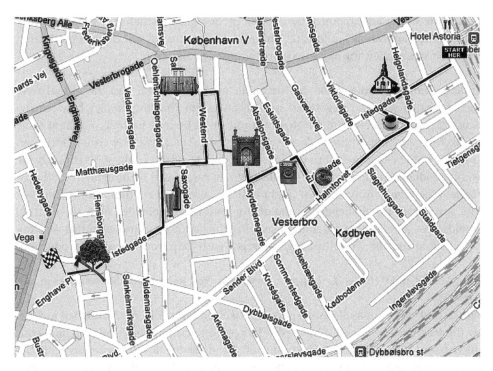

Figure 12.1
Postcard used as map and flyer designed by the students.

interviews are about. The narrator is relating and including these spaces in the overall narrative, thereby linking them to the actual space. The interviews take the listener to a different temporal setting, a near past that is still related to the situation, but distant from the concrete situation.

3. Reflection: A musical sound track represents another kind of space, an abstract space, which does not represent concrete, physical settings but brings in a space for transportation and reflection. The music adds a pulse that corresponds physically to the listener and encourages a rhythm in the transportation from one place to another. The music organizes the time in a physical way—a time that does not represent past, present, or future but provides a pulse that encourages us to time our physical behavior in a certain way.

When it comes to dramatic tension, all through the production we find an almost even relationship among the three elements (narration, narrator, and reflection). Although a narrator guides the listener through the entire production, other narratives (such as the guide in Skydebanehaven) are also framed as strong voices. These voices let the listener hear single individuals tell about their life at Vesterbro. Stylistically these little stories are supported by a sound production in which the environment of the narration appears as soundscape. This reflection points toward an open production in which space is left for more than one omniscient narrator.

Ending Remarks: Audio Walk   In the audio walk, the actual and the virtual were mixed, challenged, and negotiated to such an extent that the borders between the actual surroundings and the imaginative production became blurred, so that at some points it became impossible to decide what was actual and what was virtual. Although the time frame was attached to the space (one had to be at certain spots through the whole production), time was also challenged and negotiated by bringing in both historical time (voices from the past) and physical timing (the rhythm from the music). The space was also challenged: some of the soundscapes blended with the existing soundscape; others had a function of coloring the various narrations. In this way, the actual space and the virtual space also merged with help from the audio production.

2.2   Audio Guide: *Husker du: Lydspor i Greve?* (Do You Remember: Soundtracks in Greve?)

The second case is an audio guide named *Husker du: Lydspor i Greve?* launched in 2013 by the local history museum in Greve.[2] The project was initiated, designed, and conducted by Kamilla Hjortkjær, a curator at the museum, in collaboration with the composers Hans Sydow and Jens Toyberg-Frandzen and the graphic designer Christina Sydow.

The production consists of ten short sound compositions between one and four minutes long. The ten tracks are embedded in an app, which informs the user that it is "an alternative city walk" that takes you to ten different locations in the municipality of Greve: a train, social housing, a single-family home, a sports venue, a town of craftsmanship, a kindergarten, a shopping mall, camping, a beach, and a school.

Actual Space and Time   The ten locations are marked on a map (in the app) to show the listener where to go and listen to the specific tracks. Every mark on the map links to its sound to make it easy to navigate between place and sound. Meanwhile an introduction tells us that the tracks can also be listened to at home—information that illustrates a production less entangled in actual time and space than the previous one.

The ten productions are also available as a list, where they are accompanied with a short text and a photo collage explaining and illustrating the context of the sound. Both the photo collage and the sound consist of a mix of archival material and newly produced material. During a period of time after the project was launched, it was installed as an exhibition in which the collages were enlarged and headphones were installed with the sound that was related to the photograph.

Just as *Mit Vesterbro* intended to portray Copenhagen, so the intention of *Husker du* is to portray this specific municipality. Greve, a suburb twenty-five kilometers outside Copenhagen, covers a larger area than Vesterbro, sixty square kilometers, and with a population of only 48,000 is not as dense as Vesterbro.

Until the early 1960s, Greve was an agricultural area with small villages. During the 1960s and 1970s, the land was prepared for owner-occupied housing, and typical single-family homes and smaller townhouses were built. In the municipality's northeast corner, we also find rental housing, including social housing. In recent years, small stores in Greve have closed down and been replaced by the larger Hundige shopping mall. The ten spots selected for the audio guide represents different aspects of everyday life in Greve in the past and present, all rather central and within biking distance.

Virtual Space and Time   The ten compositions vary in content. A common characteristic, though, in their way of characterizing a certain spot is that it is addressed by a combination of memories of the past, historical audio clips, newly recorded audio material from the present, and voice-overs (in eight of the ten productions). The archival material represents the past both in content and through the media itself with compressed voices and noisy productions. The material from the present is, in contrast, smoothly recorded. All materials have gone through advanced editing that does not leave any part of the production to coincidence.

The voice-over in *Husker du* is not a traditional guide explaining what is seen or experienced, but a presentation of the citizens' memories about the past. The quotes are collected from the local population but are rewritten so that they all begin with "I remember..." This brings a steady rhythm and flow into the production and ties the single productions together. On the one hand, these quotes function as an opening toward ownership and recognizability among the citizens, almost as if the production was produced collectively. On the other hand, the stylization and the fact that they are read by an external speaker (one of the composers) also sends a different signal: the story of Greve becomes a narration from the perspective of the composer, who takes the citizens' words into his own mouth, reconstructs their sentences to give them the right flow, and designs the municipal soundscape to fit the composers' artistic ambitions.

Ending Remarks: Audio Guide   Although these productions are presented as site-specific audio guides, they do not entangle with their surroundings to the same extent as the audio walk described earlier. This has two results: First, the production does not invite a physical response or mental immersion but establishes a distance between the actual space and the virtual space. Second, because of this distancing, the production can be taken from one specific context to another without leaving essential parts of it behind.

This does not mean that the productions do not consider the space. In all productions, a soundscape consisting of sounds recorded at, or relating to, the specific narrative are embedded. But whereas the recordings underlying the soundscape in *Mit Vesterbro* supported and intensified the situated space, the soundscapes in *Husker du* appear designed and composed to such an extent that they appear more as autonomous compositions than as situated expressions: the soundscapes move between accidental background sound into more strictly composed rhythmic patterns based on the sound of the site, but not on the actual environmental sound.

The temporal dimensions in *Husker du* also differ from those in *Mit Vesterbro*. As already mentioned, the productions are organized in an overall open form, in which the order of the ten pieces can be executed randomly. Since each production is located in different locations, the overall project invites the user to pause between each of them, which again can invite dialogue among several listeners. By this we may conclude that whereas *Mit Vesterbro* is designed to be perceived as one long contemplative individual experience of time and space, *Husker du* can, with all the little breaks, be a more social experience, with room left for engagement with other listeners.

2.3   Overview and Methodological Approach

From these two examples, in table 12.1 I conclude some general characteristics of the audio walk and audio guide, and their relation to actual space and time and to virtual space and time.

From a methodological point of view, the earlier in the design process such complexity is considered, the greater the chances are to design a product that fulfills the original intensions: Is the production to be entangled, engaged, and situated in actual time and space? Is it to be designed as an open form? Or is the intention to produce an autonomous composition that can be taken from one place to another? Whatever

Table 12.1

Comparing audio walk and audio guide

	Audio walk	Audio guide
Actual space	Site specific	Site specific—but the space can be mediated in various ways
Actual time	Real time is superior to narrative time	Narrative time is superior to real time
Virtual space	Framing of or embedding the actual space	Explaining the actual space
Virtual time	Perfect timing of physical movement	More flexible; open form is possible

the overall intention is, it is important to take such considerations into account at a very early stage. Such considerations can be discussed, clarified, and systematized using table 12.1. These essential characteristics serve, on the one hand, as tools to identify and discuss the ideas one may have. On the other hand, they also suggest complex questions and scenarios that need to be further discussed.

3 Grasping Complexity: The Sonic Envelope

To reflect on and grasp the complex situation of constructing a portable audio production engaging with time and space, I draw on further theoretical considerations. This leads me to develop a figure that illustrates the relationship between the actual and the virtual in the two cases presented earlier and in a third case presented hereafter.

The English architectural historian and theorist Peg Rawes (2008) has developed the idea of "sonic envelopes" to try to grasp the complexity of experiencing the Canadian sound artist Janet Cardiff's artistic audio walks. The concept is developed on the basis of a discussion between two texts by the French philosopher Henri Bergson from the late nineteenth century and practical audio walks by Cardiff from the first decade of the twenty-first century.

A sonic envelope "represents the relationship between specific sonic images, materials and spaces in the environment and the individual's powers of perception" (Rawes 2008, 62). It takes into account both physical and psychic perceptions of both time and space and "enable[s] our understandings of the aesthetic role of the participant who interacts with an architectural or art experience" (62).

Rawes draws on Bergson's writings to unfold the complex relationship of time and space philosophically, "between forms of sound, perception and topological space" (Rawes 2008, 62). Central points are the development of his theories in dialogue with topology—a qualitative scientific knowledge of geometric forms in which connectedness, change of shapes, emergence, and perception are taken into account (as a break from the rational and objective Euclidian geometry, which excludes the dimension of time). This allows Bergson to bring in the notion of time to space to establish spatiotemporal relations. In *Matter and Memory*, he analyzes "how space and time exist as physical or material forms and as virtual modes of perception" and how time and space in their "empirical and physical forms ... enable the most abstract or 'virtual' forms of perception (such as memory) to be '*actualized*'" (70). Bergson concludes that time and space are "the diagrammatic design of our eventual action upon matter" (Bergson 1896, quoted in Rawes 2008, 70). Not only do time and space become related, but so do the physical and the psychic, so that the "the physical actions of the individual are generated in direct relation to the psychic activities of the body" (Rawes 2008, 71).

Certain effects from the work of Cardiff can be highlighted to exemplify a production that to a high degree presents both a multilayered time-space dimension and a strong relationship between the physical movement and the psychic perception. In Cardiff's *Louisiana Walk* (1996), the voice of the narrator—the artist herself—is recorded close to the microphone and placed in the foreground of the virtual soundscape. With a whispering voice, the narrator addresses the listener directly, saying, "Hello. Do you hear me? I want you to walk with me through the garden. Let's go outside ... Let's walk down the stairs. Try to walk to the sound of my footsteps so that we can stay together." A close relation is established not only in the intimate sound but also through the physical guidance of the walk. To make the production site specific, a layer of the virtual soundscape consists of binaural recordings from the situated space: for example, footsteps, wind, ocean, and a tour guide in Louisiana. The effect of this soundscape thereby is a diffusion of the borders between the actual and the virtual space, which—as far as I experienced it—creates an acute awareness of both. Other parts consist of additional sounds that support the narrated story—a murder mystery. Together with the narrative, these sounds add a fictitious layer that makes us slip between past, present, and future.

3.1 Conclusions about the Virtual and the Actual and the Sonic Envelope

To sum up the relationship between the actual and the virtual, and the sonic envelope, I have developed a model (fig. 12.2) that allows us to consider several aspects of the process simultaneously. While being a diagram of what issues should be approached in the process of designing portable audio design, the figure also illustrates how the single parameters in table 12.1 relate to one another. The intention with the model is, as with the table, to provide a tool for use in the early design process, so that the designer of the production can clarify what to be aware of, so that the production's original intentions can be executed.

To illustrate how the diagram is to be understood, I have placed the three examples discussed previously in the chapter. The conclusion is that the closer to the middle the production navigates, the greater chance there is that the recipient experiences the production as entangled in time and space.

4 Entangling the Surroundings: Excavating the Soundscape

To create an audio design that entangles a certain location, it is vital to be closely acquainted with the chosen space, since the actual soundscape should serve as a site-specific background or even foreground to the produced virtual soundscape. The aspects that appear from the investigation of the actual should be part of the creation of the virtual soundscape, to ensure that the virtual soundscape merges with the actual soundscape to create a listening experience that stresses the situated.

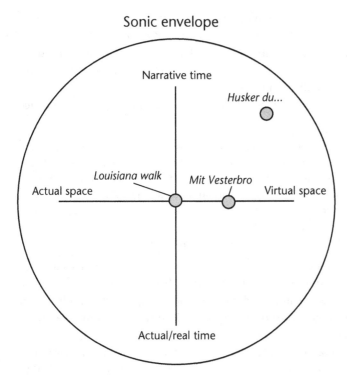

Figure 12.2
Model of the relationship between the actual and the virtual, and the sonic envelope.

I introduce two methods for doing this: the first is an exercise for gaining an auditory awareness of one's surroundings; the second is an introduction to analytical tools to systematically grasp the sounds of the existing space.

Within artworks of the historical and the neo-avant-garde, a tradition of experimenting with the surroundings can be found in the recurrent investigation of the relationship between art and the everyday—the artificial and the real.

During the 1950s and 1960s, questions about listening were explored through many kinds of artistic experiments. I have chosen to refer to two other pioneering artists, Pauline Oliveros (b. 1932) and R. Murray Schafer (b. 1933), who have both worked consciously with listening to the environment. This leads to a presentation of newer methodological tools developed by the younger Danish landscape architect Rikke Thiirmann Thomsen, based on Schafer's work, among others.

4.1 Listening to Noise and Silence

Before starting to analyze the existing soundscape of the selected location, one should consider the listening situation itself—a situation that can be experienced in various ways and on various mental levels. Emphasizing an awareness of the listening situation can help us to avoid habitual listening such as "the city is noisy," "the country is silent," or "music is pleasant." The goal is to establish a situation in which *all* sounds ‑ are heard, identified as causal events, and reckoned as "pure" sounds with certain qualities: timbre, pitch, temporality, and spatiality (far or near).

The American composer Pauline Oliveros has developed a philosophy and practice called "Deep Listening":

Basically Deep Listening ... explores the difference between the involuntary nature of hearing and the voluntary, selective nature exclusive and inclusive—of listening. The practice includes body-works, sonic meditations, interactive performance, listening to the sounds of daily life, nature, one's own thoughts, imagination and dreams, and listening to listening itself. It cultivates a heightened awareness of the sonic environment, both external and internal, and promotes experimentation, improvisation, collaboration, playfulness and other creative skills vital to personal and community growth. (www.deeplistening.org/site/content/about)

Deep Listening is as much a mode of being in the world as it is a certain methodology of listening, which is also underpinned in Oliveros's book, in which she states: "Sounds carry *intelligence*. Ideas, feelings and memories are triggered by sounds. If you are too narrow in your awareness of sounds, you are likely to be disconnected from your environment" (Oliveros 2005, xxv).

Besides the philosophical, almost ideological, content of her statements, Deep Listening is also a practical tool that can help us to understand the situation of listening to an environment. Consciously differentiating between *listening* and *hearing* helps to distinguish the process of perception (Oliveros 2005, xxii):

• *Hearing* is unconscious, based on physical abilities. It is measurable by physical and scientific measurements.
• *Listening* is a conscious, reflective perception, which is best described in psychological terms, or within cultural historical experiences.

Deep Listening is defined as a modus in which one "is learning to expand the perception of sounds to include the whole space/time continuum of sound—encountering the vastness and complexities as much as possible" (Oliveros 2005, xxiii). This modus is explained by shifting between the two modes:

• *Focal* attention (exclusive, clarifying listening)
• *Global* attention (diffuse and continually expanding to take in the whole of the space/time continuum (13)

Following Oliveros's program, it is possible, through months of intensive training, to become a certified Deep Listener. I will present only one exercise. The purpose of this exercise is to engage with the location, before starting the actual analysis, and approach the space in a more or less intuitive way.

The exercise consists of a silent listening session followed by writing down the memories of experienced sound in a private journal (Oliveros 2005, 12–17). For pragmatic reasons, I suggest limiting the listening session to only five-ten minutes (set a timer), compared to Oliveros's suggested twenty minutes. I also suggest doing breathing and stretching exercises before beginning the session to create a tension and concentration before the relaxation.

After the listening session, write down your experience with the following questions in mind (not as a checklist):

- Did the act of listening and hearing change over time?
- What made me listen and change to a mode of focal attention?
- What were the sounds I heard, and what did I listen to?
- What was at distance, and what was near?
- Did specific sounds get my attention? Why?
- How did it feel to remember sound?
- How did it feel to listen?

The purpose of this exercise is to experience a partly intuitive listening situation, which is not directed by predetermined parameters, measurements, or aesthetics, and to establish an experience that opens toward an individual perception of the soundscape. The exercise should be carried out in the design process so as to engage with the space in a creative or aesthetic way. This can be done in several ways: for instance, a significant sound that stays in mind can be highlighted in the virtual soundscape to underline it; a certain sound pattern can be continued; sounds that appeared to be missing can be added; or sounds that were annoying can be subtracted. In this way, the personal experience of the soundscape can function as inspiration for the final production.

4.2 Mapping the Soundscape

Whereas Oliveros's work is useful in unfolding a sensitive relation to the location as such, her terminology has few details. To systemize the sounds heard at the specific location—to either include them in, or exclude them from, the final production—a more systematic listening strategy based on a more general terminology can be useful. First I introduce the pioneer and Canadian composer R. Murray Schafer, and later the Danish architect Rikke Thiirmann Thomsen and her way of taking Schafer's thoughts further.

From the 1960s and onward, Schafer has paid much attention both to the study of actual soundscapes and to the construction of so-called soundscape compositions (recorded and composed electroacoustic soundscapes detached from their environment) (Schafer [1977] 1994). Besides being the first to introduce the term *soundscape* (as a counterpart to landscape), Schafer was also the first to call attention to the world's auditory environment, or acoustic ecology, as he called it (how did it sound, how did it affect the inhabitants, and how did it change and develop over the years?), while at the same time developing a terminology and methodology for mapping sound-scapes. Among these, three terms are useful in both the analysis and the composition of soundscapes (208):

• Keynote: Referring to a musical term identifying the key of a piece. The keynote sound of a landscape may not always be heard consciously; for example, it could be wind, water, trees, or traffic.
• Signal sounds: Foreground sounds listened to consciously, for example, bells, whis-tles, horns, sirens.
• Sound mark: Derives from the term *landmark* and is a sound unique to an area.

These three terms can be used in the process of analyzing the existing soundscape, and also as a compositional tool to structure the form and characteristics of the virtual soundscapes in the process of creating the audio production.

There is no doubt that Schafer was a visionary pioneer, but critiques of his work have also been raised: by favoring the sounds coming from the natural soundscape (or from classical music), he ends up rejecting all sound belonging to modernity (Groth and Hjorthkjær 2002, 139; Kreutzfeldt 2009). In spite of this critique, many theoreticians have been inspired by Schafer's work. Among these we find the Danish landscape architect Rikke Thiirmann Thomsen and her research into urban quiet places. Basically Thomsen questions the notion of silence, which she does not intend to reduce to a low number of decibels, but as a phenomenon that should to be approached holistically:

To me, silence is something that is stimulated by multisensory perception. ... Auditory atmo-spheres are mysterious. Much of their content can be invisible and implicit, and their cumulative effects can come from volatile and little-explored phenomena such as pressure changes, infra-sound, ultrasound and other barely perceptible signals. In addition, they are filled with ideas, memories, utopias and fears (Toop 2004). So we can measure the sound level in decibels, whereas there is no measure of silence. Instead, we have to discuss our way to the content and its meaning. (Thiirmann Thomsen 2012, n.p.; translation mine)

As part of the research project "Landscape Character Assessment" at the Swedish Uni-versity of Agriculture, Thomsen and her colleagues developed what they call "sonotop analysis," a method for characterizing sonic landscapes, developed from the theories of Schafer. The method is gathered in a schema or matrix (fig. 12.3), which directs the listener to give a nuanced and qualified response to an auditory experience of a specific sonotop.

The matrix was filled by first describing the most constant sounds, often background sounds (key-notes) and then the figure sounds (events), that appeared on the soundscape. The descriptions were made quickly and intuitively, with the vocabulary of the listener (based on the previously developed vocabularies). (Thiirmann Thomsen 2012, n.p.)

SOUND ANALYSIS	SITE	DATE	TIME	WEATHER	NAME					
				Specification of the sound	Ljudet i sig					
MOMENT	PARTS OF SOUNDSCAPE	PARTS OF SYNTAX	Duration	Technical	Mimicry	Direction	Metaphor	Source	Emotional	Meaning
DIRECT	Atmosphere	long-term present					...sounding as...	...of...	...valued as...	...telling about (proposal)
ANALYZE	Key note 1									
	Key note 2									
	Key note 3									
	Event 1									
	Event 3									
	Event 4									
	Event 5									
	Event 6									
	Event 7									
	Potential sound	seldom present								
DESIGN	Proposal	not yet present								

Figure 12.3
Schema developed by the Swedish landscape architects Per Hedfors and Rikke Thiirmann (from Thiirmann Thomsen 2012, n.p.).

The eight categories are explained as follows:

1. Duration: the duration of the sound
2. Technical: technical description of the sound (often using the terminology of acoustics)
3. Mimicry: the sound described with adjectives that simulate the sound
4. Direction: where the sound comes from and if it appears in a linear movement, from one place, or as "surround"
5. Metaphor: does the sound remind the listener of something else?
6. Source: what makes the sound?
7. Emotional: personally judgment of the sound
8. Meaning: judgment of the message the sound might have

I introduce the matrix here to offer a concrete tool, which can—as Schafer's three terms—be used in the analysis of an existing soundscape. But Schafer's terms and the matrix can also be used in the process of designing an audio production's virtual soundscape, as compositional tools that help to select and structure the layers of sounds. Together with the more intuitive approach, the process of designing a virtual soundscape that corresponds with the actual space can succeed.

5 Designing Portable Audio: Conclusion

Portable audio designs such as audio walks and audio guides are increasingly popular. Whether one wants to produce a guide in a museum, a city walk downloaded from the Internet, or an experimental art project, this chapter highlights the importance of a production process that is both sensitive and systematic toward the production process itself and the chosen location.

To design a production that either entangles or counterpoints the chosen space, the designer must take the specific location into account early in the design process. The actual production or composition must, in other words, begin with site-specific awareness. Such awareness entails several approaches.

One is the need to pay attention to the specific genre (is it an audio walk or an audio guide?). The two cases presented in the beginning of the chapter illustrate that the choice of genre affects the way the productions relate to space and time. In these two cases, the audio walk was more engaged with space and time, while the audio guide appeared to be an almost autonomous production. The relationship between the actual and the virtual was further discussed by introducing the term "sonic envelope," leading to an illustration in which the productions could be compared to

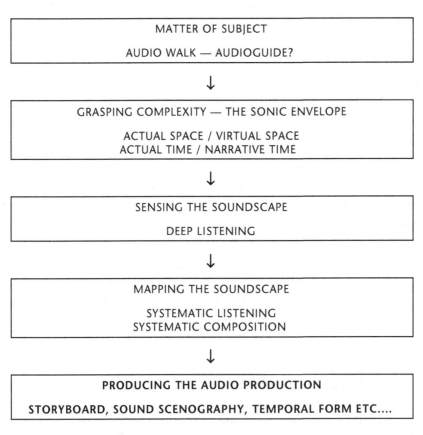

Figure 12.4
The overall portable audio design process.

each other: the closer to the middle, the more the production is entangled with the specific space.

From there the chapter emphasized the importance of getting acquainted with the specific space by approaching it both intuitively and systematically. The intuitive approach opens toward an individual and spontaneous experience of the space, while the matrix supplies tools to a more systematic approach. The benefits of these approaches are twofold: they are useful in the excavation of the actual soundscape, and they work as creative inputs, guidelines, and compositional tools when designing the virtual soundscape.

In these ways, the methodological approaches I have presented here will lead to an audio production that not only narrates the actual through the virtual but also blurs the distinction. The overall process is summed up in figure 12.4.

Notes

1. Vesterbro is a city district in the municipality of Copenhagen.

2. Greve is a suburb outside Copenhagen.

References

Beekhuis, Wendy, Lasse Byrdal, Tine Schjødt, and Ditte Sommer. 2011. *Mit Vesterbro* [My Vesterbro]. Candidate assignment, Performance Design, CBIT, Roskilde University.

Bergson, Henri. [1896] 1991. *Matter and Memory*. Trans. Nancy Margaret Paul and W. Scott Palmer. New York: Zone Books.

Brown, Ross. 2010. *Sound: A Reader in Theater Practice*. Hampshire: Palgrave Macmillan.

Chattopadhyay, Budhaditya. 2012. Sonic menageries: Composing the sound of place. *Organised Sound* 17 (3): 223–229.

Debecque-Michel, Laurence. 1999. Situationism and avant-garde. *Critique d'art* 14 (Autumn), http://critiquedart.revues.org/2397.

Fisher, Jennifer. 2004. Speeches of display: Museum audioguides by artists. In *Aural Cultures*, ed. Jim Drobnick, 49–61. Toronto: YYZ Books.

Foster, Hal. 1996. *Return of the Real*. London: October Books.

Groth, Sanne Krogh Hansen, and Kamilla Hjorthkjær. 2002. *Lydkunst: En kunstart i billede og lyd* [Sound art: An art form in picture and sound]. Det Humanistiske Fakultet, Københavns Universitet.

Haraway, Donna. 1991. *Simians, Cyborgs, and Women: The Reinvention of Nature*. New York: Routledge.

Kreutzfeldt, Jacob. 2009. *Akustisk territorialitet* [Acoustic territory]. Det Humanistiske Fakultet, Københavns Universitet.

Oliveros, Pauline. 2005. *Deep Listening: A Composer's Sound Practice*. Lincoln, NE: Deep Listening Publications.

Rawes, Peg. 2008. Sonic Envelopes. *Senses and Society* 3 (1): 61–76.

Schafer, Murray. [1977] 1994. *Our Sonic Environment and the Soundscape: The Tuning of the World*. Rochester: Destiny Books.

Schafer, Murray. 2006. The music of the environment. In *Audio Culture*, ed. Christoph Cox and Daniel Warner, 29–39. New York: Continuum.

Sonnenschein, David. 2001. *Sound Design*. Saline, MI: Michael Wiese Productions.

Stern, Jonathan, ed. 2012. *The Sound Studies Reader*. London: Routledge.

Thiirmann Thomsen, Rikke. 2012. Stille rum i byen [Silent spaces in the city]. *Seismograf/DMT*, seismograf.org.

Toop, David. 2004. A sense of foreboding. In *Haunted Weather*. London: Serpent's Tail.

Truax, Barry. 2012. Sound, listening, and place: The aesthetic dilemma. *Organised Sound* 17 (3): 193–201.

13 Alternate Reality Games

Erik Kristiansen

What. Urban games are games that take place in the real world of the players and use the properties of the city. Alternate Reality Games (ARGs) are urban games that pretend to be conspiracy theories that are really happening in the life of the players. The games are experienced through events, challenges, and collaborative puzzle solving and may evolve through the engagement of the players. A new design method, Aulaia, addresses the design of urban games in the form of ARGs. Along with the design method, several examples from real-world ARGs are given.

Why. ARGs and other urban games are usually large and complicated undertakings, which require many coordinated activities to make successful games. This design method secures a structured approach not only for the design of the game but also for its launch and running. ARGs develop along with the players and require special monitoring when running.

Where. ARGs are increasingly popular entertainment, typically used as marketing stunts and learning games. They are played worldwide by a large number of players and known as an example of twenty-first-century entertainment featuring city exploration, interactive challenges, and collective intelligence.

How. The method includes directions for idea generation, site exploration, how to write the narrative, design of the player experience, design of challenges, and how to run and monitor the game. In addition several tools are suggested to facilitate the process. Urban games are examples of highly situated games, as they depend on contextualized play. Likewise the design method benefits from both in situ design and situated action.

1 Introduction

The turn of the century saw several new entertainment forms arrive in the form of hybrid digital games that explored the city and the life of its inhabitants. Play festivals where streets turned into playgrounds and games featuring thousands of players scouting for strange clues emerged. Urban games became a genre that featured several forms of interactive entertainment, based on digital technology in some form, but extended to incorporate or add an extra virtual layer to the experiences of the city. Urban play featured several new challenges: how can we integrate physical play with virtual play? How can we design activities that include the streets and buildings of the city? And how can we make the inhabitants of a city work together toward the same goal? One answer, of course, is to design an urban game. In the emerging awareness of the city, the increasing demand for advanced interactive entertainment, and people's fascination with conspiracy theories, a form of urban play called Alternate Reality Games has grown popular and found many uses, from pure entertainment to marketing stunts and learning games. This chapter takes you on a voyage where you learn the basic principles of ARG design through the Aulaia method.

Alternate Reality Games are game experiences originating with The Beast in 2001. The first trace of the game was in the credits of a trailer for the movie *A.I.: Artificial Intelligence* by Steven Spielberg. Among the many names, a line read "Sentient Machine Therapist: Jeanine Salla." Observant cinemagoers were intrigued and followed the trail of the alleged robot therapist on the Web, where a strange story unfolded. They discovered that she apparently was a researcher and that her friend Evan had died in a boating accident on his AI-enhanced boat. Over the course of three months, over three million players (Dena 2006) explored over thirty websites, had live phone conversations, and took part in the birth of a new kind of interactive entertainment, which never revealed itself as a game. The Beast was, in fact, sponsored by Microsoft and ran as a marketing stunt for the movie *A.I.* ARGs have since continued to develop and attract hundreds of thousands of players because they provide suspense and advanced puzzle solving, relying on collective intelligence in people's own real and virtual environments. ARGs attract designers because they require multidisciplinary skills, great teamwork, lots of creativity, situated design, and the ultimate daring necessary to design and launch a performance that may change people's lives.

1.1 What Alternate Reality Games Really Are

ARGs create collective player experiences that rely on a mix of real-world and virtual clues, performances, and puzzles woven into an engaging narrative. Players seek to uncover a hidden narrative through clues, events, and puzzles orchestrated by a team of *puppetmasters* who are responsible for the game design and how the otherwise secret game is executed. ARGs are cross-media games that incorporate any device that can transmit a message, often using digital media such as trailers, cell phones, GPS, social media, and YouTube in combination with imaginative use of posters, signs, events, and old-fashioned technology such as floppy disks, typewriters, and cryptography machines. The core of any ARG is a narrative typically based on some sort of hidden conspiracy, which the players are invited to unmask. The games always take place in the real world, often in an urban setting, and the players are not playing a role but find themselves immersed in a narrative that interferes with their usual life and environment day and night, where anything becomes a possible clue. Sometimes they will be called to explore unknown venues; sometimes they will be challenged with puzzles they have to solve. ARGs are designed as collective challenges and are not meant to be solved by players on their own. Instead they have to form teams and coordinate their actions using chat forums and other social media. ARGs have been successfully used to promote ideas and new products and as learning games. On the other hand, the downside is the complexity of their design and execution. Some players may become frustrated by difficult puzzles or even become scared by dramatic events. It is the responsibility of the puppetmasters to ensure a safe and compelling player experience, often engaging many persons over a stretch of weeks. A general introduction to ARGs can be found in Kim et al. (2008) and Szulborski (2005). The design method presented here is based on studying several ARGs produced by students at Roskilde University, including my own design work, as well as larger, well-known productions.

1.2 Why ARGs Need Design Methods

ARGs are usually larger undertakings. Many of the famous ARGs have attracted hundreds of thousands of players and span several weeks of play. But even small ARGs made to introduce new students to the university campus still require much the same effort and coordination as staging a minor performance at a theater. The designers behind an ARG are called puppetmasters, although they cannot control the strings of the players but merely arrange challenges that the players may or may not undertake. The player experience is a sequence of events that he or she may interact with, which provides an experience of collective problem solving, suspense, and progression. Compared to other games, ARGs have no rules but operate only through challenges, suspense, and curiosity to engage the player. As a consequence, an ARG has to be redesigned on the go to respond to the players' changing demands. As ARGs do not reveal themselves as games, they cannot be designed in the open. This puts an extra strain on the design process, where all experiments, research, and props construction have to be kept in the dark. This calls for a design method that secures a best practice with a structured way to design the narrative as a sequence of events that engage the players combined with methods for on-the-fly redesign. The design method presented here is split into two parts: designing the game and executing the game. The design phase includes the creation of the narrative and how it is exposed to the players, and the execution phase deals with the puppetmasters' monitoring, intervention, and redesign. Little has been published on the design practices of ARGs, the main work being by Szulborski (2005) and McGonigal (2006, 2007).

1.3 Where to Use the Method

The method is meant to be used for the design of ARGs of any kind but can also be used in part for other games that share some of the features of ARGs. This may be relevant for the design of other site-oriented urban games, such as big games, pervasive games, and live-action role-playing games. Students of nongame performances like interactive storytelling, flash mobs, happenings, street theater, and the interactive and invisible theater of Augusto Boal (Boal 2003) may also find the method interesting.

1.4 How ARGs Are Designed

A motto with ARGs has always been "This Is Not A Game," better known as the TINAG aesthetic. An ARG will never acknowledge that it is a game, but at the same time neither will it expose itself as a hoax. This means that all references to real-world events must be true, and if references are made to websites or events that are fictitious, then they must be staged to look real in all details. ARGs are put to action by "inviting" persons to join by using strange clues that attract attention. These are called *rabbitholes* and may be anything from jars of honey containing letters (I Love Bees) to envelopes stamped "Top Secret" distributed in the streets (Find Holger). Often the task of a rabbithole is to point to online sites where parts of the game's narrative may be found and where players may meet other players. The narrative must be designed as an interactive narrative and exposed in small parts using many different media and even staged performances. The players have to piece the information together, often by solving *puzzles*. These are carefully designed to make the players work together. To secure the players' continued involvement, ARGs are continually redesigned by using *trailheads*, which are indirect interventions by the puppetmasters to help the players.

The design method is called Aulaia (from the Greek word for the curtain that separates the stage from the audience in a theater, which in ARG terminology refers to the puppetmasters' hidden work). Central to the process is how to design an interactive narrative and how it may be exposed using diverse media. This is accommodated in the design method by working with player activities coupled to a timeline. The second part includes methods for monitoring and interacting with the players to change sequence or put trailheads into use. The design acknowledges the importance of being situated due to its site-specific nature and the way working with props and challenges allows for influencing the design of the narrative. Part of the design process must take place at the physical site where the game is later going to be performed. Recognizing the difficulties and potentials with materials in situ and tinkering with technology pushes creativity and develops ideas, which in turn may change the background narrative.

2 Designing an ARG Using Aulaia

Designing an ARG is always a complex undertaking and therefore needs project organization. In ARG terminology, the designers, who usually also execute the game, are called puppetmasters. This title may be misleading, because the puppetmasters do not control the strings of the players, as in the old doll theaters, but are the creators, designers, constructors, and facilitators of a gaming experience and must already from the start be careful to acknowledge this role and what it entails. The puppetmasters work behind the curtain (i.e., in secrecy) and have to control a complex performance, meet hard deadlines, and monitor the game without direct interference. This calls for a team that is carefully organized and whose members trust one another. Above all the project needs a name—at least a code name that identifies it and the spirit of the team's work. The main activities of the puppetmasters consist of designing the narrative, props, puzzles, media, and events. A repository where all documents, ideas, and photos are kept and shared by the puppetmasters is essential. Likewise a *game design diary*, where discussions, design proposals, and decisions are kept. This has proved to be vital for several ARG projects, because many issues are discussed on the fly and later forgotten if not put into writing. As designing an ARG is a secret adventure and an example of designing as a performance, some secret rituals may be appropriate. One puppetmaster team wore self-made paper hats when working on their ARG. A summary of the method is given in figure 13.2 at the end of the chapter.

2.1 Getting the Idea

ARGs are based on a story that might be true, not too unrealistic while still retaining elements that seem improbable or unworldly, and therefore have the power of attracting attention and keeping engagement. Part of the narrative may never be directly used but has the important function of keeping the design team on the same track. Stories are usually based on conspiracy theories. Everyone loves conspiracies, and people are always looking for them and tending to believe, or at least find interesting, even the most absurd stories.

Most design challenges start with a problem, and most ARGs seem to be part of marketing stunts to promote new brands or products. Examples are the promotion of movies (The Beast), video games (I Love Bees), education (Find Holger), and the Olympic Games (Find the Lost Ring). Recently a number of projects are exploring the potentials of ARGs as learning games (Whitton 2009). ARGs have also been designed to promote ideas or solve problems, such as the game World without Oil, which focused on how people would cope without fuel, and the game Conspiracy for Good, which aimed at fighting the forces of social and environmental injustice through collective interactive storytelling. In connection with the identification of the originating problem, it is important to study the target group of the game closely. What are their habits and interests? Which places do they visit? What level of engagement can you expect? Engaged players (called "devotees") are ready to take a chance, for example, by calling up secret phone numbers or showing up at events. Other players may prefer to work with difficult deciphering tasks. This knowledge is essential when rabbitholes are put to use.

The challenge is to create a story that fits the purpose of the game. It should link to the problem but may do so in an unexpected way. Ideas for stories are often found in controversial organizations or strange inventions. What if a spaceship crash-landed, and the AI computer system spread over the Internet (I Love Bees)? Or what if a museum in fact was a cover-up for a research center on a life-prolonging serum (The Cliff Game; see Kristiansen 2009)? It is important that the team works together on this first phase, because the quality of an ARG lies in the way the narrative is told through the artifacts that the players pick up or find on the Internet. Another way of working with the idea is to look at it from the players' perspective. What is the player going to pick up as the first rabbithole? Among methods for idea generation, drawing a common mind map on a large piece of paper has been successful. As ARGs are linked to the real world, this method suggests beginning with an analysis of the site, where the game is going to take place. This site or sites should, of course, link to the problem that the ARG is going to solve.

2.2 Exploring the Site

All ARGs have the quality that they "invade" the player's reality. ARGs are not an activity that people attend or subscribe to but one that becomes part of the players' lives for a period of time. To do this in a reasonable way, ARGs are not just virtual phenomena on the Internet but must extensively use the place or site where the players live their daily lives. This site specificity is usually crucial to an ARG and provides a much more varied game play than just relying on a single platform. An ARG should reach you no matter where you hide! Any site has a lot to offer that can be used creatively by an ARG. To explore the possibilities and to link the site with the idea, it is important to carry out a site analysis. This can be done in several ways. *Place storming* (Anderson and McGonigal 2004) is a method originally aimed at innovating pervasive technology by playing out small improvised scenarios using daily tools given a new meaning. They suggest that working in situ, that is, at the very place where the design is to be used, increases creativity. This is supported by my own work with creativity in pervasive game design (the *site-storming* method), where I suggest using a game-based approach in situ to facilitate idea generation for pervasive games (Kristiansen 2009, 2013). The site-storming method recommends the use of the *dérive*—a special way of drifting through the city to explore it combined with mission-based cards. The cards should be designed with missions aimed at exploring the site in accordance with the ARG in question, for example, "Go to a place where you are not supposed to enter. Describe what is happening here at night." Distribute the cards and send each puppetmaster on an explorative mission. Both place storming and site storming can be recommended for the design of ARGs. Ideas should be documented by photographing what catches the eye. Print the photos, draw a map of the area, and use it as basis for developing ideas together.

2.3 Writing the Narrative

A good narrative has to be original and thoroughly worked through with many details that are unusual and irresistible, but still probable. The narrative is often inspired by an event that has happened some time ago, which some persons know of, but which no longer can be kept secret. The game Find Holger based its narrative on a secret agency that the government put to work to clean up shortly after World War II, which is claimed still to be operating. The story behind Find the Lost Ring was based on six amnesiacs who woke up in labyrinths around the world, each with a mysterious tattoo, "Find the lost ring," written in Esperanto. The ARG was composed of a prologue and twenty-six chapters, each with its own media and puzzles.

When the general idea is agreed on, the narrative should be written by a single person or a small group of persons, of which one is the lead writer. The game needs a narrative that consists of many small parts, called a *transmedia narrative*, designed for rabbitholes, puzzles, and so on, which can be enjoyed without being either complete or in perfect sequence. A practical method for developing such a narrative is to write an *ur-text* —that is, the underlying narrative first. It is important that the narrative is full of details that make it credible. The ur-text must be presented and discussed by the whole team to secure a uniform understanding of the game. The players will never experience the ur-text, only the realized parts of it. The transmedia narrative is often called *nonlinear storytelling* or *ergodic literature* (Aarseth 1997). In practice this means that the ur-text can be designed as a typical novel, but a transmedia narrative should be designed in parts, which have a more or less strict sequence but can be enjoyed in parts. These parts may be realized using any media you prefer. A typical ARG uses as many different media as possible, both virtual and physical, and is therefore regarded as a *cross-media* game. An episodic rhetoric with frequent points of suspense is recommended to maintain suspense.

2.4 Designing the Player Experience

For ARGs it is particularly crucial to design the game with the player in mind (player-centered design), as the players may interact with the game in different ways and at different speeds. When the narrative is more or less complete, the question becomes how it can be deployed. Which parts should be realized as rabbitholes? As trailheads? As additional information? As puzzles? Or as events and performances? The players will meet and interact with the game only through these channels of communication. They will never meet the puppetmasters, and there is no way directly to tell them what to do. If they get stuck, you have to make a trailhead available, which is a piece of information that brings them back into the game. Rabbitholes are the artifacts that the prospective player may pick up and thus join the game. They should be designed to beg for interaction, but without being ridiculous. If a person chooses to pick up and examine a rabbithole, then he or she becomes a player and you, as a puppetmaster, are responsible for securing an engaging player experience. A well-designed ARG will look after its players, and if their attention dwindles, it will immediately launch a trailhead, which will confront the players somewhere during their day, just as annoying commercials persistently chase you on the Internet. A good ARG will strive for variation, to make the game invade the players' lives and to speak to different player styles.

ARG players can be divided into four classes: *devotee* players, *active* players, *casual* players, and *curious* players. Devotees follow the game closely and participate as much as possible, following up on new posts immediately. Active players participate, but less frequently and not always immediately. Casual players follow the game, but mostly as witnesses. The large group of curious players hear about the game or stumble on a rabbithole but do not take part and have to be invited by more rabbitholes (IGDA 2006). A key finding is that collective behavior is encouraged by low entry barriers, but also that any ARG must rely on devotees and active players to drive the experience (Kim et al. 2009). Indeed, ARGs are usually designed to be impossible to solve alone (Jenkins 2006), for example, by requiring different language skills or by taking place in several different locations at the same time. Collaboration requires awareness of the other players' actions and close participation. When a game becomes part of a person's daily life, social aspects may become inseparable from the game (Dena 2008; Kim et al. 2009). To reach players of the different categories, collaboration may be designed to include diverse skills; a low barrier can be attending a specific place at a specific time. I Love Bees used more than one hundred pay phones spread across the United States to deliver messages at specific times.

2.5 Using Models and Docs

Even a small ARG is a highly complex design problem, where the overview is easily lost. To remedy this, the design method proposes the use of several models of the ARG. They are used to facilitate the design process and in the end as a script when the ARG is launched. Aulaia includes the following documents:

• The *game design diary* is a record of all discussions and decisions pertaining to the game, kept as a diary. It should also be kept when the game is played, as it is vital for the evaluation that precise records are available. When the game is executed, actions taken by the puppetmaster team should be recorded.

• The *concept* is a short document that states the problem and main idea on a half page, plus an overview of the necessary resources needed, a rough schedule for the design process and launch date and place, and the intended duration of the game. If the game is part of a marketing stunt or learning project, then the goals of the game have to be formulated as well, so that they can be evaluated later.

• The *site analysis* should document explorations carried out at the site where the game is going to be performed. Depending on the method used, the site can be documented in several ways. The method recommends taking photographs of the interesting features on-site and attaching them to a large map, either directly on the map or using arrows pointing to the places.

• The *ur-text* is a document in the style of a novel. It is used only to set the common ground for the puppetmasters. The players will never see this document.

• The *transmedia narrative* is the ur-text realized as operational and partly independent chunks that again can be realized using different kinds of media, from old manuscripts and plans of ingenious code systems to surveillance videos on YouTube or messages given by answering machines.

• The *media plan* includes titles of all the parts of the transmedia narrative and a short description of what they are realized as (rabbithole, media, trailhead, performance, etc.), how they should be realized, and who is responsible. Each of the responsible puppetmasters must also keep a plan of the media he or she is responsible for. The media plan should correspond to the *masterplan.*

• The *masterplan* is a timeline in the form of a graph with each media plotted in, complete with type and launch date. As rabbitholes and other game events may not be picked up or puzzles may not be solved, extra material should be shown as side lines (like tracks and points in a railway station). The masterplan acts as a planning tool that gives an overview of the game and as a script for controlling the launch of the single events when the game is executed. Points where information on the players is collected are marked as solid nodes. An example of a masterplan is given in figure 13.1.

2.6 Designing Challenges

Puzzles and other challenges are central to any ARG. They are usually used to engage the players to work together on a problem. The players should feel that they are working to unearth a mystery by solving puzzles. Puzzles may be any challenge, for example, documents in foreign languages that have to be translated, almost illegible old manuscripts, or code machines. They may be hidden and only discovered when the player examines an artifact, for example, by hiding the puzzle in a picture or in a poem. In general, puzzles should be difficult to solve and require the players to

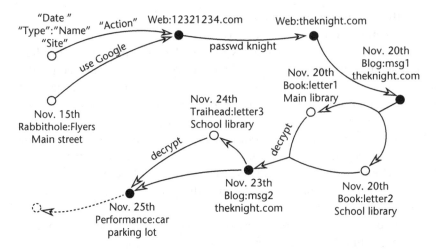

Figure 13.1

The masterplan showing part of a small fictitious ARG. Each node is a planned activity. Arrows show how the players are supposed to progress from one activity to another through an action. A split line requires the players to complete both activities, e.g., visit both libraries to collect clues. Solid nodes indicate that information on the players' progress is collected. During execution, the masterplan should be amended in accordance with the players' evolution of the game.

cooperate. If the puzzles are too easy, the players lose interest too quickly. If they are too difficult, a trailhead may be put out. As Szulborski (2005) points out, "You don't know how difficult a puzzle is, before it has been solved." Several puppetmasters have been surprised at the power of the collective intelligence of dedicated players. It seems that puzzles should be hard but include lots of information that players may sift for clues. Puzzles can be virtual or physical or a combination. They should, of course, be well integrated with the narrative. The ARG Cicada 3301 uses cryptography that requires cracking low-bit modulus RSA codes. Charlie 1 Umbra uses audio recordings that contain hidden images using SSTV techniques from 1950s. Find the Lost Ring used manuscripts written in several different languages and ancient omphalos codes to reveal GPS positions of objects to be retrieved. And The Beast required understanding a Renaissance form of music scores (lute tablature) to decode a message.

2.7 Designing Media

Using diverse media is the ARG's way to tell the story and communicate with the players. Many ARGs use rabbitholes to guide players to a social media platform or similar area where the ARG can launch messages at appropriate times. This "headquarters" can also be used to facilitate discussions between the players. Sometimes a fake Facebook profile is used for this purpose, as it can easily be linked to the narrative.

An important design principle for ARGs is that they are not a hoax. This means that even though the story is not true, every effort is used to make it appear to be true. If a mobile phone number is given, it has to be rigged so that the player can call it. Likewise any reference to persons, Web pages, companies, and so on, must lead to appropriately staged websites. Even a limited narrative quickly expands the need for media into a larger undertaking. Any ARG needs several forms of communication channels, including one-to-many, when providing information for all players; one-to-one, when communicating with a single player (rabbitholes and trailheads); and many-to-many, when facilitating discussions and collaboration between the players. The one-to-many channel is used to keep up activity by providing new material at regular intervals. Here information is dispersed for general use, often not hinted directly at the players. Rabbitholes, trailheads, and some puzzles may be directed at the player, so that he or she feels needed and has some information or ability that may be of use in the game. An interesting source for inspiration regarding media is to look at the field of media archaeology (cf. Parikka 2012). This is the study of older or rebuilt equipment that can be used for communication purposes. Tangible equipment gives a realistic feel to the ARG. The pervasive LARP Prosopopeia used rebuilt old-fashioned reel recorders as machines that enabled the players to communicate with spirits. Find the Lost Ring used "old" manuscripts, as well as rings of iron that had to be collected in different places in the world and brought to the Beijing Olympics in 2008. Anything can be used, but it is important that it is carefully designed to fit the narrative and that TINAG is maintained at all costs.

2.8 Putting It All Together

Because an ARG is secret, the design phase more or less must take place in the dark. This means that it is difficult to evaluate an ARG, as it will only be performed once, and we therefore don't know how the players will react. There are many pitfalls: rabbitholes may never be found (or removed by the regular cleaners, as happened with Find Holger), puzzles may be too difficult, information may be misunderstood, the players may find it dull, and so forth. The design strategy to answer all these problems when rehearsals are not possible is to provide extra material and to redesign the ARG while it is being played. This means that extra rabbitholes, trailheads, media, and so on, have to be prepared and kept ready. This only makes sense if we have some way of monitoring the progress of the players. Design for monitoring therefore has to be part of how everything is designed for the ARG. This is where the puppetmasters usually use social media, a blog, or a game discussion forum. If a rabbithole requires the player to create an account, we know how many and who the players are. Another way of monitoring is to use false players in discussion forums that are controlled by the puppetmasters, who interact with the real players. This can be used to facilitate discussions, provide help, and monitor progress. Designing for redesign means that all parts of the game have to be flexible and modular units, which with little or no modification can be put together in different ways.

2.9   Launching and Running

The masterplan now acts out the script when conducting the game. The launch starts by revealing the first set of rabbitholes. Sometimes it is wise to start with a single rabbithole to monitor how many players it catches. In practice, several rabbitholes of different kinds are needed to attract a player community of sufficient number. Some ARGs have used an event to promote the ARG. An ARG was designed using a spectacular performance in the university canteen as an intro. A person was dramatically performing that he was ill while losing his (secret) papers. Subsequently he was taken away by paramedics. This acted as a teaser to the real rabbitholes, which followed a few days later. From the performance, people got the idea that something was up, and it made them alert and eager to pick up rabbitholes. During the performance of the ARG, the puppetmasters are performing three functions: monitoring the players' progression, launching new media and events according to the master plan, and redesigning the game to secure the players' engagement and respond to their progression. As puppetmaster, you must provide the players with a rewarding and safe experience. You are the facilitator who makes this happen, and the players, who may know or suspect that this is not for real, may spend hours solving puzzles and searching high and low for clues. Sometimes their reaction is not the anticipated one, but sometimes the players may even respond with information that brings new value to the game. The answer is again to redesign the game immediately in response to the players' wishes for adventure. It's their game. To monitor the game, it is advisable to supplement the game's discussion forum with a log, where the puppetmasters track player progression and share it with the team.

2.10   Evaluating an ARG

As the ARG was designed to monitor the players' progress, the puppetmasters already are in indirect contact with many of the players. When the ARG ends, maybe with a surprise event, the puppetmaster team may step out from behind the curtain and evaluate the game with the players, who by now have realized that it was a game. If the game was designed as an answer to a problem, it must be evaluated according to the problem. If it was designed just for fun, it may be evaluated according the perceived enjoyment. Macvean and Riedl (2011) provide categories of evaluation directly aimed at ARGs. You may consider a focus group or an informal talk. Or you could provide a questionnaire. The evaluation could cover questions such as the following: What is your age? What is your occupation? Have you played an alternate reality game before? How and where did you get in contact with the game? What did you dislike about the game? More advanced methods of evaluation may of course be used.

2.11 How to Use an ARG

Alternate reality games may be used for several purposes. Games that have a purpose other than just fun are often termed *serious games* and include learning games and marketing games, among others. Most of the ARGs known from the media seem to be used as part of marketing stunts. The potential of ARGs to be used as learning games has also been researched (Whitton 2009). It seems obvious that if you can engage hundreds of players in searching high and low, solving complex riddles together, there must be a considerable learning potential. An example of ARG as learning game is an arts college that each year introduces new students through a semester-long symposium. One year the topic was Renaissance art and music, and when the new students logged into the campus system, they were met with a note saying that a seventeenth-century viola da gamba had been stolen and hidden on campus by a thief called "Mad Jack." The students used help and expertise from various departments, the Web, and the library to track down Mad Jack. By the end of the semester, they had, in a playful way, learned fundamentals of academic research and how to collaborate on a common project (educause 2009).

3 Conclusion

Alternate reality games have been subject to research, particularly with regard to their potential in learning environments, but very little regarding design methods. ARGs have several unusual properties that make them interesting for research. In this section, I briefly mention three aspects of theoretical interest. As games, ARGs are unusual because they do not reveal themselves as games. Typical games share several features, such as the properties of being voluntary, rule bound, having known participants, taking place in a designated area and within a specific time (cf. Caillois 1961; Huizinga 1955; Salen and Zimmermann 2004). The game genre called pervasive games (Montola, Stenros, and Waern 2009; Kristiansen 2009) extends the properties of participants, time, and place, and as such the ARGs show pervasive properties. A notable difference is the secrecy of the activity. By not revealing itself as a designed performance, the ARG shares properties with some flash mobs and the performance type known as invisible theater, developed by Augusto Boal. Another aspect is transmedia storytelling (Jenkins 2006), which refers to ARGs' use of many media and communication channels to tell the story using chunks in nonsequential order. Finally, ARGs are peculiar in their use of a particular form of user-centered design where the user not only is the object of the design but in fact considered the hero. This means that the design artifact will insist on being of use to the user, even if it has to be revamped or redesigned. This puts the user in a curious control of the design artifact (the "hero" mode), where interaction becomes particularly rewarding. This kind of hero gaming has been discussed by McGonigal (2003).

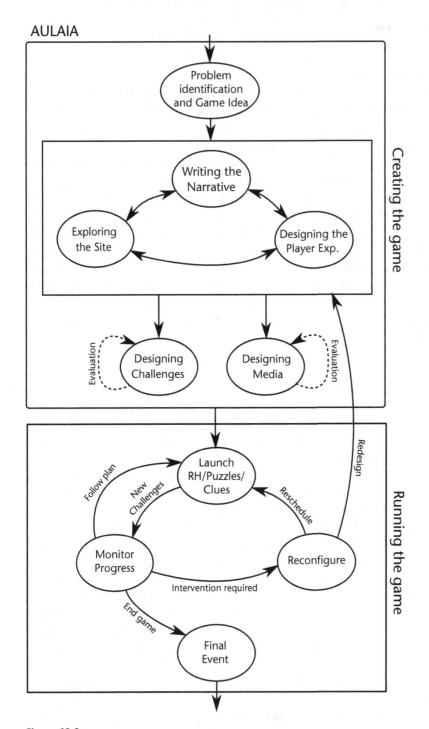

Figure 13.2

Summary of the Aulaia design method. The activities Writing the Narrative, Exploring the Site, and Designing the Player Experience should be conducted in parallel. The double arrows indicate that the activities are allowed to influence each other during design work. The dotted lines show that, if possible, evaluation may be used.

As a design artifact, ARGs show unusual properties. Ex post evaluation is not possible, as the design product (the game) is only staged once. And preproduction evaluation is difficult, as the design process is secret. Ex ante evaluation (preproduction evaluation) is also hampered by this, but some ARGs have developed "anonymous" versions of some of the trickier puzzles and evaluated them through preplay testing. It is important to stress that ARGs are performances that are not meant to be completed by the designers but rely partially on the players' engagement to evolve them. This happens not only by forcing a rescheduling of the parts of the design artifact but also by a continuous redesign process. The production of an ARG therefore relies on monitoring the success (or failure) of the usage and subsequent on-the-fly rescheduling or partial redesign of the artifact. To make monitoring smooth, most parts of an ARG have to be designed with monitoring in mind. The redesign-during-execution makes ARGs a form of collective storytelling, as the players together coevolve the story and together with the puppetmasters develop it in unforeseen directions (cf. Kim et al. 2008).

Aulaia is a structured approach for designing different kinds of narrative-based urban games, particularly ARGs, but other game genres, such as live-action role-playing games and pervasive games, may also benefit from this method. An overall view of the method including the activities described in section 2 is given in figure 13.2.

References

Aarseth, Espen. 1997. *Ergodic Literature*. Baltimore, MD: The Johns Hopkins University Press.

Anderson, Ken, and Jane McGonigal. Place storming: Performing new technologies in context. In *NordiCHI 2004: Proceedings of the Third Nordic Conference on Human-Computer Interaction* (Tampere, Finland, October 23–27), 85–88. New York: ACM Press.

The Beast. 2001. Microsoft. http://bangaloreworldu-in.co.cloudmakers.org/salla.

Boal, Augusto. 2003. From *Theatre of the Oppressed*. In *The New Media Reader*, ed. Noah Wardrip-Fruin and Nick Montfort, 339–352. Cambridge, MA: MIT Press.

Caillois, Roger. 1961. *Man, Play, and Game*. Trans. Meyer Barash. New York: Free Press of Glencoe.

Charlie 1 Umbra. 2012. http://www.reddit.com/r/conspiracy/comments/s3gek/encrypted_transmissions_found_online_currently.

Cicada 3301. 2012. http://uncovering-cicada.wikia.com/wiki/What_We_Know.

Dena, Christy. 2006. Top ARGs, with stats. http://web.archive.org/web/20060420094207/http://www.cross-mediaentertainment.com/index.php/2006/03/04/top-args-with-stats.

Dena, Christy. 2008. Emerging participatory culture practices: Player-created tiers in alternate reality games. *Convergence* 14: 41, doi:10.1177/1354856507084418.

EDUCAUSE. 2009. 7 things you should know about Alternate Reality Games. http://www
.educause.edu/library/resources/7-things-you-should-know-about-alternate-reality-games.

Find the Lost Ring. 2008. AKQA. http://www.thelostring.com.

Huizinga, Johan. 1955. *Homo Ludens*. Trans. R. F. C. Hull. Boston, MA: Beacon Press.

IGDA. 2006. Alternate Reality Games White Paper. The IGDA Reality Games SIG. http://igda.org/
arg.

I Love Bees. 2004. 42 Entertainment. http://ilovebees.com.

Jenkins, Henry. 2006. *Convergence Culture: Where Old and New Media Collide*. New York: New York
University Press.

Kim, Jeffrey Y., Jonathan P. Allen, and Elan Lee. 2008. Alternate reality gaming. *Communications
of the ACM* 51 (2): 36–42.

Kim, Jeffrey, Elan Lee, Timothy Thomas, and Caroline Dombrowski. 2009. Storytelling in new
media: The case of alternate reality games, 2001–2009. *First Monday* 14 (6), DOI: http://dx.doi
.org/10.5210%2Ffm.v14i6.2484.

Kring, Tim, Nokia, and The company P. 2010. Conspiracy for good. http://www.conspiracy
forgood.com.

Kristiansen, Erik. 2009. Games for the real world. Ph.D. thesis, Roskilde University.

Kristiansen, Erik. 2013. Design games for in-situ design. *International Journal of Mobile Human
Computer Interaction* 5 (3): 1–22.

Macvean, Andrew P., and Mark Riedl. 2011. Evaluating enjoyment within alternate reality games.
In *Proceedings of the 2011 ACM SIGGRAPH Symposium on Video Games*, 5–10. New York: ACM
Press. DOI:10.1145/2018556.2018558.

Madsen, Louise, Jacob Caspersen Kriegbaum, Karen Kirstine Baad Michelsen, Helene Drejer, Stine
Lykke Wagner, and Christian Koefoed Jessen. 2010. Alternate reality gaming—Find Holger.
Unpublished paper. Roskilde University.

McGonigal, Jane. 2003. A real little game: The performance of belief in pervasive play. In *Level
Up: Digital Games Research Conference, 4–6 November 2003, Proceedings, DiGRA 2003*, ed. Marinka
Copier and Joost Raessens. Utrecht, Netherlands: Universiteit Utrecht.

McGonigal, Jane. 2006. This might be a game: Ubiquitous play and performance at the turn of
the twenty-first century. Ph.D. diss., University of California. http://www.avantgame.com/
McGonigal_THIS_MIGHT_BE_A_GAME_sm.pdf.

McGonigal, Jane. 2007. The puppet master problem: Design for real-world, mission-based
gaming. In *Second Person*, ed. Pat Harrigan and Noah Wardrip-Fruin, 251–265. Cambridge, MA:
MIT Press.

Montola, Markus, Jaakko Stenros, and Annika Waern. 2009. *Pervasive Games: Theory and Design*.
Burlington, MA: Elsevier/Morgan Kaufmann.

Parikka, Jussi. 2012. *What Is Media Archaeology?* Oxford: Polity Press.

Prosopopoeia. 2005. IperG. http://iperg.sics.se/iperg_games5.php.

Salen, Katie, and Eric Zimmermann. 2004. *Rules of Play*. Cambridge, MA: MIT Press.

Szulborski, Dave. 2005. *This Is Not a Game*. Published by Lulu.com.

Whitton, Nicola. 2009. The potential of alternate reality games for enhancing teaching and learning. Paper presented at Next Generation Technologies in Practice Conference, Loughborough, March 10–11.

World without Oil. 2007. ITVS. http://worldwithoutoil.org.

14 Designing Software-Based Interactive Installations

Troels Andreasen, Niels Christian Juul, and Mads Rosendahl

What. This chapter focuses on software engineering principles with specific emphasis on interactive installations providing embodied, tangible, and immersive experiences for the user. Such installations may deliver light, image, sound, and movement through actuators and may provide interaction through gesticulation, voice, and sensor signals. Installations are typically driven by specialized software that differs significantly from conventional business software, and in addition may include hardware components customized for the installation. To set the context, we give a range of example installations and support the description of the approach with a single case—a bumper car competition.

Why. To some extent, standard techniques for software development can be adapted for interactive installations. However, there is a need to emphasize the unique aspects of installations, bringing tangible architecture as well as aesthetic experience, artistic expression, and leisure aspects into focus. The approach presented here has this intended purpose.

Where. Building on experience from conventional software development and with inspiration from interaction design and creative programming, this chapter considers the development of interactive installations for immersive experiences with emphasis on the special design challenges they present.

How. The approach described includes four phases: exploration, design, construction, and exhibition. The aim of the exploration is to clarify the general behavior of the installation using tools like sketching or storyboarding. The design involves a clarification of available and appropriate building blocks, as well as the linking of these blocks to provide an architectural framework comprising the intended external behavior. The construction phase takes a component-based approach to developing the final installation, and the exhibition phase concerns setting up, using, and evaluating the installation in the intended context—typically an event.

1   Introduction

When developing an interactive installation for an exhibition, it may be tempting to focus on the end product and not give sufficient attention to the intermediate stages in the development. However, without a careful development process, we may discover technical problems too late, and in the end we may be forced to make restrictions on the functionality and experience of the installation.

Not only is the interplay between an interactive installation and the location in which it is placed important; the resources available to the design team play an equally important role. Interactive installations tend to use hardware and software outside mainstream software development, and the development process should reflect this to ensure that challenges and possibilities are addressed early in the process. Thus situated design methods must be applied, not just to address the specifics of the location and the humans involved, but more broadly to address the specifics of all the available resources relevant to realizing the idea.

In this chapter, we present such a situated design process for interactive installations. We recommend a four-phase design process of exploration, design, construction, and exhibition.

2   Interactive Installations

Interactive installations are used in art exhibitions, at trade shows, or in public spaces. They are typically used at events for a limited time but may evolve and be adapted into new installations for later presentation. The installations we consider here have a relatively short development period (up to a few months) involving only a handful of developers and designers in the team. Larger projects will probably need other software engineering techniques in the design process, but they may involve the development of a prototype as a first stage, and this may well be within these limits.

Interactive installations are software-based systems for controlling light, image, sound, and movement. They may use sensors to detect audience interaction and actuators to generate effects. Such systems are often constructed as a combination of software written for the installations and modified or adapted software for various types of physical devices. They are complex systems aimed at giving a coherent experience while integrating a diversity of hardware platforms and pieces of software running on these platforms.

Interactive installations have a physical presence and aim to create an embodied, tangible, or immersive experience for the user. They can be works of art, or they can have an intended purpose, such as mediating a message or a product. The artist or creative designer and the programmer will in many cases form a closely cooperating team or even be the same person. Systems will most typically be developed iteratively until the desired expression or effect is achieved.

2.1 Examples of Interactive Installations

The following four examples show some of the characteristics and variety of interactive installations as understood in this chapter. We will explore the first of these examples in further detail in the rest of the chapter.

A Bumper Car Competition In 2011 a group of students arranged a bumper car competition at an amusement park (fig. 14.1). The bumper cars were equipped with motion sensors, and at the event, spectators and participants could follow live results on a scoreboard projected on a large screen.

Prototyping a Visualization of a Reconstructed Travel by Viking Ship In 2010 a collaboration between Roskilde University and the Viking Ship Museum in Roskilde created a pilot installation (fig. 14.2) for the museum, visualizing the journey of a Viking ship from Roskilde to Dublin. The installation forms an "experience cylinder" consisting

Figure 14.1
Bumper car competition.

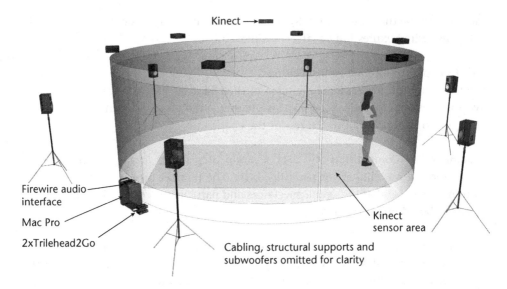

Figure 14.2
Installation for the Viking Ship Museum.

of a 360-degree screen for an immersive experience where the audience controls the visualization through movements.

Prototyping a Travel Fair Installation   In 2009 a group of students created a prototype installation for a travel fair. In the installation, a map of the world was projected on the floor, and the audience could move between countries by placing themselves on spots on the floor. Up to five people could use the installation at the same time, and images from selected countries were projected on walls while sounds and typical music from the countries were mixed together using a programmed warping sequencer with tracks in the same key.

Installation Extracting Meaning from Large Data Sets   In 2013 an installation was created for the launch of a major research project. The installation showed live Twitter feeds of selected tags related to the research project and provided an interactive word and topic visualization reflecting the tags.

2.2   Characteristics of Interactive Installations

The interactive installations we consider here are characterized by a number of properties:

• They are software-based systems with a physical presence.
• They use sensors of various kinds to detect interaction from the audience.

• They generate effects, such as light, images, sound, or movements.
• Only up to a few months are allocated to development by a team of a handful of people.
• The deadline for development is fixed by an event that will take place regardless of whether the installation is finished.
• The installation is used for a limited period.

The development process needs to address the explorative aspects of constructing systems where the possibilities and restrictions of some of the components are not fully understood beforehand. We will use the bumper car competition as an example when we explore and examine the elements of the development process in the rest of the chapter.

3   Related Design Techniques

Since a software component typically appears in the core of an interactive installation, principles and techniques for conventional software design still apply—only in slightly modified form. In this section, we briefly touch on various key techniques that relate and provide an important foundation for the approach described in this chapter. We refer to the characteristics of interactive installations mentioned earlier and in addition emphasize the need to consider that the target for the development involves not only software but typically also dedicated physical constructions, and that the requirements to input/output are predominant because the whole purpose of installations typically is to interact and experience.

Software engineering and system development are characterized by so-called process models. Important distinctive characteristics of such models are the structuring of phases and the progress through them. One extreme approach is the waterfall model (Royce 1970; Kruchten 2001), also called the linear-sequential life cycle model, because phases, in principle, must progress in sequence without ever returning to a previous phase. The iterative development model (Larman 2003) was developed as a reaction to the rigidity of the waterfall model. In the iterative model, development is performed through repeated cycles moving from phase to phase and returning when needed. Thus the model is also inherently incremental in the sense that the tasks of a phase need not all be finished when leaving a phase but can be continued when returning.

Based on iterative development and with emphasis on collaboration, an agile approach to system development has been proposed (Fowler and Highsmith 2001; Cohen, Lindvall, and Costa 2004). The focal point in agile development is that requirements and solutions evolve through teamwork in self-organizing teams.

Agile methods are thus adaptive, as they focus on adapting quickly to changing realities. Shifts in direction of development can occur often, as opposed to traditional development (such as the waterfall model), and details about future development activities are not in focus.

Agile development is a timeboxed iterative approach (Jalote, Palit, and Kurien 2004), that is, an approach where the duration of each iteration is fixed in a timebox, while the goal—what should be developed in the iteration—is adjusted to fit the available time.

Another important trend in systems development, which is basically independent of the process model, is usability studies. Usability is about how easy a system or its user interfaces are to use, and an important systematic approach to the study of this was introduced by Nielsen and Norman (Nielsen 1993; Norman 2002). In their approach, they define usability based on five quality components—learnability, efficiency, memorability, errors, and satisfaction—and combine usability with another important quality: utility. Utility addresses whether the features you need are provided by the system. Nielsen and Norman argue that usability can be studied in all phases of systems development and thus gives rise to new iterations in iterative development, but since usability studies can also be performed on already developed systems, they are not connected to the chosen process model.

While business systems developments tend to move toward more iterative and agile approaches involving users in usability testing, a more conservative approach is needed when it comes to interactive installations. Here iteration may need to be limited because development involves physical constructions that prohibit the design from being freely changed. Furthermore, the developers may prefer to guide development more by their own ideas and expressions and less by the users' involvement.

Experience and immersion in physical space often play a key role in interactive installations, so that modeling needs to prioritize these aspects, placing demands especially on input/output. Important contributions to modeling that take these aspects into account come from the fields of interaction design (Sharp, Rogers, and Preece 2007) and data visualization (Fry 2007; Steele and Iliinsky 2010; Friedman 2007). In particular, the subfield of affective interaction design (Sharp, Rogers, and Preece 2007), which deals with how design issues influence emotional responses in users, is related to interactive installation design. Because graphical projection obviously is an important technique in installations, data visualization methods aiming at providing intuitive and comprehensible images reflecting data also play a key role in interactive installation design.

4 Overall Development Methodology

The entire development process is split into four phases, each with a set of deliverables that becomes input to the following phase, as illustrated in figure 14.3. Timeboxing of each phase helps manage the project to succeed on time. The development of the

The Idea (vision)

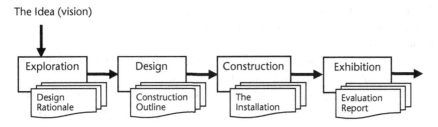

Figure 14.3
Four-phase model with deliverables.

installation for the bumper car competition mentioned in section 2 is used as an example to illustrate the development phases.

4.1 The Design and Evaluation of the Bumper Car Competition

The idea is to create an event at an amusement park extending the bumper car ride to a staged competition. Instead of offering individual rides in the cars, the ride has a goal, that is, to bump into as many other cars as possible as often as possible during the ride. For each bumper car, the number of bumps into the other cars at the scene is counted automatically and visualized to enable both riders and spectators to follow the number of bumps for each bumper car in the competition. A tournament will be set up with heats to select the overall winner of the competition during an event expected to last one day.

The development process is divided into four separate phases that each ends with a deliverable. The aim of the first phase is to explore the challenges and opportunities for the installation. The general idea of how the competition can be arranged is developed, and an analysis of whether the project is realistic with respect to manpower, technology for bump detection, and venue for the competition is performed.

The second phase of the project concerns the detailed design of the system. The system architecture is elaborated and decomposed into the various elements of data transfer and data collection, bump computation, data modeling, and visualization of both live scores and status of tournament. The third phase contains the majority of the programming and involves installing sensors in cars and other hardware at the venue. The fourth phase starts with fine-tuning and calibration of the system before the competition and ends with an evaluation after the event.

4.2 The Four-Phase Model

In general, the development of interactive installations may be separated into four phases. Each phase constitutes a timebox. Iterations over the tasks within each phase are often necessary, whereas iterations involving multiple phases should be avoided.

The constraint is not only due to the project management advantages of timeboxing but also due to practical considerations like building physical artifacts is costly or difficult to undo or redo.

In the *exploration phase*, the aim is to clarify the general behavior of the installation. An interactive installation may depend on and involve the physical surroundings (e.g., the travel fair in sec. 2) and the relationship between the components of the installation and the physical space (e.g., the experience cylinder in sec. 2). At this stage, investigations of technological options are needed and may include limited tryouts of new and existing technology (e.g., the use of Kinect as a sensor, and the availability of Twitter feeds). The deliverables of the first phase are collected in a *design rationale* as a basis for the design process.

In the *design phase*, the architecture of software, physical components, and the surrounding space should be clarified. When designing the software architecture, the main challenge is to find a way to separate it into smaller parts with limited interdependence, often inspired by the technological building blocks explored in the first phase. The separation into components makes it easier to construct, debug, and test the various parts before the whole system is assembled. The deliverables of the second phase are collected in a *construction outline* for the construction phase.

In the *construction phase*, the actual software is constructed, and we build any physical element of the installation based on the outline from the second phase. With these types of installations, it may be beneficial to create smaller programs that isolate certain features, and then later integrate them into the main system. As soon as enough building blocks are available, we put them together to have a partial working interactive installation to which we add features and components until we have the full installation working. The deliverable of the third phase is *the interactive installation* itself, including guides and documentation of the construction.

In the *exhibition phase*, the software, hardware, and other physical components are evaluated. The test should ensure that the system is reliable and that the intended overall appearance and aesthetics have been met. This includes a usability perspective, as well as a more artistic perspective. Does the installation communicate how the audience can participate in the installation? Does the installation give the intended artistic experience to the audience? The deliverables of the last phase are collected in an *evaluation report* documenting the achievements.

The four phases are separated by milestones and associated deliverables (fig. 14.3). The deliverables of each phase provide a foundation for the continuation of the project into the following phase.

Although the four phases are executed in sequence one after the other, effectively timeboxing each phase, the activities in each phase may be done in parallel and repeatedly until the end of the phase. Some activities are also present in more than one phase, but scoped to fit the goals of each phase.

5 Exploration Phase

The purpose of the exploration phase is to clarify the general behavior of the installation and decide among the technological options. At the end of the phase, we should have a general idea of what we should construct and be able to assess the feasibility of the development of the installation. The participants in the installation should have a common understanding of the goals, methods, and techniques used in the work, and the documentation of the phase should be selected so as to assist in this process. The end result of the exploration phase is a design rationale that should guide the designers and developers in the design phase.

5.1 Exploration for the Bumper Car Competition

In the exploration phase, one should get a general idea of how the bumper car competition should be arranged. There will probably be a scoring system so that drivers get points based on how many other cars they hit, and the competition could be arranged with a number of heats and a grand finale for the highest-scoring drivers. During the competition, a scoreboard should show the results of the heats and the overall standing of drivers.

A number of other aspects should be clarified at this early stage of the development. Some of these are critical for the development and may change the project fundamentally.

• Will an amusement park host the event? At this stage we need an informal agreement with an amusement park that it will collaborate.
• Can we detect bumps? The initial idea is to use Wii controllers (Wiimotes) with motion sensors. They can communicate with computers using Bluetooth. But will it actually work over the distances of a bumper car track and in the electrical field between metal floor and powered ceiling? At this stage, we should conduct some experiments to see whether the setting is realistic or if we would need a completely new idea to track the cars.
• Can we collect bump information from a sufficient number of cars? We should make some experiments where information is collected from many Wii controllers at the same time and assess how that part of the project can be realized.
• How much programming is needed, and are the necessary skills available in the development team? This assessment may depend on whether one can find software components that facilitates parts of the installation.

The exploration phase for the bumper car event showed that it was indeed possible to collect bump information from the cars using Wii controllers and Bluetooth. An amusement park indicated that they would be interested in hosting the event.

5.2 Elements in the Exploration Phase

The analytical tasks regarding software-based interactive installations include the following:

- Determine the purpose of the installation.
- Scout for information (e.g., data set) to be used in the final product as dynamic input or as built into the product.
- Scout for technological options potentially relevant to the purpose or as building block (visible as well as invisible).
- Investigate possible location, other materials, and information (experimentally narrowing down which to use in the final product).
- Experiment with technological elements for inspiration and create building blocks for the final product.
- Decide on the time (duration of event, as well as event deadline), space (location[s] and physical surroundings), and audience relevant to the final product.
- Give an overall description of the final product.

The process of exploration may be seen as a repeated iteration over the various elements. It involves exploring technological options and attaining inspiration from similar installations, as found in Igoe (2011) and Borenstein (2012). A change in location or a fundamental change in the underlying technology may affect other parts of the design of the installation.

The various results and decisions in the exploration phase are collected in the design rationale. It should contain results from the explorations in this phase and give a general impression of the installation. It would probably contain a *sketch* of the room and physical components of the installation. Computers or sensors and actuators may not be directly visible to the user, but the sketch should show how they can be placed. If parts of the installation include animations or sequences of events to be performed, one may write a script or score with a timeline where the various elements are included.

Techniques from usual software project development (Pressman 2010; Trifonova and Jaccheri 2008) may be relevant for interactive installations. Among these are various specifications used to support a common understanding. Use case diagrams describe how users interact with the system. Mock-ups show the users' interface to the system, and data models describe the collection of concepts and objects relevant to the system. These may be included in a requirement specification.

The design rationale focuses on the interactive installation and its immediate use. In parallel to this work, the team or other teams may explore arrangements for the event or exhibition in which the installation is being used. The arrangement plans might include fund-raising, public relations, legal aspects, and marketing. These plans can be seen as a separate development process, which will not be considered further in this context.

5.3 Deliverables

The result of the exploration phase is collected as a design rationale. It documents the decisions and facilitates a common understanding of the project. The design rationale contains a more mature description of the idea and how it might be realized. The description should specify sufficient relevant technological building blocks and other artifacts to assess the feasibility of the project.

6 Design Phase

In the design phase, the architecture of both software and the surrounding space should be clarified. When designing the software architecture, a main challenge is to find a way to separate it into smaller parts with limited interdependence. This makes it easier to construct, debug, and test the various parts before the whole system is assembled.

6.1 Designing the Bumper Car Competition

The design of the bumper car competition is based on the design rationale from the exploration phase. The design takes place at three levels that influence each other:

The amusement park hosting the competition imposes both constraints and options to the design. The size of the venue and the court within which the bumper cars can drive is clarified, including the actual bumper car models, sizes, and numbers. A design sketch placing the different artifacts at the scene might be helpful.

The system architecture of the involved hardware and software is developed experimentally. The goal is to decompose the system into subcomponents and to describe how everything fits together in an overall architectural plan. Experiments are conducted with Wiimotes (remote devices from the Nintendo Wii game) as sensors in the cars and how they can be mounted in the cars. The sensor data must be communicated to a computer collecting the raw data at first. The available Bluetooth technology for communication solves the purpose within the constraints (radio communication range) of the physical scene and the number of cars available (capacity of communication network).

The experiments clarify how to develop an algorithm to detect, extract, and calculate how often each car has bumped into one of the others. The algorithm must also exclude the counting of false bumps, where the car bumps into other artifacts, and the situation where the car is the victim of another car bumping into it.

The contestants, heats, car usage in each heat, and number of bumps are stored in a database on a server computer. The presentation of live scores of a running heat and the overall status of tournament, including plans for following heats and the presentation of the final result of the competition, is designed. Screen layouts on paper are extremely helpful to select among different layouts. Such mock-ups (Ehn and Kyng

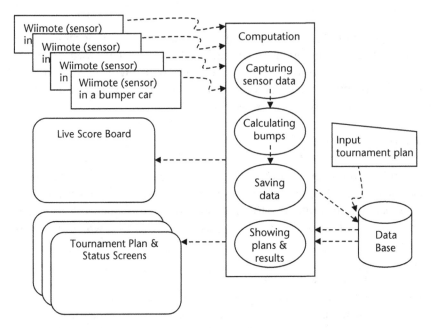

Figure 14.4
Architectural design of IT system in bumper car competition.

1991) can be tested for usability issues. Although some issues might show up only later when tested live at the scene of the competition, testing on paper helps to clarify the design.

The design of the composition of the hardware and software components constituting the current vision of the system is described in figure 14.4.

The competition is also designed in more details. Game and tournament rules are derived to specify how to win a heat, as well as the whole tournament.

6.2 The Design Process
In an interactive installation, one will normally need to design the system at the three levels exemplified in the previous section:

- The physical space
- The system architecture
- The action plan

Design Reflecting the Physical Space   The interactive installation should be situated in a location, and the design should make clear which components the installation consists of. The physical space can be clarified and illustrated with sketches of the location, layout of the room, and any other features relevant to the installations. In some situations, one will need construction drawings of components of the installations before they are manufactured.

The Design of the Systems Architecture   The hardware and software part of the system will normally be composed of a number of components and be linked to various sources of input. The software system can be described and decomposed at different levels, leading to a sequence of views of the system. At the outer level, the architecture of the system can be illustrated with a representation of the connection between external units and the software (see the left side of fig. 14.4). Software parts can further be decomposed into components, units, and libraries. One may need more detailed descriptions of some specialized parts of the system.

At this stage, it is frequently important to examine whether there are *libraries* or *open-source* code that can be used in the installation. As an example, the visualization of Twitter data was built by reusing open-source libraries realizing Twitter access. If some existing program parts can be reused in the design, it should be noted in the systems description.

Designing the Action Plan   The interaction between audience and installation can be illustrated by using rich pictures or a simplified form of storyboard. The interaction does not necessarily form a strict timeline but may contain alternatives, possibilities, and elements that may reoccur at various times. The interaction can be illustrated with small drawings of possible scenarios of the system at selected points in the use of the installation. The storyboard can assist us in decomposing the software system into smaller parts that can be programmed independently, and we may discover that seemingly independent parts are variations of the same structure and can be realized with the same software solution.

6.3   Deliverables

The iterations over all these different streams of design in the design phase result in a construction outline. It describes the overall composition of the installation, as well as the components of which it is to be built. It includes diagrams showing the architecture with its constituting components and identifies requirements to function, form, and data. The presentation may include mock-ups, storyboards, and rich pictures.

7   Construction Phase

The purpose of the construction phase is to implement software components, construct physical components, and fit it all together in such a way that the resulting installation provides the intended behavior. Repeatedly testing the components individually and in combination during the construction is obviously crucial. An important part of the construction is also to provide documentation for the installation and for the constituent components.

7.1   Construction of the Bumper Car Competition

The construction is based on the construction outline from the design phase that includes what is sketched in figure 14.4. Thus the construction involves finishing the physical cars by mounting sensors in them, and developing software components for capturing sensor data from the cars for bump calculation and for storage of bump data. A database component is developed and included for storing the tournament and heat data. In addition, components to provide output to the live scoreboard, the tournament plan, and the status screens must be constructed.

Hardware and software components, as well as the installation as a whole, are thoroughly tested and documented. Finally, a plan for the event, invitations and registration of contestants, a detailed agreement with the venue, and any other pre-event activities are also carried out.

7.2   Controlling the Construction Phase

The starting point for the construction is the construction outline delivered with the design. While the target, the final installation, will often be a coherent and unique device, the construction outline will, as indicated in the previous section, be decomposed into components that can be treated and developed individually in the construction phase.

One approach to the development process is to work in a *top-down* fashion, where one starts with a general outline and step by step breaks it into smaller parts. This is then done repeatedly until we have elements of the overall design of a tractable size and complexity. An alternative approach is *bottom-up*, where we construct components we expect will be used in the final construction, and later include them in the overall design. The components will normally be made in a more general style than in a top-down approach. One version of this is *component-based development*, where software is constructed by assembling existing components, frameworks, libraries, and services (Brown 2000).

Interactive installations tend to benefit from using a bottom-up approach to the development process. In the exploration phase, we may already start to build components that receive readings from sensors or components that produce some visual or audio effects that play a central role in the installations. The installation may also use existing components or libraries and be assembled from this mixture of components.

Installations often include experimental equipment, where bits of hardware and software, at an early stage of development, need to be fitted together. Testing and debugging such equipment should have a high priority in the process. Writing many lines of code without running the program should be avoided, and if larger blocks of code from other programs need to be included, then it is crucial to test and debug those parts in an artificial setting before inclusion in the program.

The interactive installation will often be used only for a limited period, and for this reason there may be less emphasis on the development of the system for easy maintenance and extendibility. On the other hand, it is important to identify parts of the system for potential later reuse in other contexts. Whether or not a given part has this property is often obvious, and examples of these reusable components are many: the combined software and hardware of a person-tracking device, a heart rate monitor, a bump-measuring unit, a gesture tracker, a positional sound audio system. Notice also that in some cases the installation as a whole may be considered as generic and open for inclusion of diverse content. One example of such a generic platform, mentioned in section 2, is the "experience cylinder" (Andreasen et al. 2011). Obviously, for reusable parts, it is beneficial to perform a thorough development, paying careful attention to maintenance as well as extendibility. Thus a component-based approach is important also in this context.

7.3 The Component-Based Approach

In the component-based approach, we write smaller parts of the system separately and then later compose or integrate them into the full system. The design phase will involve decomposition and will indicate candidates for components in the construction outline, but further decomposition may be needed in the construction phase. Examples of components that may be subject to further decomposition are the reusable parts mentioned earlier.

More generally, systems that use various types of external sensors will typically need some processing of the external input. In developing such components for this purpose, we may be able to find open-source code that performs some of the processing, or we may write the code ourselves. In either case, it is often advisable to start by writing a program that accepts the input and just displays readings. This will make it easier to debug and test the system and spot any problems at the hardware level or at the level of the interface to the software. If a hardware part is untested and at an experimental stage, then one should perform these tests as early as possible in the exploration phase. The outcome may change the general design of the installation if the hardware part is critical for the whole system.

Often there will also be a need for data-handling components. Part of the data handling in the installations may use software in libraries or in open-source code. We might find libraries that perform image or sound analysis or support various kinds of visualization. Such libraries or code blocks should be tested separately before being used in the installation. If the code is introduced into the program without testing, it will become unnecessarily complicated to locate any issues that might arise afterward.

7.4 Evaluation Issues in the Construction Phase

As emphasized, repeatedly testing while developing components is important in the construction phase. The collected results of these tests are obviously a contribution to construction phase development. However, evaluation of the installation as a whole should also be considered through function testing as well as usability testing.

A *function test* will examine whether the system can perform in typical uses of the system. We may reexamine a storyboard or script and check whether the various flows and choices in the story are realized in the system.

If the system is intended to be used without further explanation or guides, we may want to examine whether it is sufficiently self-explanatory. This can be done with a *usability test*, where we ask a small number of potential users to explore the installation. In an interactive installation, it may be important to tune the response to sensor input so that the effect is clear to users.

7.5 Deliverables

The main product of the construction phase is the installation. In addition, the phase delivers a final plan for the exhibition at the event, a description of the installation, and documentation of components and compositions. Finally, results of the evaluation of components and the entire installation should be included.

8 Exhibition Phase

Before the exhibition, one might need some final adjustments to the installation. There might be minor changes to the installation based on weather, light condition, or other aspects of the location. During the evaluation, one should observe the use of the installation and gather information about user experience. Experiences from the installation and the exhibition might lead to ideas for new installations or for further development of the technology.

8.1 Bumper Car Competition

The bumper car competition took place during one afternoon, and the development team had access to the bumper cars from the morning. Fine-tuning the installation consisted of calibration of sensors and final positioning of a large screen for the scoreboard so as to allow spectators and participants to follow live results. During the event, the team documented spectators' experience and afterward evaluated the event. This could lead to proposals to other amusement parks with bumper cars and be the basis for innovations in future amusement park attractions. Arranging the competition did require a number of other activities not directly related to the installation. The team would arrange a marketing campaign and fund-raising, create posters, and find prizes for the winners. Much of this needed to be done in parallel with the construction of the bumper car competition platform.

8.2 Activities in the Exhibition Phase

Choosing the most appropriate approach to evaluate a given interactive installation must necessarily involve considerations on various properties and characteristics of the given installation. The basis for the evaluation should be the purpose and intended experience of the installation. An installation may be an artist's work of art, leaving interpretation open to the audience, with no or only vague intentions regarding the viewer's or audience's experience. In this case, no or only a very brief evaluation is needed. A different type of installation might have a specific purpose that can be specified in terms of what the viewer should experience and learn, how this should be accomplished assuming specific interaction by the viewer(s), and providing specific immersive mediation by visualization, audio, or behavior of physical components. With such installations, the requirements of a satisfactory evaluation are naturally higher. We should assess the user experience, whether the message or information has been communicated and whether the installation was easy to use and understand.

8.3 Evaluation Techniques

Evaluation of interactive installations has been covered in several recent publications on aspects of deriving actual measurable results, as well as on evaluation methodology. Hornecker and Stifter (2006) report on the evaluation of a digitally augmented exhibition on the history of modern media, discussing visitors' interaction with installations from an interaction design point of view. Through their evaluation, they try to recover what makes an installation engaging and how it can provide an engaging experience for groups. The evaluation is based on analysis of log files, interviews, and observations.

Focusing on museum and scientific center installations, Campos, Campos, and Ferreira (2012) report on evaluation results for a specific installation in a science center (the 6DSpaces project) and conclude that the objective should be to deliver a memorable experience without intrusive input requirements. The simpler and more straightforward the interaction is, the better is the experience.

Gonçalves introduces a framework called M-dimensions (Gonçalves et al. 2012), defining ten dimensions (interaction style adequacy, area integration, visibility, feedback, structure, reuse, simplicity, education, entertainment, collaboration), which are evaluated individually by a five-point scale and aggregated by simple averaging to provide an overall grade. Gonçalves's dimensions are developed specifically for museum exhibitions but obviously apply to other types of installations as well. The dimensions comprise a useful separation for characterization of installations. However, rather than simply aggregating dimension scores, an obvious alternative would be to use the dimensions in specifying purpose and intended experience. Evaluation can then be performed, to the degree that the dimension aspects are measurable, by comparing intended and experimentally derived dimension values.

8.4 Deliverables

The end product of the development process is the evaluation report, containing notes on the final configuration, fine-tuning components, and overall performance of the installation, as well as analysis on how the installation was received by the audience. The report may contain ideas and proposals for further development of the installation, as well as new ideas.

9 Conclusion

This chapter describes a development model for interactive installations consisting of four phases, each with a set of deliverables, as illustrated in figure 14.5. The model focuses on the timeboxing of the deliverables during the process rather than on the activities. Some activities, such as analysis, programming, and evaluation, will typically take place in several phases of the project. The development model furthermore emphasizes that certain tasks in the project can be done in parallel so as to improve the efficient use of the resources in the development team. These elements are

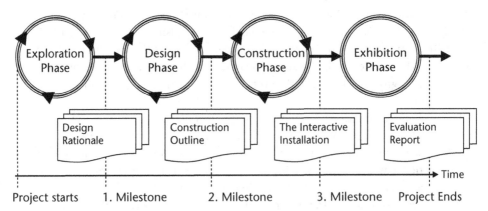

Figure 14.5

The timeboxing four-phase model.

especially important when the interactive installation is to be used at an exhibition or at an event with a fixed deadline.

References

Andreasen, Troels, John Patrick Gallagher, Nikolaj Møbius, and Nicolas Padfield. 2011. The Experience Cylinder, an immersive interactive platform: The Sea Stallion's voyage: A case study. In *AMBIENT 2011: The First International Conference on Ambient Computing, Applications, Services and Technologies*, ed. R. Emonet and A. M. Florea, 25–31. Barcelona: ThinkMind.

Borenstein, Greg. 2012. *Making Things See: 3D Vision with Kinect, Processing, Arduino, and Maker-Bot*. Sebastopol, CA: O'Reilly Media.

Brown, Alan W. 2000. *Large-Scale, Component-Based Development*. Upper Saddle River, NJ: Prentice Hall.

Campos, Pedro, Miguel Campos, and Carlos Ferreira. 2012. 6DSpaces: Multisensory interactive installations. *World Academy of Science, Engineering and Technology* 12 (61): 1089–1092.

Cohen, D., M. Lindvall, and P. Costa. 2004. An introduction to agile methods. In *Advances in Computers*, vol. 62, ed. M Zelkowitz, 1–66. New York: Elsevier Science.

Ehn, Pelle, and Morten Kyng. 1991. Cardboard computers: Mocking-it-up or hands-on the future. In *Design at Work: Cooperative Design of Computer Systems*, ed. J. Greenbaum and P. Ehn, 169–195. Hillsdale, NJ: Erlbaum.

Fowler, Martin, and Jim Highsmith. 2001. The agile manifesto. *Software Development* 9 (8): 29–30.

Friedman, Vitaly. 2007. Data visualization: Modern approaches. In *Smashing Magazine*, August 2, http://www.smashingmagazine.com/2007/08/02/data-visualization-modern-approaches.

Fry, Ben. 2007. *Visualizing Data: Exploring and Explaining Data with the Processing Environment*. Sebastopol, CA: O'Reilly Media.

Gonçalves, Lígia, Pedro Campos, and Margarida Sousa. 2012. M-dimensions: A framework for evaluating and comparing interactive installations in museums. In *Proceedings of the 7th Nordic Conference on Human-Computer Interaction: Making Sense through Design*, 59–68. New York: ACM Press.

Hornecker, Eva, and Matthias Stifter. 2006. Learning from interactive museum installations about interaction design for public settings. In *Proceedings of the 18th Australia Conference on Computer-Human Interaction: Design; Activities, Artefacts, and Environments*, 135–142. New York: ACM Press.

Igoe, Tom. 2011. *Making Things Talk: Using Sensors, Networks, and Arduino to See, Hear, and Feel Your World*, 2nd ed. Sebastopol: O'Reilly Media.

Jalote, Pankaj, Aveejeet Palit, and Priya Kurien. 2004. The timeboxing process model for iterative software development. *Advances in Computers* 62: 67–103.

Kruchten, Philippe. 2001. From waterfall to iterative development: A challenging transition for project managers. Rational Edge, Rational Software. http://web.sau.edu/GrenierKennethR/ClassPrep/csci300/Readings/From%20Waterfall%20to%20Iterative%20Development%20-%20The%20Rational%20Edge%20-%20Dec%2000.pdf.

Larman, Craig. 2003. Iterative and incremental development: A brief history. *Computer* 36 (6): 47–56.

Nielsen, Jakob. 1993. *Usability Engineering*. San Francisco: Morgan Kaufmann.

Norman, Donald A. 2002. *The Design of Everyday Things*. New York: Basic Books.

Pressman, Roger. 2010. *Software Engineering: A Practitioner's Approach*, 2nd ed. New York: McGraw-Hill.

Royce, Winston. 1970. Managing the development of large software systems. *Proceedings of IEEE WESCON* 26:1–9. http://leadinganswers.typepad.com/leading_answers/files/original_waterfall_paper_winston_royce.pdf.

Sharp, Helen, Yvonne Rogers, and Jenny Preece. 2007. *Interaction Design: Beyond Human-Computer Interaction*. Chichester: John Wiley.

Steele, Julie, and Noah Iliinsky. 2010. *Beautiful Visualization: Looking at Data through the Eyes of Experts*. Sebastopol, CA: O'Reilly Media.

Trifonova, Anna, and Letizia Jaccheri. 2008. Software engineering issues in interactive installation art. *International Journal of Arts and Technology* 1 (1): 43–65.

15 A Pragmatist Method for Situated Experience Design

Sara Malou Strandvad

What. This chapter presents a pragmatist method for situated experience design. The constituting elements of the method are (a) devices, (b) mediators, and (c) programs of action. The method derives from empirical studies and can be seen as a descriptive analysis turned prescriptive. The method is illustrated with two cases, one from film production, and the other from performance design.

Why. The method addresses, and proposes a solution to, the difficulty of making creative design processes fit into universal design methods. By offering an alternative account that broadens the perspective of what should be included in a design method, the outcome of the method may be needed to understand nonlinear creative processes.

Where. The application area of the method is experience design widely understood, unique projects that are created with the purpose of providing their audiences with an experience. Experience designs may be found in cultural industries, industries working with creativity commercially, and everyday life practices.

How. The method comprises three questions to consider while being in the process of making an experience design: (1) Which techniques are employed as devices? That is, how do conventional wisdoms within the field work as tools to construct the design? (2) Which actors become mediators in the process of constructing the design? That is, how do various kinds of actors, for example, investors and technical equipment, influence the design process? (3) What program of action does the design outline? That is, what is the intended use that the design aims to realize, and which options for use does the design give? By raising these questions, the method means to assist design processes in action. Thus the method aims to transcend the dichotomy between method (theory) and practice (action), suggesting instead that we see design practices as situated methods.

1 Introduction

In this chapter, I propose that a universal method cannot simply be realized in an experience design. As processes of creating experience designs consist in inventing something unique, universal design methods become inadequate. Also, things happen differently than planned, and thus the design method becomes one of several tools, materials, technologies, and collaborators that take part in the process of designing. Moreover, the audience plays a part in forming the experience. In that way, the neat picture of a universal method is disturbed, as the practical process of designing is wider and messier than this picture allows for.

Therefore I suggest an alternative method: a pragmatist method, which takes into account conventional wisdoms from the fields in question and considers them as important devices, yet furthers this with a consideration of their employments and limitations. Second, the method looks into the actors during production that become part of forming the evolving object: collaborators as well as materials, technologies, and other elements. Finally, the method investigates the intended use that the design prescribes and how the design is used in practice. With these three elements in mind, I suggest that it becomes possible to make a situated experience design.

To illustrate the situated design method, I employ two case studies, one from the field of filmmaking, and one from the field of performance design. In the two cases, I look into the three questions of the situated design method: how universal methods function as devices; how various actors become mediators; and how a specific program of action is installed in the design, the use of which nevertheless depends on attachments made by users. By means of the two case studies, I aim to illustrate how the process of designing entails several decisive elements, and I suggest that a situated method will bring these elements into the picture.

2 Theoretical Approach

With its ambition of presenting an alternative to universal design methods, the chapter is inspired by Schön's (1983) notion of how reflection happens in action and Weick's (1995) critique of rational planning. Yet the vocabulary of the chapter is taken from science and technology studies (STS). Within this body of literature, a refined analytical framework has been developed through detailed empirical studies of scientific work and technological developments. In this chapter, I propose applying three of the analytical concepts from these studies in a different context, namely, that of aesthetic experiences. Furthermore, I suggest translating these analytical concepts into a situated design methodology, thus turning from descriptions to prescriptions.

2.1 Transferring STS to Aesthetic Experiences

In this chapter, I transfer a vocabulary from STS to experience design. A number of previous studies have made similar moves. First and foremost, the French cultural sociologist Antoine Hennion (1989) has been pioneering in bringing a perspective from STS to use in studies of music. Similarly, the Bulgarian sociologist Albena Yaneva (2009) has proposed an actor-network theory of design. In line with these suggestions for transporting STS as a research method to be used in other fields, this chapter considers experience design with inspiration from STS. Whereas this transportation of ideas presumes similarities between the fields of creative production and the fields of science and technology, for example, in comparing the studio with the laboratory (Alpers 1998; Hennion 1989), it also makes clear that these fields represent different modes of existence, for example, since scientific work claims to uncover truth, whereas creative work obviously constructs fiction (Latour 2002).

2.2 Translating Analyses of Design into Methods for Design

This chapter not only transfers analytical concepts from STS to a different field, namely, that of aesthetic experiences, but moreover suggests turning these concepts into a situated design method. Studies within the STS literature are renowned for their analyses of design processes (e.g., Callon 1986; de Laet and Mol 2000; Latour and Woolgar 1979; Law 1989). Whereas these studies are famous for the concepts they derive from rigorous empirical analyses, as well as their research methodologies, they do not outline design methods. That is, they analyze design processes and reflect on how to study such processes; they do not advise how to manage design processes and do not outline design methods. However, using the STS analyses of design processes, it might be possible to detect some ideas to think with in future design processes. Particularly since the concepts that these studies have invented to depict design processes stem from specific empirical studies, this vocabulary seems relevant for formulating a situated design method. That is, rather than extracting a generalized framework from STS, a grand theory (such as actor-network theory [Latour 1999, 2005]) that could be moved in unchangeable form to numerous other fields of research, I suggest employing three concepts from the STS vocabulary, via two empirical cases, as inspiration for future experience designs.

2.3 A Situated Design Method

A design method inspired by STS should begin by emphasizing being situated. As Suchman (2002) has proposed, inspired by Haraway's (1988) notion of situated knowledges, design work should be considered as located, situated practices. Famously, Haraway argues that instead of holding on to the notion of objectivity, "a conquering gaze from nowhere" (1988, 581), or criticizing the notion of objectivity from a social constructivist, relativistic viewpoint, "vision from everywhere" (584), all knowledge claims are historically contingent, local, particular, embodied "views from somewhere" (590). Drawing on Haraway's view on situated knowledges, Suchman proposes that design work is positioned and takes place in specific locations. Thus designers' plans are not simply transferred into the world without alterations but form the starting point for contingent, situated actions. Suchman clarifies: "By situated actions I mean simply actions taken in the context of particular, concrete circumstances" (2007, 26). Thus a situated design method would start from the location of production, seeing the conditions as constitutive for the design.

2.4   Introduction of Concepts

As the material in the following sections is structured around three concepts from STS, devices (sec. 4.1), mediators (sec. 4.2), and programs of action (sec. 4.3), I briefly introduce these concepts here. In the subsequent paragraphs, the concepts will be discussed and put to use in relation to experience design.

The concept of *devices* describes those tools that are used to translate phenomena that are otherwise invisible into something visible. In laboratories, for example, scientific facts become established as instruments translate substances into literary inscriptions such as graphs or texts (Latour and Woolgar 1979; Latour 1987). In finance, as another example, calculative devices shape the trade by visualizing the workings of the market (Callon and Muniesa 2005; Beunza and Stark 2004). In the case studies in this chapter, I use the examples of dramaturgy and experience economy discourse to describe devices that make experience designs graspable.

The concept of *mediators* draws attention to the actors, human and nonhuman, that play a role in the design process by making connections and simultaneously altering that which is being connected (Hennion and Meadel 1986, 1989; Hennion 1995, 1997; Latour 2005). Mediators thus function by assembling, holding relations in place, and modifying them. For example, Yaneva (2008) suggests that a building undergoing renovation becomes a mediator as it surprises its renovators and makes their planned actions impossible. As the building turns out to contain different materials and elements than the renovators assumed, it resists their actions and changes their plans of action. In that way, the building becomes a mediator as it transforms action in unexpected ways, thus changing the social meanings attributed to it (2008, 17). In the design method described here, I use the concept of mediators to draw attention to various actors that become part of the design process.

Finally, the concept of *programs of action* highlights that a design prescribes a specific form of use (Latour 1991). In other words, users are configured by a design as use is defined, enabled, and constrained by the design (Woolgar 1991). Thus a design can be said to embody a script, an outline of what the design is meant to achieve, and users are expected to describe this script and act in accordance with it (Akrich 1992).

However, the extent to which use can be inscribed into designs may sometimes be overestimated (Suchman 2007). In this chapter, I discuss the problematic of programs of action in the case of experience designs.

3 Case Studies

In the following I use two case studies as illustrations, one from the field of film production, and one from the field of performance design. These cases have not been designed according to the pragmatist method. Rather, the analyses of the two cases are used to extract and illustrate this method. In that way, the descriptions of what happened in the specific cases are used as inspiration for making prescriptive suggestions about how to design future experiences. Furthermore, the two illustrations may seem like an ill-matched couple. However, they are chosen to demonstrate some variety of experience designs, and yet they have some similarities, as I employ an event of viewing the film (sec. 4.3). By means of the two case studies, I aim to illustrate how the three elements, which compose the pragmatist method, play out empirically.

3.1 *Moving Up*

Moving Up (Danish title: *Spillets Regler*), which came out in 2008, is a Danish feature film about an associate professor who engages in fraud to further his career. The film was a debut film, funded primarily by the talent development program New Danish Screen at the Danish Film Institute.

I followed the development of this project over nearly a year in 2006–2007. During my study, the project went from the stage of first draft of the manuscript through eight versions of the script to shooting and editing of the film. My empirical material on this case consists of seven interviews with the producer, two interviews with the director, a number of phone calls to the producer, three funding applications, return letters from the funding scheme, observation notes from the meeting where the project was green-lighted, four different synopses of the film, eight editions of the script, a promo of the film, and the final film.

3.2 Horsens New Theater

Horsens New Theater is a cultural center, primarily a concert and theater venue, in the provincial town Horsens in Denmark. Since the city council aims to rebrand Horsens from prison town to experience town, Horsens New Theater is meant to play a part in transforming the town into a creative hub. After hiring a new theater director in 2012, the theater has launched its ambition of becoming the best performance house in Europe. To pursue this ambition, the theater has altered its strategy from solely providing a scene for touring artists to creating events around these acts.

Figure 15.1
Still from *Moving Up* (2008). Copyright Tju-Bang Film.

Figure 15.2
Facade with light, Horsens New Theater. Copyright Frank Nielsen.

The empirical material about this case stems from a visit at Horsens New Theater, which I conducted with a group of students in April 2013. Here the theater director described the strategy of the venue together with a newly appointed performance designer.

4   Three Elements in Situated Experience Design

In the following paragraphs, I look into three elements of situated experience design. The first element considers universal design methods that are in use and functioning but contested nevertheless. The second element looks at mediators, or various objects and collaborators that influence the design process. Last, the third element concerns the programs of action that experience designs outline and how audiences attach to them.

4.1   Devices

Experience designs often build on conventional wisdom about how to proceed. Various domains of aesthetic design have their own accepted ways of designing, techniques that are taken for granted. On the one hand, such techniques provide useful guidelines and compose necessary devices to make ideas graspable. On the other hand, techniques become combined, altered, and contested, and it is through such struggles with various devices that actual designs arise.

In the case of *Moving Up*, the director was interested in making a film about an unpleasant character. The filmmakers described their work as a study of inferiority and aimed at portraying megalomania as arising from the fear of insufficiency. The project had started with an idea about a power-hungry politician but turned into a story about a psychologist with an inferiority complex and ended up as a story about an associate professor who engages in fraud to gain a full professorship. Throughout the different versions of the story, the basic plot was about a man who behaves amorally when he feels threatened.

In this case, dramaturgy was used as a device to construct the story. Based on the theme of inferiority that the director was interested in, a scriptwriter was employed to assist the director in creating a story. The scriptwriter introduced dramaturgy, understood in the classical Aristotelian sense as a three-act structure with causal-logical development from the beginning over a middle part to the end. Within this tradition, a story should be based in a conflict handled by an active main character with a clear goal that is confronted with obstacles on the way to reconciliation in the end (Breum 2006; Novrup Redvall 2010). Thus the story of *Moving Up* became composed in accordance with these principles.

However, at the same time, the director disputed this classical dramaturgical model. As an alternative, the director spoke of himself as a taste-machine, a sieve that everything in the film has to be poured into, filtered, and become imprinted by. In that way, the director positioned himself in line with the auteurist tradition, personified, for example, by the famous director Lars von Trier, who has been criticizing the conventional and effective dramaturgical model for creating superficial films, suggesting instead pursuing a director-driven strategy of making films (Novrup Redvall 2010). Thus the device of Aristotelian dramaturgy was challenged in the case of *Moving Up* by the device of auteurism.

In the case of Horsens New Theater, the theater director aims to stage compelling performances that will attract a larger audience. The venue of Horsens New Theater hosts touring acts that have a settled format and are presented in more or less the same manner everywhere they go. However, the new strategy of Horsens New Theater consists in doing more than just hosting shows. Instead of only providing a scene for visiting acts, the venue now stages them, creating local events around them. To do so, a light and sound technician has been appointed as performance designer. In collaboration with the rest of the personnel, the performance designer creates a scenography and lighting at the theater that fits the show in question. Whereas the actual show is most often designed beforehand, the places where the audience goes before and after the show are not part of the traveling design, and hence these locations are where the performance designer stages events. First and foremost, events take place in the lobby, which is decorated and lighted to frame each act specifically. Also, the facade of the venue is sometimes illuminated. In that way, each show gets its own scenography.

Creating a local scenography around traveling shows can be seen in the light of the experience economy as a way of staging experiences to attract customers (Pine and Gilmore 1999). Since the political agenda in Horsens is explicitly oriented toward the experience economy, this discourse can be said to provide a device that is employed in the initiatives of Horsens New Theater. When the American economists Joseph Pine and James Gilmore wrote *The Experience Economy* (1999), they suggested that experiences represent the next stage in the development of the postindustrial economy after the service economy. As a device for designing experiences, Pine and Gilmore advise, one should create events that are unforgettable and have a limited supply; sell the use of a product, not the product itself; put the consumer at the center of attention; activate all five senses; and enable a sharing of the experience (11–20). The performance designs at Horsens New Theater may be said to follow this advice.

Yet one central element of the performance design at Horsens New Theater is missing if it is considered solely as an implementation of the experience economy discourse, namely, that the design is created in relation to specific shows. Rather than starting from the general ambition of becoming a hot spot in the experience economy, each performance design at Horsens New Theater begins from the specifics of the act in question and employs the techniques of light, sound, and props to enhance these specifics.

In that way, both the filmmakers and the performance designers do more than apply a single technique representing the conventional wisdom in the field. The devices of Aristotelian dramaturgy and experience economy discourse are applied, and they become productive in translating ideas into tangible objects. That is, these traditions offer techniques that turn a vague thematic about inferiority and a dull venue into a story and a performance house respectively. By doing so, these tools may be seen as devices that translate something otherwise intangible into effective designs.

However, the devices of dramaturgy and experience economy discourse do not account for everything that happens during the production processes in the two cases. In the case of filmmaking, the director used himself as a tool to create a more personal story, thus including the device of auteurism; and in the case of event making, the performance designer worked with materials that were already at hand from the show in question. In that way, devices are important tools, but they become mixed with numerous other actors, as we shall see next.

4.2 Mediators

Practicalities are difficult to fit into universal methods. Often the trouble begins when design intentions informed by a universal method are to be carried out. At this point, numerous obstacles start influencing the process. Although the production process is all about practicalities, they do not seem to have a proper place in methods. Unpredictable as they are, practical matters may resist and alter design intentions, and by doing so they may be seen as obstacles to realizing the intended design.

However, practical issues in real-life situations can produce feedback to design processes and in that way become part of refining the design. The notion of iteration (which is propagated throughout this book) designates exactly such a progression through trial and error. Testing preliminary versions of a design allows reactions and practical matters to be integrated into the design. Thus, rather than real-life situations presenting an obstacle to a design vision, they may be seen as constitutive of the design. A situated method thus reverses the suggestion that design processes start from ideas that afterward meet obstacles they have to overcome to be realized. Arguing the other way around, a situated method highlights exactly how such obstacles enable and construct designs.

To illustrate how obstacles may become productive and constitutive, I use the example of the role played by an investor in the case of filmmaking, and the role played by technical equipment in the case of performance design, to exemplify two types of mediators. These two examples are not exclusive; in the case of filmmaking, numerous other actors, both human and nonhuman, came to play decisive roles in forming the design (e.g., the photographer, lead actor, location, props on the location), and likewise in the case of performance design. However, I find that the examples of investor and technical equipment are illustrative, as they indicate the diversity of sources that may influence the design.

In the case of *Moving Up*, one of the important factors in the development process became the representative of the main investor, the film consultant from New Danish Screen, a funding scheme at the Danish Film Institute that targets new talents. Rather than solely funding the project, the film consultant also became involved in defining the project.

For example, when seeking development subsidies, the filmmakers sent a first draft of the manuscript for their film. In the response letter, the film consultant noticed, among other things, that a crucial task was to develop the main character: "The story is hindered by an unclear definition of the main character's project and problem. ... His psychology should be clarified and his plot should be more fatal." After receiving this feedback, the filmmakers started debating. The director wanted to tell the story of an unlikable character, but the scriptwriter and the producer were concerned that the film would not work if it did not make the audience sympathize with the main character. The director felt that an investigation of a character's sense of inferiority could make a fine film, but the scriptwriter and producer were not so sure. They wanted development in the story by means of loss of status of the main character. The film consultant's comments put this discussion on the agenda and were used by the scriptwriter and the producer to try to push the director in the direction that they wanted. At the same time, the director used the consultant's comments to develop the story in the direction that he felt was right.

In that way, the feedback from the consultant resulted in a progression of the story along the lines sketched out by the consultant and filled out by the scriptwriter and the director. That is, the film consultant came to manage the process by outlining a scope of issues that the filmmakers had to address. By doing so, the filmmakers' discussions became structured by the film consultant's comments; the issues that the filmmakers addressed were those that the film consultant had called attention to.

In the case of Horsens New Theater, technical equipment becomes defining for the performance designs, which is also underlined by the fact that the performance designer is a professional technician. Particularly light, but also sound and props, constitutes the performance designs. Every night the lobby is illuminated differently with colored lights. At events that are staged around musical and theater acts, the lighting in the lobby is supplemented with props and sound. For example, when a house DJ performed, the lobby was transformed into nightclub for an after-party; the room was dark, filled with smoke, with loud house music playing, creating an atmosphere to continue the DJ show. On a different occasion, a tango show was boosted with a truckload of decoration props, among them a giant disco ball, which transformed the venue into dance hall.

In that way, props, light, and sound create the performance design, providing a setting that is meant to get the audience into a mood. In this way, the technical equipment becomes active. Without the enormous disco ball or without the darkness, the tango and house events would have looked quite different. Thus the equipment is crucial for the design.

If we consider the film consultant and the technical equipment as mediators, their involvement can be seen not only as something that is governed by designers (filmmakers or performance designer) but as something that alters the design. That is, the concept of mediation suggests that real-life issues (such as dealing with investors or realizing the design practically) are not elements that are simply put to use by a designer as mastermind. Rather, these elements may change the design in ways that were not intended or predicted by the designer. Thus, rather than seeing a design as a pure entity, in the sense of an intended vision materialized, the concept of mediation suggests viewing design as put together by many different actors, which add their own abilities to the evolving design, thus altering and enchanting the design (see Gell 1999; Hennion and Latour 2003). Thus with the concept of mediation it becomes possible to view design as a distributed activity.

4.3   Programs of Action

Designs build on envisioned actions and outline scopes of possibilities for audiences. However, the intended reception of an experience design and how the design is received in practice may not correspond. Thus it may be worth reconsidering the scope of possibilities that the design outlines.

As an example of how an audience received *Moving Up*, I use a screening that I attended. In December 2009 the film was shown at Roskilde University to raise awareness of the working climate among the staff. The event was organized by the HR department of the university; it was introduced by the personnel manager and concluded with a discussion with the director, and about eighty employees attended. At this event, the film was meant to spur reflection in the audience.

When the personnel manager began the introduction, a person behind me whispered to the person sitting next to him: "Is Peter Ganzler [the leading actor] coming? If not, I'm off." Thus the attraction of the event seemed to be as much to get a chance to see a movie star as to see the actual film. After the viewing, the director opened the discussion by asking the audience: "Did you recognize anything?" Nobody answered that question. Instead members of the audience raised questions about different issues such as the director's sources of inspiration, the moral of the film, and where the film was shot. As this example shows, the audience approached the event design differently than intended by the HR department.

At the event at Roskilde University, the film was meant to be seen as a representation of life in academia, which would make the audience speak their mind about their own working life. However, this did not happen. Instead the audience asked polite questions about the making of the film. Perhaps the audience did recognize something in the film; perhaps they felt that the event was not the place to speak up about problems at work; perhaps they found the film to be poor. In any case, the audience received the design differently than intended by the HR department.

In the case of Horsens New Theater, the performance design is intended to enhance the experience of shows that are staged at this venue by establishing an atmosphere that is in line with the act in question. By moving through the performance design before and after the show, the audience is supposed to get in the right mood and continue this mood afterward. By extending the atmosphere of the show, the performance design is supposed to give the audience a total experience so that the night at Horsens New Theater will become memorable.

According to the theater director, Horsens New Theater has been quite successful in making audiences use the performance designs as intended, to an even greater extent than planned. Not only does the director tell of amazing sceneries and lively audiences, but he can also measure the success of the performance designs by the turnover at the bar and how late the venue has been held open. With record bar sales and extended late-night hours, the venue has managed to make audiences prolong their stay, enhance their experiences, and really make nights out of their visits.

Perhaps the reason for the success of the performance designs at Horsens New Theater is because the design outlines a relatively open program of action, that is, entering the lobby and eventually buying a drink. On the other hand, the program of action of the HR event where *Moving Up* was shown is quite narrowly defined, that is, explicitly addressing problems in your working life at a social gathering, after viewing the film. Whereas an open program of action enables use in multiple ways, a narrow program of action necessitates highly specific use practices. A narrow program plans to make the audience behave in one particular way, and if they follow the script, a specific experience is expected to occur as a more or less automatic response to the design. Thus the design is privileged as the primary producer of the experience. On the other hand, an open program designs for the unplanned. Making the script fairly limited enables various experiences. Most important, this depends on the audience.

Turning attention to the active role of users/audiences is characteristic both within technology studies (Oudshoorn and Pinch 2003) and within literary and cultural studies (Barthes 1990; Foucault [1969] 1979; Hall 1980). As these different strands of research point out, the extent to which reception can be inscribed into a design is often overestimated. To think of reception as something that can be put into a script entails an unambiguous picture of the workings of a design; "an over rationalized figure of the designer as actor, and an overestimation of the ways and extent to which definitions of users and use can be inscribed into an artifact" (Suchman 2007, 192). Audiences behave differently than envisioned. Rather than following the intended programs of action, audiences may reject or renegotiate the script or perhaps even construct antiprograms that conflict with the original program of action (Latour 1991).

4.4 What to Do?

In this section, I sketch out what to do to use a situated method of experience design, called the pragmatist method. This method consists of three questions to be addressed in the process of making an experience design. The three questions are based on analytical abstractions that originate from empirical studies of design processes: devices, mediators, and programs of action.

(A) Which techniques can be employed as devices? To construct a design, it is necessary to use tools to move from intangible ideas to tangible objects. To do so, it is important to gain knowledge about conventional wisdom within the field and become skilled in using devices that represent this wisdom. However, it is also important to remind oneself that the device you use will produce specific results; that your design becomes formed by the tools you choose to use. For that reason, devices should sometimes be challenged—with your intentions, different devices, and the situation at hand.

(B) Which actors can become mediators in the process of constructing the design? During the process of designing, various kinds of actors may influence the evolving design. These should be acknowledged for the capacities they bring with them. For that reason, potential mediators such as, for example, external stakeholders and technical equipment should be included in the design process, and they should be recognized for their formative powers. Mediators may feed into or disturb the original idea; the important thing is that they are given a proper place in the design process (and in descriptions of the process).

(C) What program of action should the design outline? Consider how the design may work. Ask what the intended reception of the experience design consists in, and which options the audience is given. In other words, define the intentions of the design, and how these intentions can possibly be encountered by an audience. As part of this consideration, it may be a good idea to reflect on how to allow actions by the audience; that is, rather than believing that the design will automatically give them the intended experience, consider how the design can let them form various experiences themselves.

To sum up, the pragmatist method suggests paying attention to three elements while being in the process of making an experience design: the *devices* that are used to construct the design, the *mediators* that become involved in defining the design, and the *program of action* that the design represents. If we point to these three elements of concern while designing, the scope of the method may become wide, depending on the empirical situation.

5 Conclusion

In this chapter, I have sketched the pragmatist method for experience design, which highlights the situated character of this design. Accordingly, the pragmatist method is based on analyses of design processes, and the method's three elements, devices, mediators, and programs of action, are meant to turn attention to the situation at hand. By doing so, a situated method is meant to allow for multiplicity in the production process as well as in user practices. Thus, rather than excluding the mess of production and use, a situated design method takes up exactly these messy issues and scrutinizes them to account for how design is made in action. Accordingly, a situated design method aims to compose a method that bridges the gap between theory and practice, between universal design methods and how they are employed in design processes.

Traditionally, design processes are illustrated as linear processes or at least processes that make progress toward an optimum through trial and error, as the notion of iteration suggests (Lotz 2008). In that way, it is presupposed that the design process moves from an idea to a materialized version of that idea. However, the situated design method that this chapter outlines acknowledges that breaks may happen along the way; it is not necessarily the same idea that is refined throughout the process, but different ideas that are interchanged where some are given up and others come to take over. Thus rather than seeing the design process solely as a matter of stabilization of a design, we may also observe a fluidity to the design (de Laet and Mol 2000). Yet when the process is seen in retrospect, the chronology makes the process seem linear, moving from a starting point to the end result. Thus it may be worth illustrating the design process differently, with lines of development that indicate how the refinement of a design includes substitutions of the idea, together with the influences of various mediators and user practices.

Figure 15.3 shows the process of starting with ideas for a design (illustrated with dots), which meet (1) *devices* (crosses) and (2) *mediators* (triangles), by which the design evolves into (3) a *program of action* (pattern) that can be used in different ways (lines).

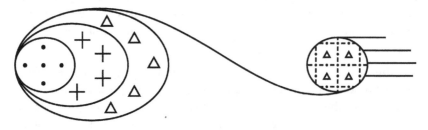

Figure 15.3
The pragmatist method.

References

Akrich, Madeleine. 1992. The de-scription of technical objects. In *Shaping Technology/Building Society: Studies in Sociotechnical Change*, ed. Wiebe E. Bijker and John Law, 205–224. Cambridge, MA: MIT Press.

Alpers, Svetlana. 1998. The studio, the laboratory, and the vexations of art. In *Picturing Science, Producing Art*, ed. Caroline A. Jones and Peter Galison, 401–417. London: Routledge.

Barthes, Roland. [1968] 1990. The death of the author. In *Image, Music, Text*, 142–148. London: Fontana Press.

Beunza, Daniel, and David Stark. 2004. Tools of the trade: The sociotechnology of arbitrage in a Wall Street trading room. *Industrial and Corporate Change* 13 (2): 369–400.

Breum, Trine. 2006. *Film, Narration, and Seduction: A New European-American Scriptwriting Model*, 2nd ed. Frederiksberg: Frydenlund.

Callon, Michel. 1986. Some elements of a sociology of translation: Domestication of the scallops and the fishermen of St. Brieuc Bay. In *Power, Action, and Belief: A New Sociology of Knowledge?* ed. John Law, 196–223. London: Routledge.

Callon, Michel, and Fabian Muniesa. 2005. Economic markets as calculative collective devices. *Organization Studies* 26 (8): 1229–1250.

de Laet, Marianne, and Annemarie Mol. 2000. The Zimbabwe bush pump: Mechanics of a fluid technology. *Social Studies of Science* 30 (2): 225–263.

Foucault, Michel. [1969] 1979. What is an author? In *Textual Strategies: Perspectives in Post-structuralist Criticism*, ed. Josué V. Harari, 141–160. Ithaca: Cornell University Press.

Gell, Alfred. 1999. The technology of enchantment and the enchantment of technology. In *The Art of Anthropology: Essays and Diagrams*, 159–186. London: Athlone Press.

Gomart, Emilie, and Antoine Hennion. 1999. A sociology of attachment: Music amateurs, drug users. In *Actor Network Theory and After*, ed. John Law and John Hassard, 220–247. Oxford: Blackwell.

Hall, Stuart. [1973] 1980. Encoding/decoding. In *Culture, Media, Language: Working Chapters in Cultural Studies*, ed. Stuart Hall, Dorothy Hobson, Andrew Lowe, and Paul Willis, 128–138. London: Hutchinson.

Haraway, Donna. 1988. Situated knowledges: The science question in feminism and the privilege of partial perspective. *Feminist Studies* 14 (3): 575–599.

Hennion, Antoine. 1989. An intermediary between production and consumption: The producer of popular music. *Science, Technology and Human Values* 14 (4): 400–424.

Hennion, Antoine. 1995. The history of art: Lessons in mediation. *Réseaux: French Journal of Communication* 3 (2): 233–262.

Hennion, Antoine. 1997. Baroque and rock: Music, mediators, and musical taste. *Poetics* 24: 415–435.

Hennion, Antoine, and Bruno Latour. [1996] 2003. How to make mistakes on so many things at once—and become famous for this. In *Mapping Benjamin: The Work of Art in the Digital Age*, ed. Hans Ulrich Gumbrect and Michael Marrinan, 91–97. Stanford: Stanford University Press.

Hennion, Antoine, and Cecile Meadel. 1986. Programming music: Radio as mediator. *Media Culture and Society* 8: 281–303.

Hennion, Antoine, and Cecile Meadel. 1989. The artisans of desire: The mediation of advertising between product and consumer. *Sociological Theory* 7 (2): 191–209.

Latour, Bruno. 1987. *Science in Action: How to Follow Scientists and Engineers through Society*. Milton Keynes: Open University Press.

Latour, Bruno. 1991. Technology is society made durable. In *A Sociology of Monsters? Essays on Power, Technology, and Domination*, ed. John Law, 103–131. London: Routledge.

Latour, Bruno. 1999. On recalling ANT. In *Actor Network Theory and After*, ed. John Law and John Hassard, 15–25. Oxford: Blackwell.

Latour, Bruno. 2002. What is *Iconoclash*? Or is there a world beyond the image wars? In *Iconoclash: Beyond the Image Wars in Science, Religion and Art*, ed. Bruno Latour and Peter Weibel, 14–37. Karlsruhe and Cambridge, MA: ZKM and MIT Press.

Latour, Bruno. 2005. *Reassembling the Social: An Introduction to Actor-Network-Theory*. Oxford: Oxford University Press.

Latour, Bruno, and Steve Woolgar. 1979. *Laboratory Life: The Social Construction of Scientific Facts*. Beverly Hills, CA: Sage.

Law, John. 1989. Technology and heterogeneous engineering: The case of Portuguese expansion. In *The Social Construction of Technological Systems: New Directions in the Sociology and History of Technology*, ed. Wiebe E. Bijker, Thomas P. Hughes, and Trevor Pinch, 111–135. Cambridge, MA: MIT Press.

Lotz, Katrine. 2008. Architectors: Specific architectural competencies. Ph.D. diss., Royal Danish Academy of Fine Arts, School of Architecture, Copenhagen.

Oudshoorn, Nelly, and Trevor Pinch. 2003. *How Users Matter: The Co-construction of Users and Technologies*. Cambridge, MA: MIT Press.

Pine, Joseph B., and James H. Gilmore. 1999. *The Experience Economy*. Boston: Harvard Business School Press.

Redvall, Eva Novrup. 2010. Teaching screenwriting in a time of storytelling blindness: The meeting of the auteur and the screenwriting tradition in Danish film-making. *Journal of Screenwriting* 1 (1): 57–79.

Schön, Donald A. 1983. *The Reflective Practitioner: How Professionals Think in Action*. New York: Basic Books.

Suchman, Lucy A. 2002. Practice-based design of information systems: Notes from the hyperdeveloped world. *Information Society* 18 (2): 139–144.

Suchman, Lucy A. 2007. *Human-Machine Reconfigurations: Plans and Situated Actions*. 2nd ed. Cambridge: Cambridge University Press.

Weick, Karl. 1995. *Sensemaking in Organizations*. Thousand Oaks, CA: Sage.

Woolgar, Steve. 1991. Configuring the user: The case of usability trials. In *A Sociology of Monsters? Essays on Power, Technology, and Domination*, ed. John Law, 57–102. London: Routledge.

Yaneva, Albena. 2008. How buildings "surprise": The renovation of the Alte Aula in Vienna. *Science Studies* 21 (1): 8–28.

Yaneva, Albena. 2009. Making the social hold: Towards an actor-network theory of design. *Design and Culture* 1 (3): 273–288.

IV Methods for Sustainability

16 Electric Vehicle Design

Thomas Budde Christensen and Niels Jørgensen

What. Vehicle design is situated design in the sense of design that is constrained by industrial context. In the automobile industry, the development of a new product, whether a conventional or an electric vehicle, is extremely expensive. The industry's response is a hybrid design approach that combines phased and iterative design. The main phased aspect is to freeze the design before implementation. Iterative aspects include the construction of digital and physical prototypes during the design phase.

Why. The hybrid design approach of the auto industry is a compromise: On the one hand, finalizing design before production avoids the costs of altering the extremely expensive facilities for mass production of cars. Moreover, a late design change may require recalling cars already sold. On the other hand, iterative techniques applied in the design phase may provide input about user preferences and inconsistencies in the design and thus reduce the risk, associated with phased design, that design decisions are based on insufficient knowledge of how the design will work in practice.

Where. Today a conventional or an electric car is typically developed in a process that corresponds to the hybrid method described in this chapter, if the car is designed for mass production. Exceptions include extreme luxury, sports, and experimental cars produced in small numbers.

How. Inside the car industry, designers of an electric vehicle must strike a balance between the hybrid method's phased and iterative elements. For example, designers must decide what components and technologies can be reused from conventional cars (an iterative aspect) versus what parts will be designed specifically for the electric vehicle (strengthening the phased aspect). Outside the car industry, the industry's somewhat conservative and change-resistant approach to design has significance for, among others, the designers of artifacts and systems of a new infrastructure for sustainable transport.

1   Introduction

The design approaches of the contemporary automobile industry may be of interest for at least three reasons. First, electric vehicle design is a crucial element of the transition to sustainable transport and thus is of interest even in countries such as Denmark that have no vehicle assembly plants. Design tasks related to integrating electric vehicles in a carbon-dioxide-neutral transport system include a myriad of small- and large-scale problems, from the design of parking lots with charging stations to the design of an entire country's power grid.

The transition to sustainable transport faces many obstacles, which call for a better understanding of all the contributing processes, including electric vehicle design. One indication at the time of writing is that it appears not to be possible for Denmark to reach the expected number of electric vehicles. The Danish National Renewable Energy Action Plan (Danish Ministry of Climate and Energy 2010) expected 80,000 electric vehicles by 2020, or an estimated 3.5 percent of all cars in the country. As a means toward achieving this target, electric vehicles have been exempted from the Danish car taxes, which add between 105 and 180 percent to the sales price of a new car. However, recent sales figures for electric vehicles in Denmark have been disappointing. The Renault Fluence ZE was introduced in the winter of 2011/2012 as the main model in an ambitious sales effort undertaken by the company Better Place in Denmark and Israel. (The Fluence ZE is shown in fig. 16.2 in sec. 4.) In Denmark, fewer than 200 of this model sold in 2012. On a worldwide scale, the Fluence ZE has been a disappointment too, with fewer than 5,000 vehicles produced altogether in 2011 and 2012. This should be viewed against the background of Renault's announcement in 2011 that the Renault-Nissan alliance was planning to produce 1.5 million electric vehicles before the end of 2016 ("Renault 2016: Drive the Change," press release, February 10, 2011). The bankruptcy of Better Place in the spring of 2013 underscored the difficulties of introducing electric vehicles.

Second, the hybrid design approach of the automobile industry may be of theoretical interest as an instance of situated design, illustrating how design is constrained by industrial context, in particular an industry's key technologies. According to our analysis of the auto industry, the technologies that influence the design processes are the mass production technologies. Today these technologies are employed to produce conventional vehicles. For electric vehicles to be price competitive, they must be mass-produced as well, and so by implication, they must be designed using the same overall process as conventional cars.

The overall hybrid process is rooted in concerns about economies of scale in the auto industry, in particular the huge investments in high-tech mass production facilities. The costs are so high that they normally require sales figures above 250,000 of a new car model to achieve a return on the investment (Orsato and Wells 2007). In turn, a mass production facility is required to attain competitive prices on the global car market. As far as we can see, the prevalent design approach in the automobile industry reflects these economic realities in a relevant way. Thus we are not advocating an alternative design approach for electric vehicles, though we will discuss one in section 5; rather, by describing and discussing the prevalent design approach, we aim to describe the challenges and constraints that face the design and proliferation of electric vehicles. The industrial context of design is related to the concept of a technological path (or trajectory) in the theory of innovation in sociotechnical systems (Geels 2004). The constraints on vehicle design tend to preserve the current dominance of conventional cars (the current path) and block or delay the transition to a CO_2-neutral transportation system (an alternative path). Another theoretically interesting point may be that hybrid design is an alternative to iterative design and thus represents a supplement, if not a challenge, to the tenet that iterative processes are always superior (see, e.g., Hevner 2007; Iansiti and MacCormack 1997).

A third reason that electric vehicle design might be of interest is that the automotive industry is the world's largest manufacturing industry. It has been a leading industry in the sense that many important manufacturing and managerial principles originate in the industry. These principles include Fordism, lean manufacturing, and business process reengineering, each of which has been defined in the research and managerial literature in terms of examples and narratives from the auto industry.

Manufacturing based on standardized parts and assembly lines was introduced at Ford Motor Company in the second decade of the twentieth century. With these and other methods for mass production, the Ford Model T was eventually produced at a rate of almost 2 million in a single year, 1924. That year, the Model T sold for $290, several times lower than when the Model T was originally introduced (Nielsen, Nielsen, and Jensen 2005). Indeed, the Model T was developed in a phased process, insofar as the design was developed from 1906 to 1908 and remained the same until 1927, when the Model A superseded the Model T. Today the basic anatomy of car plants remains the same: they are expensive, specialized organisms where parts are moved along pipelines, where they are gradually assembled and manufactured into larger parts.

Lean manufacturing (Womack, Jones, and Roos 1990) and business process reengineering (Hammer 1990) were influential management strategies in the 1990s in the United States and other Western countries. Both paradigms were inspired by methods used in Japan's auto industry. These methods attracted considerable interest as Japan in 1980 became the world's leading car producer (in terms of unit numbers), a position held previously by the United States. Lean manufacturing was inspired by the Japanese car maker Toyota in particular. The strategy can be described as a set of tools for eliminating waste in mass production, for example, by organizing the flow along the assembly line in a timely way so that there is no need of an inventory of extra parts. Business process reengineering, which targets manufacturing as well as service industries, aims at fundamental changes of a company's internal procedures, rather than fine-tuning existing ones. A famous case of business process reengineering was a reorganization of purchasing procedures at Ford Motor Company. The company had found that its staff of five hundred in the accounts payable department was far larger than the comparable department at Japanese auto maker Mazda. Ford's subsequent change of procedures led to a 75 percent staff reduction.

In the aircraft industry, another important manufacturing industry, when developing a new aircraft, Boeing uses design processes that are similar to the hybrid approach described in this chapter (Jørgensen 2006). While the Boeing processes are defined explicitly and at the company level, in the auto industry, as far as we know, it is not common to define an overall design process for a car's development. The hybrid model described in this chapter is not based on design guidelines produced in the industry; rather, it is our interpretation of how car development is actually carried out in the industry.

The term *electric vehicle* (EV) is used in the chapter for a car powered fully or partly by an electric engine. There are two important types of EVs: Battery electric vehicles (BEV) are powered solely by an electric motor; electric energy is obtained from the power grid and stored on board in a battery. The Renault Fluence ZE is a BEV. Hybrid electric vehicles (HEV) have two engines, an electric and an internal combustion engine (ICE). An ICE is the conventional, fossil-fuel-based engine. An example of an HEV is the Toyota Prius. Danish tax exemption is for BEVs, not HEVs.

In the remainder of the chapter, section 2 presents the hybrid design model, and sections 3 and 4 discuss its phased and iterative aspects, respectively. Section 5 discusses challenges of the hybrid model related to technological uncertainty, and section 6 concludes.

2   A Hybrid Design Model

Our hybrid model of the development of electric and conventional vehicles is defined in terms of three main activities in the development of a new car model: design, implementation, and production. Figure 16.1 shows the hybrid model, where the three activities are arranged in sequence (the phased aspect), and the technique of prototyping is used in the design phase (the iterative aspect).

The notion of response time (as used in fig. 16.1) is adapted from the discussion of iterative and phased approaches in Iansiti and MacCormack (1997). It is a measure of how fast designers can react to new knowledge or forecasts about technologies, user preferences, and so on. The response time is the time span from when a design decision is made to when a customer purchases and uses the car.

The notions of phased and iterative design describe the ordering in time of the three forms of activities that we have singled out in the model: design,

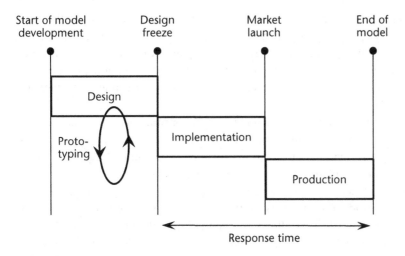

Figure 16.1

A hybrid design approach with three major phases, using prototyping inside the design phase. For a given car model, the total time consumed by the three phases is typically 6–8 years. Design covers both conceptual and detailed design (normally 2–4 years). Implementation is the construction of a mass production facility (1–6 months). Finally, a car model is typically in production for 4–6 years.

implementation, and production. The phased aspect is that design is finalized before implementation, which is finalized before production. The iterative aspect is that inside the design phase, some iteration occurs, in the sense that digital or physical prototypes are built on the basis of a preliminary design, for purposes of testing.

The model's first phase, design, comprises design decisions and activities required to make them. This includes designing a new car's platform (including frame and suspension system), other key components (including engine and other parts of the drivetrain), and the car's visual appearance. For example, the Renault Fluence ZE was designed as an EV-variant of the already existing Renault Fluence, an ICE-based car launched in 2010. In turn, the Fluence is based on the C-platform of Renault-Nissan, the same platform that the Renault Mégane III is based on. The Fluence is a four-door sedan, which is a rather conservative style. The design of the Fluence ZE's electric drivetrain generated a range of new design and engineering problems and required the combined efforts of several Renault research and advanced engineering departments (Midler and Beaume 2010). Modifications made to the conventional Fluence include stretching the frame by thirteen centimeters to make room for the battery between the rear seat and the trunk.

The second phase, implementation, is much shorter than the two other phases. This phase is significant because the cost of implementation is the main cause of the overall phased approach. Andrews, Nieuwenhuis, and Ewing (2006) estimate the price of a vehicle assembly plant somewhere between £390 million and £665 million. Such costs make it imperative to freeze the design before plant construction. The Renault Fluence ZE is produced at a Renault plant in Bursa, Turkey. The plant produces the conventional Renault Fluence and has been extended so that it can also produce the EV version of the Fluence.

The third phase, mass production, takes place at one or more plants. Renault's plant in Bursa, Turkey, is one of several plants that manufacture the ICE version of the Fluence. The plant also manufactures various versions of Renault's Mégane and Clio models. Indeed, given the plant's total production in 2012 of 292,000 cars, the couple of thousand EVs produced constitute a very small fraction. In the course of the mass production phase, a model is typically face-lifted a couple of years after market launch. A face-lift is a model update that allows the vehicle manufacturer to revitalize the styling of a model, and may comprise an update of minor exterior elements such as instrument panel, bumpers, headlights, mirrors, and minor trim changes. A face-lift does not require a redesign of core technologies or components or extensive alteration of the assembly plant or component manufacturing plants. Thus, when a consumer buys a face-lifted new car, the car is based on core design decisions made as many as six to eight years before the purchase. A wholly new-version model may be developed if the model has proved successful in the market. For example, the VW Golf has evolved through generation I to VII, launched in 1975 and 2013, respectively, each of which was a new model in the sense of figure 16.1 and had an average lifetime of approximately six years.

3   The Hybrid Method's Phased Aspect

Economies of scale are essential in the automotive industry. Economies of scale are the advantages that manufacturers can obtain when producing large quantities of the same product. Large-scale production enables manufacturers to reduce the cost per unit produced. Economies of scale in the auto industry are the chief economic mechanism or phenomenon that has influenced how new cars are designed. In this section, we first indicate the scale in which cars are mass-produced (sec. 3.1). Then we discuss the high costs of recalling and repairing cars already sold (sec. 3.2). Finally, we describe how production is organized on the basis of platforms and modules that are shared between different car models (sec. 3.3).

3.1   Mass-Market Vehicle Production

The last thirty years have witnessed a dramatic restructuring of the automotive industry. In this process, the number of independent vehicle manufacturers has been greatly reduced. By 2012, the fifteen largest manufacturers produced approximately 87 percent of all passenger cars in the world. The total number was about 65 million passenger cars (OICA 2014).

Modern mass-market vehicle production is characterized by high-volume production with economic break-even points approaching 250,000 units per car model (Orsato and Wells 2007). The break-even point is the number of units that must be sold before the manufacturer makes a profit from the investment in the model. The high number of cars that must be sold before breaking even is due primarily to the costs of the production plants. As noted in section 2, these costs are extremely high. A typical vehicle assembly plant consist of four main elements: (1) a press shop where steel sheets are pressed into body parts, (2) a welding plant where the body parts are welded together to form the vehicle body, (3) a paint shop where the vehicle body is coated and painted, and (4) a final assembly where preassembled parts are fitted onto the vehicle body to create the finished vehicle. A vehicle assembly plant only allows constrained flexibility. Fitting a new car model into an existing vehicle plant requires redesign of production lines and rearrangement of expensive tooling, for example, in the press shop.

To reach economic break-even points, high-capacity use is needed at the assembly plants. The profitability zone of European assembly plants is usually above 80 percent capacity (IHS Global Insight 2009). Thus the vehicle manufacturers need to keep up high-volume production at existing plants to pay back the large investments. This makes assembly plant owners vulnerable to changing consumer preferences and fluctuations in demand for new cars. This stimulates conservative design strategies in the industry.

3.2 The Costs of Recalling Cars Already Sold

A car model is recalled if defects are discovered after marked launch. Because of the high production numbers in mass-market car manufacturing, recalls are a potential economic disaster for the manufacturers. For example, a defective window switch discovered in 2012 caused Toyota to recall 7.4 million cars worldwide, including Yaris, Corolla, and Camry models. In addition to the direct economic costs of repairing large numbers of cars, recalls also affect the value of the model brand.

The main examples of iterative product development discussed by Iansiti and Mac-Cormack (1997) come from the software industry, in particular the development of Web browsers by Microsoft and Netscape in 1996 and 1997. On the one hand, recalling and repairing a car resembles distributing a patch to a software product. On the other hand, for a software company to distribute a new version of its software is much easier than for a car company to recall and repair millions of cars already sold. For this reason, the automotive industry must emphasize completing the design before starting mass production. A similar argument underlies the statement that "hardware is best developed with as little iteration as possible, while software can (and often should) evolve through much iteration" (Maier and Rechtin 2000, 95).

3.3   Shared Platforms and Modules

Most of today's vehicle manufacturers have developed design strategies that allow component and technology sharing across the group's models and brands. Such strategies allow for higher volumes in component manufacturing, and thus for lowering the unit costs of the components.

If a new car model is tied to the development of an entirely new platform, the development approach for the model becomes more phased, because platform development is costly and must be completed before production can commence. On the other hand, a new model can be developed in a more iterative style if the model can reuse an existing platform.

The Renault Fluence ZE shares many characteristics with the conventional ICE version of the Fluence, despite the fundamentally different drivetrain solution. In turn, the Fluence is based on the C-platform of Renault-Nissan, as mentioned in section 2. The Renault-Nissan alliance organizes vehicle development around twenty-two platforms shared between the brands of the alliance, which include Dacia, Samsung, Lada, Datsun, and Infiniti, in addition to Renault and Nissan (Renault-Nissan 2012). Approximately 85 percent of the total production volume in Renault-Nissan is produced on just five of these platforms (Sehgal and Gori 2012). The C-platform, for example, is the basis for models such as the Renault Mégane, Scenic, and Fluence and the Nissan Qashqai and Rogue (Renault-Nissan 2012).

The Renault-Nissan alliance has converted the platform strategy into a modular strategy, called the "common module family," to attain a higher degree of component sharing (Renault-Nissan 2012). The common module family was launched in 2009 and is to be applied to vehicles entering the market between 2013 and 2015. The system consists of five modules: (1) central and rear underbody, (2) cockpit, (3) engine compartment, (4) front underbody, and (5) electrical architecture.

The Renault-Nissan alliance has developed three common module families (CMFs): CMF 1 covers the largest volume of cars in the alliance, encompassing C- and D-platform vehicles, or medium-size and larger vehicles; CMF 2 covers small vehicles; and CMF 3 covers the smallest vehicles in entry markets.

The VW Group is another example of a group that has implemented a comprehensive modularization strategy for component sharing. The group comprises the passenger car brands VW, Audi, Skoda, and SEAT, as well as the luxury and sports brands Porsche, Bugatti, Bentley, and Lamborghini. Core components such as engines, gearboxes, and air-conditioning are integrated into functional systems, called modules, which are shared across multiple brands and models. Previously this system was based on a platform concept, where components and technology were shared across similarly sized car models. For example, the VW B platform was used in midsize sedans and station wagons. Today the platform strategy has evolved into a modular tool kit strategy, which aims at technology and component sharing across differently sized models (VW 2012).

The implications of shared platforms and modules are, on the one hand, that the development and manufacturing costs of a new model, including a new EV model, are lowered. On the other hand, the more iterative approach means that new models resemble existing models more.

4   The Hybrid Method's Iterative Aspects

The hybrid design process in the auto industry can be characterized as a basically phased process. However, the model also includes iterative process elements. Three iterative techniques that are widespread in the industry are discussed in this section. Each technique is a form of prototyping.

4.1   Prototypes Used in the Visual Styling of a New Model

The auto industry, according to Tovey, Porter, and Newman (2003), organizes design processes on the basis of a distinction between styling and engineering. During the styling phase, designers use sketches and clay models when working on the visual appearance of a new car model. These are used to communicate and evaluate new designs between members of the design team and between the design team and the management. A visual design is constrained by requirements following from the selected vehicle platform, technologies, and manufacturing practices, but the constraints are managed loosely in the initial design phases (Tovey, Porter, and Newman 2003). Of course, the styling phase also uses computer-aided design as a supplement to pencil sketches and clay models.

4.2   In-Firm Prototypes

Full-scale and fully functioning prototypes are also used for testing purposes before making final decisions about the design of a new model. Testing covers performance, durability, reliability, safety, and other aspects. Bakker, van Lente, and Meeus (2012) use the phrase "in-firm prototypes" for this kind of prototype, since they are used mainly in a test context defined by the company, for example, in laboratory tests or on closed raceways.

Renault has large testing facilities in Aubevoye (France), Lardy (France), and Titu (Romania). Each test facility includes a large number of different raceways and test benches, enabling Renault to test prototypes and components under different conditions. While developing the electric vehicle model Renault ZOE, Renault carried out a large number of tests, during which electric motors and batteries were tested at the Lardy Technical Center. Then the car as a whole was tested for reliability and durability in 850,000 kilometers of performance testing, at different sites with varying temperatures and road surfaces. The car additionally underwent thousands of user tests to simulate durability in real-life usage (Renault 2013).

Prototype testing has an inherent iterative character, but in the auto industry, prototyping usually does not involve communication with external stakeholders. In fact, attempts are sometimes made to hide a prototype's visual appearance, which is treated as a business secret until model launch.

4.3 Concept Cars Displayed to the Public

The auto industry produces a large volume of concept cars that are displayed publicly at fairs and auto shows and on the Internet. These concept cars may communicate, for example, a proof of principle for a promising new technology or a new design philosophy to external stakeholders outside the company.

Concept cars serve two main functions: (1) they are part of an iterative design process where engineering concepts, technologies, and visual designs are displayed to potential customers and competitors to generate feedback to the designers, and (2) they are part of the branding of the auto makers, in the sense that concept cars display technological capabilities and future styling (Bakker, van Lente, and Meeus 2012). These types of vehicles can sometimes be far from the vehicles that are actually placed on the roads, in both styling and technology. Bakker, van Lente, and Meeus (2012) analyzed 224 prototypes of hydrogen vehicles that had been displayed by auto makers between 1970 and 2008; even as late as 2013, no auto makers had introduced hydrogen-fueled cars in large-scale production.

The first version of the Renault Fluence ZE was displayed as a concept car at the Frankfurt Motor Show in 2009 ("Renault Fluence ZE: The Car of Tomorrow … Now!" press release, October 3, 2011). This first version appeared in a more futuristic styling than the conservatively styled model launched on the roads three years later. Thus, in this case, the trend where concept cars have a more radical design than the production models seems to apply to electric cars as well (fig. 16.2).

5 Challenges of Electric Vehicle Design

A major challenge of electric vehicle design is the uncertainty of electric vehicle technology. The future development of the technology is extremely difficult to predict. For example, battery-charging technology is essential for electric vehicle proliferation. Unfortunately, the design of the Renault Fluence ZE, the key model marketed by the company Better Place, relied on the assumption that battery switching would become widespread, an assumption that turned out to be wrong.

Technological uncertainty amplifies the drawbacks of the hybrid design approach. Recall from section 2 that freezing the design before implementation entails a long

Figure 16.2
Above, concept car from 2009; below, the actual Renault Fluence ZE as launched on the market in 2011–2012.

response time from design decision to market launch. This means that design decisions are made on the basis of assumptions about how the relevant technologies will develop for several years into the future. Since the development of technologies related to electric vehicles is highly uncertain, a huge financial risk is associated with investing in electric vehicle development. Design situated in the auto industry must take into account not only the industry's general economic mechanisms but also specific challenges related to introducing a new technology.

In a wider perspective, technological uncertainty is related to path dependency. In the theory of innovation in sociotechnical systems (Geels 2004), path dependency means that a system (such as the transportation system) tends to evolve along the path of the technology the system is already based on (cars with conventional engines) and resist transition efforts toward a new technology (electric vehicles). In Geels's analysis, path dependency is based on cultural habits, the interests of social actors (e.g., oil companies), and several other factors. Path dependency may further be reinforced by uncertainty about new technologies.

Whereas the previous sections have discussed characteristics of vehicle design that are common to electric and conventional vehicles (when they are mass-produced), here we focus on electric vehicles. In the following, we discuss battery technology (sec. 5.1), technologies and standards for battery charging (sec. 5.2), and so-called smart grid technology for integrating battery charging in the power grid (sec. 5.3). The end result of these constraints on the design process may be a highly conservative approach, and we discuss an alternative, the so-called clean sheet approach (sec. 5.4).

5.1 Battery Technology

It is expected that future batteries will cost less and provide larger storage capacity at a given weight (National Academy of Sciences 2013). The currently preferred battery technology for EVs, lithium-ion batteries, is already the result of a technological leap, caused by mass production of batteries for portable devices (cell phones, laptops, etc.). Producers and users of EVs do not know the speed at which battery technology will improve in the future. This is essential, because the high battery cost is a significant part of the overall cost of an EV, and also because the current limited driving range is of prime concern of customers.

5.2 Industry Standards in the Future Charging Infrastructure

The Renault Fluence ZE was designed so that it can have its battery replaced automatically at a so-called battery switching station using robot technology. Thus the Fluence ZE combines two charging options for the internal battery pack: either conventionally (for EVs) via a plugged connection to the electric grid, or by replacing the battery with a fully charged one. Renault was collaborating with electric mobility providers, such as Better Place, to deploy battery switching stations.

Battery switching increases the range of EVs. With a fully charged battery, the Renault Fluence has a claimed range of 150 kilometers. The conventional method of charging a fixed battery may take as long as six to eight hours, depending on the type of charging, so it is difficult to go beyond the vehicle's range without recharging the battery overnight. However, the future proliferation of battery switching stations is highly uncertain after Better Place, the battery switching station operator in Denmark and Israel, filed for bankruptcy in spring 2013. The bankruptcy of the Danish affiliate came only six months after Better Place had completed the full national coverage of battery switching stations in Denmark. Poor sales figures nevertheless forced the company to close down, as mentioned in the introduction of the chapter.

Compatibility issues may also arise, where a given switching station may work only with batteries of certain types. Even with regard to charging a battery via the power grid, there are competing standards, and so there is uncertainty with respect to which standards will prevail. A number of additional charging options are being explored and implemented, including so-called quick charging and inductive charging. International negotiations are carried out to design common charging standards, which will make it possible to charge cars of different brands at the same charging spot. These future standards depend on a complex development involving stakeholders such as electric mobility providers, utility companies, electric grid companies, and public authorities.

The automobile designer must consider these uncertainties early in the design process. Later, a user thinking of buying an electric vehicle will have to consider them as well. At the time of purchasing an EV, the user knows the presently available charging options, but it is difficult to predict whether, say, the number of battery switching stations will increase or decrease in the future.

5.3 Smart Grid Integration

A final area of technological uncertainty is whether and in what way battery electric vehicles can be integrated into the electricity production sector. Many governments plan to introduce renewable energy sources (wind power, solar power, biomass and hydro power) in the electricity systems. The renewable energy sources fluctuate according to the natural variations in, for example, wind condition and solar radiation (Christensen and Kjær 2012). This causes fluctuations in electricity production. These fluctuations are difficult to manage in the electric grid because the traditional power sources, such as coal-fired power stations, are inflexible in the sense that they cannot easily be turned on and off. Electric cars could provide flexibility if vehicle charging is coordinated and managed according to peaks and lows in the electricity system. The benefit for the electricity system is that vehicles could be charged in periods with high production (Christensen, Wells, and Cipcigan 2012). The benefit for the vehicle owner is cheaper charging, because prices in the electricity market are low in periods with low demand. This type of system is usually referred to as a "smart grid system."

Conversely, if electric vehicle charging is not intelligently monitored and managed, charging is likely to take place during the afternoon and early peak in the electricity system, say between 5 p.m. and 9 p.m. This will require the use of backup plants to deliver the needed electricity. Unfortunately, backup plants are typically older and less efficient and pollute more.

The future smart grid technology will be the result of complex processes, involving actors such as grid companies, EV manufacturers, electric mobility providers, public authorities, and electric vehicle owners, the outcome of which is difficult to predict. EV manufacturers take this insecurity into account when planning their investments. If electric vehicles are not successfully integrated into the power grid structure, the green image of EVs may be compromised, and political support may vanish; for example, in Denmark, the support for EV tax exemption may erode.

5.4 A Radically New, Integrated Design of Electric Vehicles?

Another challenge to the hybrid design method is that it may be overly conservative. Indeed, the design of some electric vehicles has been criticized by Lovins and Cramer (2004) for being too "incremental," that is, too similar to the design of internal combustion engine vehicles. The Renault Fluence ZE is a case in point, being a variant of a car originally designed for internal combustion engines.

Lovins and Cramer suggest a "clean sheet" design approach as an alternative to what they see as the prevalent approach to EVs, where auto makers merely introduce new components in the drive line (engine and battery) but retain the design of the car's other components. Instead a design for an electric or hybrid vehicle should be an integrated one, where other parts are redesigned, in particular with a view to reducing the weight of all components (Lovins 2011). Weight is of primary importance for an EV because of the limited capacity of the car's battery, which limits the distance EVs can drive before the battery must be recharged.

The predominant downside to the clean sheet design approach is that technologies and components will have to be developed from scratch during each vehicle development program. Economies of scale in component manufacturing similar to those associated with traditional auto manufacturing are therefore likely to be difficult to achieve, as technologies and components are developed exclusively for the dedicated vehicle instead of being standardized for use across multiple vehicles and platforms. This is ultimately likely to raise costs in both design and manufacturing.

6 Conclusion

The chapter has discussed a hybrid design model that is used in the automotive industry. The model combines two approaches: (1) a phased, sequential design approach, where one design activity is finalized before the next design activity begins; and (2) an iterative design aspect, where in-house tests, prototypes, and feedback from users are internalized in the design activities to create feedback loops between use and design phases. The chapter explores how this hybrid design approach is situated in the automotive industry and discusses the constraints and challenges under which new car models, in particular electric cars models, are designed and produced. The analysis is based on a case study analysis of the Renault Fluence ZE electric car.

Two challenges related to the hybrid approach have been discussed. One is that the phased nature of the approach entails a relatively large response time, and this increases technological uncertainty, because design decisions are taken years before the final vehicle models are placed on the roads. The Renault Fluence ZE was developed with a battery switch option, which should make it possible for users to switch batteries at dedicated stations instead of having to rely on time-consuming direct charging from the electric grid. However, the battery station operator Better Place filed for bankruptcy in spring 2013, only a year after the launch of the Fluence ZE. This illustrates the problems associated with long response time in the phased design method.

A second challenge is that electric vehicles are too similar to conventional cars. They are not designed with sufficient emphasis on weight reduction, although weight reduction may be crucial to extend the distance an EV can be driven before recharging the battery. Furthermore, EVs are designed to fit into the existing production system in the automotive industry, which is characterized by high-volume production and low unit costs. This production system makes it economically unattractive for the vehicle manufacturers to produce car models in low unit numbers. This implies that it is unattractive to experiment with alternatives to conventional cars. Thus the analysis illustrates that the integration of electric vehicles with conventional internal combustion engine cars in terms of platform and module sharing, and in terms of shared manufacturing facilities, constitutes a major design constraint for the proliferation of electric vehicles. The hybrid design model is shown graphically in figure 16.1 in section 2.

References

Andrews, Deborah, Paul Nieuwenhuis, and Paul D. Ewing. 2006. Black and beyond: Colour and the mass-produced motor car. *Optics and Laser Technology* 38: 377–391.

Bakker, Sjoerd, Harro van Lente, and Marius T. H. Meeus. 2012. Dominance in the prototyping phase: The case of hydrogen passenger cars. *Research Policy* 41: 871–883.

Christensen, Thomas B., and Tyge Kjær. 2012. What is CleanTech? Unraveling the buzzword. In *Rethinking Climate Change Research*, ed. Pernille Almlund, Per H. Jespersen, and Søren Riis, 43–65. Farnham: Ashgate.

Christensen, Thomas B., Peter Wells, and Liana Cipcigan. 2012. Can innovative business models overcome resistance to electric vehicles? Better place and battery electric cars in Denmark. *Energy Policy* 48: 498–505.

Danish Ministry of Climate and Energy. 2010. National handlingsplan for vedvarende energy i Danmark. In *National Renewable Energy Action Plan*. Copenhagen: Danish Ministry of Climate and Energy.

Geels, Frank W. 2004. From sectoral systems of innovation to socio-technical systems: Insights about dynamics and change from sociology and institutional theory. *Research Policy* 33 (6–7): 897–920.

Hammer, Michael. 1990. Reengineering work: Don't automate, obliterate. *Harvard Business Review* 68 (4): 104–112.

Hevner, Alan R. 2007. A three cycle view of design science research. *Scandinavian Journal of Information Systems* 19 (2): 87–92.

Iansiti, Marco, and Alan MacCormack. 1997. Developing products on Internet time. *Harvard Business Review* 75: 108–117.

IEA. 2011. Clean Energy Progress Report. Update June. Paris: International Energy Agency.

IHS Global Insight. 2009. Impacts of the financial and economic crisis on the automotive industry. In *Impact of the Financial and Economic Crisis on European Industries*. Report prepared for the European Parliament's committee on industry, energy and research. http://www.europarl.europa.eu/document/activities/cont/201109/20110906ATT25989/20110906ATT25989EN.pdf (accessed August 15, 2013).

Jørgensen, Niels. 2006. The Boeing 777: No chainsaw massacres, please! *Journal of Integrated Design and Process Science* 10 (2): 79–91.

Lovins, Amory B. 2011. *Reinventing Fire: Bold Business Solutions for the New Energy Area*. White River Junction, VT: Chelsea Green.

Lovins, Amory B., and David R. Cramer. 2004. Hypercars, hydrogen, and the automotive transition. *International Journal of Vehicle Design* 35 (1–2): 50–85.

Maier, Marc W., and Eberhardt Rechtin. 2000. *The Art of Systems Architecting*, 2nd ed. Boca Raton: CRC Press.

Midler, Christophe, and Romain Beaume. 2010. Project-based learning patterns for dominant design renewal: The case of Electric Vehicle. *International Journal of Project Management* 28: 142–150.

National Academy of Sciences. 2013. *Transitions to Alternative Vehicles and Fuels*. Washington, DC: National Academy Press.

Nielsen, Keld, Henry Nielsen, and Hans S. Jensen. 2005. *Skruen uden ende: Den vestlige teknologis historie* [The endless screw: History of Western technology], 3rd ed. Copenhagen: Nyt Teknisk.

OICA. 2014. World motor vehicle production, International Organization of Motor Vehicle Manufacturers. http://www.oica.net/wp-content/uploads/2013/03/worldpro2012-modification -ranking.pdf (accessed January 3, 2014).

Orsato, Renato, and Peter Wells. 2007. U-turn: The rise and demise of the automobile industry. *Journal of Cleaner Production* 5: 994–1006.

Renault. 2013. Renault ZOE: The electric supermini for everyday use. http://media.renault.com/ global/en-gb/renault/Media/Topic.aspx?mediaid=44472&mediakitid=44471 (accessed August 12, 2013).

Renault-Nissan. 2012. Alliance facts and figures, 2012–2013. http://www.renault.com/en/lists/ archivesdocuments/alliance-facts-and-figures-2012.pdf (accessed August 12, 2013).

Sehgal, Bhavya, and Pronab Gori. 2012. Platform strategy will shape future of OEMs—flexibility to drive growth. http://sandhill.com/wp-content/files_mf/evalueservewhitepaperplatformstrategy willshapefutureofoems.pdf (accessed August 12, 2013).

Simonsen, Jesper, Jørgen O. Bærenholdt, and John D. Scheuer. 2012. Synergies. In *Design Research: Synergies from Interdisciplinary Perspectives*, ed. Jesper Simonsen, Jørgen O. Bærenholdt, Monika Büscher, and John D. Scheuer, 201–212. London: Routledge.

Tovey, Michael, Sara Porter, and Robert Newman. 2003. Sketching, concept development, and automotive design. *Design Studies* 24: 135–153.

Volkswagen. 2012. Factbook 2012. http://www.volkswagenag.com/content/vwcorp/info_center/ de/publications/2012/03/Factbook_2012.bin.html/binarystorageitem/file/Factbook+2012.pdf (accessed August 12, 2013).

Womack, James P., Daniel T. Jones, and Daniel Roos. 1990. *The Machine That Changed the World*. London: Simon & Schuster.

17 Sustainable Transition

Ole Erik Hansen and Bent Søndergård

What. The chapter examines designing for sustainability as interventions in socio-technical systems and social practices of users and communities. It calls for reflexive design practices that challenge dominant regimes and shape alternative design spaces. The specific case is the reconfiguration of vision, agendas, technologies, actors, and institutions in the emergent design of an urban mobility system based on an electric car sharing system.

Why. Designing for sustainability is a fundamental challenge for future design practices; designers have to obtain an ability to contribute to sustainable transition processes.

Where. The chapter addresses design processes aimed at sustainable transition enacted in complex social settings that involve many different actors with diverging agendas.

How. The chapter outlines a conceptual and analytic framework for a reflexive design practice for sustainability, including the perspective of structural changes (transition of socio-technical systems and social practices), design as metadesign, and reflexivity in the contextual framework of the design practice (regimes/design spaces).

1 Introduction

In this chapter, we analyze designing for sustainability as interventions in social practices embedded in socio-technical contexts; thus the transition of socio-technical systems and social practices is the focal point of sustainable design. In addition, we conceptualize design as situated acting in regimes and design spaces; sustainable design becomes a question of reflexivity concerning contextual social structures and dominant regimes (fig. 17.1).

This understanding of the social situatedness of design practices as embedded in socio-technical systems or regimes and the analysis of design practices draws on Giddens's structuration theory and critical realism. Giddens (1984, 19) argues that "the rules and resources drawn upon in the production and reproduction of social action

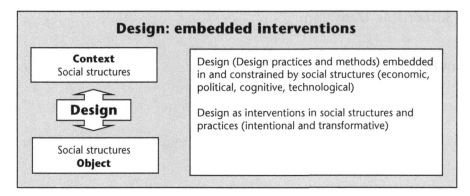

Figure 17.1
Design as embedded interventions: social structures, here seen as socio-technical systems, both form the contextual conditions and become the object of design (for sustainability).

are at the same time means of system reproduction." This implies that the constitution of social structures and agents cannot be separated, and they form a duality. Therefore designers and design practices have to be addressed as situated in the social structures constraining and enabling their actions. Social structures are enabling conditions that allow social transformative design processes. Knowledgeable agents (designers) draw reflexively on resources and rules (here perceived as socio-technical systems or regimes) and select specific elements as important for the structuration of the design spaces.

More generally, from the perspective of theory of science, critical realism (Bhaskar 1978) argues that there is a social reality, but there are different perceptions based on theoretical and normative preferences, because social reality is not fully transparent. Furthermore, social systems are open systems, and therefore outcomes are simultaneously caused and contingent (Sayer 2000). Therefore the designer's understanding of the important factors in socio-technical regimes is crucial for the interpretation of the design space, and these interpretations can change during the design process.

This chapter addresses how designers meet metadesign problems in specific design spaces. It examines designing as a process where designs evolve through cycles of learning based on acting within a specific design space, and where designers in a reflexive process may coshape alternative design spaces.

Design for sustainability has evolved as a core design issue in response to the fundamental social challenges of climate change, resource depletion, and health and environmental problems. Designing is, following Simon, a socially distributed process enacted in society as intended effort: "Everyone designs who devises courses of action aimed at changing existing situations into preferred ones" (Simon 1984, 111). Designing for sustainability calls for an intentional, normative design practice with the capacity to redefine products and practices, and capable of being reflexive and radical.

Focus is not only on grounding design in present practices and competences but on transcending given structural constraints and facilitating structural changes and shifts in social practices.

The challenge is to design sustainable social practices (Stegall 2006), expanding the focus of sustainable design from artifacts and production systems to the inclusion of everyday practices; we have "moved from largely technical concerns about efficient resource consumption and minimizing waste in our existing industrial systems to a more recent focus on the very social issue of lifestyle change" (Thorpe 2010, 3). Sustainable design, perceived as the formation of more sustainable practices, combines structural changes (on the level of socio-technical systems) and shifts in social practices (Shove and Walker 2010).

2   Analytic Framework

Designing for sustainability goes beyond eco-design schemes of more sustainable products; it concerns the transition of socio-technical systems and social practices.

2.1   Socio-technical Systems, Technological Regimes, and Design

In adopting a socio-technical transition perspective in relation to design, we depart from the understanding that socio-technical systems both form the contextual conditions for, and become the object, of design (for sustainability); we need to understand how socio-technical systems and practices are constituted and, furthermore, understand their dynamics of development, reproduction, and change.

The notion of socio-technical systems has been introduced to understand how both social and material elements structure and constitute technology and social practices. Socio-technical systems such as car-based mobility are constituted of networks of actors, institutions (rules), and artifacts (holding meaning and power, prefiguring agency). They are systems with codeveloping elements of technology, production systems, service systems (e.g., maintenance systems), markets, consumer behavior/user practices, policies (regulation, institutional frameworks), infrastructures, and cultural meaning (Geels 2004).

In this way, socio-technical systems are seen as interrelated systems of production and consumption, as interdependent material, social, and cultural elements. Thus changes to obtain more sustainable practices will involve interrelated changes of all elements. The transition perspective on sustainable development is based on the understanding that the challenge of sustainability goes beyond optimizing our present systems; we need transition, that is, radical transformations shaping systems based on other values, technologies, and so on.

It is an actor-based approach asserting the importance of actors and stakeholders, the framing of their actions, their interpretation and perception, interests and strategies, and networks and interaction, as both constitutive and dynamic properties of socio-technical systems. Socio-technical systems can be seen as semicoherent aligned systems, but closures (in terms of stable patterns of aligned elements) will always be relative and temporarily: "Tensions and misalignment may (temporarily) exist between elements, which create windows of opportunity for wider change" (Kemp, Geels, and Dudley 2012, 16). Understanding the systemic interdependencies and tensions, as well as an analytic mapping of stakeholders' perceptions, strategies, and interests, and in this way understanding restraints and opportunities, become integral parts of the design process.

We introduce the notion of "technological regimes" to emphasize the social embed-dedness and path dependency of innovation and design processes within socio-technical systems:

A technological regime is the rule-set of grammar embedded in a complex of engineering prac-tices, production process technologies, product characteristics, skills and procedures, ways of handling relevant artifacts and persons, ways of defining problems; all of them embedded in institutions and infrastructure. (Rip and Kemp 1998, 338)

The concept of regimes builds on an institutional understanding of actors, where actors (designers) are supposed to act within, and be reproduced in, a context of insti-tutionalized rules (see Giddens 1984). Regimes are dominant practices, norms, and shared assumptions that structure the conduct of private and public actors (Kemp and Rotmans 2005, 39).

Technological regimes enable action (design and innovation) by providing shared principles, norms, rules, and decision-making procedures within a given issue area; regimes provide stability and direction, but on the other hand, they tend to have a high level of inertia, leading to reproducing and optimizing (design) practices. Within regimes, actors will be inclined to perform "normal" design and technology practices characterized by path dependency and biased toward incremental improvement and system optimization.

Regimes are communities of actors sharing cognitive rules in terms of problem agendas, search heuristics, and guiding principles (Geels 2004). Technological regimes are social realities, but in the analysis of social practices and design practices it is important to include a hermeneutic understanding of how the actors and designers perceive and motivate their actions with reference to a specific interpretation of the structural conditions (Giddens 1984).

The notion of technological regimes provides an understanding of the general (global) framework structuring design practices, but we need an understanding of specific (local) design situations. For this purpose, we introduce the notion of "design spaces." Design spaces are "specific situated configurations of networks of actors, specific interpretations and discourses and structural conditions in terms of institutional and material interdependencies, all structuring design practices" (Holm, Søndergård, and Hansen 2010, 126) (see sec. 3.2 in this chap.).

The challenge of sustainable design is to change these regimes and design spaces, and that becomes a project of metadesign (see sec. 3.2) concerned with regime transformation and the constructive formation of alternative design spaces to establish new configurations of actors, agendas, and institutions enabling new openings for sustainable social practices.

2.2 Changing Socio-technical Practices Embedded in Socio-technical Systems

Designers need to understand what constitutes the persistence of social practices so as to build up a design capability to advance more sustainable practices (Scott, Bakker, and Quist 2012), as well as the dynamics of how practices emerge, reproduce, and change (Shove and Walker 2010).

Practices are composed of specific configurations of interconnected social, cultural, and material elements. Reckwitz defines practices as "a routinized type of behavior which depends on the specific interconnectedness of many elements, interconnected to one another: forms of bodily activities, forms of mental activities, 'things' and their use, a background knowledge in the form of understanding, know-how and notions of competence, states of emotion and motivational knowledge." These elements form a block "whose existence necessarily depends on the existence and specific interconnectedness of these elements, and which cannot be reduced to any one of these single elements" (Reckwitz 2002, 249–250).

With the same understanding, Shove and Pantzar (2005) suggest a more straightforward comprehension of practice as a bundle of three elements: "material artifacts, conventions and competences", where material artifacts include technologies, spatial room, and so on; conventions are social and personal meaning and norms related to the given practice; and competences include understanding, know-how, and procedures.

We engage in taken-for-granted everyday practices, but whether a practice is considered normal or appropriate relates to collectively established conventions of "normality" (Shove 2003). Practices (e.g., of mobility) are individually performed in a specific context and place; however, main elements of practices are constituted collectively at a structural level (systems of provision, collective norms, etc.). We have to operate with practice as both a structural coordinating entity and (individual) performance (Schatzki 2001).

Social practices are part of socio-technical systems. They depend on the system of provision supporting (or restricting) specific schemes of practices in mobility. Taking mobility practices as a case, these practices are embedded in socio-technical systems in terms of infrastructures, production systems of automobility, and so on, all leading to a rigidity to change (a high degree of path dependency) (Shove and Walker 2010).

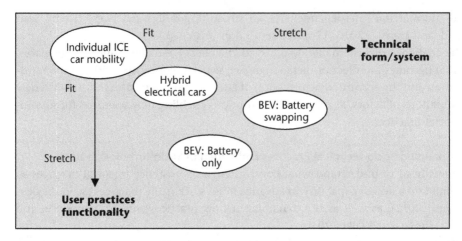

Figure 17.2
Fit and stretch pattern of electric vehicle concepts in relation to user practices and technical system. Adapted from Dijk, Orsato, and Kemp 2013, 144.

In mobility we do have a specific linkage of "the structural" and social practice in terms of a spatial specificity of accessibility to mobility options; our individual urban mobility practices are conditioned on local infrastructure, available public transportation, and institutional frameworks (e.g., price structures). Social practices and the specific local configuration of mobility systems cannot be separated, and design as intervention has to address both sides.

In introducing and designing new technologies, we will have a "fit or stretch" problem in relation to both entrenched user practices and the system of provision (the socio-technical system)—here illustrated with the introduction of different concepts of electric vehicles (fig. 17.2). Compared to the internal combustion engine (ICE) private car, the electric car concepts—such as hybrid electric cars, BEV with battery exchange systems, and BEV with battery only (no swapping)—represent different patterns of fit/stretch with existing practices and technology platforms (see also sec. 4.2).

In designing new mobility systems, we may adopt different pathways ranging from technology substitution within given user practices and socio-technical systems to pathways seeking a concurrent reconfiguration of practices and technologies (Raven and Geels 2010).

3   Intervention in Socio-technical Systems and Practices

To practice intentional design for sustainability, designers have to expand their scope and skills. This involves reflexivity in the criteria of sustainability and the acquiring of "ecological literacy," including an understanding of the interaction with ecosystems and streams of material (Stegall 2006). But it also involves knowledge of "metadesign," that idea that design has to address processes of structural change, changes of vision, discourses, and institutions, and the configuration of alternative design spaces.

3.1 Metadesign

On a general level, Giaccardi has defined metadesign "as critical and reflexive thinking about the boundaries and scope of design, aimed at coping with the complexity of natural human interaction made tangible by technology. ... Metadesign deals with the creation of context rather than content" (Giaccardi 2005, 343).

Within design research, metadesign has been used in a more narrow sense to denote "a user-centered and participatory design approach" (Giaccardi and Fischer 2008, 2). In their perspective: "The challenge is to create social and technical infrastructures that enable users to cope with the emergent aspects of reality and allow them, when needed and desired, to act as designers and be creative" (ibid.). The argument is that creating such structural conditions, allowing users to act as designers, and providing frameworks (not fixed solutions) for the integration of users can serve as a stronger design approach capable of coping with ill-defined design problems, supporting reflective practitioners, and in general supporting design as a collaborative process.

Here metadesign is limited to a second-order design practice configuring structures for a participatory design process without questioning dominant regimes structuring (and restraining) the design process. Opposed to this understanding, we operate with a notion of (sustainable) metadesign as design efforts oriented toward deliberate change of the contextual framework of design practices, the intentional transformation of dominant regimes, and the formation of specific design spaces; or, defined positively, deliberate efforts to develop alternative design spaces.

We thus call for reflexive design practices to critically scrutinize generally held convictions and socio-cognitive structures of regimes. These reflexive practices concern the discursive structures, or as Wahl and Baxter (2008, 72) put it: "Upstreams, in the immaterial dimension, the 'metadesign' of our conscious awareness, value systems, world-views and aspirations defines the intentionality behind materialized design." Metadesign, however, is not limited to the socio-cognitive aspects (discursive struggles), as claimed by Wahl and Baxter, but involves a scrutinizing of all the elements, including material and institutional elements, constituting socio-technological regimes and specific design spaces.

3.2 Design Spaces

Defining design as situated, inscribed in specific contextual frameworks and subject to reflexive processes of interpretation of designers, is central to design studies.

Buchanan (1992, 9) operates with four broad areas of design: "design of symbolic and visual communication, design of material objects, design of activities and organized services and design of complex systems or environments for living, working, playing, and learning." He identifies them as "places of invention" having their own kind of design practices, but also being interconnected (e.g., design practices exploring objects as part of larger systems and environments). They are subject to processes of conceptual repositioning resulting in a diverse set of "placements" having boundaries to shape and constrain meaning. According to Buchanan, placements in this respect provide contexts, and applied in specific situations to problems in specific circumstances, they constitute interpretive structures and sources of new ideas and options.

With this understanding, Buchanan (1992) introduces "the doctrine of placement" as a way of inscribing design practices; that is, designers, both as communities and individually, develop sets of placements that become their (personal) creative conceptual space. He holds that a perception of designers as operating in "placements," positioning and repositioning themselves within them, is vital to the understanding of design processes, in particular when looking at design in complex social settings addressing so-called wicked problems. We need to operate with specific placements, defined in specific situations and circumstances by the actors involved in the design process, as an intermediate setting and framework for understanding design processes.

Buchanan's objective is to understand the creative processes of design by focusing on the cognitive framing. By introducing the notion of design spaces (sec. 2.1), we emphasize the material and institutional settings as equally important constitutive elements in the space structuring design processes. We understand design processes as enacted in a duality of structural and interpretive/selective processes.

Operating within a design space involves knowledge of the interdependencies (material and institutional) and an understanding of how specific interpretations or translations of environmental/sustainable challenges, in combination with expectations related to specific technologies, such as electric cars, construe a set of actors, technologies, and objectives in the specific technology field (Raven and Geels 2010; Holm, Søndergård, and Hansen 2010). The role of design is to frame actors' needs and aspirations and to translate various positions and ideas into a specific technology field. Framing is especially important for sustainable design, as it becomes a means of redefining products and technologies and making them fit to everyday life experiences (Lidwell, Holden, and Butler 2003).

An integral part of this process is the formation of local niche projects and the design of (experimental) socio-technical projects that enable processes of learning, building of networks, and development of experience-based expectations (Brown et al. 2003; Raven and Geels 2010).

3.3 Metadesigners

Metadesign is always part of design processes. Design is a socially distributed process (e.g., Simon 1984), and integrating new stakeholders and forming coalitions that support a given design are part of design as a social process. Advancing new designs includes concurrent technological and discursive processes; we have to engage in discursive struggles concerning the definition of actors, meanings, and technologies (Holm, Søndergård, and Hansen 2010). In this perspective, the specific design efforts (including, e.g., niche projects and socio-technical experiments [Brown et al. 2003]) shape the specific coalitions of actors supporting and relating to the project, while metadesign concerns the framework conditions enabling the coalition of actors and the enacting of the anticipated design.

In this respect, we share Giaccardi and Fischer's (2008) call for metadesign as second-order design practices concerning the development of structure enabling the participation and development of competent actors in enacting the design. However, the limitation of their approach is its lack of reflexivity. Designing for sustainability has to reflect on and challenge the existing dominant regimes structuring unsustainable practices.

Undertaking metadesign and deliberately seeking to influence the framework conditions of design are a prerequisite in designing for sustainability. Designers have to engage in the development, challenge, and transformation of "erratic" design spaces and deliberately seek to shape alternative design spaces. This implies that designers should build on analyses of the addressed socio-technical systems, identify and understand how they constitute structural conditions, and by this insight enable a critical design practice.

4 Designing Mobility: Electric Vehicle Based Mobility Systems

The specific case of designing for sustainability is the design of an urban mobility service system (Cleardrive) in Copenhagen based on battery electric vehicles (BEVs) in an intelligent car sharing system (Cleardrive 2013). It is a study of the early formative stages of a design process, focusing on the project's structuration of design spaces through its interpretation of, and intervention in, the local socio-technical traffic system.

This is a study of a design process, where the focal design company, Cleardrive, in interaction with actors from the transport industry, the electric vehicle industry, local and national government, and potential customers—and in relation to local agendas to mitigate climate change and to reduce pollution and urban congestion—designs a mobility system replacing fossil-fueled vehicles with electric vehicles.

4.1 Mobility System: The Specific Context

The car-based mobility system is an example of a nonsustainable socio-technical system burdened with environmental problems, the use of limited resources (fossil fuels), and health problems. Policies in the European Union (EU) have focused on harmful climate effects by introducing demands on emissions and fuel efficiency, but without obtaining substantial reduction in the total energy use and related CO_2 emissions (e.g., Energistyrelsen 2013).

The transition to electric-car-based mobility systems has emerged as a central technological option, and Danish (climate) policy programs identify electric cars as one of the pathways to reducing CO_2 emission from transportation.

The Danish programs have had high expectations concerning the development and diffusion of BEVs. Through tax exemption, free-parking concepts, and support to test projects and experimentation, government and municipalities have metadesigned a design space for electric vehicles, based on the expectations that market actors could ensure a fast propagation of BEVs.

These expectations have not been met. The main reasons have been misfits with reigning mobility practices and expectations and a lack of necessary infrastructures, combined with the limited driving range of BEVs (e.g., Christensen, Wells, and Cipcigan 2012). BEV is still seen as an immature and troublesome technology that is difficult to integrate in the scheme of everyday life. On a general level, the Danish programs have adopted a strategy addressing the BEV as a technological innovation, as opposed to strategies perceiving the transformation as integrated changes of both technology and mobility practices (see Dijk, Orsato, and Kemp 2013, sec. 2.2).

The Danish regime of automobility sets specific conditions for transition. Its main characteristics are high taxation (a registration fee ranging from 105 to 180 percent of the price of the car) combined with annual fees favoring small and energy-efficient cars. The regime of transportation has been dominated by a neoliberal market approach and limited political support for investment in transforming and upgrading public transportation. This combination of factors establishes a vigorously defended "right to automobility"—a strongly held position, which was displayed in a heated debate about, and in 2012 the final rejection of, the project of establishing an urban toll ring for cars in Copenhagen intended to counter congestion and be a financial instrument for mobility investments. Denmark has strongly entrenched private car use practices, also held rigid by the commuter society, mobility practices related to summer resorts, and other factors.

The Danish strategy for development and diffusion of electric vehicles provides, together with the Danish regimes of automobility and transportation, a specific design space within which market actors can act strategically, either by taking advantage of the framework or by changing it.

The regimes of transportation and automobility function as a selection environment. The regulation and institutional framework of the taxi system of Copenhagen provide an example. A taxi service system based on electric cars could be an option for the introduction of BEV, but it would require a remake of the system or a readiness

> **Barriers to BEV taxis in Copenhagen**
>
> Attempts to introduce Taxi services based on BEV have
> experienced two major problems related to the regulation
>
> - Taxis are already subject to tax-exemption rules
>   (no benefit of adopting BEV)
>
> - The taxi branch is subject to local regulation tending to
>   protect the interest of firms and drivers within the branch.
>   Obtaining a license for a Taxi firm in Copenhagen requires
>   more than 10 years documented Taxi experience (rules
>   out new alternative and experimental projects and firms)
>
> So far central and local authorities have not deviated from
> this regulation.

Figure 17.3
Institutional barriers to BEV in the national and local taxi regulation.

to bypass established rules to enable experimental projects (fig. 17.3). Another example of path-shaping regulation is that the Danish tax exemption includes only electric cars, ruling out hybrid cars as a pathway to achieving mobility based on electricity.

4.2   The Danish Design Spaces of BEV

Since 2009, the major BEV project in Denmark has been the Danish branch of the Better Place global project developed in cooperation with Renault. Better Place has introduced a technology platform combining exchangeable batteries in electric cars with an infrastructure of exchange stations to meet the main barrier of BEV: the short driving range. Moreover, Better Place operated as a risk-taking intermediate agent; the company continued to own the batteries (reducing the risk of battery lifetime and technology obsolescence from the user) and negotiated packages of power supply (Christensen, Wells, and Cipcigan 2012). The Danish energy company DONG participated as minority shareholder in the Danish affiliate; from their perspective, BEV using "intelligent charging" (charging when energy supply is high) had the potential to be a dynamic element in an anticipated smart grid. Despite heavy investment in the infrastructure, however, the project failed. The project filed for bankruptcy in May 2013 (see sec. 5).

Better Place was in line with the Danish program of a market-based diffusion aiming at making BEV an alternative to traditional internal combustion engine (ICE) cars for private car users. Better Place was basically conceived as a technology substitution, a transition pathway based on a fit with the prevailing private car use practices. In this respect, it represents a project adapted to and reproducing/consolidating the prevailing Danish BEV design space (see fig. 17.5 in sec. 5).

4.3 Cleardrive

The Cleardrive BEV project represents an alternative to the existing Danish strategy for electric vehicles. It has defined the project as the formation of an urban mobility service system, where car ownership is replaced by access to a mobility service based on BEV and integration with public transportation—an integrated intelligent car sharing system.

Cleardrive grew from a perception of a new opening in the political agenda in the wake of the political buildup to the UN climate conference in Copenhagen in 2009—and a potential paradigm shift in mobility based on BEV. The team of entrepreneurs establishing Cleardrive drew their experiences and resources from the paradigm shift of developing IT platforms for Internet-based music services, and in the electric car technology, they saw a parallel challenge: a shift from product to service waiting for an intelligent platform, including a supporting IT system.

Cleardrive is a "project organization" devised to elaborate a business case of BEV. In this role, they have undertaken the project to develop a tailored concept of a BEV mobility system for the central Copenhagen urban area; and as networking entrepreneurs, they are seeking to build alliances, establish business relations, and raise funding for the project. In parallel they function as an analytic think tank engaging in consulting projects and international cooperation with similar urban mobility projects.

From its beginning in 2011, Cleardrive has been working to develop a concept for the Copenhagen project, including development of the related IT system. As of September 2013, the project is in a formation stage. A pilot project was launched in July 2013 on the small island Bornholm, but the launch of the Copenhagen mobility service awaits an announced new public initiative on electric cars and urban mobility (see sec. 4.5) (Cleardrive 2013; Nielsen 2013).

4.4 Cleardrive: Analytic-Based Strategic Expectation of BEV Technology

The core step has been a redefinition of strategic expectations for BEV based on interpretation of the present mobility system and the potential of the BEV technology. In contrast to Better Place's technology substitution project, Cleardrive envisioned BEV as a basic element in an integrated mobility service system. This redefinition comprised four main elements:

(1) The construction of an intelligent mobility service system. The users of BEV will be offered mobility without ownership based on an urban system consisting of:

   (a) A high number of cars distributed within the area covered by the mobility project
   (b) An IT system tracking the car fleet and giving clients smartphone-based information on availability and (energy) status of cars in the system

(2) Provision of (a) mobility service for business and public institutions and (b) a mobility service for private users, especially as an alternative to the second car (or to acquiring the first car).

(3) Initial implementation as an urban mobility service; the mobility service is defined as flexible access (pick and ride concept) to mobility within a specific area (in this case central Copenhagen).

(4) Integration with other local mobility systems; a subscription should include integrated access to public transportation systems and access to taxi service (when no cars are available).

Cleardrive's strategic expectation for BEV deviates significantly from the conceptual framing of Better Place. The substitution of private cars is considered too difficult an entry point—BEV cannot at this stage cover all functional expectations, such as full flexibility and unlimited range, related to private car use, and private car user practices are assessed as a too deeply embedded social practice to be challenged; this part of the Danish design space for BEV (regime for mobility) is considered a fixed condition.

The assessment that the market of private users was too difficult to develop led to a focus on business consumers in the first stage of the implementation process, combined with the provision of an urban mobility service. The belief is that the business market can provide a platform for diffusion to other user groups and to other cities.

Departing from a mobility service concept, Cleardrive on the one hand seeks to take advantage of the specific design space related to urban mobility in Copenhagen (e.g., linking to public traffic systems and taxis). On the other hand, it attempts to redefine the design spaces by redefining the strategic expectations; it introduces a new agenda and interpretation of BEV. This redefinition takes place as an interactive negotiation with local actors and actors of the mobility system, aimed at the formation of a technology coalition.

4.5 Development of the Technological Concept

The definition of strategic expectations and the development of the technological concept cannot be separated. The expectations defined in the process are related to an assessment of the potential of the BEV technology and how an IT platform for the service could be developed in the specific transportation context of urban Copenhagen.

The core idea of the concept is a provision of flexible access to mobility by placing a fleet of cars within the covered area (fig. 17.4). In a first rollout of the Cleardrive mobility service, the project plans to place 150 BEVs in central Copenhagen (Cleardrive 2013). The cars can be used outside the designated area but have to be delivered back within the area. Users can use their smartphone to track free cars, and the local travel card (*Rejsekortet*) or smartphone can function as a key when picking up the car. The mobility system will be run by three central units of management and service that will collect cars for charging, cleaning, and service and replace them (optimizing the mobility coverage). The project takes advantage of parking lots reserved for electric cars and for car sharing.

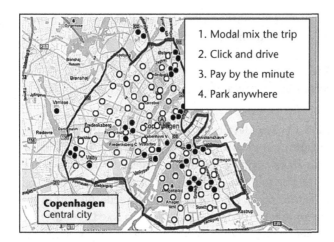

Figure 17.4
Cleardrive: pick and ride illustration of the concept: ○ free cars, ● occupied. Source: http://www
.cleardrive.dk.

A number of European cities have implemented such intelligent car mobility service systems. Most of them, however, use traditional vehicles, but there are some BEV-based systems. Daimler-Benz, which has become an important actor in urban car sharing systems, has developed a system in Amsterdam (Car2go) based on small BEVs (an adapted version of the Daimler "smart car" concept) designed to provide an alternative flexible urban transportation system using an urban charging infrastructure established by the City of Amsterdam (Car2go 2013). The other major BEV-based project is in Paris, Bolloré Bluecars. It is the result of a public–private partnership, where the industrial group Bolloré, with a basis in battery technology, has developed its own charging infrastructure and uses the Italian-produced Bluecar (Autolib 2013). In comparison, the Copenhagen project is based on battery-driven medium-size electric cars supported by centralized staffed charging facilities—choices related to Cleardrive's focus on the business segment.

The concept of an urban mobility service system rules out a piecemeal implementation. If it is going to succeed, it has to start with a critical mass (estimated at 150 cars to cover central urban Copenhagen). It also rules out the idea of a general (national) coverage; this has to be met by cooperation with other mobility providers (e.g., rental car companies).

Besides the BEV, the technological core of the project is the IT platform (central management and a communication system from the cars) and user apps devised to track and manage the car fleet and to provide an interface for the customers. In addition, the IT system will enable integration with other traffic systems. The Copenhagen project includes the idea of interfacing with the national system of travel cards (*Rejsekortet*), both to enable a seamless mobility (intermodality) including Cleardrive cars and public transportation and to enable the use of the traveling card as a key for the cars.

For business customers, Cleardrive offers an adapted mobility service product ensuring a number of ready and available at a company's address during business hours. The system ensures that only the company's employees can see the "company cars" in the system, while the employees at the same time have access to the full fleet.

4.6 Design Space: Institutional Framework and Network

The configuration of the Copenhagen Cleardrive concept reflects the specific national and local framework conditions; a tax exemption on BEVs and favorable parking conditions (parking lots reserved for BEVs, combined with no parking fee for BEVs and car sharing vehicles on the street) are important preconditions for the "pick-and-ride" concept based on a BEV fleet.

On a more general level, when negotiating and interacting with the public authorities, Cleardrive has been able to link the project to local strategies on climate and mobility. As a specific project turning general aspirations into practical solutions, it has both met policy interest in implementing a green development and fitted into an aspiration of marketing Copenhagen as a green city. In the process, the Cleardrive project has been able to subscribe to established (local) discourses, but in its interaction, it has also coproduced an alternative strategic expectation, vision, and imagined future for urban mobility. The Copenhagen project could benefit from framework conditions and local agendas, while the taxi project, on the contrary, failed to get the needed changes in the institutional framework (see fig. 17.3).

The ambition of integration with public transportation systems (intermodality) to provide integrated mobility (also including public systems of urban bikes) has faced structural constraints. The public transportation companies have, as a consequence of new regimes of market competition and tenders, adopted strategies focusing on their core services (and with limited efforts in developing new intermodal services). They have taken an interest in the Cleardrive project, but from the perspective that the project can generate traffic (e.g., attract business customers). A more active interaction with the Cleardrive project could have included focused efforts to develop a seamless shift between different transport modes, for example, between the Cleardrive mobility system and trains and buses. At this stage, however, this has been limited to a planned integration of the Cleardrive project in the travel card (*Rejsekortet*) system.

Cleardrive concentrates its efforts on attracting business customers as a shortcut to obtaining the needed critical mass. In this effort, they have the challenge to make the BEV project a sound and attractive business concept and to meet the expectations of business travel. This implies an ability to link the project to operational and corporate social responsibility (CSR) company programs, and in addition to offer an attractive package to a company's employees. This can be tricky because free cars for management-level employees are often an important part of their work contracts.

At this stage, before having an operational project, the main impact on the specific design space has been a reconfiguration of actor relations and agendas by presenting an alternative strategic expectation for adoption of BEV mobility and an alternative urban mobility service concept. This involves the inclusion of public actors, transportation actors, and private business actors as part of a network.

The Cleardrive project can be seen as an intervention giving impetus to a redefinition of the Danish BEV design space (fig. 17.5). The collapse of Better Place and the emergence of new urban mobility systems (including Cleardrive), combined with stronger interest in alternative mobility systems from both public (e.g., regions, Copenhagen) and private actors, have led to a redefined program in the Danish Energy Agency. The agency has adopted a new funding program combining development of a charging infrastructure and local mobility systems based on electric cars, and in 2014 the program, in cooperation with the region and municipality of Copenhagen, is going to call for projects within this framework. This creates an opening for the Cleardrive project, but also a challenge in terms of rival projects attracted by the program and funding.

5   Discussion of the Case

The design process of the Cleardrive project is a part of a major reconfiguration (metadesign) leading to the development of a new urban mobility system based on intelligent car sharing. BEV is seen as a part of the backbone technology of such a system, but it could integrate a variety of other cars designated for specific needs.

Cleardrive has had to operate within the confines of the existing regimes of automobility. The design process of Cleardrive in the Copenhagen project has been a combination of intelligent use of the design space at hand and a metadesign aimed at defining an alternative design space and reconfiguring the socio-technical system of mobility.

This duality—adaptation and transcendence—is manifest in relation to mobility practices. Cleardrive refrained from substitution of the "all-purpose" private car but has nevertheless developed a mobility service closely fitting the users' expectations of flexibility (it can be used instantly without making a reservation, and independently of where you are and where you want to go within the designated area). However, the Cleardrive project challenges our perception of flexibility of being related to private ownership and offers a more sustainable mode of mobility. In this perspective, the Cleardrive project can be seen as an intervention in the socio-technical system of mobility (shaping and designing new user expectations and technological options) and a deliberate effort to develop an alternative design space (a metadesign act).

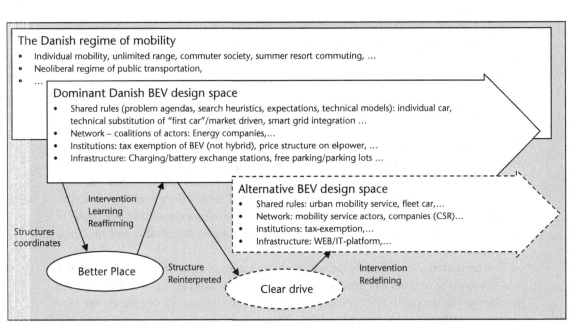

Figure 17.5
Better Place and Cleardrive as local experimentation projects constituting design spaces for BEV by acting within the Danish regime of mobility.

Within the Danish regime of mobility and the specific design space that it provides for the introduction of BEV, Better Place and Cleardrive represent two projects that have differed in the interpretation of the existing design space and in their strategic choices (fig. 17.5).

Better Place (in alliance with DONG) preserved and worked within the dominating mobility expectations in its attempt to offer an alternative to the private car; the strategy has been a massive rollout of a specific technology platform. It was a major (and expensive) infrastructural project aligned with the Danish strategy of diffusion of BEV; it was highly dependent on a rapid penetration of the private car market (Christensen, Wells, and Cipcigan 2012); and it had to close when it failed to achieve that goal.

Cleardrive has made a more radical interpretation of the technological options of BEV, linking it to intelligent urban car sharing systems and an alternative vision of flexible urban mobility. It has involved a challenge of the existing design space of mobility in the city of Copenhagen—preserved by dominant actors pleased with the exciting rationalities and expectations for the future. Cleardrive has had to assess the functional and technological capacity of BEV, seeking adaptation but also seeking to outline an alternative pathway. Its approach can be seen as a strategic intervention in a field of high rigidity by undertaking an experimental project involving a reconfiguration of agendas, actors, and technologies, the deliberate effort to shape an alternative design space, so far with the redefined program of the Danish Energy Agency (see sec. 4.6) as a provisional result.

6 Designing for Sustainability: Outline of Analytic Framework

Design is situated, and designers have to be reflexive in this situatedness. Designing takes place in social contexts and institutional settings with constraining and enabling properties (Simonsen et al., chap. 1 of this vol.). Designing for sustainability demands an active reflection on the context, and it takes a deliberate effort to change the contextual conditions by reconfiguring agendas and technologies, building coalitions of actors, and building shared visions for desired futures and sustainable technological solutions.

The presentation of the early formative design stages of Cleardrive served to display the situatedness and display design as a reflexive process and as interventions devised to change the mobility system and its structural conditions. It demonstrated how designers within a socio-technical field, by using recursive learning processes and interacting with public and private actors, have defined an alternative design space. This process involved an ongoing adjustment of strategic expectations based on interpretation and balancing how solutions fit or stretch both technologies and social practices. In addition, it illustrates how experimental projects taking advantage of specific situated conditions are needed to gain knowledge of new options and enable the formation of new alternative design spaces. Metadesign of alternative design spaces and experimental projects within existing design spaces may be perceived as mutually dependent processes.

As a general framework for such processes, we have presented designing for sustainability as a concurrent process of changing existing practices and socio-technical systems and reflection on and intervention in existing structural conditions (metadesign). In figure 17.6, we have outlined the approach and the main concepts applied, and in this way stipulate a framework for designing for sustainability.

The figure provides an analytic conceptual framework. The main point is the adoption of a transition perspective and a redefined object of sustainable design; design goes beyond the design of artifacts and systems grounded in existing practices and expectations, but involves the identification of new technologies and solutions that hold the potential to obtain more sustainable practices and socio-technical systems and objects.

Our objective has been to call for an expanded design practice, being intentional and normative with reference to principles of sustainability, being reflexive in its structural embeddedness and enacting metadesign as deliberate efforts to address the

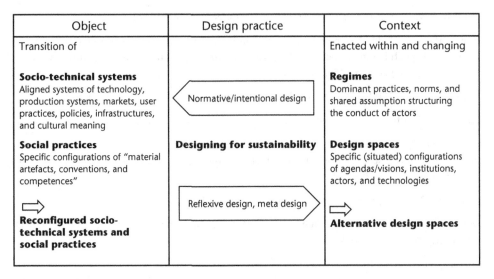

Figure 17.6
Conceptual framework for designing for sustainability.

reconfiguration of regimes embedding design practices, the latter including the formation of alternative design spaces to enable sustainable design practices.

The notion of design space, understood as specific (situated) configurations of agendas, institutions, actors, and technologies, has been introduced with the objective both to encourage a critical examination of existing design contexts and to call for a focus on openings in specific local settings or on potential alternative design spaces (alternative combinations of agendas, institutional frameworks, actors, and technologies). Designing for sustainability involves metadesign—the concurrent development of alternative design spaces and reconfiguration of existing (unsustainable) regimes and socio-technical systems.

Designing for sustainability is enacted in and addresses social realities in all their complexity. The conceptual framework and the case presented expose this complexity and forward an understanding of design as a dispersed process involving many actors. Designing for sustainability becomes an act of metadesign, redefining and reconfiguring alternative design spaces as structures conducting the conduct of the involved actors, enabling concerted action.

References

Autolib. 2013. http://en.wikipedia.org/wiki/Autolib (accessed April 20, 2013).

Better Place. 2013. http://danmark.betterplace.com (accessed April 20, 2013).

Bhaskar, Roy. 1978. *A Realist Theory of Science*. Hassocks: Harvester Press.

Brown, Halina S., Philip Vergragt, Ken Green, and Luca Berchicci. 2003. Learning for sustainable transition through bounded socio-technical experiments in personal mobility. *Technology Analysis and Strategic Management* 15: 291–315.

Buchanan, Richard. 1992. Wicked problems in design thinking. *Design Issues* 8 (2): 5–22.

Car2go. 2013. https://www.car2go.com/en/amsterdam (accessed April 20, 2013).

Christensen, Thomas Budde, Peter Wells, and Liana Cipcigan. 2012. Can innovative business models overcome resistance to electrical vehicles? Better Place and battery electric cars in Denmark. *Energy Policy* 48: 498–505.

Cleardrive. 2013. http://www.cleardrive.dk (accessed April 20, 2013).

Dijk, Marc, Renato J. Orsato, and René Kemp. 2013. The emergence of an electric mobility trajectory. *Energy Policy* 52: 135–145.

Energistyrelsen. 2013. http://www.ens.dk (accessed April 20, 2013).

Geels, Frank W. 2004. From sectoral systems of innovation to socio-technical systems: Insights about dynamics and change from sociology and institutional theory. *Research Policy* 33 (6–7): 897–920.

Geels, Frank W., and René Kemp. 2012. The multi-level perspective as a new perspective for studying socio-technical transitions. In *Automobility in Transition: A Socio-technical Analysis of Sustainable Transport*, ed. Frank W. Geels, René Kemp, Geoff Dudley, and Glenn Lyons, 49–79. New York: Routledge.

Giaccardi, Elisa. 2005. Metadesign as an emergent design culture. *Leonardo* 4 (4): 342–349.

Giaccardi, Elisa, and Gerhard Fischer. 2008. Creativity and evolution: A metadesign perspective. *Digital Creativity* 19 (1): 19–32. http://l3d.cs.colorado.edu/~gerhard/papers/digital-creativity-2008.pdf.

Giddens, Anthony. 1984. *The Constitution of Society*. Berkeley: University of California Press.

Hansen, Ole E., Bent Søndergård, and Jens Stærdahl. 2012. Sustainable transition of socio-technical systems in a governance perspective. In *A New Agenda for Sustainability*, ed. Kurt Aagaard-Nielsen, Bo Elling, Maria Figueroa, and Erling Jelsøe, 91–114. Farnham: Ashgate.

Holm, Jesper, Bent Søndergård, and Ole E. Hansen. 2010. Design and sustainable transition. In *Design Research: Synergies from Interdisciplinary Perspectives*, ed. Jesper Simonsen, Jørgen O. Bærenholdt, Monika Büscher, and John D. Scheuer, 123–137. New York: Routledge.

Kemp, René, Frank W. Geels, and Geoff Dudley. 2012. Introduction: Sustainability transitions in the automobility regime and the need for a new perspective. In *Automobility in Transition? A Socio-technical Analysis of Sustainable Transport*, ed. Frank W. Geels, René Kemp, Geoff Dudley, and Glenn Lyons, 3–28. New York: Routledge.

Kemp, René, and Jan Rotmans. 2005. The management of the co-evolution of technical, environmental, and social systems. In *Towards Environmental Innovation Systems*, ed. Matthias Weber and Jens Hemmelskamp, 33–55. Berlin: Springer.

Lidwell, William, Kritina Holden, and Jill Butler. 2003. *Universal Principles of Design*. Beverly, MA: Rockport Publishers.

Nielsen, Carl H. 2013. Bybilen: Wanted dead or alive [The urban car: Wanted dead or alive]. Trafikdage i Aalborg [Danish traffic conference], August 26–27, 2013. http://www.trafikdage.dk/papers_2013/196_CarlHenrikNielsen.pdf (accessed October 5, 2013).

Raven, Rob J. M., and Frank W. Geels. 2010. Socio-cognitive evolution in niche experiments: Comparative analysis of biogas development in Denmark and the Netherlands (1973–2004). *Technovation* 30 (2): 87–99.

Reckwitz, Andreas. 2002. Towards a theory of social practice: a development in culturalist thinking. *European Journal of Social Theory* 5 (2): 243–263.

Rip, Arie, and René Kemp. 1998. Technological change. In *Human Choice and Climate Change*, vol. 2, *Resources and Technology*, ed. Steve Rayner and Liz Malone, 327–399. Washington, DC: Battelle Press.

Sayer, Andrew. 2000. *Realism and Social Science*. London: Sage.

Schatzki, Theodor R. 2001. Practice minded order. In *The Practice Turn in Contemporary Theory*, ed. Theodor R. Schatzki, Karin D. Knorr-Cetina, Eike Von Savigny. London: Routledge.

Scott, Kakee, Conny Bakker, and Jaco Quist. 2012. Designing change by living change. *Design Studies* 33 (3): 279–297.

Shove, Elizabeth. 2003. Converging conventions of comfort, cleanliness, and convenience. *Journal of Consumer Policy* 26 (4): 395–418.

Shove, Elizabeth, and Mika Pantzar. 2005. Consumers, producers, and practices: Understanding the invention and reinvention of Nordic walking. *Journal of Consumer Culture* 5 (1): 43–64.

Shove, Elizabeth, and Gordon Walker. 2010. Governing transition in the sustainability of everyday life. *Research Policy* 39 (4): 471–476.

Simon, Herbert. 1984. *The Science of the Artificial*. Cambridge, MA: MIT Press.

Stegall, Nathan. 2006. Designing for sustainability: A philosophy for ecological intentional design. *Design Issues* 22 (2): 56–63.

Thorpe, Ann. 2010. Design's role in sustainable consumption. *Design Issues* 26 (2): 3–16.

Wahl, Daniel C., and Seaton Baxter. 2008. The designer's role in facilitating sustainable solutions. *Design Issues* 24 (2): 72–83.

18 Methods for Prevention of Environmental Impacts

Thomas Budde Christensen, Tyge Kjær, and Rikke Lybæk

What. This chapter discusses design methods focusing on the prevention or reduction of environmental impacts from manufacturing, use, and end-of-life treatment of products and services. This chapter explores four fields of approaches: (1) environmental management, (2) life cycle thinking, (3) eco-design, and (4) industrial symbiosis design.

Why. Industries, policy makers, and international organizations have a huge interest in finding efficient ways to design products and production processes so that life cycle environmental impacts are decreased.

Where. The four fields of methods were primarily developed for manufacturing industries that intended to reduce resource consumption and prevent environmental impacts; however, academia, government, and businesses outside the manufacturing sector have over the last decade also applied the methods discussed in the chapter. Life cycle thinking and eco-design are also built into a number of EU directives (under the policy umbrella called Sustainable Consumption and Production) focused on reducing environmental impacts from the manufacturing, use, and end-of-life treatment of products and services.

How. The four design approaches are mutually supportive and can be regarded as a hierarchy of scopes that can be applied to the design of industrial systems. The methods treated in the chapter constitute a "reservoir" of commonly accepted methods, tools, and procedures that have been implemented by a large number of companies worldwide with the support of governments and international institutions. The chapter also elaborates on how these four fields of more or less standardized, generic methods are situated when being implemented by industries in their local context.

1 Introduction: The Scope of Environmental Design Methods

Reducing and preventing life cycle environmental impacts from products and services are a great concern in industry, as well as among policy makers, worldwide. Prevention and reduction of environmental impacts constitute a design challenge to product design, design and management of production processes, and design of industrial systems in a larger context. This chapter presents the most commonly used methods.

Environmental problems are always local and situated in a specific context. The situated character of environmental problems can be illustrated with a case of a coal-fired power station in Copenhagen, Denmark. The power station supplies electricity to the grid and heat to the district heating system in the city. The incineration of coal causes a number of environmental problems. Among the most important are the emission of greenhouse gases (GHG), nitrous oxides, sulfur dioxides, and particulates. Some of these pollutants create environmental problems in the local urban environment close to the power station, whereas other pollutants are transported by the wind and therefore also may create environmental problems in neighboring regions. Emissions of GHG create a global environmental problem that is situated in the sense that effects are local, for example, changed patterns of precipitation in countries in Africa.

The methods for prevention of environmental problems are likewise situated in the specific context in which the environmental problems are created. Environmental problems that are caused by industries depend on their use of raw material and ancillary material, the specific product design, and the design of production processes in the companies. The methods for prevention of environmental problems therefore depend on how the companies are managed and organized, the technologies they deploy, and the markets they supply. This can also be illustrated with the coal-fired power station. Emissions to air (excluding GHG emissions) can potentially be reduced by exhaust emission equipment such as filters and sulfur scrubbers. The cost and the efficiency of such solutions depend on the design of the power station. The solutions are, in other words, situated in the local context of the power station, and their application depends on situated knowledge, the economy, and technology at the power station. Implementing an environmental management system may support the identification of potential solutions but always needs to be applied to the specific conditions and context in which the power station is operating.

The simple site-specific environmental management systems may not be sufficient to solve all environmental problems. This can be illustrated with the following example: Reducing GHG emissions from the power station was achieved at the Vattenfall power station in Copenhagen by substituting coal with wood pellets in one of the boilers. However, the environmental effect of this solution depends on the amount fossil fuel used during transporting and processing the wood pellets. The environmental benefits, the GHG balance, from the substitution are determined by the conditions under which the wood pellets are produced, processed, and transported. Assessing the specific effect of the substitution therefore requires situated knowledge about fossil fuel inputs throughout the value chain. The most commonly used method for evaluating the environmental effect (the GHG balance) of such a substitution is the life cycle approach, which goes beyond the company boundaries and encompasses the full life cycle when considering environmental solutions.

The power station case illustrates a combined need for design methods that can assist industries in reducing the environmental impact from internal activities (the company's own processes and products) and from related emissions that occur elsewhere in the value chain or the system the companies are situated in. This chapter elaborates on such methods and presents some of the most commonly used methods and approaches in this field.

1.1 Methods, Strategies, Tools, and Approaches

There are many different approaches and strategies by which environmental impacts can be prevented and reduced. OECD (2009) argues that the practices for sustainable manufacturing have evolved from a focus on dispersion and pollution control via cleaner production and eco-efficiency to a focus on closed-loop production systems, also termed industrial symbiosis systems. This development also illustrates an increased sophistication and complexity in sustainable manufacturing practices. Pollution control and cleaner production initiatives are applied to individual companies to reduce or prevent emissions to air, water, and soil; eco-efficiency strategies and life cycle management systems are incorporated in value chains to maximize resource efficiency; and closed-loop systems are implemented across the globe to enhance recycling and improve overall resource efficiency of industrial systems.

From a company perspective, the choice of methods and approach depends on the strategy and capacity of the individual company and on the character of the environmental impacts that are caused by the company's activities. Also, elements such as position in the value chain and control over product development processes play an important role when companies decided which methods to apply (WBCSD 2006). A brand holder may, for example, have a greater influence over product design than a component supplier and therefore benefit more from the implementation of eco-design methods. Finally, regulation and legal requirements can have an important impact on environmental policies and strategies in companies (Porter and van der Linde 1995).

1.2 The Structure of the Chapter

The chapter discusses methods, approaches, and tools by which industrial systems, including their products and production processes, are designed to prevent and reduce environmental impacts. The chapter explores four groups of design methods that focus on the reduction or elimination of environmental problems:

1. Environmental management: Environmental management is a cleaner production approach by which environmental impacts are eliminated or reduced through the

design of production processes at a facility. There exist a range of standardized procedures for environmental management.

2. Life cycle thinking: Life cycle thinking and life cycle assessment (LCA) are an approach to product and process design in which the entire life cycle of environmental impacts of a product or process is assessed. LCA approaches have been developed in many shapes and forms like cradle-to-cradle, ISO 14040, life cycle management, and others.

3. Eco-design: Eco-design is an approach to product development in which environmental considerations are integrated into traditional product design procedures. Ecodesign uses a number of tools and methodologies; the most prominent is the ISO 14062 standard.

4. Industrial symbiosis system design: This is a design approach in which companies strategically target by-product exchange and waste recycling to create closed-loop production systems where waste and by-products from one company become input to the next company.

The design methods that are presented and discussed in this chapter are all widely accepted, tested, and proven tools and approaches. Eco-design, environmental management, and life cycle assessment, for example, are typically based on internationally defined standards and procedures. More than 80,000 organizations in Europe and 250,000 organizations worldwide were certified against the ISO 14001 environmental management system (ISO 2012), meaning that they have implemented a sophisticated set of predefined tools and procedures. Industrial symbiosis systems differ slightly, since they have not yet developed a standardized set of methods and procedures to the same extent as the other three fields. However, industrial symbiosis is included here to illustrate that a further expansion from the life cycle perspective to the system perspective involves new opportunities for preventing and reducing environmental impacts.

These design approaches function as generic methods, tools, and procedures that need to be situated in the local context of the companies that choose to deploy them. The process of situating the methods requires a translation from generic and abstract tools and procedures to the local context of the specific company.

2   Environmental Management

Environmental management covers a broad field of methods and procedures that have matured over the last thirty years. The most commonly used environmental management system is the ISO 14001, with more than 250,000 users worldwide in 155 different countries (ISO 2012). ISO 14001 is an international standard for implementation of a predefined set of procedures and protocols that make up the environmental management system. Certification against ISO 14001 also requires third-party audits. The second-largest system in Europe is the European Commission's counterpart system, the Eco-Management and Audit Scheme (EMAS). EMAS has many similarities with the ISO system but involves stricter requirements with regard to legal compliance and transparency (European Commission 2011).

Environmental management is a facility-oriented approach that focuses on the design, implementation, and maintenance of the part of the overall management system in an organization that has to do with design implementation, maintenance, and review of the company's environmental policy.

Most environmental management systems are based on the concept of cleaner production. This concept was developed in the late 1980s by organizations such as OECD and UNIDO in collaboration with ministries from a number of countries (Christensen and Kjær 2012). The work was followed by an international standard (ISO 14001) and a voluntary system supported by the European Commission (called EMAS).

Cleaner production is a preventative and integrated approach to solving environmental problems in which companies design and implement a management system to prevent pollution and improve resource and energy efficiency in the company or facility. Pollution prevention refers to measures (including changes to processes, practices, materials, and products) that aim at eliminating environmental problems at the source.

The preventative approach was groundbreaking when introduced in the 1990s and differentiated the cleaner production approach from end-of-pipe-oriented strategies and policies of the earlier decades (Christensen and Kjær 2012). It also had an important impact on the policy and legislation in Europe, for example, with the adoption of the Integrated Pollution Prevention and Control directive in 1998 (European Union 2008) and the Industrial Emissions directive in 2010 (European Union 2010), both of which aim at encouraging and enforcing pollution prevention measures in European industries.

Pollution prevention is considered in the long run to be a more effective and attractive strategy than end-of-pipe measures, as it eliminates environmental impacts at the source, whereas end-of-pipe measures (such as catalytic converters, chimneys, filters, etc.) most often only reduce the emissions (Christensen 2008). An empirical study on environmental innovation conducted by Frondel, Horbach, and Rennings (2007) furthermore indicates that cleaner production measures also are more likely to lead to innovation than end-of-pipe measures, as cleaner production measures involve changes to the design of production processes and therefore often stimulate innovation. This can also be understood as a process of situated learning, where employees at different levels in the organization are involved in processes of reducing environmental impacts and while doing so develop skills, knowledge, and competences that will eventually make the company more innovative.

More recent eco-efficiency strategies also support the pollution prevention approach by aiming at strategies, systems, and technologies that generate a higher output with less input (WBCSD 2000; UNCTAD 2004; WBCSD 2006).

Environmental management emphasizes the continuous-improvement philosophy, which can also be found in traditional quality management systems. Continuous improvement is ensured by a consistent management system that focuses on yearly improvements to the environmental performance in line with the company's environmental policy. Involvement of employees is a specific requirement in most environmental management systems. It is considered vital for the system's long-term success to establish situated learning processes that will involve and enable employees from all levels in the organization to take part in the effort to identify, implement, and evaluate pollution preventative measures.

The implementation of environmental management systems requires the implementation of a comprehensive set of predefined procedures. This includes formulation of a corporate environmental policy with goals and aims; the planning and organization of teams and responsibilities; an assessment phase in which process data are collected and environmental hot spots identified; a feasibility phase where options to prevent and reduce environmental impacts are technically and economically assessed; and an implementation phase where changes are implemented. The whole system is finally reviewed and typically repeated annually. Each phase is described in detailed procedures, and the implementation of these procedures is audited by a certified auditor.

The implementation of environmental management systems can be regarded as a process in which a set of generic procedures are situated in a specific context of a company. This context includes the production processes and technologies that are specifically used by the company; the energy, raw material, and ancillary material that is used by the company; the company's organizational structure, management, and environmental policies and strategies; the employees' knowledge and competences; and the company's external linkages to suppliers and buyers and other relevant stakeholders.

Cleaner production measures imply that companies identify preventative ways of handling environmental problems. The preventative measures are always situated in the concrete context of the specific company. The companies, in other words, need to translate the generic and abstract idea of the preventative, integrated, and source-oriented measures into *situated* activities in their organizations. This is typically accomplished in a process where environmental managers, quality managers, and workers on the shop floor collaborate to identify the most efficient ways of preventing environmental impacts. Implementation of cleaner production at the fish-processing company Erik Taabbel Fiskeeksport in Denmark, for example, led to a series of initiatives that reduced water and energy consumption (Thrane, Nielsen, and Christensen

2009). The initiatives included changes to working routines, as well as implementation of smaller technical changes such as installing more efficient water pistols, electric engines, and pumps (Thrane, Nielsen, and Christensen 2009).

3 Life Cycle Thinking

Environmental management practices that are developed under the cleaner-production umbrella focus primarily on site-specific solutions to environmental problems. During the last twenty-five years, these methods have proved effective when looking at environmental problems from a single facility and have assisted companies in identifying, treating, and eliminating environmental problems. However, the site- and facility-specific character of environmental management has a significant downside—namely, the risk of problem shifting. Problem shifting occurs when an applied solution to a problem reduces or eliminates the problem at one place while unintentionally generating problems elsewhere, for example, when problems are shifted to other life cycle stages, to other substances, to other environmental problems, to other geographical places, or into the future (UNEP-SETAC 2005).

Life cycle assessment is a comprehensive methodology that can be applied to avoid problem shifting. Vestas Wind Systems, for example, used the LCA methodology to document life cycle environmental impacts associated with the manufacturing, installation, operation, and end-of-life treatment of their V112 wind turbine (D'Souza, Gbegbaje-Das, and Shonfield 2011). The life cycle assessment shows how much time it will take before the environmental impacts associated with manufacturing the turbine and its components are outweighed by the environmental benefits that come from the renewable energy that the turbine generates. The life cycle assessment identifies break-even points between two and five months depending on the characteristics of the energy system in which the turbine is implemented and depending on the wind conditions at the site where it is installed (D'Souza, Gbegbaje-Das, and Shonfield 2011).

The life cycle approach is used in industries by company managers when designing environmental policies and strategies; by product managers and designers when deciding on, for example, product designs or product modifications; and by procurement departments when sourcing raw materials and components. It can be used by industry consortia or policy makers when comparing products or designing policies. And it can be used by consumers and product users when deciding on product choice.

The life cycle assessment methodologies have continuously been refined over the last twenty-five years. A number of large programs have contributed to the development of consistent and comprehensive standards and procedures. The United Nations Environment Programme (UNEP) and the Society of Environmental Toxicology and Chemistry (SETAC) have partnered to develop tools and manuals for life cycle assessment (UNEP SETAC 2011). SETAC was one of the pioneer organizations, and the life cycle assessment methodologies developed under SETAC became the reference work for international standards on LCA.

The International Organization for Standardization (ISO) has developed a standard that is one of the most used for LCA and commonly applied in academia as well as in industry and policy. The standard was first issued in 1997 and later revised, resulting in two standards: ISO 14040 (Environmental Management—Life Cycle Assessment—Principles and Framework) and ISO 14044 (Environmental Management—Life Cycle Assessment—Requirements and Guidelines). The two standards also support a series of standards on labeling, eco-design, and carbon footprinting.

The Joint Research Centre (JRC) under the European Commission has also developed a set of guidelines, tools, and handbooks that further specify the ISO 14040 and ISO 14044 standards to achieve greater consistency and quality assurance (JRC 2012). The JRC initiative was undertaken after the adoption of the European Union's Integrated Product Policy in 2003, which aimed for life-cycle-based policies and actions to prevent and eliminate environmental problems, and the EU's Sustainable Consumption and Production and Sustainable Industrial Policy Action Plan in 2008 (JRC 2012). The JRC handbook consists of eight technical documents (plus two more under development) that provide guidelines and recommendations on how to perform life cycle assessments.

The process of conducting an LCA can be divided into five iterative elements: First, a scope and goal definition identifies the decision context, the intended application, and the target group for the analysis. Second, the scope definition defines the system boundaries, the functions of the system that is analyzed, and the functional unit that it studies. Third, the life cycle inventory includes the generation and collection of life cycle data on resource consumption and emissions from the product system. Fourth, the impact assessment examines potential and actual environmental and health effects related to the life cycle of the product or process. Fifth, the lifecycle interpretation evaluates the results, including reflections over the completeness, sensitivity, and consistency and the creation of recommendations derived from the analysis (JRC 2012). Figure 18.1 illustrates the iterative character of the five elements.

4   Eco-Design

Eco-design is a concept that covers the integration of environmental considerations into product development. Product design plays a vital role in reducing environmental impact, as the product design determines critical issues such as material use, options for process technology, product durability, energy consumption, and recycling options in the end-of-life phase (McAloone and Bey 2008).

Most of the eco-design tools and methodologies consider the importance of integrating environmental concerns in the early design phases. Early integration of

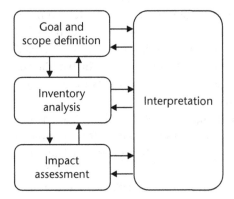

Figure 18.1
Traditional framework for LCA.

environmental concerns will offer more flexibility to designers and provide a wider range of options to reduce the potential environmental impacts caused by the product over its entire life cycle.

Eco-design draws on a variety of tools and methodologies. Most of the tools and approaches are based on life cycle thinking, meaning that they consider all environmental impacts from resource extraction to manufacturing, transport, consumption, and end-of-life treatment. The tools differ in scope and depth and have different approaches to stakeholder involvement (such as the involvement of suppliers and product users).

In 1997 the United Nations Environmental Programme (UNEP) published the report "Ecodesign: A Promising Approach to Sustainable Production and Consumption." The report was later followed by the Design for Sustainability (D4S) project, which aimed at going beyond the traditional elements of designing for environment and eco-design by incorporating social, economic, and institutional aspects into product development along with environmental aspects (Spangenberg, Fuad-Luke, and Blincoe 2010). A practical guide to D4S can be found in "Design for Sustainability: A Step by Step Approach" (UNEP 2009).

One of the most extensive eco-design programs, Design for the Environment (DfE), is carried out by the U.S. Environmental Protection Agency. The program has existed since the beginning of the 1990s and today covers a broad range of industries and products (automotive, electronics, furniture, printing, laundry, etc.). Design for the Environment includes a set of tools and methodologies for industries and sectors and often includes a broad stakeholder involvement procedure. The international standard on eco-design, ISO 14062, is a methodology for integrating environmental concerns into product development. The standard specifies possible actions and activities aimed at integrating environmental aspects into different stages of product development based on a generic model of product design that consists of a set of sequential steps from planning and conceptual design to detailed design, testing/prototyping, marked launch, and product review. ISO 14062 is part of the ISO 14000 series, which additionally covers standards on environmental management and life cycle assessment, and should be seen and used in the light of this overall framework.

Other frameworks and systems include eco-design tools and methods such as the eco-efficiency framework developed by the World Business Council for Sustainable Development (WBCSD 2000, 2006) and the cradle-to-cradle framework (McDonough and Braungart 2002).

Using the various eco-design frameworks requires a process where the eco-design tools are combined with situated knowledge about product characteristics and functions, manufacturing processes, and market conditions. Possibilities to conduct design changes are furthermore determined by situated knowledge, competences, strategies, and policies in the involved companies and industries.

Some companies and industries may find it easier to deploy the tools than others. The structure and economy of an industry may significantly influence opportunities for integrating environmental concerns. In the car industry, for example, the substitution of the conventional internal combustion engine with the battery electric drivetrain is shaped by the mass production regime, which makes it expensive and unattractive for the vehicle manufacturers to experiment with alternative drivetrain solutions in small-scale unit numbers (Orsato and Wells 2007; Christensen 2011).

5   Industrial Symbiosis Design

Industrial symbiosis is an approach to environmental design that covers the integration of multiple value chains. The idea is to improve resource efficiency and reduce waste and pollution by the design of closed-loop production systems. Industrial symbiosis design is a more open concept than the ones previously discussed and does not involve the same extent of international consensus regarding standardized methods and procedures. However, it is included here to illustrate the opportunities that arise if the scope is expanded from a single value chain or life cycle to include the integration of multiple value chains or life cycles.

5.1   Origin of the Industrial Symbiosis Concept

The concepts of industrial ecology and industrial symbiosis began to appear in academic literature in the late 1980s and have since become widely used by researchers and companies across the globe. The industrial ecology metaphor was derived from a couple of articles by Frosch and Gallopoulos (1989) and Ayres (1989), which emphasized design of closed-loop industrial systems, recycling via extensive waste and by-product exchange between companies, and material and energy cascading as promising strategies to improve resource efficiency and reduce environmental strain. The concepts and tools that are covered by the industrial ecology umbrella have been refined and developed over the last twenty-five years, and the ideas that originate from the industrial ecology literature can today also be found in the concepts of cradle-to-cradle (McDonough and Braungart 2002) and circular economy (MacArthur Foundation 2012; Su et al. 2013).

5.2 Features of Industrial Symbiosis

Industrial symbiosis usually applies to sophisticated industrial systems in which a number of companies are involved in waste and by-product exchange, utility sharing, or supply synergies (Center of Excellence in Cleaner Production 2007; Chertow 2007). The approach has been used in a number of different countries and industries. Researchers at the Center of Excellence in Cleaner Production (2007) have identified an industrial symbiosis system in heavy industries in Australia; Martin and Eklund (2011) have studied industrial symbiosis systems in biofuel industries in Sweden; Sokka, Pakarinen, and Melanen (2011) studied industrial symbiosis systems in forest industries in Finland; Yang and Feng (2008) studied industrial symbiosis in sugar industries in China; and Maes et al. (2011) studied mixed industries in industrial parks in Belgium. Some studies (Gibbs and Deutz 2007; Heeres, Vermeulen, and Walle 2004) looked at eco-industrial parks, which represent a special variant of industrial symbiosis where the symbiosis principles have been applied to a specific location in the early planning stages in Europe and the United States.

The textbook example of industrial ecology is the Kalundborg industrial symbiosis in Denmark (Jacobsen 2006), where a group of companies involving a large power station (DONG Energy), a pharmaceutical company (Novo Nordisk), an enzyme factory (Novozymes), a gypsum plant (Gyproc), a biomass refinery (Inbicon), a refinery (Statoil), two waste-handling companies (RGS 90 and Kara/Novoren), and the municipality of Kalundborg have successfully managed to reduce raw material and energy consumption by developing a complex by-product exchange system (fig. 18.2).

The most important driver for the creation of industrial symbiosis synergies is that businesses, by using each other's residual or by-products, can reduce costs (Heeres, Vermeulen, and Walle 2004; Jacobsen 2006). Besides the economic effects of the symbiosis, there is also an environmental benefit, which is related to the reduction of the total resource and energy consumption (Jacobsen 2006; Chertow 2007). Such environmental benefits might additionally save the companies the costs of having to add end-of-pipe technologies and reduce future legal compliance costs.

Identifying opportunities for industrial symbiosis is a matter of local context and local conditions. Opportunities must be identified on the basis of knowledge about local conditions, for example, about quantities and qualities of waste and by-products,

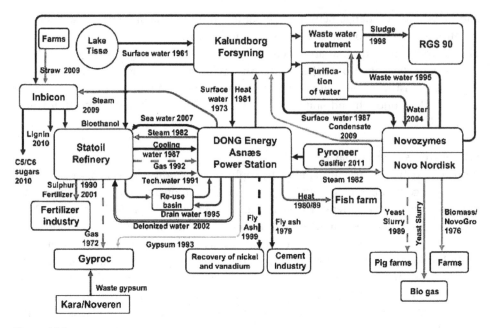

Figure 18.2
In the Kalundborg industrial symbiosis, more than thirty different waste and by-product exchange systems were in operation by spring 2013. The dates indicate when the exchange systems were implemented.

about energy and material use by the companies involved, and about actual technologies and production processes employed by the companies. This type of knowledge is inherently situated in the companies themselves, and the creation of industrial symbiosis systems therefore requires the mobilization of local, situated knowledge and competences.

The most successful industrial symbiosis systems, like the Kalundborg industrial symbiosis, have evolved over several decades where incremental steps have been taken to expand and sophisticate the industrial by-product exchange systems. In Kalundborg, this process was governed by a group of company managers who met regularly to discuss industrial symbiosis opportunities and in that process build trust and mutual understanding.

5.3   The Role of Colocation

Colocation is often seen as an indispensable element of industrial symbiosis needed to make the waste and by-product exchange function (Jacobsen 2006). From an environmental perspective, it is furthermore meaningful to reduce transport distances, as they can cause environmental impact. However, focusing on colocation as a requirement for industrial symbiosis risks overlooking potentials associated with the creation of linkages between companies that are not colocated. Additionally, the potential for industrial symbiosis is likely to be significantly larger if colocation is abandoned as a necessity and instead only regarded as a factor that may be important in cases where the local conditions require colocation. It may prove to be a good idea to transport waste or by-products over longer distances if the environmental and economic burden associated with long-distance transport proves less significant than the environmental improvements achieved from local by-product exchange. Such types of industrial symbiosis may be more difficult to identify but are nevertheless potentially just as relevant. The advantages of abandoning the requirement of colocation are supported by a study of German industries conducted by Sterr and Ott (2004), who found that extending the geographical scope of traditional eco-industrial parks would increase potentials for by-product exchange and provide a more promising frame for the creation of sustainable closed-loop economies.

Chertow (1999, 2000) has identified five generic types of industrial symbiosis systems. The importance of colocation varies between the five types. The five types are (1) through market-based waste exchange, where companies achieve multiple benefits but rely on a low degree of coordination; (2) where waste is exchanged within the boundaries of a single company located in one site or across multiple sites; (3) among colocated companies (eco-industrial parks); (4) among local companies that are not directly colocated but located in close proximity; and (5) among companies in a regional setting, typically involving a larger number of companies, but without overall coordination of the waste exchange. These different types of industrial symbiosis systems illustrate the complexity under which such systems are organized, and demonstrate that the conditions for waste use and by-product exchange differ widely across industries, sectors, and geographic conditions, as well as from company to company. The role of colocation is therefore determined by context and as such is an element of the industrial symbiosis concept that is always situated in the local conditions in which the industrial activities take place.

5.4 Summary and Discussion

This chapter has presented four approaches to reducing and eliminating environmental impacts. Each approach covers a number of design methods. These methods have continuously been developed by large organizations such as the United Nations, the European Union, the International Organization for Standardization, national governments, and industries and are widely used in industry and by policy makers across the globe.

The process of developing the methods also illustrates another type of situatedness; namely, the methods are situated in the system of stakeholders and organizations that have developed them. The chapter has described the historical process by which environmental management systems, life cycle assessment approaches, and eco-design approaches were developed. These processes have institutionalized a set of commonly agreed-on methods and procedures that companies can implement to eliminate or reduce environmental impacts. Changing designs of products, processes, and systems can be assisted by the knowledge that has been produced over the last twenty-five years of work with environmental management systems, life cycle approaches, eco-design, and industrial symbiosis.

The first approach presented in the chapter, environmental management, focuses on how production processes can be designed and managed to prevent and eliminate environmental problems. The environmental management approach covers a set of methods and procedures that have been adopted by a large number of industries across the globe. The second approach is the life cycle thinking approach. Life cycle thinking goes beyond the boundaries of a single company and looks at products and processes in a sequential flow from cradle to grave. The approach also covers a number of tools and methods that have been developed internationally, and like environmental management is widely used across industries, academia, and government. The third approach, eco-design, encompasses methods to integrate environmental concerns into product development. Eco-design is based on the life cycle approach and includes methods and procedures by which product developers and designers can reduce or eliminate environmental problems arising from manufacturing, use, and end-of-life treatment of products and services. The fourth approach is industrial symbiosis, which is a systems design approach linking otherwise separated companies by means of physical exchange of materials, energy, water, and by-products. This requires a process in which situated knowledge is mobilized, as illustrated in the case.

The four fields are mutually supportive and can be regarded as a hierarchy of scopes that can be applied to the design of industrial systems (fig. 18.3). Environmental management is traditionally applied to single manufacturing sites and is the simplest in the sense that it involves the least number of stakeholders. The design focus is primarily on processes and their optimization. The life cycle approach is in some situations more effective because it avoids problem shifting, but on the other hand, it is also more complicated and requires more knowledge and resources to implement. Eco-design usually requires life cycle knowledge and can be regarded as a practical way of integrating knowledge about life cycle environmental impacts into product development. Industrial system design is usually based on the combination of multiple LCAs in a process where by-product exchange and waste recycling are explored across otherwise separated value chains (Chertow 2007). This provides a larger variety of options and possibilities but also increases complexity. Steering the design process is also complicated by the need for multiple actors to collaborate to change the system design. The identification of opportunities depends on local

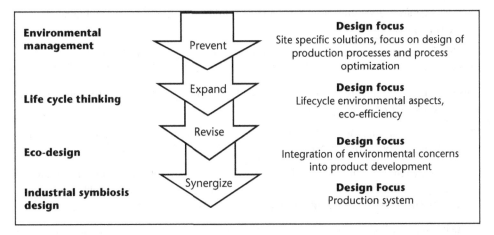

Figure 18.3
Design methods for preventing and reducing environmental problems (inspired by OECD 2009).

conditions (including, e.g., technology and economy) and also on situated knowledge about these conditions. This was illustrated in the case of Kalundborg industrial symbiosis, where local knowledge about opportunities plays a vital role in the development (historically, as well as for the future) of the industrial symbiosis system.

The use of the design methods presented here often requires translation from the generic and abstract form, which often focuses on procedures, tools, forms, and frameworks, into the local context, which could be, for example, a manufacturing company. This process can be seen as one in which the generic methods are contextualized, or situated. This is illustrated in the environmental management section, where the idea of pollution prevention as a generic method is situated in the local context when the abstract idea of pollution prevention in a specific company is translated into product changes that eliminate the environmental problem at its source.

References

Ayres, Robert. 1989. *Industrial Metabolism, Technology, and Environment*. Washington, DC: National Academy Press.

Center of Excellence in Cleaner Production. 2007. Regional resource synergies for sustainable development in heavy industrial areas: An overview of opportunities and experiences. Curtin University, Perth.

Chertow, Marian R. 1999. 1999 industrial symbiosis: A multi-firm approach to sustainability, 1999 Greening of Industry Network Conference. https://gin.confex.com/gin/archives/1999/papers/SUindustrial.pdf.

Chertow, Marian R. 2000. Industrial symbiosis: Literature and taxonomy. *Annual Review of Energy and the Environment* 25: 313–337.

Chertow, Marian R. 2007. "Uncovering" industrial symbiosis. *Journal of Industrial Ecology* 11 (1): 11–30.

Christensen, Thomas Budde. 2008. Eco-efficiency i CSR. In *Corporate Social Responsibility*, ed. Jan Stentoft Arlbjørn. Copenhagen: Børsen Forum.

Christensen, Thomas Budde. 2011. Modularised eco-innovation in the auto industry. *Journal of Cleaner Production* 19 (2–3): 212–220.

Christensen, Thomas Budde, and Tyge Kjær. 2012. What is CleanTech? Unraveling the buzzword. In *Rethinking Climate Change Research*, ed. Pernille Almlund, Per H. Jespersen, and Søren Riis, 21–43. Ashgate Studies in Environmental Policy and Practice. Farnham: Ashgate.

Donnelly, K., Zoe Beckett-Furnell, Siegfried Traeger, Thomas Okrasinski, and Susan Holman. 2006. Eco-design implemented through a product-based environmental management system. *Journal of Cleaner Production* 14: 1357–1367.

D'Souza, Niel, Erhi Gbegbaje-Das, and Peter Shonfield. 2011. Life cycle assessment of electricity production from a V112 turbine wind plant. PE North West Europe ApS: Copenhagen, Denmark, February 2011.

European Commission. 2011. EMAS—Factsheet, EMAS, and ISO 14001: Complementarities and differences. Published by the European Commission, DG Environment. http://ec.europa.eu/environment/emas/pdf/factsheet/EMASiso14001_high.pdf (accessed April 20, 2013).

European Environmental Agency (EEA). 2012. Material resources and waste—2012 update. In *European Environment State and Outlook 2010*. Copenhagen: European Environment Agency Publication Office.

European Union. 2008. Directive 2008/1/EC of the European Parliament and of the Council of 15 January 2008 concerning integrated pollution prevention and control. *Official Journal of the European Union*.

European Union. 2010. Directive 2010/75/EU of the European Parliament and of the Council of 24 November 2010 on industrial emissions (integrated pollution prevention and control). *Official Journal of the European Union*.

Frondel, Manuel, Jens Horbach, and Klaus Rennings. 2007. End-of-pipe or cleaner production? An empirical comparison of environmental innovation decisions across OECD countries. *Business Strategy and the Environment* 16: 571–584.

Frosch, Robert A., and Nicholas E. Gallopoulos. 1989. Strategies for manufacturing. *Scientific American* 189 (3): 152.

Gibbs, David, and Pauline Deutz. 2007. Reflections on implementing industrial ecology through eco-industrial park development. *Journal of Cleaner Production* 15: 1683–1695.

Heeres, R. R., W. J. V. Vermeulen, and F. B. Walle. 2004. Eco-industrial park initiatives in the USA and the Netherlands: First lessons. *Journal of Cleaner Production* 12: 985–995.

ISO. 2012. *Forging Action from Agreement: How ISO Standards Translate Good Intentions about Sustainability into Concrete Results*, 2nd ed. Geneva: International Organization for Standardization, ISO Central Secretariat.

Jacobsen, Noel Brings. 2006. Industrials in Kalundborg, Denmark: A quantitative assessment of economic and environmental aspects. *Journal of Industrial Ecology* 10 (1–2): 239–255.

JRC. 2012. *The International Reference Life Cycle Data System (ILCD) Handbook*. Joint Research Centre, European Commission. Luxembourg: Publication Office of the European Union.

MacArthur Foundation. 2012. *Towards the Circular Economy: Economic and Business Rationale for an Accelerated Transition*. Cowes, UK: Ellen MacArthur Foundation.

Maes, Tom, Greet Van Eetvelde, Evelien De Ras, Chantal Block, Ann Pisman, Bjorn Verhofstede, Frederik Vandendriessche, and Frederik Vandevelde. 2011. Energy management on industrial parks in Flanders. *Renewable and Sustainable Energy Reviews* 15: 1988–2005.

Martin, Michael, and Mats Eklund. 2011. Improving the environmental performance of biofuels with industrial symbiosis. *Biomass and Bioenergy* 35: 1747–1755.

McAloone, Tim, and Niki Bey. 2008. Environmental improvement through product development: A guide, Version 1.0. Danish Environmental Protection Agency, http://www2.mst.dk/udgiv/publications/2009/978-87-7052-949-5/pdf/978-87-7052-950-1.pdf.

McDonough, William, and Michael Braungart. 2002. *Cradle to Cradle: Remaking the Way We Make Things*. New York: North Point Press.

OECD. 2009. Sustainable manufacturing and eco-innovation, synthesis report, framework, practices and measurement. Organisation for Economic Co-operation and Development, Structural Policy Division, OECD Directorate for Science, Technology, and Industry, Paris, France.

Orsato, Renato, and Peter Wells. 2007. U-turn: The rise and demise of the automobile industry. *Journal of Cleaner Production* 15: 994–1006.

Porter, Michael E., and Claas van der Linde. 1995. Green and competitive: Ending the stalemate. *Harvard Business Review* 73 (5): 120–134.

Sokka, Laura, Suvi Pakarinen, and Matti Melanen. 2011. Industrial symbiosis contributing to more sustainable energy use: An example from the forest industry in Kymenlaakso, Finland. *Journal of Cleaner Production* 19: 285–293.

Spangenberg, Joachim H., Alastair Fuad-Luke, and Karen Blincoe. 2010. Design for Sustainability (DfS): The interface of sustainable production and consumption. *Journal of Cleaner Production* 18: 1483–1491.

Sterr, Thomas, and Thomas Ott. 2004. The industrial region as a promising unit for eco-industrial development: Reflections, practical experience, and establishment of innovative instruments to support industrial ecology. *Journal of Cleaner Production* 12: 947–965.

Su, Biwei, Almas Heshmati, Yong Geng, and Xiaoman Yo. 2013. A review of the circular economy in China: Moving from rhetoric to implementation. *Journal of Cleaner Production* 42: 215–227.

Thrane, Mikkel, Eskild H. Nielsen, and Per Christensen. 2009. Cleaner production in Danish fish processing: Experiences, status, and possible future strategies. *Journal of Cleaner Production* 17: 380–390.

UNCTAD. 2004. A manual for the preparers and users of eco-efficiency indicators, version 1.1, United Nations Conference on Trade and Development. http://unctad.org/en/docs/iteipc20037 _en.pdf (accessed January 2, 2014).

UNEP. 1997. *Ecodesign: A Promising Approach to Sustainable Production and Consumption.* Paris, France: United Nations Environment Programme, Industry and Environment, Cleaner Production; The Hague: Rathenau Institute; Delft, Netherlands: Delft University of Technology.

UNEP. 2009. Design for sustainability: A step by step approach. United Nations Environmental Programme, Sustainable Consumption and Production Branch, and Delft University of Technology. http://www.d4s-sbs.org/d4s_sbs_manual_site_S.pdf (accessed January 28, 2013).

UNEP-SETAC. 2005. *Life Cycle Approaches: The Road from Analysis to Practice.* Published by the United Nations Environment Programme (UNEP) and Society of Environmental Toxicology and Chemistry. Paris: SETAC.

UNEP-SETAC. 2007. *Life Cycle Management: A Business Guide to Sustainability.* Published by the United Nations Environment Programme (UNEP) and Society of Environmental Toxicology and Chemistry. Paris: SETAC.

UNEP-SETAC. 2011. *Towards a Lifecycle Sustainability Assessment: Making Informed Choices on Products.* Published by the United Nations Environment Programme (UNEP) and Society of Environmental Toxicology and Chemistry. Paris: SETAC.

WBCSD. 2000. *Eco-efficiency: Creating More Value with Less Impact.* Geneva: World Business Council for Sustainable Development.

WBCSD. 2006. *Eco-efficiency: Learning Module.* Geneva: World Business Council for Sustainable Development.

Yang, Shalin, and Nanping Feng. 2008. A case study of industrial symbiosis: Nanning Sugar Co. Ltd. in China. *Resources, Conservation, and Recycling* 52 (5): 813–820.

19 Transferring Methods to New Contexts

Margit Neisig

What. Sometimes design methods gain credibility widely. They are transferred because they have gained legitimacy, not because of the specific solution. They are not universal but extremely complex social constructs. They have become trusted schemes, rules, norms, or routines, and thereby authoritative guidelines. Thus the institutional perspective explains the proliferation process, but as they are transferred, the new contexts are different.

Why. The knowledge about contextual dependence of design methods and how to cope with this situatedness is relevant to designers to avoid the "blindness" so difficult to escape when transferring design methods. As design methods are often recognized as being universal, unexpected problems arise in many cases when methods are transferred to new contexts. Designing for a sustainable transition needs to take these lessons into account.

Where. The knowledge is applicable when transferring design methods from one context to another to create sustainable developments. The transfers that are investigated in this chapter are to (1) new types of organizations, (2) new social settings, and (3) completely different cultural settings.

How. The analysis unfolds through three case studies, in which design methods that have gained credibility in one context are transferred to very different contexts. The social construction of technology (SCOT) theory, the actor-network theory (ANT), and the information ecology perspective help us to understand why blindness is produced, how and why translation processes take place, and why and how the design method and the context have to coevolve as an ecology. The learning points from these cases are summarized in ten prescriptive learning sentences on how to transfer design methods in a situated way.

---

1 Introduction

This chapter focuses on the difficulty of transferring design methods to new organizational, social, and cultural contexts when pursuing sustainable development. Three case studies illustrate how proliferation, adoption, and adaptation (or rejection) of design methods take place, and how different theoretical perspectives can help to understand these processes and guide awareness when transfer processes are planned. The point is not to explain and illustrate each of the theories in depth but to draw practical methodological attention points and theoretical reflections when design methods are transferred.

These are the three illustrative cases:

1. The jam session method was developed and used by IBM for internal purposes. In 2006 it was transferred and used in relation to the third World Urban Forum conference (WUF3), organized by UN-Habitat with Vancouver, Canada, as the host city.[1] The conference is dedicated to socially sustainable urban development.

The jam session uses the collective intelligence of a large number of participants to brainstorm, develop, and select ideas. It is applicable in processes involving up to several hundred thousand participants geographically spread worldwide in a process supported by IT.

2. The concept of living labs (LL) is well rooted in Finland. During the Finnish EU presidency in 2006, it was made the starting point for building a common European Network of Living Labs (ENoLL). This chapter investigates the formation of the Helsinki-Tallinn living lab.

LLs are about a systematic user co-creation that integrates research and innovation processes through exploration, experimentation, and evaluation of innovative ideas, scenarios, concepts, and related technological artifacts in real-life use cases. The method thereby enables a broad sustainable focus on innovations in technology and other areas.

3. Cradle to Cradle (C2C) is developed by Braungart and McDonough. The concept is American and gained momentum in the Netherlands and northwestern Europe but has also been transferred to Chinese eco-cities as demonstration projects for inspiration to the huge urban development taking place. This chapter investigates the Huangbaiyu case.

C2C aims at eliminating waste by making any substantive processes part of a closed circuit. The method is applicable to redesigning the relationship between human, natural, and built systems to gain sustainability.

2 Theoretical Perspectives When Design Methods Are Transferred

The theoretical perspectives considered in this chapter all address the interlinkage of technology with organizational, social, and cultural contexts. However, not only technologies but also design methods can be highly context dependent.

Institutional theories understand the transfer of a design process as a process of gaining legitimacy by isomorphism, which is a similarity of the processes or structures of one organization to those of another, be it the result of imitation or independent development under similar constraints. This perspective helps to understand the proliferation and adoption of the successful design concepts as they become trusted authoritative guidelines for social behavior (Scott 2004). Each of the three cases illustrates that the design method has achieved success or recognition in its original context.

The social construction of technology (SCOT) theory (Bijker, Hughes, and Pinch 1987) attaches importance to understanding the relationship between social and technical processes and regards them both as human (social) constructions. In that way, design methods are seen as highly complex social constructs. The three cases show that not only is it difficult to transfer this complexity from one context to another, but the actors also became blind to certain parts of the complexity that were taken for granted.

Actor-network theory (ANT) (Law and Hassard 1999; Latour 2005) contributes by addressing the translation process and the "black box."

Translation is the process of forming a network (Callon 1986). It occurs in four steps: (1) problematization, (2) interestment, (3) enrollment, and (4) mobilization. Translation involves negotiations among human and nonhuman actors. Negotiations establish common sets of definitions and meanings. The outcome of successful negotiations is an actor network characterized by aligned interests.

A *black box* is a device, system, or object viewed in terms of its input, output, and transfer characteristics without any knowledge required of its internal workings. That is possible when it is stable and need not be contested anymore. Then it can be "black-boxed" (Callon 1987). Inside the black box, the device, system, or object constitutes a whole network of other, perhaps complex, associations. A stable network can similarly be punctualized (Law 1992), that is, black-boxed to look like a single-point actor or node in another larger network. When this happens, it is replaced by the action itself and the "seemingly simple author of that action" (Law 1992, 5). However, black boxes are contextual and seen from a specific perspective.

As institutional theories contribute to the understanding of the proliferation and adoption process, both the SCOT theory and ANT contribute to the understanding of the adaptation process, when a design method is transferred to a new context.

The theories of information ecologies (Nardi and O'Day 1999; Pór 2000) understand design methods as part of a holistic system of people, practices, values, and technologies in a given local environment. There is a constant coevolution of skills, technologies, practices, and so on. It creates a dynamic picture, where the focus is on relationships rather than the individual parts. This understanding thereby opens up an interpretation of an information ecology as a complex *adaptive* system in which one part cannot change without affecting *the whole system*, which has to coevolve.

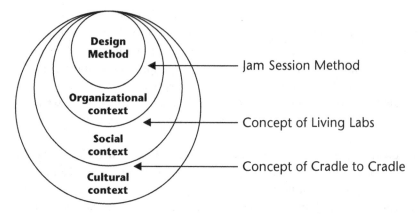

Figure 19.1
The cases highlight different aspects of new contexts.

The three cases are chosen to illustrate different aspects of the new contexts when transferring design methods. As outlined in figure 19.1, the jam sessions case illustrates a transfer process from one type of organization to another. The LL case illustrates a transfer process involving extremely new social settings. And the C2C case illustrates a transfer process to completely different cultural settings.

3   The Jam Session Method

3.1   The Design Method and Its Original Application
IBM has used online jam sessions since 2001. The method is used to develop best practices, foster good management, and change IBM's corporate values (Hempel 2006; Bjelland and Wood 2008). The largest jam session held at IBM was InnovationJam in 2006. About 150,000 people from 104 countries participated; about two-thirds of the active participants came from IBM and employees' families, and the rest from partners, universities, and customers from sixty-seven companies (Bjelland and Wood 2008). The goal was radical innovations with the power to transform industries, alter human behavior, and create new business opportunities for IBM.

Habitat Jam was the first time a jam session was used outside IBM. IBM has since applied jam sessions as a method on several occasions and is now selling jam sessions to customers as a service.

3.2   InnovationJam 2006
During two seventy-two-hour sessions, participants posted more than 4,600 ideas while debating IBM's most advanced technologies and considering applications to real-life problems and future business opportunities. The themes of InnovationJam

were prestructured into six themes with selected subthemes (Bjelland and Wood 2008).

As a prelude, a Web site that informed participants about the technologies addressed by InnovationJam was created (Hempel 2006). It also allowed for discussions in preparation.

Jam phase 1 was conducted as a seventy-two-hour online brainstorming session. Extensive planning behind the scenes and an orchestrated effort by up to two hundred facilitators and moderators were conducted. During the jam session, IBM's eClassifier text-mining tool was used to scan discussion forums to identify emerging themes and help participants to quickly capture the essence and prioritize the underlying discussions in each forum. IBM's tool SurfAid provided real-time measurements on the user behavior and the demographic participation.

The jam session was followed by a postjam phase 1. About fifty senior executives and professionals from around the world spent one week in New York to review the results from phase 1 to synthesize the thirty-one "Big Ideas." The method used by IBM to identify the most valuable comments started by using the text-mining tool eClassifier. The tool studied words in common phrases and classified items into categories. Then the reviewers worked in subgroups focusing on a group of related ideas (health, environment, the Internet, etc.). Only after both computer and human treatment could the top management review the results from the jam session and search for important ideas.

The next step was a second seventy-two-hour online jam to refine and develop the "Big Ideas." Jam phase 2 was also followed by a postjam phase 2 in New York, which again involved technology-supported categorization and assessing ideas of value to the company.

Only three months after the first jam session, IBM's CEO announced the allocation of $100 million for the launch of ten new business units (IBM 2006). It is worth noting that the entire process had senior management focus and commitment, and considerable resources were put into both the process and the realization of the nominated ideas.

3.3   Why the Design Method Has Gained Popularity

Globalization and the network economy are some of the driving forces behind the jam session method: globalization because the method is suitable for involvement independent of geographic location, and the network economy because the network's collective intelligence is harvested.

Collective intelligence is a shared or group intelligence that emerges from the collaboration and competition of many individuals and appears in consensus decision making. IBM wants to tap into the collective intelligence to shorten innovation time, meeting customer expectations and exploiting scattered talents; but Lesser et al. (2012) also point out that:

key study findings indicate that successful Collective Intelligence efforts need to:

• Address sources of resistance, including operational challenges, conflict with existing charters, perceived loss of control, and shifting roles and responsibilities
• Integrate Collective Intelligence into the work environment, both technologically and culturally
• Act on what is discovered, communicating value and outcomes to both the organization and the individual.

3.4   The Transfer and Problems Arising in the New Context

The World Urban Forum (WUF) is an organization assembling energy and ideas from civil society and the private sector in a dialogue with local, regional, and national governments in advising the United Nations, in particular the CEO of UN-Habitat, in charge of the international program for issues relating to human settlements.

As host of WUF3 in June 2006, Canada committed itself to bringing ideas into action and to making the event more inclusive. Habitat Jam was a special seventy-two-hour Internet event preceding WUF3 (UN-Habitat 2006a). The focus of Habitat Jam was to solve some of the world's most critical issues related to urban development. Over 39,000 people came as equals to learn, share, and be heard. Participants came from all over the world, from government, industry, academia, youth and women's groups, and poor communities around the world. Seventy-eight percent were slum dwellers, young people, or grassroots women. The aim was to provide input to the WUF's agenda and to initiate a dialogue about how to put ideas into action. After the jam session, the government of Canada contracted the International Centre for Sustainable Cities (ICSC) to analyze the more than four thousand pages of transcripts from the jam dialogue and identify the best actionable ideas. With a team of jam consultants, ICSC restricted the field to seventy actionable ideas, all of which were then further analyzed and described with stories, photos, and links to similar projects and reports. The results were published as a book and a CD, which was given to each of the ten thousand participants in WUF3 as part of their registration kit (UN-Habitat 2006b).

Habitat Jam was the first of its kind, the largest public consultation ever held on sustainable urban development. It was a demonstration project sponsored by the Canadian government in collaboration with UN-Habitat and IBM. It took place on December 1–4, 2005, but unlike IBM's InnovationJam, the Habitat Jam combined IBM's advanced online tools with face-to-face meetings.

Habitat Jam involved a culturally, linguistically, technologically, and educationally diverse audience in a forum where all comments were treated alike. Language and lack of computer access were barriers to be overcome. Through special partner organizations, more than twenty-five thousand people who lacked Internet access were able to participate via live workshops, focus groups, World Urban Café jam sessions, and Internet cafés to share their ideas and stories with others in the Habitat Jam (UN-Habitat 2006a).

The seventy actionable ideas were chosen because they were practical, represented ideas from different parts of the world, had relevance for the WUF3 agenda, and could potentially have a major impact on urban problems. In all cases, the selected ideas were based on experience from a city, group, or community that had a story to tell about bringing those ideas into action (UN-Habitat 2006b).

Unlike IBM's InnovationJam, however, the best ideas had no funding. It is hoped that WUF3 participants or those who discover Habitat Jam on the Internet will find ideas and directly use them in their own situations (UN-Habitat 2006a).

In the evaluation, Habitat Jam was described as an outstanding success in terms of inclusion, global range, and the number of actionable ideas generated by the participants (UN-Habitat 2006a). The summary report (UN-Habitat 2006a) concludes that it was amazing what just three months of effort could do to reach the marginalized and bring their voices into WUF3. However, for future jams, the report recommends getting broader participation from politicians, senior officials, and the private sector to bring the ideas into practice.

3.5 Theoretical Reflections Illustrated by the Case

Seen from an institutional perspective, the proliferation of the jam method was inspired by the legitimacy that the method had gained by being successfully used internally by IBM, which told the success story and provided assistance to let an isomorphic process take place. The schemes, rules, norms, and routines from the jam concept became trusted, authoritative guidelines for social behavior; the method was adopted.

But this case also shows the complexity of transferring the jam method from one context to another. The ANT contributes by addressing the translation process (the adaptation of the method) and the "black box." A lot of translation had to be done to bring the concept/network into play.

The Habitat Jam had to cope with not having Internet and computers in many slum areas, and not everyone being able to understand English. But they also had to cope with finding relevant people to take part in the jam session, and how to place the results in the mind of the WUF3 participants, and afterward the many decentralized decision-making processes regarding urban development. Therefore they needed a lot of "human networks" to support the translation process. How to harvest collective intelligence in the innovation of global urban development ends up being a rather different process from harvesting collective intelligence in the innovation of IBM's business lines.

As foreseen by both the SCOT theory and the ANT's black box, the actors also were blind to certain parts of the complexity that are taken for granted. In this case, the blindness was toward the organizational settings needed to bring the ideas from vision to reality, that is, the organizational and financial structures, as well as leadership power, to "act on what is discovered and address sources of resistance" (Lesser et al. 2012).

Highlighting the limitations of the Habitat Jam, its success requires ideas and recommendations from the event to live on *after* the event. They must be at the center of WUF3 and influence the issues in dialogue and networking sessions. They must control the agenda of governments and organizations, whose role is to improve the lives of the world's urban citizens. And investments must be made to implement the ideas.

If one compares with IBM's internal JAM, this is the major difference. A global company like IBM was able to put both managerial and financial power behind the ideas generated by the method. The weakness of Habitat Jam is the lack of powerful key decision makers to support the activity, sponsor funding to realize the best ideas, back the best idea makers to move forward, remove resistance or obstacles to projects and efforts, and help to maintain momentum, networking, and progress. That is also why the report recommends an even broader participation by politicians, senior officials, and the private sector.

Whether Habitat Jam is a successful ecology according to the theoretical perspective of an information ecology depends on whether all necessary parts of the ecology are coevolved—and in this case, something is still lacking regarding the decision making and implementation system.

4 The Concept of Living Labs

4.1 The Design Method and Its Original Application

The fundamental idea of living labs (LL) is to cast users in the role of everyday innovators.[2] To move from a user-centric model with users as objects of the product development to a user-driven model means involving users as both stakeholders and activators in the research, development, and innovation processes. Users are equal partners with the public sector, academia, and business.

LLs represent an "open innovation," as termed by Henry Chesbrough (2006). A network of LL partners is seen to form an ecosystem, which can consist of dozens or even hundreds of different partners. In LL cases, the best possible partners will be identified. The result is an ad hoc network with the users as involved actors. Joining and resigning from an LL ecosystem is voluntary for each partner (Helsinki Living Lab 2007).

Helsinki Living Lab is an ecosystem of the LLs and their collaborators in the Helsinki metropolitan area (Helsinki Living Lab 2007), and it has inspired the European Network of Living Labs (ENoLL). It represents an open innovation process by the inclusion of lead users, interdisciplinary teams, and users/citizens, as well as complex multidisciplinary and cross-cultural knowledge. This facilitates the development of a whole product,[3] which is what the mass market requires (European Commission 2009). That is one of the reasons why Helsinki has gained a reputation as a highly innovative region.

4.2 Why the Design Method Has Gained Popularity

The overall objective of creating ENoLL is to develop a future European innovation system (ENoLL Strategy Wiki 2013). The European Commission study (2009) shows that the LLs build bridges between ideas and technology and between development, market access, and complete development.

ENoLL was first launched by the Finnish EU presidency in 2006. The network originally had nineteen members. It has been extended to over three hundred members through six waves, and a seventh wave is planned during 2013. All ENoLL members offer innovative services unique in one way or another (European Commission 2009).

The LL movement was originally strong in the northern part of Europe, with a strong tradition of usability and participation and high IT availability among small and medium-size businesses and citizens. The network is now broadly based across Europe, but with a concentration in western Europe (European Commission 2009).

The LLs have developed into an innovation infrastructure now the basis for several pilot projects in a cross-border network interconnecting "smart cities" (Lemke and Luotonen 2009; ENoLL Strategy Wiki 2013; European Commission 2012). This is aimed at new and revolutionary Internet technologies that are also seen as helpful to tackle climate change and sustainability issues (Lemke and Luotonen 2009).

Today the development of new Internet-based services may best be characterized as a market of isolated solutions for many applications using different standards. This inhibits more widespread use of Internet-based services that are also seen to reduce carbon disclosure. Therefore common open platforms for Internet-based services have high priority (Lemke and Luotonen 2009; European Commission 2012).

4.3 The Transfer and Problems Arising in the New Context

An ideal case for discussing transfer issues deals specifically with the transfer of the LL method from Finland to Estonia in enhancing Helsinki-Tallinn cross-border cooperation and thus metropolitan regional integration.

The empirical part consists of data from research (Lepik, Krigul, and Terk 2010) based on the analyses of fourteen interviews conducted among Tallinn and Helsinki city officials, representatives of technology enterprises, and field experts, using structured interviews and discussions. The topic of the LL was quite new to most of the interviewees. It was possible to think in terms of a field or technology, but not in terms of concrete environments that should be created for the LL. Formation of concrete ideas presumes a deep understanding of functioning mechanisms. In this case, an important element is missing: interest of potential users. Interest occurs with knowledge about the method's potentials.

The article points to a hypothesis that part of the factors found in the study may be general and valid not only in cities with post-Soviet history but wherever the transfer takes place from a region with higher technological or institutional level to a lower one.

Besides a few high-tech companies within the ICT industry, the majority of Estonian high-tech companies are small and financially weak. This is a problem: in richer countries like Finland, the companies are able to invest in development of an idea that may not pay off immediately, and this is extremely important in considering the LLs. For Estonian high-tech companies, this kind of investment is usually not available.

After the interviews, several roundtables and seminars were organized. The findings indicated that there was a danger of a deadlock. A great effort had to be made to work out exact tasks to start the project and involve the citizens. Realistic ideas necessary for city development and attractive to domestic technology companies would be vital to show that the process was serious and that companies and people would not just be wasting their time. The project also needed involvement from the top political level, that is, from the Mayor.

Uncertainty about the required amount of investment from private companies and the workload for key officials made it necessary to move from the awareness phase to a trial phase. Even with the Finnish experience available, a large number of unanswered questions existed. Under these conditions, the idea of creating a cross-border Estonian-Finnish LL became extremely ambitious: there was a need to transfer not only the method itself but also people who had experience using the method.

Unlike Estonian companies, Finnish companies have financial coverage for participating in technological innovations and ability to multiply the solutions worked out in the LL. Several Finnish companies have daughter companies in Tallinn, thus making participation in the LLs even less complicated.

However, Finnish participation in the Tallinn LL not only increases its capacity but also guarantees a positive attitude of the stakeholders and all citizens. For Finnish companies, Tallinn was a good test ground: east European cities are specific markets for new technologies and new ways of organizing citizens' life. Developing new solutions that are different from Finnish solutions, involving citizens of Tallinn, and multiplying the process later in central or eastern Europe or in other places constitute a promising business idea that is useful to Tallinn at the same time.

Now, several years after this research was done, the Helsinki-Tallinn LL is up and running and has succeeded in building the relationships between developers and users.

4.4   Theoretical Reflections Illustrated by the Case

This case illustrates a transfer process to new and different social settings although Helsinki and Tallinn are extremely close geographically. The case illustrates a proliferation process inspired by the legitimacy that the method had gained by being successfully implemented in Helsinki. This provided a success story and also assistance for an isomorphic process to take place. Here the schemes, rules, norms, and routines from the Helsinki LL are seen as trusted, authoritative guidelines, and the method was adopted in Tallinn.

However, as Lepik, Krigul, and Terk (2010) emphasize, an LL is a highly complex and difficult concept to transfer, as not only technology but also ideology, knowledge, institutional cooperation experiences, and ways of thinking and acting need to be transferred. And it also requires political support and the enhancement of social networks.

In this case, too, some of the actors were blind. Some Tallinn actors were blind toward the understanding of the new concept. The actors had to have a certain level of maturity, but that is what they earned by getting involved. The initial interest had to be nurtured. The blindness was also toward the need to develop the actors before getting any potential interest for the concept. A "chicken or the egg" situation existed.

ANT contributes by addressing the translation process and the black box. A lot of translation had to be done to bring the LL networks into play. The Helsinki-Tallinn case shows the need to let all the different actors gain not only awareness but also experience (playing roles in the network) to find their own translation of the meaning of the concept. It was not possible to transfer the concept only with the help of trained Finnish people.

The understanding of the LL concept is in close harmony with the theoretical perspective of information ecologies, as the proliferation of LLs is seen as a growing ecology, constantly adapting to local conditions (including power relations).

The European Commission study (2009) mentions that the tools and methods used in the LL approach vary considerably from LL to LL. A high degree of nonhomogeneity and unevenness can be found throughout Europe, owing to a number of factors:

- Different interpretations of a relatively new concept
- The necessity of adapting the LL approach to different cultural and institutional contexts
- Different types of technological infrastructure available
- A variety of business application domains and priorities
- Different nature and role of the actors

LLs might be seen as prosperous ecologies, as the European Commission (2009) identifies five areas to which LLs contribute:

1. Opportunities for vertical integration of technologies (technical advantage)
2. Potential for coevolution of related technologies (horizontal integration)
3. Access to users and user groups
4. Sharing of infrastructure costs
5. A "springboard" to the market

5   The Concept of Cradle to Cradle

5.1   The Design Method and Its Original Application

Cradle to Cradle (C2C) has been conceived almost as a new industrial revolution. The method focuses on redesigning products in such a way that at the end of their life they are disassembled and become either biological or technical nutrients, that is, part of the biological cycle, or recycled in industrial production. The perspective is not limited to minimizing resources but extends to completely eliminating waste. The design thinking has been developed by Braungart and McDonough over the past fifteen to twenty years (McDonough and Braungart 2002) and has become a widespread vision and shared language. Some large multinational companies like Nike, Ford, BASF, and Steelcase (McDonough 2002) have been showcases for the concept, helping it to gain credibility and trust. The C2C concept is extremely popular in the Netherlands. After the broadcast of a compelling documentary on the concept in 2006, many initiatives began to implement the concept. However, there has been a shared concern that unless clear strategies and concrete successes were achieved, the surge of enthusiasm around the concept would remain hype and fail to institutionalize real and tangible change toward sustainable development. The optimal design of a societal infrastructure based on the C2C metabolisms is a discussion that has only just begun. However, the province of Limburg, with the city of Venlo in the forefront, has developed into a test bed as a C2C region, and it is now scaled up for wider application funded by the European Commission as part of INTERREG IVB North-West Europe (NWE) (Booth et al. 2012).

5.2   Why the Design Method Has Gained Popularity

C2C is generally seen as a solution to the problem of a lack of sustainability in the relationship between humans and nature: increased use of resources and increased waste and emissions. The huge growth of urban development is also a concern. In 1950 only about 30 percent of the world's population lived in cities. In 2008 the world's urban population for the first time exceeded the rural population. In 2050 about 70 percent of the world population will live in cities, or six billion people (United Nations, Department of Economic and Social Affairs, Population Division 2012).

Over the past thirty years, Chinese cities have grown by 400 million people, equivalent to the total population in the United States and Mexico (Lu 2011).

According to the Worldwatch Institute (2013), sixteen of the world's twenty most-polluted cities are Chinese, and rapid economic development has strained the government's ability to protect the environment. During the first decade of the twenty-first century, the Chinese government sought to raise awareness and interest in the environment by establishing a number of eco-cities as demonstration projects (Hald 2009). These were also used as a platform for international cooperation and technology exchange. In this context, the C2C concept was tested in Huangbaiyu.

5.3   The Transfer and Problems Arising in the New Context

Huangbaiyu is a model village created by William McDonough and Partners in collaboration with Tongji University in Shanghai, the Benxi Design Institute, and the China–U.S. Centre for Sustainable Development (CUCSD).[4]

The final village master plan developed by William McDonough + Partners in October 2004 outlines six basic principles for the design of Huangbaiyu (May 2008–2009):

1. Buildings will primarily be built of locally sourced and rapidly renewable materials that can be returned safely to the ecosystem as a biological nutrient or of man-made materials designed to safely be reused for construction of new buildings in the future as a "technical nutrient" in a circular economy.
2. Supply of buildings with energy will be based on locally sourced quickly renewable materials, including animal, human, and agricultural waste.
3. Human habitation will be centralized and consolidated to optimize the use of valuable productive land while enhancing habitats and allowing for the natural environment of the development.
4. Quality of life will be improved through development of community, convenience, and comfort.
5. Materials will be used in the C2C cycles.
6. The village will be supplied by solar energy.

The master plan for Huangbaiyu included four hundred centralized houses, all with the same appearance, a reconstructed school, a plant for the gasification of biomass to supply energy for heating and cooking, and a lake. It also included the use of renewable energy, a common water system, a closed loop for material and waste streams, and improvement of habitats and agriculture (May 2008–2009).

In Huangbaiyu, according to the plan, the living standards of the approximately 1,400 people (400 families) would be improved, coal burning would be reduced, and peasants who had lived scattered throughout the valley would be gathered in the eco-city to release more land for agriculture (May 2008–2009). In China much farmland is lost to urbanization, factories, and desertification. Therefore the government wishes to increase the effectiveness of the remaining agricultural land.

Traditionally, the villagers used wood from the surrounding hillsides to cook and heat their homes. Each family was assigned an area to cut wood, and they managed carefully not to overexploit the hills. The water was pumped from hand-dug wells, and washing was done in the river. It was old-fashioned sustainability (Toy 2006).

In Huangbaiyu most of the farmers complement their livelihood with the sale of maize, keep small flocks of sheep or pigs, and raise vegetables in small gardens. These other sources of income were what threw a spanner in the works of the otherwise large-scale project (Toy 2006). The income that farmers stood to lose with less room for additional crops did not appear to be part of the planners' calculations.

Toy (2006) describes how the construction of Huangbaiyu was mainly privately funded, and the price of moving may also have blocked the villagers. If their income was taken into account, the price was outside the peasants' reach. The price of an eco-house was twice the cost of an ordinary house (Toy 2006).

In the summer of 2005, forty-two houses were expected to be completed, with at least forty families who moved into the eco-city. While the masonry had been completed, however, significant problems with the functionality of the houses existed: there was no electricity, no water, and no gas. The houses remained largely in this state until the end of 2008. Conflicts of interest, desire for speed, personal greed, a global perspective, technical inexperience, faulty materials, lack of supervision, and poor communication, among other things, were the reasons for the failed realization of the demonstration project in Huangbaiyu (Toy 2006).

Of the forty-two completed houses, only three used a combination of hay and compacted soil. The remainder were built out of hay and compressed bricks of coal dust, which triggered a debate about whether coal dust is a health risk (Toy 2006).

Only one house had solar panels; the rest were built to burn wood but have now been modified to use gas from biogasification. None of the houses faced south as originally planned, because the building contractor changed orientation to fit feng shui. Inexplicably, the new houses also got garages, although none of the villagers could afford a car (Toy 2006).

According to Shannon May, a U.S. researcher who has followed the project (May 2007, 2008), it was unsuccessful from the start.[5] Her studies show that whatever Huangbaiyu needed, it was not 42 new houses, let alone the 360 planned to follow. Even if the houses were more affordable and people's incomes increased, they would not want to spend the money on new houses. They would rather send their daughter to college or get surgery for Grandmother or open a small shop. The project was based on a flawed assumption that people wanted a new house (Toy 2006).

What the Huangbaiyu experiment shows is the danger of trying to impose a new way of life on people without fully understanding their needs and the realities of their lives. May criticizes the political discourse according to which eco-cities in poor rural areas are forced on the people without proper inclusion or analysis of their everyday practice, let alone involvement of the rural people themselves in decision making. In Huangbaiyu the city council was involved in the decision, but no involvement of the citizens themselves or any kind of ethnographic investigation took place beforehand.

The case of Huangbaiyu shows how C2C as a design principle does not in itself meet the requirements of sustainable urban development. The C2C philosophy looks only at the ecological dimension, not the broad concept of sustainability, in which the social and participatory dimension is also important. In the case of Huangbaiyu, this was later admitted by McDonough (Sacks 2008).

5.4 Theoretical Reflections Illustrated by the Case

This case illustrates a transfer process to completely different cultural settings. Also in this case, the concept, C2C, has gained trust and legitimacy. This happened through successful stories told by trusted parties, global sustainability constraints, and a compelling vision that led to an isomorphic adoption of the method seen as authoritative guidelines (the institutional perspective).

The C2C case also shows blindness to certain parts of the complexity of the social construct of the design method that are taken for granted. In this case, the blindness is toward social involvement and social justice, as C2C is taken solely as an environmental concept. But in the Western cases, C2C has been rooted in a social movement. When transferred to different cultures, such as China, this social movement rootedness cannot be taken for granted. The lid of the black box, according to ANT, has to be opened.

The C2C case shows that if the concept is not rooted in a local involvement or a social movement, the translation processes simply fail, and strong elements of original culture and traditions (the local actor network) take over (in this case, e.g., feng shui, coal dust bricks, and the need to stay dispersed). In the theoretical perspective of an information ecology, the C2C/Huangbaiyu case shows a failed ecology, in which people, practices, values, and technologies did not form a holistic system but reverted to separate parts again.

6 Conclusion

As the three cases show, sometimes design methods become extremely popular and gain credibility and trust. They spread from one arena to another, but not always with the same successful achievements as in the original context.

The problem is that often the organizational, social, and cultural contexts of a design method are neglected in the practical world, and unexpected problems arise. But which practical attention points can be learned from the three cases when trying to pursue sustainability in a broad sense through transferring design methods?

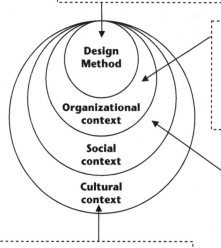

1. Adapt the design method to cope with the different situations. It might be helpful for the proliferation of a concept or method if it is seen as a growing ecology, constantly adapting to local conditions. People, practices, values, and technologies have to be understood as a holistic system in a local environment.

Design Method

Organizational context

Social context

Cultural context

2. Be aware that not only the design method has to be adapted, but also the organizational settings into which it is transferred. The leadership, organizational, and financial structure needed to bring the ideas from visions to reality also has to be developed.

3. A lot of human networks are needed to support the translation process.

4. If the concept or method should live on after the transfer process, it is not possible to make a transfer only by help of trained experts. Different actors must be allowed to gain not only awareness but also experience (getting roles in the network) to find their own translation of the concept.

5. The actors need a certain level of maturity in order to understand the concept, but that is what they get by getting involved. The initial interest has to be nurtured.

6. Be aware that the process might end up being rather different.

7. When transferring sustainability concepts do not focus solely on environmental issues. Do not ignore social involvement or social justice seen from local cultural perspectives.

8. Be aware if a concept used to be rooted in a social movement. This rootedness cannot be taken for granted when transferred to different cultures.

9. You need to recognize that the translation processes may simply fail, and strong elements of original culture and traditions may take over. So make your ethnographic studies carefully and adapt the concept to the local culture.

10. If this is not possible, then adapt the local culture to the concept through intensive change management or forget the project.

Figure 19.2
Ten prescriptive sentences on how to transfer design methods in a situated way.

First of all, the design methods presented in this chapter are complex social constructs developed to address complex problems. The complexity of the social constructions makes it difficult in practice to transfer the design methods from one context to another. However, when it is done, it is important to develop networks, leadership skills, and values to handle broad participatory processes while ensuring anchoring regarding decision making. This requires actors to be ready for change, but at the same time actors get ready by assuming roles in such processes. This type of development seems to be a prerequisite for harvesting collective intelligence across organizational, social, cultural, and professional barriers.

When it comes to the kind of complex problems regarding a sustainable transformation of the world's urban development, evidence suggests open innovation strategies that in a broad sense involve the users. This is required to achieve a workable knowledge transfer. To summarize this into a prescription of how to transfer design methods in a situated way is not simple, but the cases can be summarized in ten learning sentences, shown in figure 19.2.

Notes

1. UN-Habitat is the United Nations agency for human settlements. The WUF is a biennial conference, which was established by UN-Habitat with the participation of a wide range of partners.

2. According to Ståhlbröst (2008), the concept of living labs started to develop in the late 1990s, and one of the first institutions to mention it was the Georgia Institute of Technology.

3. A "whole product" is a core product augmented by everything needed for the customer to have a compelling reason to buy. The concept was first introduced by Regis McKenna (1986).

4. CUCSD is a nonprofit organization. The U.S. Secretariat, with McDonough as chairman, raises funding through a Founder's Circle: mostly Fortune 500 corporations that make multiyear commitments of $50,000 per year to sit on the U.S. Board of Councilors for the CUCSD. It worked through local municipal (Benxi), district (Nanfen), and township (Sishanling) governments to implement the project and selected a local businessman, Dai Xiaolong, to act as developer and investor (May 2008).

5. Supported by Intel, Shannon May lived for fifteen months in the city as she worked on her Ph.D. dissertation. May has created the website http://www.shannonmay.com (accessed February 1, 2013) on Huangbaiyu.

References

Bijker, Wiebe, Thomas P. Hughes, and Trevor Pinch, eds. 1987. *The Social Construction of Technological Systems: New Directions in the Sociology and History of Technology*. Cambridge, MA: MIT Press.

Bjelland, Osvald M., and Robert C. Wood. 2008. An inside view of IBM's "Innovation Jam." *MIT Sloan Management Review* 50 (1): 32–40.

Booth, Colin A., Ab Oosting, Nii Ankrah, Felix N. Hammond, Kim Tannahill, Christopher Williams, Helma Smolders, Joni Braas, Linda Scheepers, Ajay Kathrani, Lali Virdee, Tereza Kadlecova, Olaf Lewald, Marita Mess, Bertrand Merckx, Marc Renson, Amélie Cousin, Tiphaine Cadoret, Roy Vercoulen, Eva Starmans, Alexandre Bertrand, Alina Beloussova, Liette Mathieu, Jean-Marc Meulemans, and Jeannot Schroeder. 2012. Beyond sustainability: Cradle-to-cradle business innovation and improvement zones in NW Europe. In *The Sustainable City VII: Urban Regeneration and Sustainability*, ed. Marco Pacetti, Giorgio Passerini, Carlos A. Brebbia, and Giuliano Latini, 515–527. Southampton: WIT Press.

Callon, Michel. 1986. Some elements of a sociology of translation: Domestication of the scallops and the fishermen of St. Brieuc Bay. In *Power, Action, and Belief: A New Sociology of Knowledge*, ed. John Law, 196–233. London: Routledge & Kegan Paul.

Callon, Michel. 1987. Society in the making: The study of technology as a tool for sociological analysis. In *The Social Construction of Technological Systems: New Directions in the Sociology and History of Technology*, ed. Wiebe E. Bijker, Thomas Parke Hughes, and Trevor J. Pinch, 83–103. Cambridge, MA: MIT Press.

Chesbrough, Henry W. 2006. *Open Innovation: The New Imperative for Creating and Profiting from Technology*. Boston: Harvard Business School Press.

ENoLL Strategy Wiki. 2013. http://enoll-strategy-towards-horizon2020.wikispaces.com/home (accessed February 4, 2013).

European Commission. 2009. DG Information Society and Media. Study on the Potential of the Living Labs Approach including Its Relation to Experimental Facilities for Future Internet Related Technologies. Final Report, March 9, Brussels.

European Commission. 2012. Europe's Information Society. Thematic Portal—about ICT PSP. Archived September 13, 2012. http://ec.europa.eu/information_society/activities/ict_psp/about/index_en.htm (accessed February 4, 2013).

Hald, May. 2009. *Sustainable Urban Development and the Chinese Eco-City: Concepts, Strategies, Policies, and Assessments*. FNI Report 5/2009. Lysaker, Norway: Fridtjof Nansen Institute.

Helsinki Living Lab. 2007. Convergence of users, developers, utilizers, and enablers. Helsinki Living Lab Tekes-Project, Art and Design City Helsinki Ltd., Helsinki. http://www.forumvirium.fi/sites/default/files/hll_brochure.pdf (accessed February 2, 2013).

Hempel, Jessi. 2006. Big Blue brainstorm. *Bloomberg Businessweek*, August 7.

IBM. 2006. IBM invests $100 million in collaborative innovation ideas. IBM.com, News Room, news release, Beijing, China, November 14. http://www-03.ibm.com/press/us/en/pressrelease/20605.wss (accessed January 24, 2013).

Latour, Bruno. 1987. *Science in Action: How to Follow Scientists and Engineers through Society*. Cambridge, MA: Harvard University Press.

Latour, Bruno. 2005. *Reassembling the Social: An Introduction to Actor-Network-Theory*. Oxford: Oxford University Press.

Law, John. 1992. Notes on the theory of the actor-network: Ordering, strategy, and heterogeneity. http://www.lancs.ac.uk/fass/sociology/papers/law-notes-on-ant.pdf (accessed February 4, 2013).

Law, John, and John Hassard, eds. 1999. *Actor Network Theory and After*. Malden, MA: Sociological Review.

Lemke, Max, and Olavi Luotonen. 2009. Open innovation for future Internet-enabled services in "smart" cities. Discussion paper, draft 0.2, INFSO-F4, 14. September.

Lepik, Katri-Liis, Merle Krigul, and Erik Terk. 2010. Introducing Living Lab's method as knowledge transfer from one socio-institutional context to another: Evidence from Helsinki-Tallinn cross-border region. *Journal of Universal Computer Science* 16 (8): 1089–1102.

Lesser, Eric, David Ransom, Rawn Shah, and Bob Pulver. 2012. Collective Intelligence: Capitalizing on the crowd. IBM Global Business Services, executive report, IBM Institute for Business Value, Somers, NY, January.

Lu, Ding. 2011. Introduction: China's great urbanization. In *The Great Urbanization of China*, ed. Ding Lu, 1–11. Series on Contemporary China 30. Singapore: World Scientific.

May, Shannon. 2007. A Sino–U.S. sustainability sham. *Far Eastern Economic Review*, April.

May, Shannon. 2008. Ecological citizenship and a plan for sustainable development. *City* 12 (2): 237–244.

May, Shannon. 2008–2009. Huangbaiyu—the project—the facts, 2008–2009. http://www.shannonmay.com/Huangbaiyu_Facts.html (accessed February 2, 2103).

McDonough, William. 2002. Cradle to cradle case studies. http://www.mcdonough.com/writings_c2c_case_studies.htm (accessed February 2, 2013).

McDonough, William, and Michael Braungart. 2002. *Cradle to Cradle: Remaking the Way We Make Things*. New York: North Point Press.

McKenna, Regis. 1986. *The Regis Touch: New Marketing Strategies for Uncertain Times*. New York: Basic Books.

Moore, Geoffrey A. 2009. *Crossing the Chasm*. New York: HarperCollins.

Nardi, Bonnie A., and Vicki O'Day. 1999. *Information Ecology: Using Technology with Heart*. Cambridge, MA: MIT Press.

Østergaard, Søren Duus. 2008. IBM innovation jam: Experiences and techniques. IBM Corporation, March. http://www.epractice.eu/files/Soren%20Duus%20-%20IBM%20Innovation%20Jam.pdf) (accessed February 4, 2013).

Pór, George. 2000. Nurturing systemic wisdom through knowledge ecology. *Systems Thinker* 11 (8): 1–5.

Sacks, Danielle. 2008. Green guru gone wrong: William McDonough. *Fast Company Magazine*, November.

Scott, W. Richard. 2004. Institutional theory. In *Encyclopedia of Social Theory*, ed. George Ritzer, 408–414. Thousand Oaks, CA: Sage.

Ståhlbröst, Anna. 2008. Forming future IT: The Living Lab way of user involvement. Ph.D. diss., Luleå University of Technology.

Sudjic, Dejan. 2006. Making cities work: China. BBC, June 21. http://news.bbc.co.uk/2/hi/asia-pacific/5084852.stm.

Toy, Mary-Anne. 2006. China's first eco-village proves a hard sell. *Age* 26.

Turkama, Petra. 2010. *ENoLL: Nordic Network of User-Driven Innovation and Livinglabbing*. Oslo: Nordic Innovation Centre.

UN-Habitat. 2006a. Habitat Jam: Summary report. http://www.globaldialoguecenter.com/docs/habitat_jam_report_en.pdf.

UN-Habitat. 2006b. *From Ideas to Action: 70 Actionable Ideas for the World Urban Forum 3*. Nairobi: UN-Habitat.

United Nations, Department of Economic and Social Affairs, Population Division. 2012. *World Urbanization Prospects, the 2011 Revision: Highlights*. New York.

Worldwatch Institute. 2013. Filthy air choking China's growth, Olympic goals. http://www.worldwatch.org/filthy-air-choking-chinas-growth-olympic-goals (accessed February 4, 2013).

Appendix: Questions for Discussion

This appendix provides three questions for each chapter to inspire discussion and reflection.

Chapter 1

• Discuss the four different concepts of "situatedness": situated knowledges, situated practice, situated learning, and situating contexts. What kinds of interrelatedness can you see between the concepts?
• Discuss and compare the different types of methods organized in the book's four parts: methods for projects, methods for collaborative processes, methods for aesthetic experiences, and methods for sustainability.
• Discuss the characteristics of each of the methods presented in tables 1.1 through 1.4. How can you use these tables to navigate through the book?

Chapter 2

• What is the main risk in each of the analysis, construction, process, and vision projects?
• Why is a project design that focuses equally on all four basic elements of a design project rare in practice?
• How can an equal focus on three or all four basic elements be maintained throughout a project?

Chapter 3

• How can study processes be designed to create productive learning environments, where students are acting as co-designers in relation to experimental use of new technologies?

• How can learning situations supporting a flexible communicative setup be designed to foster creative and challenging communication among group members?
• Describe two examples from your practice—either from teaching or from project work—where you gained experience with planning or redesigning an artifact, a prototype, a product, or a learning situation.

Chapter 4

• Discuss how you would (could) appropriate the MUST method's four principles to your own current (or earlier) design project.
• Discuss which concepts are central to your design project and their relation to the project.
• Choose three different techniques that can support participation in your design project and discuss how to use them.

Chapter 5

• What different ways to learn about the specific situation can you use in activity 1?
• Why are there both an ex ante and an ex post evaluation in SDSM?
• What will always be the problem in developing a methodology with a broad reach?

Chapter 6

• How does each of the two techniques support collective analysis of qualitative data? (Give concrete examples from the case or from your own work.)
• How do the techniques support inductive or abductive reasoning? (Give concrete examples from the case or from your own work.)
• How can you and your group use these techniques in your own current or future work?

Chapter 7

• For which states of consciousness could it be beneficial to develop rituals in your group?
• How can you use portable equipment (e.g., light, music, colors, your body) to create states of consciousness and spheres that foster creativity?
• Do you already have rituals—perhaps as the expression of a habit—which you can stop using or develop?

Chapter 8

• What are the central advantages of customer journey design methods in comparison with other approaches that also center on user experiences?
• What are the central contributions made by the participatory design tradition in relation to making and playing with customer journeys?
• What are the arguments for developing and using tangible participatory design tools—and what disadvantages might there be?

Chapter 9

• What are the typical challenges of facilitation, especially when using visual methods and materials in different group contexts?
• How can novice facilitators deal with challenges and develop a practice as reflexive facilitators?
• How can the novice facilitator gain more comfort with using visuals to develop a facilitation practice with visual methods?

Chapter 10

• Why do you think urban pedagogy stresses the importance of taking the lived experiences of urban inhabitants as the point of departure for design and learning processes?
• What do you think is the most important outcome of the situated design process presented in the case study?
• Discuss how you can use the Urban Co-creation method as part of a university project, and what other tools and techniques you might use.

Chapter 11

• Why is the time right for working with situated design in urban planning, and what can culture-led spatial design offer the design process?
• Give examples of the components of a situated and emergent design process.
• What is the role of the designer when design is a process of assembling existing spatial qualities?

Chapter 12

• What kind of portable audio production do we want to design, and how do we want it to engage with time and site?

• What are the auditory characteristics of the chosen site?
• How does the final production relate to the chosen site? To what extent does it entangle, and to what extent does it counterpoint?

Chapter 13

• How may alternate reality games (ARGs) be used for purposes other than pure entertainment?
• What is transmedia storytelling, and how is it used in ARGs?
• How may players engage in and change the flow of an ARG?

Chapter 14

• Discuss what constitutes the domain of interactive installations. What's in and what's not? How do the four examples in section 2 complement each other? Give another example of an interactive installation.
• Describe at least two activities in each of the four phases of the development model.
• Which evaluation activities can occur in each of the four phases of the development model?

Chapter 15

• Why are universal methods not fit to describe creative processes?
• What do the concepts of devices, mediators, and programs of action describe?
• How can experience design become situated?

Chapter 16

• List five activities during the design, implementation, and production of a new car model that are—or may become, in some cases—very costly.
• Explain the concept of economies of scale.
• List some arguments for and against the chapter's assumption that electric vehicles should be designed following the same hybrid design process that is used by the auto industry today to design conventional cars.

Chapter 17

• Discuss the relation between design practices and technological regimes. Discuss how different kinds of design practices within the automobility regime may be needed in the development of new mobility practices. This could include the design of news cars, transport systems, social mobility practices, transport polices, and so on.

• Discuss how alternative local design spaces for mobility systems and practices can be constituted. Discuss how designers—as meta-designers—can be part of the development of such alternative design spaces.

• Departing from the case of battery electric cars, discuss how the design of Cleardrive has developed as a reflexive process, and discuss how it has changed the design space.

Chapter 18

• What are the main features of cleaner production?

• What are the main advantages associated with the life cycle approach compared with the site-specific environmental management approach?

• What is the general idea in industrial symbiosis?

Chapter 19

• Why is it so difficult to escape "blindness" (or the black box) when transferring design methods to new organizational, social, or cultural settings? Which consequences might be the result of this kind of blindness?

• Give examples of blindness and its consequences from other cases you know about.

• Discuss how the prescriptive learning sentences from this chapter may be applied to the cases you know about, and whether they might solve unexpected problems in relation to the transfer process.

Contributors

Lars Birch Andreasen is Associate Professor of Interaction in Virtual Learning Environments at Aalborg University, Copenhagen. He holds a Ph.D. in educational studies from the Danish University of Education. He is a member of the coordination group for the Danish master's program in ICT and learning (MIL). His research deals with collaborative and dialogic learning, social media and new technologies, information literacy, and problem-based learning. His recent publications include a book chapter in *Increasing Student Engagement and Retention Using Mobile Applications: Smartphones, Skype, and Texting Technologies,* and an article in the new peer-reviewed *Journal of Problem Based Learning in Higher Education* 1, no. 1.

I am engaged in situated design methods because of my interest in studying dialogic learning, for example, online interaction as a specific situated practice.

Troels Andreasen is Associate Professor of Computer Science at Roskilde University. He holds a Ph.D. from University of Copenhagen, Denmark. His main research interest areas are information retrieval, fuzzy logic, intelligent systems, ontology, and language technology. He is working on principles for concept extraction from text and a generic approach to intelligent behavior within interactive installations.

I find the design and development of "experiences" to be an important new interdisciplinary area linking humanities and technology and consider situated design to be an inevitable approach in this area.

Richard Baskerville is Board of Advisors Professor in the Department of Computer Information Systems, Georgia State University. His research specializes in security of information systems, methods of information systems design and development, and the interaction of information systems and organizations. His interests in methods extend to qualitative research methods and the design science research paradigm. He is the author of *Designing Information Systems Security* (J. Wiley) and more than 200 articles in scholarly journals, practitioner magazines, and edited books. He is Editor Emeritus of the *European Journal of Information Systems* and associated with the editorial boards of the *Information Systems Journal, Business & Information Systems Engineering*

(Wirtschafts informatik), *Journal of Information Systems Security*, and the *International Journal of E-Collaboration*.

I believe all design activity is necessarily situated; the tension between the necessarily unique situation and the urge to be methodical is the stuff of life.

Keld Bødker, Ph.D., is Associate Professor at Roskilde University, Denmark. He has conducted participatory design research focusing on how IT designers can cooperate with users and management in the process of clarifying goals, formulating needs, and designing and evaluating coherent visions for change. Publications include *Participatory IT Design: Designing for Business and Workplace Realities* (MIT Press, 2004), as well as papers for international conferences and journals.

We know from empirical research in information systems that classic methods as "prescriptions for how to do a project" don't work that way, so situated design methods are needed because they provide much more relevant support to a design project.

Thomas Budde Christensen is Associate Professor in the Department of Environmental Social and Spatial Change, Roskilde University. He has a Ph.D. in environmental innovation in the auto industry and has been working with environmental innovation and implementation of environmental technology in the transport sector and in the energy sector. Lately he has been involved in research projects regarding cleantech, industrial symbiosis, and sustainable biofuels. His publications include articles in *Journal of Cleaner Production, Energy Policy, Sustainable Development*, and *European Journal of Sustainable Development*.

Situated design methods are needed to deliver sustainable development.

Henriette Christrup is Associate Professor of Performance Design at Roskilde University. Since 2004 she has performed research and teaching in creative leadership in performance design, as well as experiences and self-creation connected to performative spaces. She has for many years been engaged in experimenting with design, research, and development methods taking inspiration, among other things, from art, therapy, and heart research. Her publications include *On Sense and Sensitivity in Performative Processes* (Edward Elgar, 2008), *Joyful, Collective Design Processes* (Routledge, 2010), and *Self-Creation and Performance Spaces* (Tusculanum, 2013).

I wish to contribute to transformations—in persons, relations, and the surrounding world—by using the Wheel of Rituals when working in the unknown in situated design processes.

Martin Severin Frandsen is affiliated with the Centre for Action Research and Democratic Social Change at Roskilde University and a member of Supertanker, a group of urbanists based in Copenhagen. His research interests cover urban sociology, participatory design and planning, community development, urban pedagogy, and pragmatist philosophy. Recent publications in English include "From 'Troublemakers' to Problem Solvers: Designing with Youths in a Disadvantaged Neighbourhood" (Proceedings of the 12th Participatory Design Conference, 2012), and "From 'Book Container' to Community Centre," in *The International Handbook on Social Innovation* (Edward Elgar, 2013).

Through situated design processes, urban inhabitants can learn about the urban environment and how to change it.

Karin Friberg finished her M.S. in information technology, interdisciplinary IT development, in 2006 at Roskilde University. Her thesis "Electronic Medical Record: A Question of Safety" constitutes the empirical case in chapter 6 of this volume. Since then, she has been working as an information architect and business analyst at the Danish National Police. Her primary task is business development, including optimizing business workflows, eliciting business demands, and specifying requirements for critical business systems.

I am engaged in situated design methods to get a deeper understanding of underlying problems, their causes, and consequences, for the purpose of identifying possible solutions or initiatives.

Lisbeth Frølunde is Associate Professor of Visual Communication and Digital Media at Roskilde University. Recent publications are "Animated War," in *Convergence* (Sage, February 2012); "Machinima Filmmaking as Culture in Practice: Dialogical Processes of Remix," in *Computer Games and New Media Cultures* (Springer, 2012); and "Dialogical Ethics and Reflections on Unfinalizability," in *Knowledge and Power in Collaborative Research: A Reflexive Approach* (Routledge, 2012). Her research concerns film and multimedia production processes, media literacy, digital culture, and visual methods. Lisbeth is experienced as a workshop facilitator across the IT and design industry, education, and counseling. Her background includes working as Concept Developer for the LEGO Group, harnessing children's input to multimedia design (games, software, online communities, robot toys). She holds a Ph.D. in media studies and education, an M.A. in expressive arts therapy, and a B.F.A. in fine arts.

My engagement with situated design methods stems from an interest in creative learning as a collaborative, dialogic, material process.

Sanne Krogh Groth holds a Ph.D. in musicology from the University of Copenhagen (2010) with a historical study of the Swedish electro-acoustic music studio EMS. Her M.A. is in musicology and theater studies with a thesis on contemporary sound art. Since 2011 Groth has been an assistant professor of performance design at Roskilde University, with research in the fields of sound and performance studies, sound art, performance art, and contemporary music. She is editor in chief of the contemporary music and sound art magazine Seismograf.org.

Roskilde University has an extraordinary tradition of combining theory and practice. Being part of this book project has not only documented and reflected our daily work but also complemented and qualified our future teaching and research.

Sune Gudiksen is a Ph.D. fellow in co-design of media, services, and business models at Aalborg University. He is the author of several design and innovation articles, including "Making Business Models," in *Co-design*, and "Business Model Design Games," in *Creativity and Innovation Management*. He is especially interested in the underlying principles behind the creation and application of collaborative tools and techniques, mostly within media, services, and business models. He is the owner of the new blog initiative www.businessmodeldesign.org, where he posts regularly about design, tools, cases, and business model issues from a design and innovation point of view.

Situated elements are what determine the difference between generic design tools that are applicable in every situation and design tools that are carefully prepared according to each case.

Ole Erik Hansen is Associate Professor of International Regulation and Environmental Planning at Roskilde University. He is doing research in global environmental politics and transition of sociotechnical systems. His publications include contributions to *Design Research: Synergies from Interdisciplinary Perspectives* (Routledge, 2010) and *Rethinking Climate Change Research: Clean Technology, Culture, and Communication* (Ashgate, 2012).

My background is in analyzing the transition of socio-technical systems, and I find it very important to participate in the development of situated design methods to develop more sustainable products and processes.

Morten Hertzum, Ph.D., is Associate Professor of Computer Science at Roskilde University. His research interests include user-centered design, participatory design, usability evaluation methods, achieving benefit from IT, and information seeking and visualization. Currently his empirical work concerns IT in health care. He has published in, among others, *Information Processing and Management, International Journal of Human-Computer Interaction, International Journal of Human-Computer Studies, Communications of the AIS*, and *Information and Organization*.

I am engaged in situated design methods because the local context is a rich source of information and circumstances decisive to the success of design projects.

Niels Jørgensen is Associate Professor of Computer Science at Roskilde University. His previous research includes the organization of open-source development projects ("Developer Autonomy in the FreeBSD Open Source Project," *Journal of Management and Governance*, 2007, vol. 11). His current research includes a study of the strengths and limits of the concept of exemplary learning in design studies (Aalborg University Press, 2013). At Roskilde University, he directed the development and launch in 2008 of the university's new interdisciplinary bachelor's program in design, humanities, and technology.

I am engaged in situated design methods because I believe that there is no single design method that fits all situations—not even iterative design.

Niels Christian Juul is Associate Professor of Computer Science at Roskilde University. He holds a Ph.D. from University of Copenhagen, Denmark. His main interest is IT security and privacy. He is currently working on design principles for privacy-friendly IT systems, for example, in the health-care sector. Additionally he studies drivers of, and barriers to, new technology, especially information technology.

It is exciting to reflect on a multifaceted and multidisciplinary practice where aspects of humans and technology are intertwined at all abstraction layers and to be enlightened on both humans and technology.

Finn Kensing is Director of the Center for IT Innovation, University of Copenhagen, Denmark. He has published explorative, experimental, and interventionist research in the fields of participatory design, health informatics, computer-supported cooperative work, and human-computer interaction. He is the coauthor of *Participatory IT Design: Designing for Business and Workplace Realities*, which presents theory, methods, and practices for introducing sustainable IT in organizations. Recent keynotes include the Participatory Design Conference 2008, the International Workshop on Personal Health Record 2011, and Medical Informatics Europe 2012.

Situated design methods are needed, since all design situations are unique.

Tyge Kjær is Associate Professor in the Department of Environmental Social and Spatial Change, Roskilde University. He has been researching environmental planning for thirty years and has been involved in an extensive number of research projects in collaboration with industries and public authorities. He has published numerous articles, papers, and reports about environmental planning.

Situated design methods are an epistemological imperative because the complex character of nature and social systems requires a situated epistemology.

Erik Kristiansen holds an M.A. in general linguistics and computer science and received his Ph.D. in performance design from Roskilde University in 2009. He has worked with pervasive game design and game design methods for several years, including research into playful design, particularly the design of interactive museum exhibitions. His research interests also include the reconstruction of Renaissance musical instruments and Danish design history, as well as research into the physical context of nondigital games. He is currently a researcher in performance design at Roskilde University.

I am engaged in situated design methods because situated design for me is working with messy design—that is, the challenge of creating design methods for a messy world where users are just as engaged as they are unpredictable.

Rikke Lybæk, Ph.D., is Associate Professor in the Department of Environmental Social and Spatial Change, Roskilde University. Since 2001 she has been researching industrial ecology and industrial symbiosis in Europe and Southeast Asia. She has published articles in *Journal of Industrial Ecology, Progress in Industrial Ecology,* and *Journal of Sustainable Development.*

Designing more intelligent artifacts, services, and systems is the basis for a sustainable future.

Margit Neisig is Assistant Professor at Roskilde University. She has a Ph.D. in socio-technological planning and has many years of practical experience in management of change/transition concerning technology, learning, and development using design methods in both product, organizational, and regional development. She has worked as head of department in Tele Danmark Development; director of the Development Department, County of Funen; and HR director, Municipality of Fredensborg. She has been a consultant for several organizations and taught within her field at a number of universities.

As complex human constructs, situated design methods may have an enormous transformational impact toward the creation of sustainability in a broad sense.

Jørgen Lerche Nielsen is Associate Professor of ICT and Learning at Roskilde University. He is conducting research in designing networked problem-based learning processes, collaborative learning, students' activities in group work, and the roles of the professor as supervisor for study groups in their situated learning processes. His recent publications include book chapters in *Exploring the Theory, Pedagogy, and Practice of Networked Learning* (Springer, 2012), *Increasing Student Engagement and Retention using Mobile Applications: Smartphones, Skype, and Texting Technologies* (Emerald Group Publishing, 2013), and an article in the new peer-reviewed *Journal of Problem Based Learning in Higher Education* 1, no. 1.

I am engaged in situated design methods because of my interest in studying aspects of problem-based learning, students' activities in group work, and the roles of the professor as supervisor for study groups in their situated learning processes.

Lene Pfeiffer Petersen holds a master's degree in geography and urban planning from Roskilde University. She has several years of experience in conducting and facilitating participatory processes for students, mainly within the academic environment of Roskilde University. Her research interests are everyday life studies, participatory processes and learning, and group dynamics. Publications include "From 'Troublemakers' to Problem Solvers: Designing with Youths in a Disadvantaged Neighbourhood" (Proceedings of the 12th Participatory Design Conference, 2012) and (in Danish) "Tips and Tricks for Group Formation," in *The Sociology of Project Work* (Samfundslitteratur, 2013).

Situated design processes can provide children and youths with vital skills for becoming urban citizens and active members of their communities.

Jan Pries-Heje is Professor of Information Systems at Roskilde University. He is also head of a research group on user-driven innovation and head of studies for the master's program in project management and process improvement. He serves as Chair to IFIP

Technical Committee 8 on Information Systems. His research focuses on designing and building innovative solutions to managerial and organizational IT problems. He has published more than 200 scholarly books and papers. He is senior editor for *Journal of the AIS*, specializing in design science research.

I am engaged in situated design methods because I never believed in a one-size-fits-all way of doing things.

Mads Rosendahl is Associate Professor of Computer Science at Roskilde University. He has a Ph.D. from Cambridge University. His main focus of research is in the area of programming languages and program analysis with a special focus on abstract interpretation and complexity analysis. He is currently part of an EU project on creating software analysis tools that enable energy-saving optimizations of software on modern hardware.

Situated design gives a solid framework for design and construction of software that uses experimental hardware and software.

Kristine Samson is Assistant Professor of Performance Design at Roskilde University. She received her Ph.D. in performative aesthetics in urban space and is now doing research on the performative city and how culture, art, and events become part of urban planning. She has written several works on urban design, site specificity, and spatial performance: "The Becoming of Urban Space" (Routledge, 2010), "Aesthetic Performativity in Urban Design and Art" (Museum Tusculanum 2014), and (with Louise Fabian) *DIY Design: From Ludic Tactics to Strategic Planning* (Routledge, 2014).

I am engaged in situated design methods because I find it necessary to invent alternatives to master planning while making use of the vast social, material, and aesthetic resources at hand in cities today.

Jesper Simonsen is Professor of Participatory Design and Director of the university strategic research initiative Designing Human Technologies at Roskilde University. Since 1991 he has conducted research in collaboration with industry on participatory design, developing theories and methods for participatory design in an organizational context. His publications include *Participatory IT Design: Designing for Business and Workplace Realities* (MIT Press, 2004), *Design Research: Synergies from Interdisciplinary Perspectives* (Routledge, 2010), and *Routledge International Handbook of Participatory Design* (Routledge, 2012).

I am engaged in situated design methods because participatory design—a process of investigating, understanding, reflecting on, establishing, developing, and supporting mutual learning between multiple participants in collective reflection-in-action—can only be accomplished by situated design methods.

Bent Søndergård is Associate Professor of Socio-technical Planning at Roskilde University. He is doing research in sustainable transition, environmental innovation, and governance with a focus on transition of socio-technical systems. His publications include contributions to *Design Research: Synergies from Interdisciplinary Perspectives* (Routledge, 2010) and *Rethinking Climate Change Research: Clean Technology, Culture, and Communication* (Ashgate, 2012).

My engagement in design and situated design methods is based on the need to merge design studies and sustainable transition and the question of how we have to understand, both on a conceptual level and in practice, design and the social practice of designing.

Sara Malou Strandvad is Associate Professor in Performance Design, Department of Communication, Business, and Information Technologies, Roskilde University. She has authored various publications in the field of cultural sociology, including articles in *European Journal of Cultural Studies*, *Cultural Sociology*, and *Visual Studies*. Her research concerns organizing processes in creative industries, currently focusing on valuation processes.

I am engaged in situated design methods because the students I teach are required to design events and need methods to do so that are academically qualified.

Connie Svabo, Ph.D., is Associate Professor and Head of Studies in Performance Design, Department of Communication, Business, and Information Technologies, Roskilde University. From 2010 to 2013 she was project leader for the theme "Experiencescapes" in the Danish national innovation network on knowledge-based experience economy, and her coauthored chapter in this book grows out of this research-industry collaboration. Her primary research focus is the project Transforming Trash—Excavating Futures, which explores recent examples of trash art and analyzes them as contemporary archaeological, cultural, and artistic practices with potential for envisioning desirable futures. She has published over a dozen papers and book chapters.

Situated design methods address the tinkering and negotiation that are crucial when things are made to happen.

John Venable is Associate Professor and former Head of School at the School of Information Systems, Curtin University of Technology, in Perth, Western Australia, where he has held various positions since 1997. He is currently Director of Research in the School of Information Systems and Codirector of the Curtin Business School Not-for-Profit Research Initiative, which conducts research aiming to improve not-for-profit and charitable organizations and the third sector. His other research interests include problem analysis and solving, systems analysis and design, organizational culture and change management, knowledge management, and technology-supported teaching and learning.

My goal is to enable people to design better ways to improve their and other people's lives. Uncritically applying standard design methods to nonstandard problem situations is a recipe for failure—and all problem situations are nonstandard in some way.

Index

Note: Page numbers followed by an "f" or a "t" indicate figures or tables, respectively.

Printed in the United States
by Baker & Taylor Publisher Services